BUSINESS IN GOVERNMENT AND SOCIETY

Ethical, International Decision Making

Frederick Maidment

William Eldridge
Kean University

Prentice Hall
Upper Saddle River, New Jersey 07458

Library of Congress Cataloging-in-Publication Data

Maidment, Frederick.
    Business in government and society : ethical, international decision-making / Frederick
    Maidment, William Eldridge.
        p. cm.
    Includes bibliographical references and index.
    ISBN 0-13-769217-X
        1. Business ethics.   2. Political ethics.   3. Social ethics.   I. Title.   II. Eldridge, William
    (William H.), d. 1999.
HF5387.M3334 2000
174'.421—dc21

99-045118

Editor: Elizabeth Sugg
Production Coordination: Linda Zuk, WordCrafters Editorial Services, Inc.
Cover Designer: Bruce Kenselaar
Director of Manufacturing and Production: Bruce Johnson
Managing Editor: Mary Carnis
Marketing Manager: Shannon Simonsen
Manufacturing Manager: Ed O'Dougherty

© 2000 by Prentice-Hall, Inc.
Upper Saddle River, New Jersey 07458

Printed in the United States of America

10   9   8   7   6   5   4   3   2

ISBN 0-13-769217-X

Prentice-Hall International (UK) Limited, *London*
Prentice-Hall of Australia Pty. Limited, *Sydney*
Prentice-Hall of Canada Inc., *Toronto*
Prentice-Hall Hispanoamericana, S. A., *Mexico*
Prentice-Hall of India Private Limited, *New Delhi*
Prentice-Hall of Japan, Inc., *Tokyo*
Prentice-Hall Pte. Ltd., *Singapore*
Editora Prentice-Hall do Brasil, Ltda., *Rio de Janeiro*
Prentice-Hall, *Upper Saddle River, New Jersey*

To the memory of William Eldridge:
friend, teacher, scholar, colleague.
He is sorely missed by all who knew him.

CONTENTS

6   CURRENT ISSUES IN THE MODERN GLOBAL ENVIRONMENT   115

7   CURRENT ISSUES FOR THE MODERN BUSINESS ENTERPRISE   145

8   CURRENT ISSUES FACING GOVERNMENT

14 ETHICS WITH CONSUMERS AND PRODUCTS   303

15 STRATEGIC RESPONSE TO A CHANGING GLOBAL ENVIRONMENT   331

16 MEETING THE CHALLENGES OF THE FUTURE   351

PREFACE

A strong ethical background in the social issues that confront business, government, and society is necessary to successfully guide executives of organizations in today's rapidly changing environment. *Business in Government and Society: Ethical, International Decision Making* provides the student with the necessary background to meet the challenges of this rapidly changing environment in an ethical and honorable way. The book is based on the authors' more than 30 years experience in the classroom and in both government and industry. The style and content have been shaped by their experiences and interactions with hundreds, if not thousands, of students, businesspeople, public servants, and colleagues.

The book is organized into 16 chapters, each dealing with various aspects of business, government, and society, with a strong ethical and international viewpoint. Each chapter begins with a list of the concepts the student will learn and ends with an extensive list of questions that will enable the student to test and improve understanding of the material. Each chapter is followed by a series of cases designed to illustrate real-life ethical dilemmas facing managers in the fulfillment of their obligations, and real-life incidents are featured in the text to help illustrate the concepts.

Business, government, and society are three interacting systems within which individuals must operate. This book places managers and their organizations within the context of a complex society. Business is examined and discussed from both an ethical and an international perspective, requiring that the student understand the capitalist system and its rivals in the context of the Industrial Revolution and the development of the modern post-industrial economy.

Government and its problems in an evolving and changing world are discussed so that the student will understand the role of government in the society and the changes that role has undergone during the twentieth century, as well as its importance as the twenty-first century begins. The relationship between government and industry is of particular importance as the new millennium begins. The way these two institutions of modern society coexist will have a great deal to do with the success of developed as well as lesser and least developed countries in the next several decades.

Religion, social structure, and culture all play a role in how well a society will do in the next century. How society reacts to and supports its means of production and government, with all the rules and regulations associated with that interaction, becomes an important and possibly defining activity of the society. The tools are there. The important decision·will be how those tools—whether wielded by industry, the government, or society as a whole—will be used for the benefit of the individuals in the society.

The importance of **ethical decision making and strategic management in an international context** is presented in relation to the problems and opportunities faced by business, government, and society. For decisions to be successful and for the society to develop in a just and ethical way, standards of decision making and their consequences need to be set and maintained. This means that organizations must take the long view on what their decisions will mean and how those decisions will be implemented. Organizations must pass a standard of ethical performance; this book provides guidance in achieving such a standard in a variety of cultural contexts. All organizations, whether public or private, need to view their decisions through the ethical prism of the long-term good of the society and their other stakeholders.

Government and its role in society, especially with regard to its relationship with business, is a major concern of this book. Government sets the minimum level of conduct for organizations through its role in passing laws and other forms of regulation. But ethical behavior generally goes beyond mere adherence to the law. The law, in fact, may be unethical or even immoral, as was the case in Nazi Germany; in that society, obeying the law was an immoral act. Individuals need to look beyond the law for ethical and moral behavior. Using only the law as a guide is insufficient to the achievement of an ethical and moral society. The law provides a starting point, not a finishing point.

Social issues are a major focus of the book, specifically how those issues are affected and shaped by the actions of business and government in particular and society as a whole. Social issues are examined from the perspective of their ethical impact on the society as well as any international implications and overlap they may have. All factors of the society are interrelated; every action, whether originating in business and industry, government, or society as a whole, has both intended and unintended consequences. Thinking these actions through by using the tool of strategic management and an ethical approach to decision making is one of the keys to the success of any action.

The global economy is a major focus of this book. In today's world, global competition is a fact of life. Unfortunately, what would be considered ethical behavior in one setting may not be considered ethical in another society. Culture and laws differ, and organizations need to learn how to deal with these differences effectively and ethically. The origins of these differences can be found in the history and the culture of various societies. Every society has developed along different lines and each has its own unique culture and institutions. Dealing in an ethical and moral way with these societies' differing institutions will be one of the major challenges facing business and industry in the future.

Business in Government and Society includes a variety of features designed to help the student learn:

1. The development of an integrated ethical decision-making model in the text.
2. A unique international approach to business, government, and society.
3. Over 50 cases.
4. Over 120 incidents based on real-life events.

5. A list of the concepts the student will learn, at the beginning of each chapter.

6. A unique combination of ethical principles and an international perspective.

7. An extensive list at the end of each chapter of questions for review.

In addition, the text is accompanied by an instructor's manual that provides the instructor with:

1. Approaches to determining grades for students.

2. A course syllabus, including a course outline, a bibliography for the course, an assignment schedule, and course objectives.

3. Lecture outlines.

4. Answers to questions in the case studies.

5. Examination questions.

There is also an accompanying workbook for the text. The workbook gives the student practice in thinking about these issues and provides the instructor with additional material for the course.

Business in Government and Society offers a unique solution to the problems of combining the material from a traditional course in business and society and a course in business ethics with an international focus. It brings together these three important areas in the business curriculum into a single text; it is our belief that such combination will be a beginning of a trend in this area. It is impossible to discuss the topics of business, government, and society without discussing the international environment as well as the ethical implications of decisions made by managers in an ever-shrinking world. Everything is interrelated, and the consequences of decisions are going to be even more important from an ethical and international perspective than they have been in the past. The world is becoming a much smaller place, and we need to learn how to live together on this small planet.

ACKNOWLEDGMENTS

We need to thank many people for helping us develop this book. First, our wives and families, as well as our colleges, students, and friends have helped in the development of this book. In particular, we would like to thank the reviewers who helped us shape the book in its final form: Guy Adamo, Berkeley College; Bonnie Bolinger, Ivy Tech—Terre Haute; Chris W. Grevesen, DeVry Institute; and Norma J. Gross, Houston Community College.

FOREWORD

These are the times that try men's souls.   Thomas Paine

The story of the ebb and flow of American society can be told in this one simple phrase written by Thomas Paine over 200 years ago. Paine wrote the phrase during the darkest hour of the American Revolution: when the cause was all but lost; when the fledgling thirteen colonies seemed utterly defeated by the power of the British Crown; when the sunshine patriot and summer soldier had deserted the army, the nation, and the idea that "all men are created equal. That they are endowed by their creator with certain inalienable rights. And, that among those rights are life, liberty and the pursuit of happiness."

Other times would follow to try men's souls. The abolition of slavery and the Civil War, would try the nation in ways that could only be captured by President Lincoln, who determined that "It is rather for us to be here dedicated to the great task remaining before us. . . . that this nation, under God, shall have a new birth of freedom—and that government of the people, by the people, and for the people shall not perish from the Earth."

Other times to try the nation's soul would follow: World War I, the Great Depression, World War II, and the Cold War would all try the soul of the American nation, and new trials continue to vex the American spirit.

Today, we are faced with a nation and leaders that seem to have lost their way. Almost daily, we are assaulted by reports of large corporations terminating thousands of employees in the face of what we are told is the best economy in the world. At the same time, the media report that the very same executives who "terminated" those employees, together with their careers, their livelihoods, and their families, reward themselves with ever more money, ever more perks, ever more stock options, and ever more benefits.

Our religious institutions seem less concerned with souls and more concerned with their parishioners' wallets. Tales of fallen prophets abound, whether it is a Jimmy Swaggert or a Jim Baker. Not only do the feet of many of our ethical and religious leaders seem to be made of clay, but they seem to be taking their congregations into a moral and ethical wilderness of shifting and sinking sands from which there will be no escape, no pardon, and no reprieve.

The government fares no better. Whether it is on the local, state, or national level, unethical actions and corruption abound. In some of our major cities, nearly a quorum of former members of city councils could be found in the local federal prison. In Missouri, both the state attorney general, the officer specifically charged with enforcing state laws, and the speaker of the state House of Representatives were convicted of felonies and are currently serving sentences. Both the Pennsylvania state attorney general and the chief justice of the New York state court of appeals, the highest judicial officer in the state, were convicted of felonies.

The federal government has certainly been no stranger to ethical lapses, corruption, or breaking the law. Vietnam, Watergate, selling arms for hostages, the Contras, and now Whitewater, File-Gate, Travel-Gate, campaign financing, and Monica Lewinsky all become part of a federal montage of unethical behavior and illegal activity. If a special prosecutor is getting a little too close, some damaging information is leaked. Whether the leak is true or not is unimportant—the image on the evening news is all that counts. Illegal campaign contributions? Everybody does it. We are all guilty, so nobody is guilty. Destroy a person's life, career, family? It is all part of the game: a "sport" that everyone plays inside the Washington beltway, as Vince Foster, the long-time Clinton friend and aide from Arkansas, said in his suicide note.

Corruption does not build trust. Special prosecutors do not inspire. "No controlling legal authority" does not provide the nation with the moral leadership it so obviously and desperately craves.

Although the United States may have won the Cold War, the price of that victory was higher than we could ever imagine. Rot, cynicism, and moral decay are everywhere. Employees distrust their bosses. Nearly every survey concerning employee–employer relations tells us that employees do not trust their companies and have no loyalty because it has been more than adequately demonstrated that their companies have no loyalty to them.

Our religious organizations are under siege and parishioners generally ignore their religious leaders. Churches, synagogues, and mosques are in the business of moral and ethical education, but few would argue that they are succeeding. Building empty cathedrals somehow seems more important than feeding hungry souls.

The citizenry is deserting the government because the government has deserted them. Every year, with each election, voter turnout is lower, and the legitimacy of the government may soon be called into question. President Clinton was elected with less than 25 percent of the vote of the eligible voters. The citizens are giving up on the government because the government no longer represents them. It has become imperial—often simply for sale to the highest bidder. Campaign finance reform was killed by the very special interests it was designed to control, and the average citizen has less and less say in the government.

This seems to be resulting in a kind of unspoken agreement between the government and the citizenry: "(1) don't get us into a real war where a lot of Americans get killed, (2) don't mess up the economy, and (3) don't raise our taxes." This seems to be the attitude of many in the country, and who is to say that they are not right!

The soul of the nation is, indeed, being tried. Whatever else a country or society may be, it is a community. In a shrinking world of expanding global competition and communication, the society needs to have a clear idea and mission of where it wants to go and what it wants to become. Whatever else may be going on, that mission, ideal, dream, is not being articulated on any level in the society. There is no Franklin Roosevelt who can inspire and rally the nation in the face of the Great Depression. Roosevelt faced the greatest domestic economic disaster in the history of the United States. Today, we face another great domestic as well as international disaster. The main component of that disaster is not economic, but rather, one of the soul: the way we treat each other, live with each other, and communicate with each other.

The first thing that American society must do is to determine what it wants to become in the twenty-first century. Today, the United States is in a position not unlike the one occupied by the United Kingdom a hundred years ago. The British mistakenly thought that things would continue as they had been—and they could not have been more wrong. Times changed and the British Empire no longer exists. In a hundred years, could the same be said of the United States?

The American nation must decide what it wants to be in the next millennium. Will it be a land that Lincoln foresaw in his Gettysburg Address, whose ideals were so eloquently expressed by Jefferson in the Declaration of Independence, or will it be something else, something uninspired, something less wanted, or something less desirable?

Certainly, there are areas that need immediate improvement if the nation is to succeed. The education system is in need of reform, as is the political system. Businesses must be held more accountable for their actions; a quick look at the ethical problems of the tobacco industry is more than enough evidence of that. Health care is another area that needs attention. Whether Americans want to admit it or not, health care is rationed in the United States based on the ability of the patient to pay. Those that can pay for it get the best health care in the world, and those that cannot pay for it don't.

For American society again to be a moral and ethical society, embodying the finest hopes of humanity, it must renew its once-high ideals. Those ideals will not always be met, but the attempt to continue to strive to meet them is the essence of a just and ethical society. The journey, not the arrival, is the key.

The concept of equality; the importance of the individual and human rights, balanced with the real needs of the community; the necessity for true economic and political freedom; and the moral commitment to defend, promote, and tolerate those freedoms for others as well is the essence of a just and ethical society and the best and only true hope for an ethical and just world.

Frederick Maidment
William Eldridge

The Study of Ethical Decision Making in Business, Government, and Society

Concepts : You Will Learn ■ ■ ■

the reasons for the study of ethics in business, government, and society

the basic concepts of ethics

the basic reasons to study ethical decision making

how the concepts of ethical decision making are applied to business, government, and other segments of society

the reasons that ethical decision making has become especially critical in an age of government regulation, media scrutiny, and public distrust of its institutions

INTRODUCTION ■ ■ ■

Many believe that we are in an era when citizens are deeply suspicious of the ethical standards of nearly all of our nation's institutions. Presidents of the United States have become embroiled in scandals involving their personal lives, governmental activities, and campaign financing. Our country's largest corporations have been found guilty of such activities as racial discrimination, illegal sales practices, insider trading, money laundering, and other improper practices.

Judges, prosecutors, and police officers have been convicted of various crimes and sent to jail. Religious leaders have been found guilty of various improper acts. Military officers and noncommissioned officers have been embroiled in sex scandals. Clergy have been convicted of misusing their followers' funds and exploiting their followers improperly.

As a result of the ethical problems in so many areas, there has been a reawakening of the subject of ethics in schools, corporations, and government.

The scandals have made people realize the high cost of low ethical standards. Although most people have some concept of what *ethics* means, they are often too busy to think about ethics within a structured decision-making model.

The author's experience is that important decisions are too often made quickly without the benefit of a structured decision-making model.[1] This means that wrong decisions are often made with negative ethical consequences for the organization and the people involved. It is useful to have a structured decision-making model that would be certain to include ethical considerations in the decision-making process.

The study of ethical decision making in business, government, and society is a difficult one because there is no clear understanding of what *ethics* means. One can read various philosophers' discussions of ethics, but it is difficult to read writings that were written in a completely different time. Concepts that seemed valid 100 years ago seem irrelevant in an age driven by computers, fax machines, and television sets.

Religious concepts that seemed to provide ethical guidance have been challenged by the courts, the public, lawmakers, and the actions of the clergy. Legal ethics have been challenged by the public, lawmakers, and the actions of the legal community. Political "ethics" seems to have disappeared in the middle of a series of scandals. Business ethics has become an oxymoron, and ethics in the society seem more difficult to find.

Some people laugh at the idea that ethics of any kind exist in the business world today. They suggest that U.S. companies are so driven by the need to achieve good short-term profits that the concept of ethics no longer exists. Downsizing of businesses, governments, and not-for-profits has created greater stress on the people involved.[2] As a result, they may be more likely to engage in unethical conduct to obtain the results they need at the moment. However, if organizations engage in unethical conduct, it can have a very negative impact on the organization. People do not want to support organizations that engage in unethical conduct. People do not want to work for organizations that could put them in difficult ethical situations.[3]

Bad ethics are usually bad for the organization, but how does one go about deciding what constitutes ethical behavior in a society that seems to have lost its ethical moorings? How does any organization define its ethical code in such a fiercely competitive world?

President Clinton and Vice President Gore justified their massive fundraising practices by observing that it was necessary to engage in such activities because the other side was doing it.[4] Speaker Gingrich said similar things. Consultants who run negative campaigns against their opponents justify them because they "work."

Companies often justify questionable marketing and sales practices by claiming that they are just reacting to competitive practices.[5] Some police officers and attorneys have admitted to misconduct relating to cases because of the pressure to win. A recent survey of military officers indicated that it is a common practice to falsify combat readiness reports to increase an officer's chances for promotion.[6] The military has always prided itself on its high ethical standards. Nevertheless, many in the armed services contend that "the state of ethical conduct is abysmal".[7] If winning becomes everything, ethical standards are likely to lose.

BUILDING AN ETHICAL CODE ■ ■ ■

It is clear that constructing an ethical code in the latter half of this century has been much more difficult than previously. In part, fewer people seem interested in discussing ethics as a topic. If gangster rap is an acceptable form of "music," what does *music* mean? If police departments cover up the abuse of citizens or intimidate minority citizens, what does "to serve and protect" mean? How does one approach the topic of ethics in a country whose public schools rank in the middle among industrial countries?

In schools, instructors are being asked to make subjects clearer for their students.[8] In the world outside the schools, ambiguous managerial problems rapidly become ethical dilemmas. Ethical decision makers generate a number of alternatives and weigh the consequences of each.

Society demands that managers respect certain values and will impose sanctions on managers who do not respect the values of the culture in which they operate. Students must be willing to examine their own beliefs, consider the beliefs of others, and explore various options when analyzing cases or real-world situations. It is important to follow the steps in the decision-making model precisely. It is also useful to put them in writing.

DECISION-MAKING MODEL[9] ■ ■ ■

The first step in making any decision is to define the problem or situation carefully and in writing. One should also do research, obtain advice, and then re-define the problem. This is the most important step in the process. Unless it is done well, one is not likely to reach a positive result.

Sometimes it is useful to step back from a problem and see if it can be reformulated as an opportunity. Some problems actually provide a chance to reexamine one's operations and determine if the organization can make improvements. It is often useful to bring in people from the outside to take a look at the situation. They may have different perspectives which could be useful. Only when one is absolutely certain that one has adequately defined a problem should one move forward. This is particularly true if the situation has important ethical implications.

The next step is to explore the options that may exist to help one deal with the situation. It can be useful to put all the options on flipcharts or a blackboard. This is the time for some creativity rather than judging the options. One should want to generate as many plausible options as possible. The options should be written out, addressing the situation at hand and stating the reasons the option will solve the problem. The third step is to evaluate each option suggested. Some organizations assign specific people to argue the pros and cons of each alternative.

One consideration in evaluating options should be the culture of the organization. The culture of an organization is its values, beliefs, practices, and ways of doing things. For example, McDonald's has a very strong marketing culture. They do an extraordinary job of meeting the needs of their customers, especially young people and working women with children.

Colleges often have a "publish or perish" culture. That is, professors must publish articles or books or they will not advance. This puts pressure on

BOX 1.1   The Decision-Making Technique

1. *Identify the problem.* What is really the problem in this situation? This is, perhaps, the most important step in the decision-making technique. Many of the decisions that are incorrect were because of the failure to define the problem.

2. *Review the pertinent data.* What things indicate that there is a problem, and how and why are they important? Most organizations have many activities going on at the same time; the key is to determine the relevant factors.

3. *Generate alternatives.* What can you do that will help to solve the problem? Remember, doing nothing is always an alternative.

4. *Select alternatives.* Of the various alternatives developed in step 3, which one do you select?

5. *Implement the alternative selected.* Go out and implement the alternative selected.

6. *Review.* Did the alternative selected and implemented solve the problem? What other problems have been created?

Adapted and expanded from Certo, Samuel C., & Peter, Paul J., *Strategic Management Concepts and Applications.* New York: Random House Business Division, 1988.

BOX 1.2   Sticking with the Model

Many organizations and individuals get themselves into ethical and other problems because they stray from the proper model for decision making that has been outlined in this book. Although unimportant decisions may be handled quickly, it is dangerous to try to resolve important issues without considering all the alternatives within a structured model. An effective model would allow a meaningfull discussion of the issues and would permit a full review of the ethical considerations presented by the situation.

Too often, decisions are based on considerations that have little relationship to what is in the best interests of the larger society. An institution that does not consider the interests of others will lose the power given to it. An ethical decision maker reaches out to different people and groups in order to reach proper and ethical decisions. Many organizations do not take the time to define their business adequately and how they are going to earn money. Each organization must find its own distinctive competence.

Private companies that do not clearly understand what they do well and how they are going to meet the needs of their customers are not likely to survive in a fiercely competitive international economy. They drift into ventures that do not succeed because they have not done their homework and utilized the appropriate decision-making model. As a result, the organization does nothing well and falls into a pattern of trying to reach the market with vague appeals. This will not work in an economy that offers customers very specific choices. The customer is not likely to buy from an organization that cannot specifically define the reasons that one should purchase its product or service.

Successful organizations also consider carefully all the available alternatives. It has been the authors' experience that organizations spend far too little time planning and developing strategies for the future. A great deal has been written about the importance of implementing a vision. This has been useful, but an organization must have a meaningful vision to implement. One of the functions of senior managers is to develop plans that benefit the entire organization and all the stakeholders.

The death of communism did not mean that people have abandoned their doubts about the ability and intentions of senior management. Workers and middle-level managers often see senior

BOX 1.2 (continued)

managers as the enemy. They are often perceived as "hangers-on" who do little except collect large salaries. Senior managers need to be seen as bringing something of value to the table other than simply giving orders to underlings. They need to ensure that decision making is done properly, that the right questions are asked, and that alternatives are examined properly and thoughtfully. Workers need to have confidence that their superiors are concerned about everyone's welfare.

When decisions are made without adequate use of a proper model, they are likely to be poor ones. It is the responsibility of senior managers to make proper decisions. Too often, major decisions are made with little involvement of others and no meaningful analysis.

instructors to write almost continuously in order to achieve tenure or obtain promotion. Some law firms and accounting firms are work factories. They ask their new associates to work a prodigious number of hours to build large client billings. An associate must work hard and bring in new clients to be made a partner.

The best-run consumer goods companies are extremely dedicated to customer service. Many of the newer high-tech companies are rather informal. Conversely, many older institutions have a much more formal and structured culture, often based on a military model.

Even the best options or strategies are not likely to succeed if they are so contrary to the organization's culture that the workers are unwilling to carry them out. If the best option is contrary to the organization's culture, one has two choices. One can choose another option or one can go about changing the culture of the organization.

A good option addresses the definition of the problem that was determined previously.[10] One can look at the strategy and find that the organization's key members agree that it will resolve the situation in the best manner possible. A good strategy also effectively assigns the human and financial resources necessary to carry it out. A strategy that does not reallocate the organization's resources is not likely to be effective.

The next step is to implement the strategy selected. It is at this stage that tasks for individual units and people should be outlined. It is also important

BOX 1.3 Nominal Group Technique

One way to improve on traditional brainstorming, which can be easily dominated by one person, is to use the nominal group technique, which forces everyone to participate. In this technique, all participants are asked to list 10 or so alternatives to a particular problem. After they have been given some time to write down their alternatives, they are poled by the facilitator, with each participant giving one of the alternatives they have created individually until all the lists are exhausted. The facilitator writes them all down, usually on a flipchart or a blackboard, and they are grouped together based on the similarity of the responses. This is an excellent way to generate numerous responses to a problem while getting input from those who are somewhat reluctant to participate in the typical brainstorming session.

that the subunits and personnel know what's expected of them. It is at this stage that the who, what, when, where, why, and how questions need to be answered. Participants should also be given the opportunity to "buy into" the strategy option. People are more likely to accomplish something if they have had some input into the decision-making process.

One should then monitor the implementation of the strategy option and the tasks assigned to the various people. It is useful at this stage to define precisely what is to be accomplished and how progress will be measured.[11] Advocates of management by objectives argue that the tasks relating to achieving the strategy ought to be as measurable as possible. That is, one ought to make tasks as quantifiable as possible. The more the goals can be measured, the more likely they will be accomplished. It is useful to establish regular updates regarding the progress of the strategy's implementation. Many organizations have monthly, quarterly, and annual reviews.

The next step is to reward individuals and units making progress toward achieving the objectives and the strategy. Employees respond well to rewards. If employees do not receive some sort of recognition, they are likely to believe that their efforts are not appreciated.[12] This will probably lead to less than optimum results. Conversely, good rewards are likely to lead to even better results in the future.

ETHICAL DECISION MAKING   ■ ■ ■

One can use the decision-making model described above to analyze problems that contain ethical elements. In these cases, the definition of the problem needs to include the ethical implications for each of the stakeholders involved. How will the solution affect the ethics of the various interests as well as the ethics of the entire organization?

In the best-run organizations, the self-interest of the entire organization is consistent with the self-interests of each of its components.[13] That is, the organization finds methods of allowing individuals to achieve their goals in ways that benefit the organization. Part of this includes recognizing the ethical considerations of each party.

Workers are interested in their own success. However, they also want to be part of something larger than themselves. In the United States, we value individuality, but we also value teamwork. Many Americans want success, but they want to succeed in a way that will not interfere with their religious or ethical values.

Despite all the recent emphasis on the drive for career success, it is clear that we have values beyond earning money. On March 24, 1997, a *Time* magazine cover article was about Americans' conception of heaven. The article observed that the overwhelming majority of Americans polled believed in the concept of an after life. Respondents also recognized the traditional dichotomy between those who believed that the path to heaven is through "good works" and those who believe that "faith" is the path to the eternal hereafter.

Clearly, Americans have concerns about ethics. Stakeholders expect to have their interests and points of view considered during the decision-making process. Although the decision maker may choose to reject the views of the stakeholders, he would be wise to listen to them.

BOX 1.4 Slippery as a Rock

The symbol of the Prudential Insurance Company has been the Rock of Gibraltar, and its slogan, "Solid as the Rock of Gibraltar!" Unfortunately, the actions of the company have not always met the standards of its symbol or slogan. Prudential's investment securities department was found guilty of selling improper investments to its customers. Its insurance department was found guilty of deceptive sales practices and selling improper insurance coverage to its elderly customers.

- What are the ethical responsibilities of the company, given their actions?
- How can the company recover its reputation?
- How could Prudential prevent this from occurring in the future?
- Why do you believe that these events occurred?

Ethical decision making would seem to include the following consideration: How does this decision affect other people besides myself? One element of ethical decision making is to consider how the choices made will affect the various individuals involved. The judge who approved the fine imposed on Prudential (see Box 1.4) pointed out that the company had defrauded many of its policyholders. The company, whose symbol was the Rock of Gibraltar, had broken faith with the people who had relied on their judgment and the faith in the company that had been established through many years of marketing and sales activities.[14]

Ethical decision making would have recognized that earning a profit is only one of a company's objectives. A company has responsibilities to its customers as well as to its shareholders. One should not treat people as things that can be manipulated. Texaco settled a 1997 lawsuit relating to discrimination against its minority employees. Companies that treat people as tools to be thrown away are engaging in poor business ethics. The iron-clad rule of responsibility states that those who abuse their power will lose it.[15]

Ethical decision making also recognizes the needs of the group. When an employee decides to steal money from an employer, he or she is also violating the group's norms. The person is stealing from fellow employees, shareholders, and customers. When police officers steal money from drug pushers, take

---

BOX 1.5 Texaco

An executive who had spent most of his working career with Texaco was let go by the company. Unfortunately, this executive was not like many others and did not go quietly. This particular person had been the secretary for many of the meetings that had been held in the executive suites of the organization, and as part of his effort to develop accurate minutes, he had recorded the meetings. While the minutes reflected the business of the meetings, the tapes went further and revealed the attitudes of many Texaco executives toward women and minorities. To say that these attitudes as revealed on the tapes reflected what can only be called a stone-age attitude on matters of race and gender would be putting it mildly. Texaco was highly embarrassed by the tapes and was eventually forced to establish programs for minorities and women as well as cash payments to many employees.

bribes, or make false arrests, they are violating the group's value system. They erode the confidence that citizens need to have in law enforcement authorities. They also erode the confidence that police officers need to have in each other. One does not want to ride in a patrol car or answer a domestic violence call with a partner who has less than total integrity.

Although it is useful to consider group values and the effect of one's actions on others, it is also dangerous from an ethical standpoint simply to accept a group's norms without question. If the group is unethical, one's own conduct will also be unethical. Many examples exist of this type of unethical "groupthink".[16]

During investigations of organized crime, it is difficult to obtain evidence because of the "code of silence" that permeates groups of criminals. The same problem often exists during investigations of police corruption. Similar problems can occur within governmental or business organizations. As this is being written, the FBI Crime Lab is being investigated for providing inaccurate analyses which were designed to assist prosecutors unfairly. If this is true, it would represent a pattern of group misconduct.[17]

It is not sufficient for an individual to adopt the standards of a group. One has an ethical obligation to reject group norms that harm other people. On March 21, 1997, Liggett & Myers admitted that its product, cigarettes, caused cancer.[18] The tobacco companies may have adopted an ethical standard that put the group's interests above the public's welfare.

The Nuremberg trials held after World War II ruled that one could not avoid legal responsibility for one's acts by claiming that one was simply following group norms or the orders of superiors.[19] One has to recognize that if the group norms are unethical, one should not follow them. It can be difficult to oppose group norms that are unethical. This can take some moral courage. Unfortunately, there is little evidence that Americans, or anyone else, are willing to demonstrate great moral courage. Surveys of military officers indicate that they routinely inflate combat readiness figures to increase their chances for promotion.[20]

Prudential salespeople were willing to sell policies that were not needed by their customers, to satisfy group norms. People interviewed for this book stated because of downsizings and other corporate changes, they feel under great pressure to do whatever is necessary to meet corporate objectives.

Ethical standards that only ask what is good for oneself will not resolve ethical questions involving other people. Appeals to group norms allow one to broaden one's perspective but do not answer questions involving ethical issues affecting constituencies more extensive than the person's social grouping. Such decisions do not adequately consider the needs of the larger society.

Another ethical standard is to appeal to the values of the larger culture. A person would ask himself or herself whether his or her actions were consistent with the values of the culture. One would conform one's values to those of the culture.

The U.S. culture has many values, some of which are contradictory. It seems to value success but asks a fearful price of the successful. It values individuality but asks people to believe in teamwork. It asks people to be humble but values self-confidence bordering on arrogance. It values competition but asks people to cooperate. It values "equality" but asks people to be judged based on "merit." It rewards material success but also claims to value "ethical" behavior.

The contradictory nature of U.S. society makes ethical behavior difficult. Distrust of nearly every institution seems to grow daily. New scandals and revelations of improper conduct seem to disclose a society that has lost its ethical moorings. A country that values competition may also find it difficult to develop a climate of ethical cooperation.

Many people interviewed by the authors laughed at the concept of a book entitled *Business in Government and Society: Ethical, International Decision Making*. They indicated that they saw little evidence of ethics in the business world. They suggested that everyone is looking out for himself or herself and has no time for ethics. Some stated that their organizations show no loyalty to workers. As a result, the workers have no loyalty to the organization.[21]

Lack of loyalty can also result in a lack of ethics. Employees begin to think more of their own welfare and less of the company's. This leads to lower performance and greater pressure on employees. When pressure becomes too great, employees may be tempted to commit unethical acts. This is particularly true if employees believe that top management supports or condones improper behavior. Employees and managers can be placed into difficult situations if the ethical standards of the group result in action that would damage the public interest.

REACHING ETHICAL DECISIONS　■　■　■

It may become more difficult to make ethical decisions if U.S. society becomes less and less ethical. One of the bases of ethical decision making is to treat others as one would want to be treated. If society and its members no longer are ethical, why should one behave ethically? What is ethical behavior in a society that may be growing less ethical because its members seem less willing to treat each other with dignity and respect?

One way to judge the ethical standards of a society is to watch how people treat each other on the nation's roads and highways. In recent years there has been a sharp increase in the number of drive-by shootings and other dangerous activities.[22] Many drivers carry weapons because they are afraid to drive on the nation's highways or into the country's cities.

The Simpson verdicts seem to have added to the "us versus them" mentality that has grown in recent years. Various groups benefit by creating an environment of confrontation. In a climate that rejects compromise or appeals to what divides people, the level of integrity and respect for one another is likely to decline. Applying ethical standards can be difficult. However, the failure to make the effort will lead to unethical decisions and poor results. Application of "the law" does provide a floor from which decision makers can operate.

Legal principles represent society's decisions regarding what is ethical in a particular situation. If a decision maker has serious questions about what is ethical, the person should consult with legal counsel. An opinion provided by a competent attorney will also protect one against charges of "bad faith" or deliberately unethical conduct. Asking an attorney at least shows a desire to conform with the law.

In addition to the usual steps involved in making any decision, an ethical decision maker would also follow certain procedures that would increase the likelihood of making an ethical decision:

1. Does the definition of the problem contain ethical elements? What are they?

2. Are the ethical elements significant enough that one should check with an attorney for legal advice? Lawyers' time is expensive and one cannot turn to them every time one has a problem. In addition, while lawyers will provide legal advice, they do not want to be in the position of solving business problems for people. The manager will have to solve them.

3. Even if legal counsel advises that one can move ahead without negative consequences, one still may have ethical decisions to make.

4. Ethical decision makers should think about the long-term consequences of their decisions. For example, the discharge of employees will weaken loyalty to the organization. In addition, an organization's reputation for attracting and retaining good employees can be damaged by poor decisions regarding their workers.

5. Ethical decision makers are concerned with the interests of all the stakeholders in the organization. It is useful to write out a discussion of how the decision would affect each major stakeholder. For example, a decision to move a plant or corporate headquarters might result in savings to a company. It would also result in changes to the communities in which they operate and significant dislocations for employees, who are required to move from one location to another. Moves also have an impact on the employees' and community's perception of an organization's loyalty. Frequent or sudden moves raise ethical questions and doubts as to an organization's loyalty to its stakeholders.

6. Ethical decision makers are also concerned about how their decisions affect other people. They are concerned about whether their decisions treat other people with respect. Failure to treat people with dignity will result in resentments and covert aggression against an organization.

One will usually get what one gives. If the organization does not treat its stakeholders with respect, it will not receive respect in return. All organizations exist with the consent of society. If stakeholders lose confidence in an organization, it will decline. For example, a large retail outlet store is located on a major interstate highway. It sells a variety of items to the public. It is positioned at the middle of the market. Its managers decide that it can increase its profit by reducing by 10 percent the wages it pays to the young people who do much of the selling by working at the counters and in the aisles. As a result, the best of the younger workers leave and sales begin to decline. They tell their friends how "stingy" the store has become. The store finds it difficult to attract the best young people as workers and develops a reputation as a store with mediocre personnel with less than cooperative attitudes.

The other side of this might be a large firm that sells retail merchandise in the center of a big city. Its manager decides its profit margin can be increased by reducing the quality of its merchandise. When it does so, it also increases its rate on the return of merchandise because of customer complaints regarding the quality of the goods. The company soon develops a reputation as an organization that sells inferior goods. As a result, it loses customers to competitors and finds it difficult to attract upscale customers or high-quality workers.

A corporate employee told the authors that the ethical infrastructure of many organizations seems to have broken down. This belief coincides with many similar statements made to the authors during the preparation of this book. There is little respect for some U.S. institutions because they have not developed a well-defined ethical structure based on treating people with dignity and respect. People want to believe that they are being listened to and understood.

Ethical managers need to spend a great deal of their time asking questions and listening to employees. An organization is less likely to make ethical blunders if people are doing a better job of listening to each other. Doing this is an example of good ethical management also being effective management. The best managers reach out to their employees by asking questions and listening to the answers. In this way, managers can draw out answers from employees.

Such a technique involves employees in the decision-making process. This approach is even more important in an environment where it is useful to have decisions made at the lowest possible level. An ethical manager makes effective use of questions and listens to the answers. Good questions also help clarify one's own thoughts. One must understand the situation well before one can ask good questions.

BOX 1.6   Ethical Advocate

A book on ethical decision making would not be complete without suggesting that all large organizations ought to employ the services of an ethical advocate. The role of the ethical advocate would be to encourage an organization to take a proactive approach to implementing ethical standards. The ethical adovate's major responsibility would be to argue that ethics are important to the organization. That is, the advocate would regularly ask the organization if its actions are legal, fair, and balanced. The advocate would ask the organization to comply proactively with laws and the intention of the laws. The ethical advocate would be concerned that the organization treat all its stakeholders with respect. The advocate would identify all the stakeholders involved and look for solutions that will treat each of them fairly. Good ethical advocates would be concerned with how the organization's activities affect the remainder of society. An advocate would help the organization develop standards for treating people with respect, dignity, and fairness.

An ethical advocate is needed in a climate where there is increasing pressure on organizations to defeat the competition, to win, to reduce costs, and to increase revenue. The perception of the ethics of businesspeople by the public is so poor that advocates are needed to restore public confidence. If ethical advocates had been employed by cigarette manufacturers, they might have avoided their billions of dollars of liability and the considerable adverse publicity they have received. An ethical advocate could have argued against "spiking" cigarettes with additional nicotine, and focusing much of the marketing effort on children.

An ethical advocate's role would be to raise the appropriate ethical issues when major decisions are being made. The advocate would raise the questions that some employees would like to raise but are inhibited from raising by organizational pressures. This also permits a fuller discussion of the issues by all the participants and reduces the likelihood of the group making a major mistake.

A primary area of focus for the ethical advocate should be the relationship between the organizations and its employees. People are the most important resource of the organization. Failure to treat employees in an ethical manner is likely to prove very costly for an organization. For example, in 1997, a jury found that the Miller Brewing company had wrongfully discharged an employee and awarded him more then $20 million. Although these types of awards are rare, they do reflect the

BOX 1.6   (continued)

public's desire that employees be treated with dignity rather than as disposable parts that can be thrown away when it is convenient for the organization to do so. Although the awards can be costly to the organization, even more costly may be the wave of adverse publicity, which indicates that the organization is not a good place in which to work. If the organization is unable to attract qualified workers, it is not likely to succeed.

The ethical advocate should be an advocate on behalf of the consumer as well as the employee. The shame of the tobacco companies is that they violated their duty to the consumer. This will particularly hurt an organization in the future. Once consumer confidence has been lost, it is very difficult to recapture that confidence.

People are becoming more demanding and more skeptical about advertising and other claims for products and services. This might be another area in which an ethical advocate could be helpful. The ethical advocate could review the marketing activities for the company to determine if they comply with the high ethical standards that the company wants to maintain.

Example

Advertisements that promise unbelievable results are usually seen as being unbelievable by potential buyers, who want to know specifically what the product or service will do for them. Although it is important to emphasize the benefits of one's product, one would be careful not to oversell the benefits. There are a large number of consumer agencies and advocate groups who want to bring actions against businesses that promise more than they can deliver. Ralph Nader has built an entire career around representing consumers. There are lawyers and politicians who are able to justify their positions by bringing suits against businesses that produce fraudulent advertisements.

One role for the ethical advocate could be to review all the advertisements and marketing materials produced by the business. An ethical advocate could also be appointed to review the materials sent out by political campaigns. An ethical advocate could also review the service that the organization provides to its customers. A common complaint among purchasers is that they do not receive the services that they were promised by the seller. This adds to the general level of distrust that people have in the business community.

The appointment of ethical advocates who make an effort to understand the position of the customer would be helpful in restoring public confidence in the business community. Ethical advocates can act as advocates for customers, which would bring another perspective to business organizations. Ethical advocates could be appointed to review any major decision that affected vital consumer interests. Important marketing programs should be checked by the ethical advocate to be certain they meet the ethical standards developed by the organization.

Another area for review by an advocate should be the company's actions with respect to the environment. Protection of the nation's environment has become an issue of increasing importance to politicians and to citizens. If an organization's activities do damage to the environment, the negative consequences can be deadly. It is useful to have an ethical advocate argue on behalf of protecting the environment.

ASKING ETHICAL QUESTIONS

The first question to ask in developing an ethical organization is to determine the values that the organization would like to have. The ethical manager might begin by questioning employees, customers, suppliers, and other stakeholders in the organization about their values and skills.

Like all other people, employees want to be understood and have their contributions valued. Too many organizations do not do an adequate job of talking with employees.[23] This can lead workers to believe that management views them only as tools to earn profits. This can lead to improper and unethical conduct. Generally, people want an organization to have the following values:

1. People are valued as individuals and treated with dignity and respect.
2. People are valued for the contributions they make to the organization.
3. People are valued equally regardless of their gender, race, religion, or ethnic origin.
4. The organization values diversity and promotes its benefits. The organization will benefit from the various perspectives and abilities of each organization member.
5. If an organization expects loyalty from its workers, it must give loyalty in return. This means that employees will be assisted so that they can perform up to their maximum potential within the organization. Loyalty to employees also means that layoffs will be only a last resort. Senior managers need to look for new marketing and revenue-enhancement opportunities before laying people off. One of the reasons for the distrust of business leaders is that employees do not believe that their managers did a good job of planning. If there were too many employees, what were they doing before they were laid off? There are almost always new areas that a business can enter and new ways of earning money. Managers could use the abilities and skills of their employees to find new business opportunities.
6. Employees and managers should want to exhibit ethical behavior for its own sake. Ethical behavior toward employees, customers, and others should be expected and rewarded.
7. Ethical organizations try to resolve conflicts in a win–win manner.
8. Ethical organizations use coercive power sparingly. They try to resolve conflicts through empathetic discussions rather than through punishments.
9. Ethical organizations consider carefully how the use of power affects the people involved.
10. Ethical organizations seek to establish what social philosophers have called an environment of harmony in which people create positive relationships with one another.

The example discussed in Box 1.7 demonstrates what can occur if an organization develops a harmonious environment characterized by positive relationships among the parties. In these types of relationships, the parties are able to achieve a great deal more than in business situations characterized by win–lose confrontations.

An ethical organization will seek to find situations where all the parties in the organization can benefit. There is a great deal that needs to be done, and it is an uncreative group of senior managers who are not able to find new activities for their employees to perform in ways that will benefit the organization and the employees.

Ethical organizations do seek to find solutions to problems that allow everyone to believe they have gained something. This is commonly called a win–win solution. In many cases, organizations have not thought how they

■ ■ ■   BOX 1.7   DSX Corporation   ■ ■ ■

The DSX Corporation has been having difficulty increasing its profits. The senior management of the company has often laid people off when this happened previously. Senior management has recently worked with an outside consultant on ethics. Senior management now recognizes that its previous actions created a climate of distrust. Layoffs alienated employees and often hurt customer relations. In addition, it created an effect that resulted in profits fluctuating up and down.

This time, senior management decides to work with employees to create a harmonious environment that will help them deal with the corporation's problems. They decide to distribute forms to identify the skills of employees that were previously not known to the senior managers of the company. The results indicated that many employees have participated in community activities that involved marketing and selling. These skills were not limited to employees who had marketing and sales positions within the organization.

After the results of the survey, the company decides to embark on a new marketing and sales campaign rather than laying off employees. It asks employees if they would be willing to be retrained as salespeople. A meaningful percentage of the employees agreed to be trained in marketing and sales. The company brings in an outside consultant who works with the employees to train them how to market and sell the company's products.

The company asks its newly trained salespersons to market the company as an institution and to sell its products. Working together, the managers and employees discuss how to develop such a program. They decide to build on the strengths of the existing employees and of the company. They realize that it is possible to expand their business relationships with their current customers. Additionally, they decide to launch higher-quality, higher-price versions of several of their existing products and services.

They develop a variety of sales plans that assign large account relationships to various managers within the company. Each of the salespeople within the company are assigned to improve customer relationships and to introduce specific customers to the benefits relating to the higher-priced, higher-quality products.

could better utilize their employees' talents. One of the reasons for the low level of confidence that employees have in their managers is that the employees remember making suggestions only to have them rejected. Ethical organizations search out the ideas of customers, employees, and other stakeholders.

Ethical organizations build strong supportive teams that work well in a harmonious environment. This will take a different approach to management than the traditional top-down approach. However, this means that managers must support team members if they want employees to support them. These teams are marked by the following characteristics:

1. There exists a mutually supportive climate where everyone's contributions are valued.

2. The organization's mission statement is well defined and it has a clear idea of the exact customers' needs which are satisfied by their products and services. One cannot build a strong team and an ethical organization if one does not have a very precise understanding of how what the organization does will benefit the people who buy its products and services. An organization that is incapable of performing these tasks well may find it easy to slide into unethical behavior be-

cause they are also incapable of earning a profit in an honest manner. If an organization is incapable of being honest with itself, it is likely to have difficulty being honest with others. Organizations that do not know how to satisfy customer needs are not likely to be successful.

3. An ethical organization builds relationships with other members of the community. It establishes good relationships with customers, suppliers, shareholders, and the area in which they operate.

The organization will be able to generate enthusiastic support of its stakeholders because they treat them ethically and with respect. An organization will generally get what it gives. If it makes an effort to treat people well, it will also be treated well. Ethical organizations also believe in the Golden Rule, which states that one should treat other people as one wishes to be treated. There are few ethical principles that have stood the tests of time and of critical analysis as well as this one. In addition, this is an ethical principle in which most managers profess to believe.

The ethical organization will also ask whether its actions will contribute to the common good. It understands that its actions will have an effect on others and that it should consider the rest of society in making its decisions. As a result, the ethical organization considers a number of alternatives carefully before making a decision.

An ethical organization also thinks about how its decisions would appear to the public and how it would need to explain its actions. An ethical organization recognizes that the actions of top management will determine the ethical standards of the entire organization. An ethical organization develops codes of conduct to help employees guide their activities. It also allows employees to expose unethical conduct by the organization. They allow employees to act as advocates for ethical conduct without fear of adverse reactions from the organization.

THE ROLE OF THE ETHICAL PERSON   ■ ■ ■

Regardless of the ethical standards of the organization, individual employees retain responsibility for their own ethical conduct. They cannot avoid the consequences of their own unethical conduct by blaming the organization's failures. Acting ethically in the face of unethical practices requires courage.

What is a person to do if he or she is asked to perform unethical acts or observes unethical conduct within an organization? There are some steps that a person might consider when confronted with such situations:

1. The employee should consider the facts carefully, being certain that he or she understands the situation accurately. What appears unethical to a new worker may not seem unethical to a more experienced professional.

2. The employee should check the code of conduct of the organization. The code of conduct may provide guidance for the employee as to how the situation could be resolved.

3. The employee should consult with others, which could include one's boss, fellow employees, and personnel from the human resource area. These people

could provide useful advice regarding the employee's problem. If the ethical problem relates to the activities of one's superior, one faces a more difficult problem. In these cases, one could face severe reprisals for exposing unethical conduct.

4. If an employee confronts a situation involving a superior's unethical conduct, he or she faces a severe ethical crisis. The person may need to become a "whistle blower" and to understand that resources are available to someone who feels the need to expose an organization's wrongdoing. Going public with accusations of wrongdoing is considered an act of disloyalty by many organizations and can lead to actions of reprisal by senior management. Therefore, employees should attempt to resolve the situation internally.

5. The employee should first define the problem and then explore all possible options for dealing with it. There are groups of people who have been confronted with ethical issues and the problems of those who could be classified as whistle blowers. These groups may have additional solutions for the employee to explore. Employees should attempt to find win–win solutions to ethical problems that confront them. That is, they should seek to avoid unnecessary confrontations. All of us are rather unprepared for the responsibilities of adulthood and the situations that are encountered. Therefore, it is useful to try to find amicable solutions to problems rather than escalating them unnecessarily. The human resources department usually has people who can act as mediators and resolve interpersonal problems.

6. The employee should check with people outside the organization. Certain companies develop a closed culture that may tolerate unethical conduct. As a result, it is useful to discuss the problem with other people, to gain different perspectives.

7. The employee may want to ask himself or herself how the situation can be analyzed in terms of one's own ethical or religious teaching. Can one justify the actions based on one's own conscience?

8. An employee might also ask how he or she would react upon seeing an account of one's actions on television or in the newspaper. Would the person feel any sense of shame if these events became known? There has been renewed interest in the topic of shame as a guide to ethical conduct. It can often be difficult to decide what is ethical. It may be easier to decide by considering if one would feel any sense of shame for participating in the action if it became known. Some jurisdictions have given extensive publicity to people who have committed crimes. Ethical violations by companies or other organizations may lead to significant adverse publicity for the individual and the institution. This can lead to a loss of sales, public funding, and trust in the organization. One might consider the issue of shame to oneself or the organization resulting from the actions.

9. An employee may also wish to contact an attorney about the situation. At the very least, the attorney can advise you about your legal rights and may also be able to give you some practical advice about the ethical situation.

10. An employee should also write out all the alternatives that may be generated by the parties involved in the situation. One can then evaluate all the options that might allow one to find ethical solutions.

BOX 1.8 John TV

In an effort to reduce prostitution in Kansas City, pictures, names, and addresses of persons arrested, but not convicted, of attempting to purchase the services of prostitutes are shown on television. This rogues' gallery is an attempt to reduce the demand for the "oldest profession" by publicly humiliating the "Johns" who use the services of prostitutes. These Johns have been arrested but have not been convicted of any crime. One response has been a suit filed in federal court claiming that the privacy and presumption of innocence of the accused men has been violated. The city has responded that these arrests are a matter of public record and that the act of putting their mug shots, names, and addresses on television is simply an extension of the police blotter. For their part, the Johns have become objects of public ridicule. Interestingly, some prominent former and current public officials have found their way onto this program.

SUMMARY

Today we study ethical decision making in business, government, and society because there is a crying need for some form of an ethical approach to the problems of the society. Schools, the government, business—indeed all areas of American life—suffer from a lack of ethical behavior. This creates a difficult situation because it is often unclear what ethics means in an era of downsizing and short-term profits. Bad ethics are usually bad for the organization and can result in terrible consequences for that organization as well as for the individuals involved. Ethical codes are one answer to the problem of attempting to make ethical decisions. Violations of a code of ethics become important because the code of ethics should reflect the core beliefs of the organization.

A way to achieve ethical decisions is to develop an ethical decision-making model. This means more than the traditional model of:

1. Define the problem
2. Review pertinent data
3. Generate alternatives
4. Select alternative
5. Implement alternative
6. Review

It means that ethical considerations need to be taken every step of the way. The core values of the organization and the individual become paramount in making decisions; and the decisions made by individuals and the organizations controlled by those individuals, will, of necessity, reflect those values. It is the duty and obligation of senior management to incorporate ethical values into the organization because without those core values the organization and the individual will lose their way in a morass of conflicting demands.

In addition to the usual steps involved in making any decision, an ethical decision maker should also follow certain guidelines that will increase the likelihood of making ethical decisions:

1. Does the definition of the problem contain ethical elements?
2. Are ethical elements of such significance that one should check with an attorney for advice?
3. Even if legal counsel advises that one can move ahead without negative consequences, one still may have ethical decisions to make.
4. Ethical decision makers should think about the long-term consequences of the decisions.
5. Ethical decision makers are concerned with the interests of all the stakeholders in the organization.
6. Ethical decision makers are also concerned about how their decisions affect other people.

To be successful in ethical decision making, it is necessary to take the long view of the situation, something that Americans are notorious for not doing. Temporary short-term advantages that may result from ethically questionable actions can only result in long-term problems. Ethical decision making asks how a decision affects other people; it addresses issues other than simply making a profit for the organization; it recognizes the needs of the larger group; and it considers group values.

It is not sufficient to simply adopt the standards of the group. The individual must be willing to think and act on his or her own. In Nazi Germany, the standard of the group resulted in some of the greatest crimes against humanity in history—a story that seems to be repeating itself in Kosovo today. "Just following orders" is simply not acceptable.

Society has many values and some of those values are contradictory; that makes ethical decision making difficult. A country that values competition may find it difficult to develop a climate of ethical cooperation. A lack of loyalty on the part of organizations toward their employees may encourage those employees to think more of their own welfare than that of the organization. This may be particularly true if employees believe that top management supports or condones improper behavior. Senior management engaging in unethical behavior encourages that kind of behavior. It is likely that people will want the organization to have the following values:

1. People will be valued as individuals.
2. People will be valued for the contributions they make to the organization.
3. People will be valued equally, regardless of their gender, race, religion, or ethnic background.

Questions

1. How would you define an ethical organization?
2. What are some characteristics of an ethical organization?
3. What would be some elements of a code of conduct in a business owned by you?

4. If you were working for a governmental agency, what elements would you put in a code of conduct?

5. What elements would you place in a code of conduct for a financial institution?

6. Name some key steps you would want to take in making a decision.

7. What additional elements would you want to include when the decision includes ethical considerations?

8. What are some components that you would include in a code of conduct for police?

9. What is the standard of ethics in your school or place of work?

10. What ethical standards would you like to have your organization adopt?

11. What are some of your own ethical standards?

12. What are some ethical standards you would like to have others adopt?

13. How does the law relate to the concept of ethics?

14. Do you believe that you can study ethics?

15. How would you teach ethics to others?

16. What suggestions do you have for this course's instructor?

17. What suggestions might you have for a textbook on ethics?

18. How might cultural differences explain different approaches to ethical concepts?

19. How might the implementation of workplace diversity change the concept of ethics in an organization?

20. Might men and women have different views with respect to ethics? As to which issues?

CASE I

You are the president of a state college located in the center of a densely populated area. You assumed your position only six months previously and have recently accepted the official seals of your office. You are informed that a campus police officer recently engaged with a minority student in a high-speed chase over a minor traffic offense. You are further informed that the police officer drew a gun and pointed it at the student.

The campus community is extremely upset about the incident. They believe that it reflects a racist attitude by police. They are also concerned that the police are too willing to use their weapons. The incident is similar to cases involving confrontations between police and minority youths in nearby large cities.

You have just met with the parents of the student involved in the incident. They have demanded that any charges against their son be dropped. They also demand that the police officer be fired. Their attorney has discussed bringing a lawsuit against the school. The media has been calling frequently to discuss the incident. The police director was just in your office and demanded that you support the campus police. The head of the student government has called your office to make an appointment.

1. What are the ethical obligations of the parties involved in this matter?
2. What are the president's ethical obligations?
3. If you were the president, how would you solve these problems?

CASE 2

You are the president of a small company in a midwestern state. You have just been informed that your company's plant is emitting pollutants into the air that exceed legal limits. The cost of repairing the stacks emitting the pollution is about $1 million. This would eliminate the company's profits and would provoke an outcry from shareholders because it would mean the end of their dividend. It could also result in the need to lay off a certain number of employees. In addition, the company would need to obtain a construction permit to repair the plant. This might alert local authorities to the problem before it can be repaired. This could result in substantial penalties being imposed against your company.

1. What are your ethical responsibilities in this case?
2. How do you weigh the various interests involved?
3. What is your ethical obligation to the company?
4. What is your ethical obligation to shareholders?
5. What is your ethical obligation to employees?
6. What is your ethical obligation to the public?

CASE 3

You have recently been elected governor of a small but highly populated state. You had been elected on a "no new taxes" pledge which you repeated up and down the state. During the campaign you were so busy trying to get elected that you had little time to think about the needs of the citizens. You have just been informed that the state's bridges have deteriorated badly and need substantial repairs. The cost of these unexpected repairs is estimated at $250 million.

1. What are your ethical responsibilities as governor?
2. What actions do you adopt?
3. Why?

References

1. Drucker, Peter F., *An introductory view of management,* Harper College Press, New York, 1977.
2. Bachler, Christopher, "Workers take leave of job stress," *Personnel Journal,* January 1995.
3. Robin, Joseph P., "When bad management becomes criminal," *Inc.,* March 1997.
4. Weiner, Tim, "Money, money, money!" *New York Times,* March 2, 1997.
5. Finnel, Tom, "Raising the bar on market conduct," *National Underwriter,* June 23, 1997, v. 101.
6. Green, Brian, "Downward indicators on readiness," *Air Force Magazine,* September 1994.
7. Kemp, David, "There are no gray areas," *U.S. Naval Institute Proceedings,* June 1997.
8. Drucker, *An introductory view,* plus various other works by various authors.
9. Ibid.
10. Kreitner, Robert, *Management,* 4th Ed. Houghton Mifflin Company, Boston, 1987.
11. Seashore, Stanley, "Criteria of organizational effectiveness," *Michigan Business Review,* July 1965.
12. O'Reilly, Brian, "The new deal: what companies and employees owe one another," *Fortune,* June 13, 1994.

13. Drucker, *An introductory view.*

14. King, Carole, "States tallying Pru policyholders seeking relief," *National Underwriter,* June 9, 1997.

15. Fitzpatrick, Beatrice, "Make the business case for diversity," *HRMagazine,* May 1997.

16. Janis, Irving Lester, *Groupthink: psychological studies of policy decisions and fiascoes,* Houghton Mifflin, Boston, 1982.

17. Burerham, David, "The FBI," *Nation,* August 11–18, 1997, v. 265, n. 5.

18. Kadlec, Daniel, "Populist hero or bottom feeder?" *Time,* March 31, 1997, v. 149, n. 13.

19. Rice, Earle, Jr., *The Nuremberg Trials,* Lucent Books, San Diego, CA, 1996.

20. Kemp, "There are no gray areas."

21. O'Reilly, "The new deal."

22. Sanders, William B., *Gangbangs and drivebys: Grounded culture and juvenile gang violence,* Aldine de Gruyter, Hawthorne, NY, 1994.

23. Leabs, Jennifer, "Show them where you're headed," *Workforce,* November 1998.

Origins of the Modern Global Environment

Concepts ▪ You Will Learn ■ ■ ■

the origins of agrarian, industrial, and information-based civilization

the importance of the development of the great Western European empires in the spread of Western civilization

the reactions to the abuses of industrialization

the modern global environment in the major trading areas of the world

THE PREINDUSTRIAL WORLD ■ ■ ■

Agarian Civilization ■ ■ ■

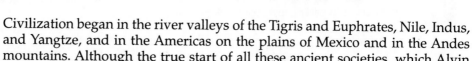

Civilization began in the river valleys of the Tigris and Euphrates, Nile, Indus, and Yangtze, and in the Americas on the plains of Mexico and in the Andes mountains. Although the true start of all these ancient societies, which Alvin Toffler has called the *first wave,* has been lost to the ages, they all had certain things in common.[1]

The first was that they were all based on agriculture.[2] The technological level of these societies had advanced to the point where the food supply was more certain if the groups stayed in one place and grew crops rather than pursuing their old hunter-gatherer ways and simply moving on after snatching whatever food they could from the environment.

A second development was that of the specialization of labor. Just as in the old hunter-gatherer days, people developed particular talents that made them more valuable to the society. With the tribe settling into one location, additional occupations became established. Some became farmers, some warriors, and some priests. The tribe grew and prospered, and the original village slowly turned into a city that was the center of the society.

Housed in the city were the marketplace, the ruler, the priests, the military, and craftspeople who designed items for the use of the general populace, including goldsmiths, silversmiths, blacksmiths, and armorers. These functions of order, exchange, production, religion, and protection represent some of the major aspects of society, even today.

The function of order was provided by the king or prince, or by the government. They established units of measure, laws for the people to live by, punishment standards for criminals, and helped to establish customs that soon became traditions in the society.

The function of exchange became the basis of marketing. One of the marks of civilizations is that the people in the society are interconnected. Self-sufficiently is the exception; interdependence is the rule. If a society develops specialization of labor and production, it must also develop a means of redistributing those goods so that all the members of the society can hope to survive.[3]

The earliest and most successful means of redistributing those goods was the marketplace.[4] People would take their surplus and exchange it with other members of the society for their goods. This barter economy worked well, but it was slow and cumbersome. The response was a medium of exchange: something that was generally agreed to have a certain, reasonably set value. Gold,

---

BOX 2.1 Hammurabi's Code

An eye for an eye, a tooth for a tooth.

One of the earliest legal codes was established by Hammurabi, a king of the first dynasty of Babylon who reigned from about 1790 to 1750 B.C. The code was inscribed on a stele of black diorite some seven feet high and was discovered in Susa, Iran at the turn of the twentieth century. The laws are grouped by subject, such as offenses against property, administration of justice, and assaults. It is obvious that the stele was designed for public display, perhaps to inform people of the rules of the state and the consequences of breaking those rules. Certainly, it was an attempt at order and the elimination of chaos in early Babylonian society.

BOX 2.2 What's a Cubit?

"Make thee an ark of gopher wood; rooms shalt thou make in the ark, and shall pitch it within and without with pitch. And this is the fashion which thou shalt make it of: the length of the ark shall be three hundred cubits, the breath of it shall be fifty cubits and the height of it, thirty cubits." Genesis 6:14–15

Webster's *Third New International Dictionary* defines a cubit as "any of various ancient units of length based on the length of the forearm from the elbow to the tip of the middle finger and usually equal to about 18 inches, but sometimes 21 or more." So the ark was anywhere from 450 to 525 or more feet long, 75 to 88 or more feet wide, and 45 to 52 feet high.

precious stones, silver, and other items were generally accepted as appropriate means of exchange. However, it was not long before the rulers stepped into the picture with a standardized medium of exchange—money. This was important for several reasons: (1) it did set a common standard of value for trade purposes, and (2) it gave the government great control over the economic activity of the society. That control made the rulers rich and set them apart from the rest of the society. The modern version of this kind of activity can be seen in the actions of the treasury departments of various governments or the actions of the Federal Reserve in the United States. When the chairman of the Federal Reserve says that the price of certain stocks is too high, the prices of those stocks plummet.

Religion came to be an important aspect of the society in civilization. Most nomadic groups had a shaman or believed in some form of what today would be called a religion. People feared the unknown, whether before, after, and during life. Would the crops be good this year? Would barbarians attack the village? Would I be killed, and if so, then what? These were all questions that all civilizations and people have. For some societies, such as ancient Egypt,[5] life and death became an obsession with elaborate rituals and ceremonies involving the trip to the other world, whether paradise, hell, or someplace in between. Appeals to the god(s) had to be made, and sacrifices were sometimes felt to be appropriate to please and placate the gods. If the gods were pleased, the harvest would be good. If not, the people would suffer. These were secrets that only the priests could know. Only they knew the right words, the right sacrifice, and what signs could be read in the entrails of the victim. In an uncertain world of high risk and easy death, the masses needed to be assured, and religion provided that assurance.

Finally, the society needed to be protected against barbarians and other external threats. While religion addressed the unknown, it was the responsibility of the ruler to address the known threats to the society. At first the people themselves would take up arms against the invader. The history of ancient Greece and early ancient Rome are full of stories of citizens taking up arms and defeating the larger, better equipped, better trained invaders.[6] But even these stories and traditions faded with time as empires grew and the need for specialized armed forces became manifest. The city, the society, the civilization had to be

BOX 2.3

"And they came to the place which God had told him of; and Abraham built an altar there, and laid the wood in order and bound Isaac his son, and laid him on the altar upon the wood. And Abraham stretched forth his hand and took the knife to slay his son. And the angel of the Lord called onto him out of heaven, and said, Abraham, Abraham: and he said, Here am I. And he said, Lay not thine hand upon the lad, neither do thou any thing unto him; for now I know that thou fearest God, seeing thou hast not withheld thy son, thine only son from me. And Abraham lifted up his eyes, and looked, and behold behind him a ram caught in a thicket by his horns; and Abraham went and took the ram and offered him up for a burnt-offering in the stead of his son."   Genesis 22:9–13

One of the distinguishing aspects of the Judeo-Christian tradition is that human sacrifice was not practiced, even during the earliest of times.

■ ■ ■ **BOX 2.4   Human Sacrifice** ■ ■ ■

Human sacrifice was one of the characteristics of many early religions. The Israelites mention human sacrifice as part of the religion of the Cannanites in the Old Testament. It was not uncommon for early civilizations in the Americas and elsewhere to sacrifice war prisoners as the Aztecs did to their god, Huitzilopochtli. Cannibalism was also practiced by the Aztecs, as the flesh of the sacrificed victims was eaten for religious motives as a kind of communion with their deities.

■ ■ ■ **BOX 2.5   Horatio at the Bridge** ■ ■ ■

One of the early legends of the Roman Republic concerned the defense of Rome against an invading Etruscan army. According to the legend, an Etruscan army approached Rome from the west, moving on the wooden Sublician Bridge, then the only span over the Tiber. Horatio volunteered to hold the bridge against the Etruscans while the Romans demolished the bridge behind him. Fighting the Etruscans, even as the bridge collapsed, Horatio became a hero of the early Roman Republic for his bravery in almost single-handedly defeating a much larger force and saving Rome from the Etruscan attack. Horatio is important because he symbolizes the strength and bravery of the individual citizen in overcoming great odds. Horatio was a symbol of the Republic.

---

protected because they had many enemies, and the larger and more prosperous a civilization became, the greater the need for protection. Rome had its legions;[7] China had its wall, the British Empire had its navy, and Russia had its winter and its mud. All conspired successfully to defeat the enemy for a very long time, but all were eventually compromised. The Germanic hords and Attila the Hun eventually overran Rome's legions; China's wall was eventually breached by the Mongols; Britain's Royal Navy was made obsolete by the airplane; and Russia's winter and mud were made irrelevant by atomic weapons.

The Age of Discovery and Exploration

After the demise of the Western Roman Empire in 456, Western European civilization went into a sharp decline that is known as the Middle Ages. Other areas of the globe continued to grow and expand. The Arabs established several great centers of learning, such as that at Madrid in Spain,[8] which later became models for great European universities in Rome, Paris, and Bologna.[9] Great advances were made in a number of areas, including algebra, architecture, and literature. In the Americas, the Mayas, Aztecs, and Incas were probing deep into the stars, making new discoveries in astronomy.[10] To call this period a dark age is a uniquely European perspective, but in Europe it was a dark age, with only a few glimmers of light, such as Charlemagne, Alfred the Great, and Wenceslaus.[11]

Europe eventually awoke from its slumber in an era known as the Renaissance. It was as though the pent-up energies of over 500 years of darkness were slowly released. The civilization was allowed to flower in ways that had not been seen since the glories of ancient Greece and Rome. Many giants of Western art, music, and literature lived during this time and to some degree were contemporaries: Michelangelo, Leonardo da Vinci, Vivaldi, and Dante being among the notables. The Renaissance started in Italy and moved slowly through the rest of Europe, but wherever it went, the dark was replaced by light. Science began to flourish and at times challenged the Church and its dogma.[12] Galileo claimed that the Earth moved around the sun, but he was silenced by the Church. Copernicus, however, spoke the same fact from the grave, and the Church could not silence a dead man.

The roots of this flowering could be traced to the travels of Crusaders and merchants who ventured outside the boundaries of Europe. Merchants brought spice, silk, and other goods from the East. Crusaders discovered entire new societies, and although they may have sacked and burned their share of them, their glories were not completely lost on the knights of the Cross.

Commerce led eventually to exploration, and exploration led to discovery. During the latter part of the Renaissance, trade by Europe with India and China was controlled by the city–state of Venice, whose only true rival in the eastern Mediterranean was the Ottoman Empire. These two civilizations fought for many years over control of these trade routes. Venice, which could trace its role in this trade back to such famous explorers as Marco Polo,[13] had established many of the routes, and the Ottoman Empire straddled most of them. For their part, the other states of Europe were tired of the monopoly that Venice had on these goods from the East. Although they could not openly support the Islamic Ottomans in their continuing wars against Venice, they could go to war against Venice in their own right, or they could find another way to China.

Stories of a rich and prosperous land to the West had persisted since ancient times in the legend of Atlantis.[14] Like Galileo, educated men knew that the world was round, not flat. You might sail far enough west so that you would not have enough food or water to get back, but you would not fall off the end of the Earth. Prince Henry the Navigator, of Portugal, started to send ships south around Africa in an effort to find an alternative route to the East,[15] and finally, Spain sent an Italian sailor west in search of the Indies, only to have him find a "new world."

■ ■ ■   BOX 2.6   Nicolas Copernicus   ■ ■ ■

Nicolas Copernicus was a Polish astronomer who founded modern astronomy. As canon of the cathedral of Frombork, he was able to study the Earth and the universe. Essentially, his radical idea was that the Earth rotated around the sun and that the Earth was not the center of the universe. This was a highly controversial idea and ran straight into the orthodox dogma of the Church. After all, in the Bible, in Genesis, God made the Earth on the second day and the sun, the moon, and the stars on the fourth day. If Genesis, the acknowledged word of God was wrong, what else could be in error?

Copernicus was not unaware that his ideas were completely revolutionary and that he could pay a high price for them, something that many of his supporters did after his death. He had an anonymous manuscript of his ideas circulated among his friends for comment. When word leaked out regarding the existence of the manuscript and curiosity increased concerning his ideas and their author, most of his friends urged him to publish it. He did so, under the title *Revolutions of the Heavenly Spheres*, just before his death in 1543.

The age of exploration and discovery represents perhaps the greatest military, societal, religious, and cultural exploration in the history of the planet. Western European civilization may have slept for nearly 1000 years, but when it finally awoke and had driven the sleep from its eyes, it was more than ready to take on the world, and did.

The explorations of Columbus, DeSoto, and Cortez, as well as those of Hudson, Cabot, and LaSalle, are in every history book. This impetus for exploration continued into the nineteenth and twentieth centuries with people such as Livingstone, Perry, Lewis and Clark, and Armstrong. It will continue into the twenty-first century as the people of this planet prepare to venture beyond the confines of the Earth and the moon and start to explore the solar system, probably starting with Mars. What has happened since the Renaissance is that European society, especially European society–based technology, has continued to expand. The leadership of the movement may have been in Italy, Spain, France, Britain, Germany, or the United States, but it has always been an expansion based on European traditions and on scientific progress. These traditions have included a respect for the individual and for a democratic society that may be traced to ancient Greece. A thirst for knowledge, a desire for wealth, and a belief in the final vindication of the cause of individual freedom and liberty have marked this advancement. Unfortunately, until very recently, a total disrespect for other cultures, values, and peoples has also marked this expansion. Societies that were in the way were either pushed aside or destroyed.[16] Little could stand in the way of the advance of Western civilization, and those societies that tried or had the misfortune to be in the way soon found themselves sharing the fate of the gooney bird: extinction, and like the last stuffed bird, the only remnant of the glories of the old culture to be found.

The only certainty of Western civilization is that it will continue to expand. The society is becoming more inclusive as other nations adopt various forms of democracy and other Western ideas. This is not to say that countries such as Japan, China, or South Africa will have societies like that of the United States, but that eventually they will probably become democratic capitalistic societies with their own Chinese or South African twist, and Japan is well on its way.[17]

THE INDUSTRIALIZED WORLD ■ ■ ■

Beginnings of the Industrialized World ■ ■ ■

The industrialized world started in Great Britain a little before the time of the American Revolutionary War. As a part of what was then British society, many of the founders of the United States were engaged in various scientific activities. The two most famous of these were Jefferson and Franklin. In addition to being a publisher, writer, politician, diplomat, and businessman, Franklin was the most famous scientist of his day.[18] Jefferson, a young man in 1776, and one of the great contradictions in U.S. history, would win fame as an architect, politician, statesman, diplomat, and educator.[19] But nothing he would ever do would be as important as his writing one particular sentence of the Declaration of Independence: "We hold these truths to be self-evident; that all men are created equal, that they are endowed by their Creator with certain unalienable rights, that among these are Life, Liberty and the pursuit of Happiness."

Franklin and Jefferson may have been among the last of the true Renaissance men, in the great tradition of Galileo, Leonardo, and Michelangelo, but they lived during the beginning of a great explosion of technology in which they both played a role. During that time, mechanization began to replace workers who had traditionally worked as craftsmen. This first took place in the textile industry, in the form of the production of cloth.[20] It then moved to other parts of the industry, especially the manufacture of shoes and hats.

The principles learned from the experience of the textile industry were then applied to other industries and in other countries. The United States and Germany soon followed Great Britain, as did, to varying degrees, the rest of Europe. People were being replaced on the farm by machines, and machines were replacing craftspeople. Production soared, but poverty in the cities became worse, while poverty in the country became intolerable and sometimes deadly.[21] Famine was a specter that haunted Europe as the division between the haves and have-nots grew wider. Production was up but there were few with enough money to buy and the political situation became very unstable in much of the industrialized world.

Reactions to the Industrial Revolution ■ ■ ■

The poverty, poor working conditions, and other problems associated with the industrial revolution did not go unanswered. Printers struck in Philadelphia as early as 1790[22] and the Luddites did everything possible to try to combat, if not stop, the industrial revolution. Conditions in the factory continued to decline, which did not go unnoticed. The first group to address the inequities of capitalism were the utopian socialists.[23] These people tried to establish communities, built around the factory, where the workers had decent housing and working conditions. They tried to provide for their workers, and some of the utopian socialists were briefly successful in establishing communities that were productive. Robert Owen was a leader in the development of this idea in England, but his and similar attempts were not widely accepted or successful.

Even in literature there was a reaction to the life of workers. In England, this was the era of the romantic literature of Bryan, Keats, and Shelly,[24] fantasies that could be read as an escape from the numbing existence of the factory. Dickens remained the great muckraker of English literature—the new movement of

■ ■ ■ **BOX 2.7 The Luddites** ■ ■ ■

The Luddites were a group of English workers who attempted to forestall the progress of industrialization by destroying wide-frame looms that made hosiery of an inferior quality but on a mass production basis, using far fewer workers and thereby suppressing wages. The acts of the Luddites were acts of desperation. At first they had sought relief from the British government, but any help from the government proved either unenforceable or blocked by the interests of the mill owners. The movement was then suppressed by the army, several leaders of the movement being killed, and latter by legislation passed through Parliament. Some of the Luddites were hanged and some were sent to penal colonies. The Luddites represent an attempt on the part of workers to control their destiny in the face of rapid technological change, and as with most such movements, they were brushed aside.

romanticism did not address the needs of the society but rather, the need to escape from the terrible working conditions, child labor, and the plight in which most people found themselves.

The roots of socialism and communism can be found in the reaction to capitalism and the excesses of the industrial revolution. Conditions in the factories were frequently terrible, so terrible that in the United States they were used as a justification for slavery.[25] Conditions on the plantation may not have been that great, but they were frequently better than conditions in the factory. The fact that the slaves were not free to make any changes in their conditions, and could be bought and sold like cattle, was not an issue, because owners of factories could do the same with their investments.

Many of these conditions came to a head in Europe in 1848. During that year Karl Marx's *Communist Manifesto*[26] was widely read and revolts occurred all over Europe. Efforts in Germany and Poland and by the Paris Commune were all attempts by workers to seize power, but none were successful.[27] The repression that followed drove many Europeans to leave for the United States and represented the first great wave of immigration from places other than the British Isles. Germany was especially well represented, to the point where in certain units of the Grand Army of the Republic, orders had to be given in German rather than English because the recruits could not speak or understand English.[28]

The union movement also started to gain strength in both the United States and Europe at this time. In the United States the unions had been under political attack for many years. Starting with the Danbury Hatters case,[29] they were, in fact, deemed unconstitutional by the Supreme Court, thus illegal for 100 years. This did not, however, prevent them from growing and becoming a force in U.S. society, but it did change their approach compared to that of their European cousins. Unions in the United States have been far more concerned

---

■ ■ ■ BOX 2.8 The Communist Manifesto ■ ■ ■

"There is a specter haunting Europe. It is the specter of Communism."*

These are the first words of the *Communist Manifesto* by Karl Marx. The *Manifesto* is a declaration of grievances against the established order in Europe. It is a revolutionary document in the great tradition of the American Declaration of Independence and the French Declaration of the Rights of Man. The *Manifesto* is, as is communism, a reaction and challenge to the established order. Unlike the Declaration of Independence and the Declaration of the Rights of Man, which dealt primarily with political questions, the *Communist Manifesto* focuses on economic questions in addition to its political thesis. When the *Manifesto* was written, conditions for the working classes in an industrializing Europe were steadily declining. Times were tough and things were bad for the vast majority of the population. The *Manifesto* and communism/socialism gave voice to the grievances of these people and were highly influential in the organized labor movement in Europe and to a lesser degree, in the United States.

"Workers of the world unite! You have nothing to lose but your chains!"*

*Karl Marx, *The Communist Manifesto* (Chicago: H. Regnery Co., 1955).

with economic than with political issues.[30] European unions, on the other hand, had long been concerned with both political and economic issues, to the point where in many countries one of the major political parties is still the "Labor" party.[31]

The Age of Empire

The industrial revolution touched off a second wave of colonial expansion for the nations of Europe. The first wave of expansion had ended with successful revolutions in English North America and Spanish America. Essentially, after 1810, the first great colonial empire, the Spanish Empire, had come to an end.[32] The vast holdings Spain had held in Latin America were virtually all independent of the mother country, and with the exception of a few islands in the Caribbean and some holdings elsewhere, the empire started by Ferdinand and Isabella was over. Spain itself had become a backwater country. Exhausted by colonial wars, Napoleonic wars, and a bankrupt economy, Spain essentially dropped out of the mainstream of European history.

This did not mean that the quest for empire was over. On the contrary, a new era of empire building was about to begin. For a country to have a successful industrial revolution, it first had to have a source of raw materials. The necessary raw materials of iron ore, coal, and others were well developed in most of Europe, and new sources had to be found. The other consideration was markets. You had to have someplace to sell your finished goods, and a colony guaranteed a market. As a result, after the Napoleonic wars, many of the nations of Europe, but especially France and Britain, together with the United States and later Germany, entered into a contest of global imperial expansion.

The French felt perhaps the greatest need to expand an empire, to guarantee raw materials for their factories and markets for their goods. Relieved of almost all of their colonial possessions through a series of wars with the British in North America, Europe, and India, the French led the expansion of colonial powers into Africa.[33] The French took large sections of North Africa and parts of Asia, frequently subduing local populations possessing a high culture. Their conquests included French West Africa, Indo-China, various islands in the South Pacific, and parts of the Middle East, as well as attempts at establishing a government in Mexico while the United States was busy with its Civil War.[34]

The British Empire, which with the exception of the 13 American colonies had been very successful, continued to have vast holdings throughout the world. Although the British had lost half of North America in the American Revolution, they still held half of it in Canada. India was all British, and parts of the Caribbean, as well as Australia, New Zealand, and the Pacific Islands, belonged to the British. But when they saw the other European powers begin to take an interest in expanding their colonial possessions, the British started to acquire parts of Asia and Africa. They expanded their holdings to include Burma, Malaya, Rhodesia, South Africa, Singapore, Egypt, and Sudan and even for a time challenged the United States over the fate of Hawaii.[35] During this time British literature featured the works of Rudyard Kipling,[36] the soldiers' poet, who penned such classics as *Gunga Din, Fuzzy-Wuzzy,* and *Danny Deaver.* Kipling often wrote and spoke of the "white man's burden" as the rationale for the expansion of the empire. The task was to bring Christianity, education, and the benefits of modern society to the "savages," some of whom had ancestors who were civilized while the British were still living in huts. This argument completely fell apart with the Boer War, where the British attacked the Boers, a group of Europeans who had settled the southern tip of Africa around 1500 at Cape Town.[37] Empire was about commerce, raw materials, and markets, obtaining them for yourself and keeping them from others.

Later, as the colonies became more British, the British Commonwealth developed, especially after World War II.[38] The British realized the absurdity of a medium-sized island off the coast of Europe controlling vast areas of Asia, Africa, Australia, and New Zealand, but they still wanted the markets and the access to the raw materials. The Commonwealth helped to ensure that, if only for a short time. Today, the British Empire is no more, and the Commonwealth is simply a vestigial association of English-speaking countries.

Two other countries attempted to build empires but were unsuccessful: Germany and Japan. Prior to World War I, Germany had acquired a few possessions in Africa and in the South Pacific.[39] But after the war, these possessions reverted to various other colonial powers that had been on the winning side. Japan also sought to establish an empire. Although coming late to empire building, Japan was initially successful in the Russo-Japanese War, where for the first time in centuries, a European power was soundly defeated by a non-European power.[40] The Japanese had beaten a European country at its own game. Between World War I and World War II, the Japanese invaded China and established a regime in Manchuria.[41] Many scholars date this conflict as the beginning of World War II. Millions of Chinese were killed in this struggle against the Japanese Empire. The Japanese were generally very successful in their war against China until they attacked the United States.

This brought the United States as well as most of the European allies into the war in the Pacific and Asia and spelled the end of the Japanese Empire.[42] As Admiral Yamamoto said: "I will run wild in the Pacific for six months, but after that I can guarantee nothing!"[43] and he was right. For six months the Japanese did run wild, not only in the Pacific but in most of Asia, expanding their victo-

---

BOX 2.9 Pearl Harbor

"Yesterday, December seventh, 1941 is a day that will live in infamy."*

On December 8, 1941, President Roosevelt addressed a joint session of Congress, requesting a declaration of war against Japan. The day before, aircraft of the Imperial Japanese Navy attacked and sank or damaged much of the U.S. Pacific Fleet. The attack was without warning and completely suprised the U.S. forces stationed in Hawaii. This attack lead to direct U.S. involvement in World War II and, after over four years of hard fighting, the eventual defeat of Japan, Germany, and all the axis powers. It led to the Cold War and the eventual victory of the United States in that conflict and to U.S. dominance of the world from a military, economic, and political perspective after the war.

"With confidence in our armed forces, with the unbounding determination of our people, we will gain the inevitable triumph—so help us God."*

*The President's War Address, December 8, 1941.

ries into much of Asia, including the Philippines, Malaya, Singapore, Indo-China, Indonesia, and Burma. The Japanese were particularly brutal in these assaults and victories. There are very good reasons why Japanese victories are often referred to as the "Rape of Hong Kong," the "Rape of Singapore," and the "Rape of Nangking." But the Japanese attempt at a traditional empire was doomed from the beginning and ended in 1945 on the battleship USS *Missouri*.[44]

Two other empires survived World War II[45] and the postcolonial era. The Soviet Empire established itself in Eastern Europe by dominating those countries and East Germany after World War II. Fighting on the Russian front had been terrible and there has never been a complete count of all the Russian dead. The Soviet Union already had an empire that it had inherited from the Czars which extended from the Baltic to the Pacific. But the Soviets wanted a buffer between themselves and the rest of Europe that they did not control, so the Warsaw Pact was established, and the "Cold War" against the United States and the rest of the Western world was begun.[46]

The Cold War was not really cold. It was only cold from the perspective that the two major world powers did not face each other directly, in combat—they used surrogates. Americans fought Vietnamese and Koreans, Russians fought Afghanis and provided "advisors" to Cuba and Angola, but direct fighting between the United States and the Soviet Union was too dangerous. Both had atomic weapons, and nobody was prepared to risk such a conflict. In the end the Soviet Union lost the Cold War together with its empire.[47] Many of the nations of the Warsaw Pact now want to join NATO, and some have, while the republics of the old Soviet Union are going their separate ways. The Soviet Empire is no more.

The only empire left is the American Empire. Most Americans do not think of their country as an imperial power. It goes against everything the founding fathers stood for, but it is an empire, nonetheless. Jefferson added the Louisiana Purchase in 1803, and vast tracks of land were added to the country after the Mexican War. Essentially, parts of or the entire states of Texas, Oklahoma, New Mexico, Colorado, Kansas, Arizona, Utah, Nevada, and California were added to the country and taken away from Mexico.[48] Alaska was purchased from the Russians, and both Hawaii and the Pacific Northwest were acquired after disagreements with the British. Finally, the remnants of the Spanish Empire were taken over by the United States after the Spanish-American War. Cuba, the Philippines, and other small possessions were added to the U.S. sphere of influence.

The United States is the only great power left in the world, and there are only a few with even the potential to rival it. A United Europe, a reformed Russia, China, and perhaps India are the only countries even with the potential to consider becoming a great power. In many ways the United States is unique in the age of empire because it did not deliberately seek the status of "indispensable nation."[49] Yet that is what it has become. It is the "last" empire.

The Modern Global Environment　

In his book *The Third Wave*,[50] Alvin Toffler made the case that modern society is at the beginning of a third era of development. The first was the movement from nomadic societies to agriculturally based civilizations, the second was from agriculture to industry, and the third, ongoing, is from industry to a society based on knowledge. Several important events over the last several years have changed the way the world operates.

The Cold War is over. The former Soviet Union and the United States have, for the first time in the post–World War II era, signed an agreement that actually reduces the number of nuclear weapons.[51] Each country did this for its own reasons, and each expects to gain certain benefits from the treaty that may be viewed as only the first step in what is hoped to be a gradual march away from nuclear destruction.

The Soviet Union lost the Cold War. The countries on the Pacific rim are only the most prominent examples of the Soviets losing the struggle for the hearts and minds of the people of the less developed world. Countries such as Japan, Korea, and Singapore are simply the most prominent examples of the success of the capitalist model. Although they have recently experienced economic difficulties, the reforms that have been instituted will help to lead them back to economic health and stability. At the end of World War II, most of the Pacific rim countries were economic disasters, whereas today, they are economic dynamos. They produce goods and services based on economies that are the envy of the entire world, including the United States. Their success has not been lost on the Russians or the Chinese. The two Koreas provide the most striking example: Two countries with virtually identical cultures, languages, history, and leveled economies in the early 1950s have become as different as one could possibly imagine in only 40 years.[52]

The Russians and the Chinese have begun to introduce various forms of Sino and Russian capitalism, and the Russians have signed a document that may become regarded as the first step in the "treaty" to end the Cold War. The United States won the Cold War. The countries that are advancing economically, and although more haltingly, politically, are those that have adopted free enterprise. This is not to say that armed conflicts will cease or that armed forces will not continue to be necessary and sometimes used. It is to say that the rules have changed, the main arena has switched, and other participants are and will be involved.

The new great conflict is "industrial war." It is simply too dangerous and too expensive for the United States or anyone else to wage traditional war directly, and the "proxies" that have been so useful in their respective causes are learning how expensive modern war is and how much they have to lose.[53] Also, there is the nightmare of nuclear proliferation, as exemplified by the Princeton undergraduate who designed a nuclear bomb some years ago. Atomic weapons, and the availability, opportunity, and temptation to use those weapons, make war on almost any level a far too dangerous occupation for all the people on the planet.

Industrial war provides the protagonists with the means and opportunity to vanquish the "enemy" while securing and not destroying the spoils. The Russians have recognized that they cannot maintain a huge military and wage industrial war successfully. The military soaks up the resources necessary to wage a successful industrial conflict. Resources, which are always limited in any society, are needed for investment, research and development, and training and education to make a society more economically competitive. Munitions, and their means of delivery, divert the resources needed to produce goods and services. Indeed, armaments produce no economic good other than demand-pull inflation through the injection of wages and other payments into the economy with no corresponding products or services, as well as the diversion of resources that could be used to produce economically productive goods.

The developed and less developed countries must now compete for markets in which to sell products as well as for materials to make goods. Many developing countries, former European colonies,[54] are now using their resources to produce goods and services for both domestic and international consumption instead of sending them to their former imperial masters. These former colonies are drawing on the lessons learned from their past of exploitation to assist them in the new world of global competition.

In Western Europe, the Common Market has proven to be the key in assisting the former colonial masters to make the transition to industrial democracy from imperialism.[55] In Eastern Europe, the death of the Soviet Empire is obvious.[56]

Some republics of the former Soviet Union have broken away from Moscow, and the two Germanys have united into what will eventually be a powerful economic force. The eventual outcome of these events remains to be seen, but it is certain that if these countries remain on their current course, Europe will be an economic force in the years to come.

In contrast, the U.S. experience has more in common with a rich uncle than with a society accustomed to the rigors and discipline of a competitive international economic environment. The United States has many advantages over other countries: Few societies possess the vastness or the degree of development of natural resources; U.S. technology is still the finest in the world, but many countries are gaining or ahead of the United States in certain areas; Wall Street has only two rivals, Tokyo and London; and no other economy offers as strong a tradition of economic freedom as does the U.S. economy.

But the U.S. society has two major weaknesses. The first is an aging industrial base that is not being adequately replaced with new technology. In the pursuit of short-term profits, U.S. corporations have not replaced their worn-out plant and equipment at a rate equal to or greater than the one at which they have been consumed. Basic industries such as steel and autos are using obsolete factories. These obsolete production facilities cannot hope to compete effectively with modern factories outside the United States. There is no way that a steel mill based on 1890s technology can compete effectively with one based on current technology. The second problem facing the U.S. economy is the specter of a relatively undertrained and poorly educated labor force compared to those in other industrial countries.[57] This workforce is not prepared to meet the challenges that will come as a result of the internationalization of markets. Real unemployment, including the counted and uncounted or discouraged workers, continues at rates that would not have been politically acceptable in the first two decades of the post–World War II era. This unemployment exists because the people in the labor force do not have the necessary skills to do the jobs that are available. One of the few economic certainties facing the U.S. worker is that in the future there will be fewer low-skill jobs and an increase in the number of jobs demanding a high degree of skill. Many unemployed workers have come from industries that have either been severely hurt by foreign competition or have moved offshore and exported jobs once held by U.S. workers. The jobs these workers once held required a low degree of skill and were easily learned by others. They often were paid wages far in excess of worldwide rates, and the ability of these workers to learn what is necessary for highly skilled positions is often questioned.[58]

The combined weaknesses of technological obsolescence and an unskilled workforce do not bode well for the United States. We may have won the Cold War only to find ourselves woefully unprepared to wage the industrial war successfully. As the French after World War I, the country's leaders are perfecting new techniques designed to win a conflict that is already over, and as the French, will find their "Maginot Line" pointed in the wrong direction.

It is now time for Americans to reconsider their role in the world and how they intend to live in the third millennium. Will the United States continue to waste valuable time, talent, and resources on obsolete and irrelevant projects, or will it rechannel those assets into the education and training of the populace and reinvestment in a new high-technology industrial base? Will the United States continue to pursue policies in the name of short-term profits and military preparedness, which divert its best minds and drain its resources, or will it again exercise the high moral, economic, and technological leadership of which it was once so proud? Finally, will the United States be a winner or a loser in the industrial war? Will it opt for obsolete ideas, thinking, and leadership, as England did after World War II, or will it move toward bold, innovative, and original approaches to the future?

SUMMARY

Civilization started in the river valleys of the Middle East, India, China, and the Americas. These early cultures, based on agriculture, represented the primary focus of civilization until about 200 years ago, the beginning of the industrial revolution in England.

During the period from the fall of Rome to the Renaissance, Western Europe fell into a dark age during which progress more or less came to a halt. This did not happen in the rest of the world, however. This period was the time of the great flowering of Islamic culture in the Middle East and even as far as Moorish Spain, but Europe was, by any measurement, a backwater in the affairs of the human race. This started to change with the advent of the Renaissance. During this period, Europe started to grow again and to expand into the Age of Discovery.

The Age of Discovery represents perhaps the greatest military, societal, religious, and cultural expansion in the history of the planet. The explorations of Columbus, DeSoto, and Cortez as well as those of Hudson, Cabot, and LaSalle, are described in every history book. What has happened since the Renaissance is that European society has continued to expand.

The industrialized world started in Great Britain a little before the period of the American Revolution. Franklin and Jefferson may have been among the last of the true Renaissance men, in the great tradition of Leonardo, Michelangelo, and Galileo, but they lived during the beginning of a great expansion of technology. The first evidence of the industrial revolution came in the textile industry, but others soon followed. Abuses were common and there were many reactions to those abuses, but progress continued. Communists, socialists, and unions all succeeded in humanizing industry to some degree, and the reforms that these movements promoted have led to a better work environment and modern Western standards of living.

In an effort to develop markets and guarantee raw materials, European societies expanded into Africa and Asia during the nineteenth century. This empire building resulted in the spread of Western ideas and institutions to parts of the world that had not developed them on their own. The French, British, Germans, Italians, Belgians, and Americans all sought to develop empires. Although the empires eventually dissolved, they did succeed in spreading European ideas and institutions.

After World War II only two empires were left standing: the Soviet Empire and the American Empire. Although Americans do not like to think of themselves as an imperial power, U.S. troops have been stationed on the Rhine River longer than were the Roman legions. The natural struggle for dominance between these two empires became known as the Cold War. Although it was often not "cold" but "hot," as the Angolans, Vietnamese, Afghans, and other peoples will testify, direct confrontation between the United States and the USSR did not materialize. Eventually, the United States won the Cold War and the Soviet Union broke up into many different countries, of which Russia is the largest and most important, but only one.

Today, the United States is the primary and most important political, economic, military, and industrial power on earth. But the conflict has changed and so have the rules. Now the major arena of conflict is in the economic sphere. Although we face the probability of continuing terrorist attacks and small wars, the chief avenue of conflict in the future is expected to be economic.

The historical factors of production remain the same today; the key is to learn to use them in the most efficient and productive way possible. The factors of land (raw materials), capital (money and machinery), and entrepreneurship (organization and management) are all easily transferred from country to country and from market to market. Because of this, labor becomes the key to the success of any society in the post–Cold War world. A highly educated and trained workforce is needed if a society is to be successful in the next century. Unfortunately, the United States is not doing as good a job as it might do in this area. International education tests rank the United States no better than average among industrialized countries. The workforce is simply not prepared to excel in the coming global competition that is bound to result from the internationalization of markets. One of the few economic certainties facing the U.S. worker is that in the future, there will be fewer low-skill jobs and an increase in the number of jobs demanding a high degree of skill. This change in the demands on the labor force, coupled with the technological obsolescence of many U.S. factories, does not bode well for the United States. The central question for the United States is whether it will opt for old ideas and old ways of thinking, as the French did with the Maginot Line between the world wars, or will move toward innovative and original ideas to develop and enhance its position in the future.

Questions

1. What was the first level of economic development? Give examples.
2. What was the second level of economic development? Give examples.
3. What were the Middle Ages in Europe, and why were they important?

4. In the year A.D. 1000, what was probably the leading culture on Earth?

5. What was the Renaissance, and why was it important?

6. What role did technology play in the expansion of European civilization?

7. What was the importance of the individual in Western thought and philosophy, and how does the U.S. Declaration of Independence embody that tradition?

8. What was the importance of the textile industry in the industrial revolution?

9. What were some of the reactions to the industrial revolution, and why are they important?

10. Why is 1848 considered to be such an important year in the development of modern European civilization?

11. What were some of the obstacles faced by unions in the United States?

12. What was the principal way in which U.S. unions differed from European unions?

13. What was the chief rationale for the establishment of European colonial empires after 1784?

14. Why did the French seek to colonize Africa in the nineteenth century?

15. What was the significance of the Boer War in terms of the rationale and political support for British imperialism in Africa?

16. What was the political significance of the Russo-Japanese War in terms of European imperialism?

17. Who won the Cold War?

18. Why was the Cold War never really "cold"?

19. In the post–Cold War era, what is likely to be the main arena of conflict between societies?

20. What two factors are likely to hamper the role of the United States as the dominant society in the post–Cold War era?

CASE 1

There was great chaos in the land. People would receive widely different punishments for the same crimes. It just did not seem right. Some were killed for stealing a loaf of bread, while others were released with only a slap on the wrist. The people were upset, as they should be. There was no consistency, and really, there was no law. The question was: How does a ruler bring a consistency of justice to his or her people? How can the ruler eliminate the chaos that was so obviously taking over in the land?

1. If you were the ruler, what would you do?
2. Why is consistency needed in an ethical society?

CASE 2

The order had finally come. The Empire of Japan was going to go to war with the United States and there was nothing you could do about it. The die was cast. You knew the United States. You had spent several years there and had seen the gigantic industrial base of the country. You knew that even if the Japanese Empire was to have the kind of initial success you expected, in a long war, Japan was doomed. Your only hope was that the Americans would give up, but you knew that would not happen. Once they had been attacked directly by Japan, they would not stop fighting until their battleships sailed into Tokyo Bay to take the surrender of whatever would be left of Japan. You know this, but there is nothing you can do to stop it.

1. If you were Yamamoto, what would you do?

References

1. Toffler, Alvin, *Future shock,* Random House, New York, 1970.
2. Ibid.
3. Toffler, Alvin, *The third wave,* William Morrow, New York, 1980.
4. Ibid.
5. Wells, H. G., *The outline of history,* Garden City Publishing, Garden City, NY, 1931.
6. Gibbon, Edward, *History of the decline of the Roman Empire,* Encyclopedia Britannica, Chicago, 1990.
7. Ibid.
8. Brett, Michael, *The Moors: Islam in the west,* Orbis Publishing, London, 1980.
9. Leff, Gordon, *Paris and Oxford: universities in the thirteenth and fourteenth centuries,* Wiley, New York, 1968.
10. Portilla, Miguel, *Time and reality in the time of the Maya,* University of Oklahoma Press, Norman, OK, 1988.
11. Asser, John, *Alfred the great: Asser's life of Alfred and other contemporary sources,* Penguin Books, Harmondsworth, Middlesex, England, 1983.
12. Ginerich, Owen, *The eye of heaven: Ptolemy, Copernicus, Kepler,* American Institute of Physics, New York, 1993.
13. Hull, Mary, *The travels of Marco Polo,* Lucent Books, San Diego, CA, 1995.
14. Abels, Harriette, *Lost city of Atlantis,* Crestwood House, Mankato, MN, 1987.
15. Wells, *The outline of history.*
16. Keller, Albert, *Colonization: a study of the founding of new societies,* Ginn, Boston, 1908.
17. Maidment, Fred (ed.), *Annual editions: international business,* 1999/2000 Dushkin/McGraw-Hill, Guilford, CT, 1997.
18. Wright, Edmond (ed.), *Benjamin Franklin: his life as he wrote it,* Harvard University Press, Cambridge, MA, 1989.
19. Peterson, Merrill (ed.), *Thomas Jefferson: a reference biography,* Scribner, NY, 1986.
20. Bland, Celia, *The mechanical age: the industrial revolution in England,* Facts on File, New York, 1995.
21. Ibid.
22. Coleman, Penny, *Strike: the bitter struggle of American workers from colonial times to the present,* Millbrook Press, Brookfield, CT, 1995.
23. Levitas, Ruth, *The concept of utopia,* Syracuse University Press, Syracuse, NY, 1990.
24. Bornstein, George (ed.), *Romantic and modern: reevaluations of literary tradition,* Pittsburgh University Press, Pittsburgh, PA, 1977.
25. Coleman, *Strike.*
26. Marx, Karl, *The communist manifesto,* H. Regnery Co., Chicago, 1955.
27. Wells, *The outline of history.*
28. Sears, Stephen W., *Chancellorsville,* Houghton Mifflin, Boston, 1996.

29. Coleman, *Strike.*

30. Ibid.

31. Blanchard, Paul, *An outline of the British labor movement,* George H. Doren Co., New York, 1923.

32. Wells, *The outline of history.*

33. Keller, *Colonization.*

34. Alba, Victor, *The Mexicans: the making of a nation,* Praeger, New York, 1967.

35. Adams, James, *The British Empire, 1784–1939,* Dorset Press, New York, 1991.

36. Seymour-Smith, Martin, *Rudyard Kipling,* St. Martin's Press, New York, 1990.

37. Adams, *The British Empire.*

38. Charmley, John, *Lord Lloyd and the decline of the British Empire,* St. Martin's Press, New York, 1987.

39. Keller, *Colonization.*

40. Esthus, Raymond, *Double eagles and rising sun: the Russians and Japanese at Portsmouth in 1905,* Duke University Press, Durham, NC, 1988.

41. Ogata, Sadako, *Defiance in Manchuria: the making of Japanese foreign policy, 1931–1932,* University of California Press, Berkeley, CA, 1964.

42. Nalty, Bernard C., *Pearl Harbor and the war in the Pacific: the story of the bitter struggle in the Pacific theater of operations,* Smithmark Library Distributions of America, New York, 1991.

43. Hoyt, Edwin, *Yamamoto: the man who planned Pearl Harbor,* McGraw-Hill, New York, 1990.

44. Pearl Harbor.

45. Gaddis, John, *We now know: rethinking cold war history,* Oxford University Press, New York, 1997.

46. Ibid.

47. Ibid.

48. Bauer, K. Jack, *The Mexican war, 1846–1848,* Macmillan, New York, 1974.

49. Campbell, Colin, and Bert Rockman (eds.), *The Bush presidency: first appraisals,* Chatham House Publishers, Chatham, NY, 1991.

50. Toffler, *The third wave.*

51. Cimbala, Stephen, *Strategy after deterrence,* Praeger, New York, 1991.

52. Kang, T. W., *Is Korea the next Japan? Understanding the structure, strategy, and tactics of America's next competitor,* Free Press, New York, 1988.

53. Gaddis, *We now know.*

54. The World Bank, *World development report, 1991: the challenge of development,* Oxford University Press, New York, 1991.

55. Caveman, Mark, *The European community: an essential guide toward knowing and understanding,* Bookmasters, Mansfield, OH, 1993.

56. Maidment, *Annual editions: international business.*

57. United States National Commission on Excellence in Education, *A nation at risk: the imperative for educational reform: a report to the nation and to the Secretary,* The Commission, Washington, DC, 1983.

58. Maidment, Fred (ed.), *Annual editions: human resources, 1997–1998,* Dushkin/McGraw-Hill, Guilford, CT, 1997.

THE ORIGINS OF MODERN BUSINESS MANAGEMENT

Concepts ┇ You Will Learn ■ ■ ■

business practices prior to the industrial revolution

the importance of the industrial revolution in the development of modern society

the development of modern ideas in management and why they are important

INTRODUCTION ■ ■ ■

Business before the Industrial Revolution ■ ■ ■

The mark of civilization has always been trade and the specialization of labor.[1] Going back to ancient times, the great civilizations of the river valleys were based on the idea that specialization of labor led to a surplus of goods that could be traded.[2] Business has been around since the dawn of civilization. It is just that historians have chosen not to call it that. Some of the earliest forms of writing that have been found from the ancient world have been accounts on clay tablets.[3]

The attitude of the ancient civilizations toward business and commerce was generally not a positive one. Although there were some great trading civilizations, such as Phoenicia, the view of commerce as being a rather base occupation was the common perception of the ancient world. Business is about the accumulation of wealth and the *Bible* says that the likelihood of a rich man entering the Kingdom of Heaven is about the same as a camel going through the eye of a needle. The ancient Greeks shared this philosophy. In the *Republic,* Plato referred to men engaged in trade as "men of copper," the most common and base element available to the Greeks and near the bottom of his social strata.[4]

The Middle Ages and the Awakening

During the Middle Ages the Church shared these ideas with the ancients. Although the Church itself accumulated great wealth as an institution, most of its members were poor serfs, only a few members of the nobility having any assets. The Church told the serfs to look for a better life in the hereafter while it acquired great tracts of land and built monuments in the form of cathedrals. It was this desire to build St. Peter's in Rome, and the selling of indulgences to finance the construction, that eventually led a young monk in Germany named Luther to revolt against the Roman Church and start the Protestant Reformation.[5]

Unlike prior reformers such as Jan Hess,[6] Luther had the support of many of the secular nobility in Germany, who saw the Church as a kind of money-gathering machine that they were not in control of, but which they wanted to control. So they supported Luther as an opportunity to gain control over the wealth of the Church, and in the process they touched off several hundred years of war in Europe as well as the Protestant Reformation.[7]

Among the many things begun by the Protestant Reformation was the movement started by John Calvin. The Calvinists are the other great leg of the Protestant Reformation. This movement, which includes the Presbyterian and Reformed churches, had as a part of its doctrine a unique and different idea, that of predestination.[8] To oversimplify, this concept was based on the idea that being prosperous, wealthy, and successful was a sign that God loved one and that such good fortune was preordained. Wealthy people were predestined to be rich, and poor people were predestined to be poor. It meant that a person could go ahead and accumulate wealth and not worry about what would happen when he or she died. It also made concentrations of money and wealth available for investment. Banking, loans, and finance became possible, and great trading societies and guilds arose in Europe. It is no coincidence that the Reformation and the Renaissance occurred during much the same period. Both were based on questioning the established order: one for religious reasons and the other for secular reasons. Many ideas of Aristotle, other ancients, and the Church simply did not stand up to the tests of the day, and no matter how much the Church and its supporters tried, the facts still came through.

The Age of Discovery

The voyages of Columbus and the explorers who came after him, which represent a great breakthrough in civilization, were based on the acquisition of wealth. The Spaniards, English, French, Dutch, Swedes, and Portuguese were all looking for wealth, specifically gold. Only the Spanish found gold, but the rest of the explorers found many other forms of wealth in the New World,[9] including land, furs, timber, tobacco, cotton, rice, and sugarcane. European civilization was expanding and the New World brought the hope of a fresh start to many and the hope of gaining wealth and position that was otherwise denied to them in Europe. So they came to the New World, and although many failed in their struggle, many others succeeded in establishing themselves.

BOX 3.1 Galileo

Galileo was one of the great minds to come out of the age of discovery. A true son of the Renaissance, Galileo made many important discoveries that put him at odds with the established doctrine of the Church. A great supporter of the Copernican theory of the universe, Galileo was constantly at odds with the dogma of the Church that the Earth was the center of the universe, as Ptolemy had postulated during ancient times.

The Copernican system was named after a Catholic priest, Nicolas Copernicus, who developed the idea of the Earth traveling around the sun. Although Copernicus may have postulated a revolutionary theory on the way the universe worked, he had either the good sense or great fortune to die prior to its general publication. Galileo, on the other hand, did not die prior to his support of the Copernican doctrine.

Because of his support of the Copernican theory, Galileo was tried for heresy by the Church. He was convicted, primarily on the basis of a letter to him from Cardinal Bellarmine, found by the Papacy just prior to the trial, which is now believed to have been forged. Galileo spent the rest of his life under house arrest at a small estate near Florence. During the eight years of house arrest at the end of his life, Galileo continued to write and do research. He continued his earlier work on the principles of mechanics and his astronomical observations.

Galileo's work and life are important for a variety of reasons: His discoveries contributed greatly to our understanding of the universe, his struggles with the established order placed him squarely in the line of the greatest revolutionaries of all time, and his intellectual honesty and determination to know the truth could not be suppressed, even by the most powerful dogma of the established power structure of the time. Finally, Galileo's and Copernicus's ideas have won the day. Their revolutionary ideas are now the accepted ones, and the dogma that the establishment and the Church fought so hard to defend are now on the ash heap of history.

The Industrial Revolution

A little less than 300 years after the discovery of the New World, the industrial revolution began in England.[10] This is really the beginning of modern society and the modern corporation. Although the earliest forms of corporations had been established by the English in the form of the great trading companies of Hudson Bay, Virginia, and East India, it was the industrial revolution that made possible and practical the great corporations of today.

Manufacturing started in the textile industry, which has always been the beginning of industrialization. In fact, in most countries today, textiles are the first industry to be mechanized. A look at the developing world will clearly demonstrate that the establishment of a modern textile industry is the first step on the road to industrialization. This is then followed by industries that are somewhat more complex, often involving the use of interchangeable parts, followed by the advent of the assembly line.

The assembly line and the industrial process probably first reached its optimum point in the River Rouge plant of the Ford Motor Company shortly after the turn of the century.[11] A huge industrial complex employing thousands of workers, raw materials would go in one end of the plant and come out the other as automobiles. Although the approach has been modified over the years and subcontractors tend to play a much bigger role than they did in the past, the River Rouge plant represents a model, an ideal on which much of modern industry has been based. Jobs were broken down into their simplest forms and the work was performed as much as possible by machines. The semiautomated assembly line, if not the totally automated line, has become the ideal of modern society, and mass production, often with individualized customization of a mass-produced product, has become the expectation.

IDEAS ABOUT THE MANAGEMENT OF ORGANIZATIONS

Attempting to find better ways to manage organizations has been a preoccupation of civilizations for a very long time. Probably the first recorded management consultant was Jethro, Moses' father-in-law, who advised Moses on how to organize the Israelites after they had left Egypt (Exodus 18: 13–26). The military was also a focus of attempts to organize. War is serious business, and most generals will tell you that most wars and battles are won before they are even begun. One of the principal ways to achieve victory is to be better equipped, better trained, and better organized than the enemy. Also, an army needs specific objectives to be achieved and a plan to achieve them. Finally, as with all enterprises, the army needs to be motivated and well led. The planning, organizing, training, controlling, and equipping of an army are all part of leadership, but they will mean little if the organization is not well led and knowledgable as to the objectives of the organization. Ancient generals, emperors, and kings knew that if they were going to be successful, they were going to have to lead. If they did not lead, all they could hope for would be a footnote in history. The same can be said of organizations today. Just as managing IBM or Mitsubishi is a great managerial task, so was building the Great Wall of China.

Classical Management Theory

Classical management theory really began with the industrial revolution in about 1790.[12] The early factory needed a continuous flow of materials and labor. Owners and managers of the early factory had to plan, direct, organize, control, and staff[13] the organization as they still do today. Classical management theory focused on the "best way" to perform certain tasks. This problem resulted in two avenues of thought concerning management: the classical scientific school and the administrative school.

Classical Scientific Management

As organizations grew to be more and more complex, managers needed new theories and models to help them meet the new situations they were facing. One of the earliest studies was done by Charles Babbage, a British mathematician and inventor. In his *On The Economy of Machinery and Manufacture*, published in 1832, Babbage wrote of his observations of the factory floor and determined that certain definitive principles of management existed. The most important one was the division of labor, and he promoted the division of work

BOX 3.2   Management Time Line

	1890	Classical management theories
Muckrakers expose unethical business practices	1900	
	1910	
		Behavioral school
	1920	
The Great Depression begins	1930	
	1940	Quantitative school
World War II		
Deming lectures in Japan	1950	Systems approach
		Neohuman relations movement
Peter Drucker writes his first book	1960	
	1970	Contingency approach
Introduction of the personal computer		
	1980	Excellence, Japanese management, benchmarking
	1990	
First U.S. government budget surplus since 1961	1998	

into separate functions that one person could master in a very short period of time.

The father of the school of scientific management was Frederick W. Taylor, who believed that science could be applied to management to produce better-run organizations.[14] Taylor thought this could be achieved in four coordinated ways:

1. By developing a science of management
2. By selecting workers scientifically
3. By educating and training workers scientifically
4. By creating cooperation between management and labor

As part of this process he developed time-and-motion studies and determined how much a worker should be able to produce given the appropriate tools and materials. In this manner he was able to determine the quickest way to perform tasks. He also recognized the importance of fatigue and how it decreased the efficiency of workers, so he instituted breaks for the workers.

Other management theorists are also included in this school. Frank and Lillian Gilbreth took Taylor's ideas off the factory floor and applied them to other environments outside the area of production.[15] Henry Gantt, the inventor of the Gantt chart, promoted the concept of a bonus system to reward outstanding workers, and Henry Metcalf suggested that systems be employed for cost control and the flow of information.[16]

Classical Administrative Management

The classical administrative school of management can be traced to the writings of Henri Fayol, a French manager who, after he retired from business, developed his 14 points.[17] Fayol knew that management was not a personal talent that people were born with, but one that could be taught and learned. From his own experience as a manager he knew that management required specific skills, and he is acknowledged as the founder of the administrative branch of the classical school.

One of the most interesting and remarkable classical management theorists was Mary Park Follett.[18] A political scientist by training, she was the first successful modern female management consultant in an era when women in polite society simply did not do that sort of thing. Her work in the 1920s focused on how important it was that goals and methods to deal with conflict and change be shared among managers. She also addressed the importance of individual and group motivation in accomplishing goals, as well as the impact of the human element in organizations. Mary Parker Follett was known for her insistence on "organized thinking" for both individual and group success and encouraged the development of management as a profession.

Max Weber was an Austrian who could probably be described as a Renaissance man. He wrote extensively on social, political, and economic issues and was an early translator of Sanskrit. He also developed the "theory of bureaucracy," a rational organizational theory based on the control of knowledge.

■ ■ ■ BOX 3.3 Henri Fayol's 14 Points ■ ■ ■

1. *Division of work.* Specialization of workers allows them to be more efficient.
2. *Authority.* Authority and responsibility are intertwined; someone has to be in charge.
3. *Discipline.* Workers must conform to the needs of the organization. Without discipline organizations cannot be successful.
4. *Unity of command.* A person can work for only one superior.
5. *Unity of direction.* The organization needs to have a specific plan.
6. *Subordination of the individual to the group.* The interests of the organization come first.
7. *Renumeration of personnel.* Workers should be fairly paid and that pay should reflect their value to the organization.
8. *Centralization.* The organization needs a balance between centralization and decentralization.
9. *Scalar Chain.* The chain of command is established to promote order and discipline in an organization.
10. *Order.* Everything should have its place. The objective of order is to avoid loss and waste.
11. *Equity.* Justice should be practiced by persons in authority. Lack of justice and equity creates disorder.
12. *Stability of employment.* Reducing employee turnover will save money and generate loyalty on the part of employees.
13. *Initiative.* Managers should encourage employees to act independently when necessary.
14. *Esprit de corps.* Morale is an essential ingredient for a successful organization. Organizations that are motivated can do anything. Organizations that do not have motivated personnel can do very little.

Weber's ideas were first published in *The Theory of Social and Economic Organizations*.[19] He said that bureaucracy developed in concert with capitalism and believed that bureaucratic organization was the best way to administer governments, universities, religious institutions, business, and the military. Weber felt that these bureaucratic organizations would be staffed with competent technical career professionals who would be judged by their superiors and promoted based on their performance. Weber placed a high value on technical knowledge: "The primary source of the superiority of bureaucratic administration lies in the role of technical knowledge which, through the development of modern technology and business methods in the production of goods, has become completely indispensable. Capitalism is the most rational base for bureaucratic administration and enables it to develop in the most rational form, especially because, from a fiscal point of view, it supplies the necessary money resources."[20]

The classical school of management established many of the ideas and forms of business that are in use today. Both the scientific and administrative sides may be seen in every organization. The scientific side may have been used more on the factory floor, but the administrative school provided the form of organization that is in use today. If carried too far, these ideas can lead to severe problems for the economy and society. The old Soviet Union, perhaps the most rigid bureaucratic system in history, illustrates the fact that unresponsive and rigid decision making and a lack of commitment among workers can lead to disaffection and chaos in a society. Only with the added human touch can organizations hope to achieve success, as was realized by the behavioral school.

The Behavioral School

The behavioral school of management was a response to the need to develop a more realistic picture of worker and human motivation in management. Over the years it had become obvious that the application of classical management principles often led to increased efficiency and production, but at the cost of a decrease in harmony among workers and conflicts between workers and management. The difference between the classical approach and the behavioral approach focused on the worker doing a particular job.

Hugo Munsterberg was one of the first people to address the psychological needs of workers. In his book *Psychology and Industrial Efficiency* he argued that productivity could be enhanced in three ways:[21]

1. Through finding the best possible person—finding the workers best suited for the job
2. Through creating the best possible work—the ideal psychological conditions for maximizing productivity and performance
3. Through the use of the best possible effect—the best psychological influence to motivate employees

The results of Munsterberg's work can be found in the use of psychological tests of new employees to determine their fitness and qualifications for a job, and in the use of learning theory to better train employees. Also, the use of modern vocational techniques to identify the skills needed on a job and to

---

■ ■ ■ BOX 3.4 Elton Mayo and the Hawthorne Studies ■ ■ ■

Elton Mayo and his Harvard co-workers were called into the Hawthorne plant after other researchers, who had been experimenting with work area lighting, had not achieved any results. These experimenters could not explain the fact that when light increased in the factory, production went up, but when it was decreased, production did not go down. In a new experiment, conducted by Mayo and his associates, two groups of six women were placed in separate rooms. One acted as a control group, for which conditions remained the same, and the second operated as the experimental group, for which working conditions were varied. A number of conditions were changed, including breaks, control over the environment, and other factors. Generally, it was found that manipulating environmental factors had little to do with increasing production.

This study led Mayo and his team to an important observation: that special attention often leads people to increase their efforts. Workers' morale remained high and production increased because the workers felt that they were an important part of a group effort and participated in making decisions that affected them. Employees work harder when management pays special attention to them and is concerned about their welfare. This special kind of treatment gave birth to the management school of human relations and their results became known as the Hawthorne effect.

---

determine a candidate's skills for a particular job are based substantially on Munsterberg's contributions.

Probably the most famous study ever conducted by management theorists was the Hawthorne experiments,[22] named after the Western Electric plant in Cicero, Illinois at which the study was conducted. This research formed the basis of much of the behavioral school of management. Another pioneer in the behavioral school of management was Oliver Sheldon.[23] Sheldon was concerned with the obligation of businesses to treat workers fairly. He also said that corporations had a responsibility beyond their immediate stockholders, to the society at large. Sheldon argued that corporate responsibility extended to the community and the society as a whole: that organizations had a responsibility to their communities, and that communities had an expectation that organizations would fulfill those responsibilities.

Through increased and more sophisticated knowledge of human and worker behavior, managers have been able to adopt approaches that have led to greater productivity. The behavioral approach has enhanced the understanding of group behavior, personal relations, human motivation, and the satisfaction derived from work over and above money. Communication and leadership have been enhanced and management is now better able to understand and motivate employees. But the behavioral school supplies only part of the answer.

The Quantitative School: Management Science and Operations Research

The quantitative approach to management came out of practices followed in World War II. During the war the allies applied the principles of quantitative analysis to solving certain problems, especially those associated with supply and logistics.[24] One of the major applications arose from the battle for control of North Atlantic shipping lanes. The allies faced two problems: (1) how to keep German U-boats from sinking so many freighters, and (2) how to determine the best possible mix of armaments and other war supplies to put on vessels before they left port. The allies were successful on both fronts, and this led to application of these principles to management after the war.

One way to describe the quantitative approach to management is to show how it differs from the behavioral and classical schools:

1. *Use of computers.* Computers are used to help calculate and assemble data to be used in decision making with quantitative models. Computers were used originally during World War II.

2. *Use of quantitative models.* Management science attempts to use mathematical models. Managers that use quantitative tools are better able to control their businesses and therefore are better managers.

3. *Emphasis on decision making.* Quantitative tools are designed to help managers plan and make decisions.

4. *Evaluation.* Quantitative techniques imply measurement, which is exactly what is needed for evaluation. It is not possible to evaluate something objectively that is not measured.

Management science is a well-established part of the problem-solving tools of most large organizations, including corporations and the civilian and military branches of government. It has made its greatest contributions in the planning and controlling functions of management in virtually all of the functional areas of organizations.

The management science approach does have certain limitations. In the first place, it was not developed by managers but by technocrats and mathematicians, so it is little wonder that some managers may be suspicious of it. Second, it is often difficult to explain because it uses levels of mathematics not usually associated with the competencies of many workers. Third, it is only a partial answer to many of the problems faced by managers on a daily basis.

OTHER THEORIES OF MANAGEMENT ■ ■ ■

The Systems Approach ■ ■ ■

Systems theory is based on the idea that everything is part of a larger whole. As stated by the founder of general systems theory, Ludwig von Bertalanffy, a biologist: "To understand an organized whole, we must know both parts and the relations between them."[25] This envisions the world as being a collection of systems operating at different levels. Each system is part of a hierarchy ranging from the very general to the highly specific. Being able to identify systems at the various levels has helped translate a somewhat abstract theory into an understandable format.

Essentially, there are two types of systems, closed and open. A closed system is one that does not interact with any other system; it is self-contained. An open system, on the other hand, is one that interacts with the surrounding environment. Virtually no system is totally closed; rather, it is a matter of degree,

BOX 3.5 Levels of Systems

System Level		Practical Example
Supranational	General	United Nations
National		United States, Italy, Japan
Organizational		Microsoft, General Motors
Group		Family
Organism		Person
Organic	Specific	Liver, heart, kidney

some systems being more open than others. A hydraulic system is a more-or-less closed system, whereas the political system in the United States would generally be considered to be open to every citizen.

Systems theory has the advantage of organizing things into a coherent whole. It allows a manager to see things in context. It prevents the manager from focusing only on his or her part of the organization and becomes a useful matrix on which to arrange the various elements of the organization. Another positive aspect of systems theory is that it attempts to integrate various management theories into a coherent whole. Various aspects of management have been heavily influenced by systems theory, including organizational behavior and operations management, even though they are very different in origin and emphasis.

There are, however, critics of the systems approach. Many feel that it does not provide the answers that a manager needs, but rather, a way of thinking about organizations and their problems. Others feel that it is long on intellectual appeal and buzz words, but short on practicality. But whatever the criticism, it does provide managers with a logical and consistent approach with which to view an organization.

The Contingency Approach

The contingency approach is an effort to determine through research which managerial techniques are appropriate in specific situations. Different managerial responses are required by different situations. What works in one situation is not necessarily going to work in another. As Fred Luthans, a major writer in the contingency management approach literature, has written: "The traditional approaches to management are not necessarily wrong, but they are no longer adequate."[26]

Generally speaking, the contingency approach to management views each situation as being somewhat uncertain. What may appear to be working now may not work in the future. Conditions, personnel, and the economy may all change. What is needed is an alternative plan to deal with those changes. For example, just because someone has been a successful military officer does not mean that she or he will be able to use the same techniques successfully to manage a group of research scientists. The two situations are very different and what may have been the basis of great success in the military may prove to be the foundation for disaster in another setting.

In the real world, the success of any management technique is dictated by the situation. As business conditions become more fluid and unstable, rigid systems of authority and power become less likely to be successful because they cannot be used as quickly to respond to accelerating changes in the environment. Less rigid, more adaptive organizations, on the other hand, tend to be more successful in these rapidly changing environments.

The characteristics of the contingency approach to management may be described as (1) an open system perspective, (2) a practical research orientation, and (3) a multivariate approach. The open system approach is fundamental to the contingency view of management. It makes the basic assumption that all systems are open and subject to changes in the environment. No system exists as a solitary unit. All systems are seen as interacting with each other and influencing each other. In addition to the external changes, contingency management also recognizes that there can be changes in internal systems.

BOX 3.6   The U-2 Incident

Toward the end of the Eisenhower administration and prior to the development of spy satellites, the United States, through the Central Intelligence Agency (CIA), was engaged in aerial surveillance of the Soviet Union. This was accomplished by high-flying U-2 spy planes that were capable of flying great distances at elevations that were too high for Soviet technology to shoot down. The United States had engaged in these flights for a period of several years and the Soviets were incensed that they were unable to do anything about it. The United States continued these flights until just before a scheduled summit between the major powers, when one of the U-2s, piloted by Francis Gary Powers, was brought down about 1000 miles inside the Soviet Union. At first it was thought that the Soviets had shot down the aircraft, but recent evidence indicates that they had penetrated the U.S. base in Iran from which the U-2 had taken off and sabotaged the plane. What followed is an absolutely classic example of what happens when an original plan somehow unravels and the alternatives have not been very well thought through:

1. The Soviets announced that they had shot down the plane. The U.S. government denied any involvement, secure in the knowledge that the pilot had probably been killed, and that if he had not, possessed a cyanide capsule. Unfortunately for the CIA, the pilot had been given an option as to whether to use it.

2. The Soviets announced that they had captured the pilot alive, and were interrogating him. The U.S. government denied any wrongdoing, and said that the Soviets had shot down an innocent pilot who had simply wandered off course—1000 miles off course—roughly the equivalent of a Soviet airplane flying over St. Louis on its way to Cuba.

3. The Soviets publicly displayed the wreck of the airplane, which was still identifiable, as well as much of the surveillance equipment carried on board. In addition, the Soviets displayed Powers, who was alive and well. The U.S. government ceased to deny anything.

The U-2 incident is remembered because it was such a fiasco. All the plans and assumptions of the U.S. government failed to account for the possibility that the pilot might live and that the Soviets might be able to identify the aircraft should it crash. When alternative plans work, nobody notices, but when they do not or when they do not exist, everyone knows it.

Personnel can change, and products come and go. Divisions are downsized and people are "rifed." Nothing remains the same for very long.

The contingency approach to management also fosters a very practical approach to research. People who do research in the contingency area of management are concerned with developing tools and techniques that will help to solve problems faced on a daily basis. Theory is often useful, but practical results that provide better and more effective management are emphasized.

Contingency theory assumes that there is more than one answer to a particular problem and that whereas there may not be a wrong answer, there may be an answer that is more "right" than others, an optimal answer. Researchers try to determine how a combination of variables interact with each other to produce a specific outcome. For example, a person who is not authoritarian by nature may be very successful in managing a highly unstructured environment such as a research lab or a college or university.

The contingency approach is a recognition on the part of managers and management theorists that each situation is different and that each situation may change with little or no notice to the people in the organizations. Managers have got to be flexible and address each new situation as it comes along. "Plan Bs" must be ready when conditions change. Managers must be prepared to answer "What do we do if . . . ?" because that is the only question that is absolutely certain to be asked. The contingency approach to management recognizes that the only constant is change and that managers and their organizations must be ready to deal with it.

Management by Objectives

Perhaps the best known management theorist in the United States is Peter Drucker, and perhaps the best known approach to management is Drucker's management by objectives (MBO).[27] This is a management system based on objectives set in agreement with the parties involved, and measurable and observable. Unfortunately, MBO is as often abused as it is used by management, but whether applied properly or improperly, it is certainly a widely used management tool.

The heart of the MBO system is a four-stage cycle. The cycle starts with the setting of objectives. Both the manager and the subordinates participate in this process. Challenging, consistent, and fair objectives are necessary as the starting point for the cycle. All objectives are put in writing and are derived from the objectives of the organization. The process calls for negotiations between the manager and subordinates to determine the objectives for the subordinates. A manager who simply dictates such objectives is not engaging in MBO, nor is an employee who is simply allowed to determine his or her own objectives.

The second step is to develop plans of action to accomplish the goals set by the manager and employees. It is the responsibility of the manager to make certain that the plans of his or her subordinates do not work at cross-purposes with each other and that they complement each other so as to achieve the greatest possible efficiency in the organization's quest to achieve its goals.

As the plans are turned into action, the manager and employees need to review periodically the results of the plan. Is the plan behind or ahead of schedule in achieving its objectives? Results need to be reviewed on a regular basis, perhaps at three-month intervals. This allows the manager to review the objectives to determine whether they are still valid. Circumstances can change that may make the achievement of an objective once thought to be very reasonable, virtually impossible, and the objectives may need to be reconsidered. The situation can also be reversed: An objective once thought to be difficult has become easy. Periodic reviews give managers the opportunity to supply feedback and to make needed course corrections.

At the end of a complete MBO cycle, usually a year after the objectives were set, the final performance is compared to the goals and objectives that were set. Superior and subordinates meet to discuss the results. MBO emphasizes results, not personalities. Appropriate rewards or suitable corrective action is then taken.

One MBO cycle is then followed by another, with each cycle contributing to the process of learning and mastering MBO. It often takes several years for even a medium-sized organization to implement an MBO system successfully.[28] People who support the MBO concept feel that higher motivation and greater productivity will result from the application of realistic objectives and more effective control.

A system that is as widely used in management as MBO is bound to generate controversy. MBO is seen to have four strengths in the management of organizations:[29]

1. It encourages self-management and personal commitment.

2. It forces organizations to develop top-to-bottom objectives.

3. It emphasizes results.

4. It blends planning and control into a rational system.

On the other hand, MBO is seen as having four major weaknesses:[30]

1. Managers can use the objectives as a threat.

2. Inflexible managers and rigid bureaucratic systems can easily destroy MBO.

3. It takes too much time and too much paperwork.

4. It is often sold as a cure-all.

Strategic Management   ■ ■ ■

Strategic management is an ongoing process of ensuring a competitive fit between an organization and its ever-changing environment. Strategic plans, which typically include budgeting, long-range planning, and strategic planning, require constant and systematic updates. Strategic management involves strategic planning, implementation, and control.

The strategic management process begins with the formulation of the grand strategy.[31] Managers must ask themselves: "What business do we want to be in?" Mission statements and overall organizational objectives are developed. Strategic managers broadly determine how the mission of an organization is to be accomplished. During this process, planners engage in a situation analysis of both the internal and external situation of the firm. This is sometimes called a SWOT (strengths, weaknesses, opportunities, and threats) analysis.

Every organization should be able to identify what it is good at and what it is not good at. It should also be able to identify those opportunities in the environment that will make maximum use of its strengths while minimizing the importance of its weaknesses. At the same time, because the environment is competitive, the organization must be able to identify the threats that are in the environment. Competitors will also have plans, and if taken to their ultimate conclusion, those plans will often include something fairly unpleasant for the organization, such as going out of business.

The next step in the strategic management process is formulation of the strategic plan. The strategic plan translates the ground strategy into policies, budgets, and plans. These plans should:[32]

1. Be results oriented in measurable terms with time limits
2. Identify the activities needed to accomplish the objectives
3. Assign authority and responsibility
4. Estimate the length of time needed to accomplish the objectives
5. Determine the necessary resources
6. Serve as a guide to communicate and coordinate the activities of the plan

Strategic plans are the responsibility of top management and often require months of preparation before they can be implemented. Such plans require filtering down in the organization if they are going to be implemented. Senior management generally does not sell directly to the customer. Other members of the organization at lower levels accomplish the goals set by senior management. Senior management needs to address four central issues concerning the implementation of strategic plans:[33]

1. Organizational compatibility with the planning process, new approaches, and with the strategy
2. Compatibility with the culture of the organization
3. Appropriateness and availability of personnel to implement the plan
4. Assessment of the success of the plan and the ability of management to take corrective action

For strategic plans to be successful, they must be accepted by management. Resistance by middle managers can destroy an excellent strategic management program. It is not unusual for middle managers to attempt to stop strategies so as to protect their own self-interests. In a competitive environment it is absolutely crucial to gain commitment because timely implementation of the strategic plan can prove the difference between success and failure.

Control is the final step in the process. Just as an automobile needs slight adjustments in course to arrive successfully at point B from point A, so does a strategic plan. Evaluation is ongoing and based on feedback. Corrective action is then taken so as to keep the plan on course.

Strategic planning is a widely used tool for developing and implementing plans for the organization. It has the advantage of providing the organization with purpose and direction. Strategic planning can be summed up by asking five questions:

1. *Where have we been?* What is the history of the organization, and how did we get where we are today?

2. *Where are we now?* What strengths, weaknesses, opportunities, and threats face the organization?

3. *Where do we want to go?* What are the mission and eventual objectives and goals of the organization? Another way to ask this question is: What do you want to be when you grow up?

4. *How are you going to get there?* What is the plan? How are you going to implement it?

5. *How will we know when we have arrived?* What will the standard be?

Japanese Management

In the 1950s, an American statistician, W. Edwards Deming, was invited by the Japanese to present his ideas on quality control. Deming believed that quality is built into the product. This idea spread rapidly through Japan and has led the Japanese to be a world leader in product quality. The idea is simple: continuous quality improvement in products.

Included in this process were several unique ideas. One was just-in-time (JIT) inventory, a technique used to reduce inventories to a minimum by having materials delivered to the factory "just in time." Called Kanban in Japanese, such programs have several unique qualities:[34]

BOX 3.7 W. Edwards Deming

W. Edwards Deming was an American scholar, teacher, author, and consultant who applied the use of statistics to quality control and was able to establish what is today called the Japanese school of management. Unable to get U.S. firms to adopt his ideas after World War II, he found an eager audience in Japan, which was rebuilding itself after the war. Japanese firms quickly adopted his ideas in the form of quality control, quality circles, and other techniques. They honored Deming by creating the Deming Prize for his contribution to Japan's rise as a major economic power. Interestingly, Deming's ideas were not adopted in the United States, and he was often laughed at by his colleagues as having strange ideas. It was not until the 1980s that his concepts were taken up by U.S. firms and only after the Japanese had made great inroads into the U.S. market.

One of the great contrasts in U.S. universities occurred between Deming and Peter Drucker, arguably the two most important management theorists in the second half of the twentieth century. Both were on the same faculty at the New York University Graduate School of Business Administration (now the Stern School). Drucker, a native Austrian, had been widely accepted and praised by U.S. industry for decades, from the 1950s to the present day. The American Deming, by contrast, was ignored and generally dismissed by U.S. industry as something of an eccentric, until his students, the Japanese, started outselling, outproducing, and "out-everythinging" U.S. firms in the American market. Deming's ideas were then rediscovered by U.S. industry, but it was decades late and they had to be bludgeoned by their Japanese counterparts. Unlike many great artists, scholars, and scientists, Deming lived long enough to see this happen, dying at the age of 93 knowing that he and his ideas had been vindicated.

1. *Closeness of suppliers.* Because of the very short lead times, suppliers have to be located close to their customers.

2. *High quality of materials purchased from suppliers.* The customer depends on the quality of the goods.

3. *Well-organized handling of materials.* Since the lead time is so short, materials need to be handled in a quick and efficient manner.

4. *Strong management commitment.* As with many programs, they will not work unless upper management is truly committed to its success.

Implemented successfully, JIT enhances organizational effectiveness in a variety of ways. It reduces unnecessary labor expenses and investment in inventory. JIT emphasizes the need to produce only items the customer wants and only in quantities desired by the customer.

Deming and the Japanese also developed the idea of quality circles,[35] groups of workers dedicated to improving the quality of their product and communicating their ideas to management. This is a very different approach from that used by most U.S. firms for many years, which consisted of using workers' muscle but not their brains. Nobody knows more about installing seats in automobiles on the factory floor than the person who actually does it. Yet for years U.S. firms were not interested in this person's suggestions on how to do that. Quality circles are important because now management wants to know.

Excellence

In their book *In Search of Excellence*,[36] Tom Peters and Robert Waterman set out to find what was good about management in the United States: what worked and what did not work. Much to their surprise, they found that rules, policies, and procedures really did not contribute to the effectiveness of organizations. What did contribute and what became hallmarks of successful organizations were very different.

The first characteristic is a bias for action. Excellent companies do not wait for things to happen to them; they make things happen. Peters and Waterman found that the most successful companies have a need to get on with things and a willingness to experiment and try new approaches.

The second characteristic of excellent companies is closeness to the customer. Organizations are driven to provide unparalleled service and quality. They listen to the customer. In some organizations, workers from the factory floor may actually visit customers so as to better understand their needs.

Autonomy and entrepreneurship was the third characteristic discovered in the search for excellence. Excellent companies encourage people to take reasonable risks by tolerating mistakes. They encourage innovation. Organizations that do not tolerate mistakes will ensure that nobody ever takes a risk, and to be intolerant of mistakes is to destroy all innovation and progress.

Productivity through people is the fourth characteristic of excellent organizations. Excellent organizations recognize that it is people who perform the jobs and tasks in an organization, not machines. Employees are treated with dignity and respect, and enthusiasm and trust are encouraged. It is rank-and-file employees who are responsible for the real gains of any organization because they are the ones who actually do the job.

Excellent organizations are marked by a hands-on management that is able to communicate its values and vision to employees. This is a part of what leadership is about. Excellent companies tend to have excellent leadership: leaders who have a vision, a concept, a dream of what they want the organization to become and are able to communicate it to employees and have them adopt it as their own. The management of these companies is also involved on a daily basis with the operation of the firm.

Excellent companies tend to stick to their knitting—to the businesses they know. The acquisition of any business is made only if the other firm is in a business that is closely related to the primary business of the acquiring organization. These businesses tend to generate their own growth and not to merge with other organizations, something that is rare in the modern business environment—but then, excellence is rare.

The seventh characteristic of excellent organizations is that they tend to have a simple structure with clear lines of authority and a small headquarters staff. The smaller the headquarters staff, the less it can bother the people who are actually involved in serving the customer. There is a reason for the old joke that one of the great lies in life is: "I'm from the home office. I'm here to help."

The final and eighth characteristic of excellence is a simultaneously loose and tight approach to management: loose in that responsibility and authority are pushed down to the lowest possible level of the organization, but tight in that the core values of the organization are never compromised and never negotiable.

Since Peters and Waterman wrote their book, some of the companies they selected as excellent have fallen on less than excellent times. The reasons that a firm runs into difficulty are sometimes unclear and certainly vary from one organization to another, but it is certain that management that will lead to excellent companies tomorrow requires much more than adherence to a single set of rules.

Benchmarking

One of the techniques to come out of the excellence movement has been the concept of benchmarking.[37] Here the idea is to try to find those firms that are the very best at fulfilling particular functions in a business. Every business has certain functions that are common to all businesses: data processing, human resources, and order processing, for example. The question is: Who does them best, and how is it possible to learn from them? Such research can be done on an industry-specific basis or by looking at all businesses in general. The purpose is to identify the outstanding organization in a particular area, investigate and discover how your operation compares with that organization, learn how and why they are able to do a better job, and then to incorporate into your operation as much as possible of what they are doing better. Benchmarking is useful because it provides a standard for comparison of how well an organization is performing a particular task, and ideas on how to do it better and with greater efficiency.

SUMMARY ■ ■ ■

Business organization was fairly simple prior to the industrial revolution. The accumulation of wealth was not as acceptable then as it is today. Society viewed commerce as one of the lower forms of human activity and believed that government, the military, and the priesthood offered more valuable occupations.

With the coming of the Renaissance, the Reformation, and the age of exploration, the accumulation of wealth became more acceptable than it had been in the past. Rather than viewing the rich as somehow unworthy of heavenly bliss, the Reformation, especially the doctrine of predestination, gave religious sanction to wealthy people, who did not have it under the doctrine of the Roman Catholic Church. The age of exploration gave people in Europe the opportunity to become very wealthy. The Spanish were the only ones to find gold, but other forms of wealth, such as land, crops, and furs, were obtained by the English, French, and Portuguese.

The modern business world began with the industrial revolution, which led to the establishment of factories and other ideas about production and the use of land, labor, and capital. As these organizations grew, there was a need to better manage them so as to optimize output. Management theorists began to appear in an effort to try to determine if there were any common principles that could be applied to industrial organizations.

The first attempt was by the classical school, which included people such as Frederick W. Taylor and Henri Fayol. This school of management sought to find common basic principles of management that could be applied to most, if not all, organizations. The second school was the behavioral school, which arose from the developing disciplines of psychology and sociology and represented an attempt to apply to the workplace what was being learned in these disciplines. Elton Mayo and the Hawthorne study probably represent the most widely known facet of this area. The third school of management, developed during and after World War II, is known as the management science or quantitative school. This approach to management utilized highly sophisticated mathematical models and computers to attempt to find optimum solutions to problems faced by managers, especially in the area of logistics. None of the schools of management that developed over the past 100 or so years has proven to be completely satisfactory. Even taken together, they do not represent a complete answer to the needs of management.

Other attempts at management have included the systems approach, which views everything as a system with a hierarchy and interaction between subsystems. The contingency approach views the world as full of uncertainty, with volatile conditions that are likely to change, for which management must be prepared. Because managerial techniques that work today may not work tomorrow, managers have to be prepared to change their approach to maximize their effectiveness.

One of the ways that management theorists have tried to improve their techniques is through use of management by objectives. Developed and popularized by Peter Drucker, this approach involves the setting of objectives and evaluation of the success in setting them. Although it has become a very popular technique, its limitations must need to be considered when adopting the procedure.

Strategic management is another attempt to try to develop a successful approach to management. In essence, strategic managers ask five questions:

1. *Where have we been?* How did the organization get to where we are today?
2. *Where are we now?* What is the current situation?
3. *Where do we want to go?* What are the objectives and goals of the organization?
4. *How do we want to get there?* What is the plan?
5. *How will we know when we have arrived?* What standard will we use to measure success?

In the past thirty years the Japanese have also contributed heavily to the management process. Building on the work of W. Edwards Deming, they helped to develop a new insistence on quality and the philosophy of Kanban or just-in-time inventory. Japanese ideas on management have greatly influenced managers in the United States and the rest of the world, but application of these ideas must be attended with caution, as they are based on experience in a highly homogeneous society and may not work as well outside Japan.

Excellence, or rather, the search for excellence, has been another avenue of management thought. Peters and Waterman attempted to find those characteristics common to all organizations that are considered to be excellent. What they found was more of an attitude on the part of the organization and the employees rather than a collection of policies and procedures: a conviction that it is ultimately people who make an organization work, not machines or policies.

Yet another technique to come out of the search for excellence and the Japanese quest for quality is benchmarking. Essentially, the idea behind this technique is to find the very best operation of a particular function and study it in an attempt to learn how to do it better yourself.

Human beings have been concerned with management since the dawn of civilization. Armies, governments, religions, and corporations have all sought to try to learn how to do things better, and it is unlikely that they will stop trying in the future.

Questions

1. What was the attitude of ancient civilizations toward business and why was it important that it change?
2. Why was the Protestant Reformation so important to the development of business?
3. What role did the Renaissance play in the development of business and industry?
4. Why is the industrial revolution so important to the start of the modern business environment?
5. What were the four things that Frederick W. Taylor thought could be achieved through scientific management?
6. What were Henri Fayol's 14 points?
7. Hugo Munsterberg argued that productivity could be increased in what three ways?
8. What were the Hawthorne experiments and why are they important?

9. In what four ways does the quantitative approach differ from the behavioral and classical schools?

10. Define *systems theory.*

11. In the contingency approach, explain the statement: "Different managerial approaches are required by different situations."

12. Why does the contingency approach assume that there is more than one "right" answer?

13. What is meant by the term *management by objectives?*

14. What are the four stages of management by objectives?

15. What are the four strengths and four weaknesses of management by objectives as identified in the text?

16. What is strategic management?

17. What is SWOT analysis?

18. According to the text, what five questions must be answered in strategic management?

19. Who started the concept of what is now called *Japanese management?*

20. What four qualities must just-in-time inventory techniques have?

21. What are quality circles?

22. According to Peters and Waterman, what are the eight characteristics of excellence?

23. What is benchmarking?

24. How does benchmarking lead to greater efficiency and productivity?

CASE I

It had been a tough day, but perhaps a rewarding one. Ferdinand looked over at his wife, Isabella, as she lay on their bed. Their marriage, although happy enough, had been more a union to drive out the hated Moors from Spain than one of love. But she had been a good wife.

That Italian navigator had made an interesting proposal. He said the world was round and that you could reach the Indies by sailing west. Most sailors disagreed with him and said that he would fall off the end of the Earth. Some scholars said he was right but that his calculations of the distance were terribly wrong.

Ferdinand knew that the Venetians and Turks controlled the trade with the East. The two were bitter rivals but still managed to demand and get outrageous sums for their wares. Breaking that monopoly was a cherished dream of all in the West, and being able to control the new route to the East would ensure great profits for Spain and for himself personally.

Money was not a problem. The loot from Granada would more than foot the bill for the three ships that Columbus requested. Finding crews among the superstitious sailors would be more difficult, however. Sailing west was thought to be a form of suicide and whatever else these sailors may be, they were not interested in that.

Ferdinand and Isabella had decided to sleep on the decision. There was much to gain if Columbus proved right and, really, not that much to lose if he didn't. Still, he didn't want to waste the three ships and the lives of the sailors who would be on them. Ferdinand pulled the blankets over himself and extinguished the candle. He wondered what riches or disasters awaited the Italian beyond the western horizon. Probably some of both, he thought, as sleep enveloped him.

1. If you were Ferdinand, whose counsel would you listen to, the practical sailors' or the scholars'?
2. If Ferdinand were to do a SWOT analysis, what would be some of the strengths, weaknesses, opportunities, and threats?
3. If Isabella and Ferdinand cannot agree, then what?

CASE 2

Those fellows from back East sure did seem like a strange bunch. They made it colder and hotter, lighter and darker, trying to figure out what would make them work harder and faster. Her group had been picked out to help these fellows here at the Hawthorne plant, and whatever it was they were looking for, the ladies were bound and determined to maintain production. They would show these men what good workers they were. Yes, sir, a fair day's work for a fair day's pay was their motto, and by gosh, they were going to do it.

Elton Mayo and his team were somewhat perplexed by the results of their experiments. They had made it colder and warmer, lighter and darker, and all kinds of combinations of the two—to no avail. The women continued to produce at the same rate as they had before. The only thing that seemed to work was when they had made it so dark that the ladies literally could not see what they were doing, a fact that was brought home to him when he entered the room and promptly tripped over one of the chairs. They knew one way to lower production, but hadn't found any way to increase it. Mayo wondered how the study was going and what results they were going to get. It didn't look like what he and the team had expected.

1. What do you think of the attitude of the ladies in the experimental group?
2. What do you think of Mayo's attempts to manipulate the environment of the workers?
3. If you were Mayo, how would you try to interpret the data you have been able to generate so far?

CASE 3

It was the worst possible thing that could have happened to the company. The corporation's number one product, its best seller and most profitable item, had been used to randomly kill several people. The police had no idea who had done it, but autopsies had been performed on the victims and they apparently had been killed by taking a Tylenol that had somehow been tainted and poisoned. The question was, what to do now. The nation was terrorized by the prospect of poisoned Tylenol, and sales for the product were falling off the table. Tylenol was Johnson & Johnson's leading product. The company could not afford the loss of such an important product, but they may have lost it anyway. The real question now was how to maintain the company's other products while attempting to salvage Tylenol.

1. If you were the CEO of Johnson & Johnson, what would you do?

References _____

1. Robischon, Mary, Bruce Levine, and Martin Glaberman, *Work and Society*, Wayne State University, Detroit, MI, 1980.

2. Ibid.

3. Rawlinson, George, *Egypt and Babylon from sacred and profane sources*, John B. Alden, New York, 1885.

4. Plato, *The Republic*, B. Jowett, ed. Modern Library, New York, 1982.

5. Schweibert, Ernest G., *The Reformation*, Fortress Press, Minneapolis, MN, 1996.

6. Ibid.

7. Ibid.

8. Ibid.

9. Wells, H. G., *The outline of history*, Garden City Publishing, Garden City, NY, 1931.

10. Bland, Celia, *The mechanical age: the industrial revolution in England*, Facts on File, New York, 1985.

11. Harris, Jacqueline C., *Henry Ford*, Franklin Watts, New York, 1984.

12. Bland, *The mechanical age*.

13. Maidment, Fred (ed.), *Annual editions: management*, 1997–1998, Dushkin/McGraw-Hill, Guilford, CT, 1997.

14. Taylor, Frederick W., *The principles of scientific management*, Harper & Brothers, New York, 1911.

15. Gilbreth, Frank, *Motion study: a method for increasing the efficiency of the workman*, Hive Publishing, Easton, PA, 1972.

16. Gantt, Henry, *Gantt on management: guidelines for today's executives*, American Management Association, New York, 1961.

17. Fayol, Henri, *General and industrial management*, Lake Books, Belmont, CA, 1987.

18. Follett, Mary Parker, *Mary Parker Follett—a prophet of management: a celebration of writings from the 1920's*, Harvard University Press, Boston, 1995.

19. Weber, Max, *The theory of social and economic organization*, Free Press, New York, 1964.

20. Ibid.

21. Munsterberg, Hugo, *Psychology and industrial efficiency*, Houghton Mifflin, Boston, 1973.

22. Mayo, Elton, The human problems of an industrial organization, Macmillan, New York, 1933.

23. Sheldon, Oliver, *The philosophy of management*, Pitman, New York, 1965.

24. Stoner, James, and Freeman R. Edward, *Management*, Prentice Hall, Englewood Cliffs, NJ, 1992.

25. von Bertalanffy, Ludwig, *General systems theory: foundations, development, applications*, Braziller, New York, 1968.

26. Luthans, Fred, *Introduction to management: a contingency approach*, McGraw-Hill, New York, 1976.

27. Drucker, Peter, *Management: tasks, responsibility, practices*, Harper & Row, New York, 1974.

28. Ibid.

29. Giegold, William, *Management by objectives: a self-instructional approach*, McGraw-Hill, New York, 1978.

30. Ibid.

31. Eldridge, William, "Where angels fear to tread," in Jack Rabin, Gerald J. Miller, and W. Bartley Hildreth (eds.), *Handbook of strategic management*, Marcel Dekker, New York, 1990.

32. Ibid.

33. Ibid.

34. Adair-Heeley, Charleene, *The human side of just-in-time: how to make the techniques really work*, AMACOM, New York, 1991.

35. Robson, Mike (ed.), *Quality circles in action*, Gower, Aldershot, Herts, England, 1984.

36. Peters, Thomas, and Robert Waterman, *In search of excellence: lessons from America's best run companies*, Harper & Row, New York, 1982.

37. Bogan, Christopher, *Benchmarking for best practice: winning through innovative adoption*, McGraw-Hill, New York, 1994.

The Origins of Modern Government

Concepts : You Will Learn ■ ■ ■

the role of government in a complex modern society

how self-interest relates to the role of government

the role of power in our society and government

the various types of governmental systems that have been adopted by nations throughout the world

how governmental units relate to other entities in society

the regulatory and other roles of governmental units

how to apply ethical concepts to governmental situations

INTRODUCTION   ■ ■ ■

We are taught in schools the basic terms associated with government, and pictures of the nation's presidents hang on the walls. However, the basic origins of government are often not examined in school. In a society in which individuals are absolutely free to do what they want, there is little need for government. Government becomes necessary to perform functions essential to create a civilized society. Furthermore, government has been given a variety of activities to perform which private businesses will not, or cannot, perform.[1]

The most important function of government is to determine the laws that will govern the lives of citizens of that society.[2] The issues of how laws can be made is discussed next.

Which Laws; Whose Laws?   ■ ■ ■

In a perfect world made up of people who are equally concerned with the interests of others as well as their own, there would be little need for laws. In such a society, people would find ways of resolving conflict and working through differences. However, people are not angels and it can become necessary to enact laws that govern people's conduct.

The issue can be stated as: Who will decide which laws are necessary and who will make these laws? One question is to determine society's relationship to the individual. In the United States, the powers of government have been limited with respect to the individual; in other societies, the individual is subordinate to the government and individual rights are sharply limited.[3]

The fundamental question that needs to be answered by a society is whether the individual or the state is of first importance. Next we look at some ways of looking at this question and how government could be organized.

Premodern Societies

Leaders often emerged through battles for land or superiority.[4] They became the rulers of their area and had the ability to impose laws on their subjects and organize their governments as they saw fit. If one were the absolute monarch, one would need to decide several major questions.

How are goods and services to be produced? A society could have goods produced by government, by private-sector entities, or by a mix of the two. In premodern societies, this issue was less complex because the needs of society were less complex.

In England, commercial establishments developed to meet the needs of the public. They tended to be small organizations that were created without governmental assistance. The vast majority of people worked on farms and produced the food necessary to feed the population.[5]

In both England and the United States, the vast majority of people lived and worked on the farms until the beginning of the twentieth century.[6] The agrarian nature of these countries helped shape a strong sense of independent action and a distrust of central government.

Until the industrial revolution, goods and services were produced by small establishments with little government involvement.[7] The industrial revolution created large private corporations that produced vast quantities of items for the marketplace.

Many workers and governmental officials believed that there were many abuses associated with the working conditions during the industrial revolution.[8] As a result, governments began to enact laws that had an impact in the workplace. The reaction to abuses of workers during the industrial revolution resulted not only in legal changes but also in a change in attitude toward governmental intervention in the economy.

The writings of Karl Marx also changed the attitude of many people toward governmental involvement in the economy.[9] The popularity of Marx was an understandable reaction to abuses in the private sector. Much of the debate in the modern era has been between those who want government to be more involved in the economy and those who urge less involvement.

Balancing Society's Interests with an Individual's Right to Act
In premodern societies the ruler could issue decrees and use force to compel obedience. An unjust ruler could establish laws primarily to support his or her own interest. A wise ruler could ask for guidance from various sources to help determine laws, and accept, reject, or modify their advice.

One requirement of any society is to create an environment of relative peace and stability.[10] Without a sense of tranquillity it is difficult to develop a system for commerce or other activities. The ruler would need to find ways of determining laws that would promote this stability.

A first rule would be to prevent people from injuring one another physically.[11] The ruler needed to issue decrees that outlawed crimes such as murder, manslaughter, and assault. Closely following these laws would be those prohibiting the taking of property through force. As a result, it became unlawful to commit acts such as robbery, burglary, or theft.[12]

It was necessary to establish courts that could rule on criminal matters so that people would not have to resolve these matters among themselves. In England, the king appointed judges who traveled around the country to try criminal cases.[13]

Resolving Disputes among Individual Parties

Another important question for a ruler to address was how to resolve conflicts among its citizens. Some rulers developed codes relating not only to criminal matters but also to govern commercial matters and disputes among the ruler's citizens.

In England, judges were appointed to resolve these disputes. The decisions of the judges were written down by lawyers who then were able to use them to guide the actions of their clients. These decisions, which became known as precedents, guided judges and lawyers with respect to situations of similar facts.[14] The monarch reserved the right to reverse the decisions of judges. This power was to be a major irritant to American revolutionaries.

Many rulers in premodern society governed wisely, but some were unable to resolve the conflicts within society. As a result, other groups wanted a greater share in the governing process. Opposition to increased taxes helped lead to the American Revolution, which ousted the English king as the ruler of the colonies. The citizens of other countries also challenged the authority of their rulers.

Modern Societies

Many observers regard the American Civil War and the industrial revolution as the beginning of modern society in the Western world.[15] It was during this period that machines began to do much of the work previously done by human beings. The American Civil War marked a new stage of warfare which involved civilian populations.

The industrial revolution changed the relationship between business and labor.[16] Previously, most people worked on farms or in small commercial establishments. As a result, there was a relatively close relationship between bosses and their subordinates. The growth of very large business organizations changed the relationship between bosses and workers. Business organizations were based on the pyramid structure of the military. This meant that there could be substantial distances between the boss and the workers. This not only created problems in the workplace but also affected the political environment.

The industrial revolution resulted in certain people acquiring incredible wealth while many workers lived in poverty. The disparity led Karl Marx, among others, to question the fundamental fairness of the system.[17] The hardships of

World War I further loosened the ties between rulers and the governed.[18] It was during the middle of World War I that the communists took control in Russia, which then became known as the Soviet Union.

In many other nations, there was a rebellion against the existing economic and political systems. The turmoil caused by the Great Depression and World War II further changed the fundamental nature of the role of government in relation to the rest of society.[19]

In the United States, the Great Depression shook the nation's confidence in the free enterprise system. Herbert Hoover had been an American hero prior to the onset of the Great Depression. He had been instrumental in creating businesses and jobs and had been the architect of a variety of programs to aid the poor. Hoover may have been the most qualified person ever to seek the U.S. presidency.

Despite his achievements, Hoover was not prepared to deal with the crisis caused by the events surrounding the Great Depression. Prevailing economic theory stated that government should not become involved in the economy and that economic downturns would be self-correcting. Hoover believed in the orthodox economic view and was incapable of solving the problems associated with the Depression.

Although Roosevelt ran on a platform calling for a balanced budget, he quickly realized that a higher level of governmental intervention was necessary to deal with problems of the Depression.[20] Under Roosevelt, the federal government intervened to provide jobs and other assistance to people who could not find employment in the private sector.

At the same time that Roosevelt was expanding the scope of the federal government in the United States, citizens of other countries were supporting political leaders who promised economic health. In Germany, Hitler came to power. In the Soviet Union, the Communist Party solidified its control. In other countries there were battles among the supporters of various leaders who promised to deal with the worldwide Depression.

The Impact of World War II   ■ ■ ■

Only the governments of the allies could mobilize sufficient resources to defeat Germany and Japan. As a result, it became necessary to place more human and material resources in the hands of the national government.

With the victory of the allies over the axis powers, citizens often saw themselves as agents of a national governmental enterprise. In addition, the education of the nation's children was placed into the hands of vast governmental bureaucracies, which further enhanced the role of government in the economy. The GI Bill of Rights permitted returning veterans to go to college.[21] This reinforced the relationship between citizens and their government and added to the government's role.

After World War II, the other remaining superpower in the world was the Soviet Union, which had adopted a policy of state ownership of all major interests. This was a policy that appealed to many Americans, who believed that the private sector distributed rewards inequitably. However, Soviet communism was also seen as imperialist and totalitarian. This alarmed many Americans, who believed in the concept of due process and religious liberties.

BOX 4.1 McNamara and Vietnam
Groupthink at Work:
J. Dexter

Was Robert McNamara's tenure as Secretary of Defense under Kennedy and Johnson a demonstration of groupthink at work? Compared with Irving Janis's original work into groupthink, the answer is yes. McNamara's recent book, *In Retrospect: The Tragedy and Lessons of Vietnam*, provides examples of classic groupthink in action.

Groupthink is defined by Janis as "a mode of thinking that people engage in when they are deeply involved in a cohesive in-group, when the members striving for unanimity override their motivation to realistically appraise alternative courses of action" (Janis, 1982). The result of groupthink is a diminishing of the capabilities of a group to consider thoroughly all realistic alternative courses of action. Social pressures, urging conformity, become stronger than individuals' senses of morality or common sense.

Robert McNamara served for seven years in the Department of Defense during the Vietnam conflict, acting as secretary under both Kennedy and Johnson. McNamara left his post as president of the Ford Motor Company to become part of the political team at the request of John F. Kennedy. His book *In Retrospect* gives examples of groupthink at the highest levels of government. McNamara states that his associates during his tenure as Secretary were "young, vigorous, intelligent, well-meaning, patriotic servants of the United States" (McNamara, 1995a). Indeed, in the book *In Retrospect*, McNamara makes no apologies for the actions of himself or his staff. Rather, McNamara explains away poor decisions by stating that his staff was acting with incomplete information in a time that was as turbulent on the home front as it was in Southeast Asia.

McNamara was a participant in the Tuesday Lunch Group, a group that met with President Kennedy as a counterpart to the Security Council. These lunches were continued under Johnson. Both Johnson and Kennedy preferred these smaller, less formalized meetings. In his article "Rethinking Groupthink: Walt Rostow and the National Security Advisory Process in the Johnson Administration," Kevin Mulcahy states: "The Tuesday lunch was the refuge of an embattled President insulating himself from all but those who would offer no disagreement." Mulcahy further asserts that the members of the Tuesday lunch "were cut off from reality—Johnson's National Security Advisory process [was one that] fostered 'groupthink'." Indeed, Mulcahy states that Walt Rostow acted as the group's mindguard: He "cleverly screened the inflow of information and used his power to keep dissident experts away from the White House" (Mulcahy, 1995).

McNamara makes continued reference to groupthink in his book. At one point McNamara states: "My influence—and therefore my responsibility as a key participant in Vietnam decision making—continued until I left the Pentagon in late February, 1968. I had been skeptical and grew increasingly skeptical, of our ability to achieve our political objectives in Vietnam through military means, but this did not diminish my involvement in the shaping of Vietnam policy" (McNamara, 1995a).

In Retrospect is McNamara's "journey of self-disclosure and self-discovery" in response to his involvement with the Vietnam conflict (McNamara, 1995a). Even though McNamara admits to failings of both the Kennedy and Johnson administrations, he makes no apologies for his actions; rather, McNamara states that he wants to "show the full range of pressures and the lack of knowledge that existed at the time—I want to put Vietnam in context. . . . It is not easy to put people, decisions and events in their proper places in the jigsaw puzzle that is Vietnam. . . . One reason the Kennedy and Johnson administrations failed to take an orderly, rational approach to the basic questions underlying Vietnam was the staggering variety and complexity of other issues we faced" (McNamara, 1995a).

In a speech made at the John F. Kennedy School of Government at Harvard University, McNamara gave several reasons why he believed the United States failed in Southeast Asia. One of the reasons was the lack of understanding of the problem during the turnover of office between

BOX 4.1 (continued)

Eisenhower and Kennedy. Eisenhower was most concerned with Laos. Eisenhower was evasive while being questioned by Kennedy as to what to do to keep Chinese communists out of Laos. At one point Eisenhower said that he advised against unilateral action by the United States. At another, he said that if Laos was lost to the communists, "We'll (the free world) lose all of Southeast Asia." Three weeks before Kennedy's inauguration, Eisenhower said: "If necessary, we're going to have to go in there unilaterally" (McNamara, 1995b). The Kennedy administration seemed unable to handle these conflicting statements.

Another cause of decision-making failure, according to McNamara, was that there was not one person, either military or civilian, who spent 100 percent of his or her time working on Vietnam. While in the late 1950s and early 1960s the military's focus seemed to be on getting advisors and teachers into Vietnam, even their duties were a bit unclear. Advisors believed that their task was to train certain South Vietnamese military officers in English, but what was lacking was contact with the "peasants." No one made a satisfying case to the citizens of South Vietnam that a vague promise of democracy, an ideology with which many were unfamiliar, was better than the solid promises being made by the communists. As McNamara said: "[T]hey [the advisors and teachers] continually confused the South Vietnamese leaders with the South Vietnamese population." McNamara states that the South Vietnamese leaders were easier to convince of the benefits of democracy, partially because they were more committed to "Western values" than the general Vietnamese population (McNamara, 1995a).

Another reason for decision-making failure, as pointed out by Ernest May after McNamara's Harvard speech, was that the best and brightest of both the Eisenhower and Kennedy administrations truly believed that the fate of the civilized world hinged upon what happened in Laos. May asserted that theology also played a part in the groupthink taking place, saying that the administrations sat around believing that Laos was a "land-locked country of three million hamlets, populated by people devoted primarily to singing songs, making love, and raising opium" (McNamara, 1995b).

Lam Quang Thi, who had been a general in the Army of the Vietnam Republic, writing for the Pacific News Service stated that the real problem of Vietnam conflict was lack of a clear objective and the resulting confusion over how to attain it. Thi asserted U.S. global policy during the Cold War focused on the containment of communism at all costs. That belief led to direct involvement in both Korea and Vietnam, as cabinets under Eisenhower and Kennedy thoroughly believed that the "domino effect" would start should Laos fall under communist control. The objective—to contain communism—was sufficiently vague as to allow for escalation of military involvement without a clear idea as to how the whole ordeal would end (Thi, 1995).

Even McNamara's diehard critics say that the book *In Retrospect* serves a purpose: defining who we were as a nation at one particular point in time. Indeed, the book serves to show all how the highest councils of government work: "Men ceremoniously defer to one another within established hierarchies, waltzing around one another's fragile yet gigantic egos, as they consummate their lust for power in the name of service" (How, 1995).

It is obvious that groupthink did occur with McNamara and others during the Southeast Asia conflict. Whether or not McNamara is entirely to blame, however, is harder to ascertain. Arthur Schlesinger states that if only one senior advisor had questioned the Bay of Pigs incident, Kennedy would have canceled his actions. There was "no atmosphere of assumed consensus" (Coffey, 1994).

McNamara's book *In Retrospect* provides examples to support the assertion that groupthink occurred in decision-making processes involving military action in Southeast Asia. As McNamara said: "Over and over again, as my story of the decision-making process becomes shockingly clear, we failed to address fundamental issues; our failure to identify them was not recognized; and deep-seated disagreements among the President's advisors about how to proceed were neither surfaced nor resolved." (McNamara, 1995a). According to Janis's definition of *groupthink*, McNamara certainly does suggest that groupthink occurred while he was Secretary of Defense.

■ ■ ■ BOX 4.1 *(continued)* ■ ■ ■

References

Coffey, R. E., C. W. Cook, and P. L. Hunsaker (1994). *Management and Organizational Behavior.* Burr Ridge, IL: Irwin.

How, P. (Summer 1995). They Died for Nothing, Did They Not? *Sewanee Review* [on-line]. Available: http://homer.Prod.Oclc,org:3050/fe . . . m 1/fs_tulltext. Htm%22:fstxt45.htm.

Janis, I. (1982). *Groupthink: Psychological Studies of Policy Decisions and Fiascoes,* Boston: Houghton Mifflin.

McNamara, R. (1995a). *In Retrospect: The Tragedy and Lessons of Vietnam.* New York: Vintage Books.

McNamara, R. (1995b). *In Retrospect: The Tragedy and Lessons of Vietnam,* speech at the John F. Kennedy School of Government, Harvard University [on-line]. Available: http://ksgwww.harvard.edu/~ksgpress/mcnamara.htm.

Mulcahy, K. (Spring 1995). Rethinking Groupthink: Walt Rostow and the National Security Advisory Process in the Johnson Administration, *Presidential Studies Quarterly* [on-line]. Available: http://homer.prod.oclc.org:3050/FE . . . ml/sx_fulltext.Htm%22:/fstxt.htm.

Thi, L. Q. (1995). A Vietnamese response to McNamara: War Was Lost in Washington, Not Saigon, *Viet Magazine,* 408 [on-line]. Available: http.//www.viet.net/vietmag/408/408_nv_response.html.

Political parties in the United States have attempted to strike a balance between allowing the private sector to operate and permitting governmental intervention when necessary. The Democratic Party has generally favored more governmental involvement in the economy. The Republican Party has generally been supportive of existing governmental activities but reluctant to expand them. Both parties have sought to find a middle ground between offering governmental services and claiming credit for economic growth in the private sector.

Many of the questions that existed in the premodern age still need to be answered. However, the issues are vastly more complex in an economy driven by technology and information. Private-sector forces want the government to leave them alone, but new forces have emerged that demand regulatory attention.

■ ■ ■ BOX 4.2 E-Mail ■ ■ ■

The explosion of the use of e-mail has created many new problems that result in calls for additional governmental regulations. Employees are now concerned with violations of their privacy, and employers are concerned with employees' abuse of the system. People are discovering that they have overflowing e-mail boxes. Some messages are from bosses, but many represent communications from fellow employees, which are often not necessary.

Bosses want employees who will make their own decisions and will respond to customer needs without the need for intervention from higher authorities. This was one of the reasons for recent downsizings and the implementation of technology. However, employees have found that e-mail allows them to communicate quickly and easily with senior management. This allows them to get advice before making decisions. This has the opposite effect than that intended when the technology was installed.

The opportunities for legal actions and governmental intervention tend to increase as complexity grows. The explosion of e-mail may require governmental intervention to resolve issues such as the employees' right to privacy, access to e-mail by law enforcement officials, and actions of employers based on interception of e-mail messages.

The development of the Internet has opened up new learning and educational possibilities. However, access to the Internet has also permitted children to obtain sexually explicit material which many parents find extremely offensive. The issue becomes how to take advantage of the new technology without creating even greater problems than existed previously. Citizens want the advantages of the new technology but also seem to want government to protect citizens from themselves, and changed social situations also create additional incentives for governmental intervention.

BOX 4.3 Don't Ask, Don't Tell

The military has traditionally prohibited homosexuals from joining the armed forces. However, attitudes about homosexuality have changed, and some homosexuals want to serve in the military. There was thus a need to develop new policies that reflected the needs of the military as well as those of new recruits. As a result, the government adopted a position sometimes called "Don't ask, don't tell." Under this policy, the recruit would not tell the military that he or she is a homosexual, and the military would not ask questions about a person's sexuality.

Although the policy has been made a matter of law, there are times when the policy implications have to be interpreted. In addition, there has been a reaction to the policy in the military because of the change it brings to the military culture. The military has been a decidedly masculine culture since its inception, which may make it difficult to adapt to the changes brought about by having women and gays in the military. Shifts in power relationships among the ranks within the military have been necessitated. This has led to situations that call for additional regulations to deal with new problems created by the change in circumstances.

BOX 4.4 *Roe v. Wade*

The *Roe v. Wade* decision, which found that a woman's privacy right to make a decision about an abortion outweighed the government's interest in the matter, has had an enormous impact on society. Controversy over the issue has resulted in the two sides coming into conflict. As a result, the government has become involved in lawsuits and decisions over whether abortions should be paid for with government funds.

WHO WILL PRODUCE GOODS AND SERVICES?

In the United States, the private sector is primarily responsible for producing goods and services. However, the government plays a major role in regulating the activities of businesses and generally establishing the rules of competition. In addition, governments provide many of the services that the private sector cannot or will not provide.[22] People often gripe about paying taxes, but taxes pay for schools, roads, the military, facilities for higher education, sewer plants, garbage disposal facilities, welfare, and other necessary functions.

One reason for the relatively poor image of government is that it often is required to perform activities that people do not know much about or want to pay for. In addition, governmental organizations are subject to a variety of changes that reflect political trends ranging from people supporting an activist government to those strongly against governmental involvement.

While Americans seem willing to permit the private sector to produce products and services, they also want government to protect them from unsafe products and improper business practices.[23] Among other issues for societies is how much citizens should pay for the government's regulatory and other services.

Under the American system of democracy, there is no consistent, rational, long-term planning process to determine which services should be provided and how much they should cost. Instead, these questions are decided by the pull and tug of political forces. As noted earlier, the Democratic Party has generally favored more government activities and greater regulation of business, whereas the Republican Party has favored less governmental activity and less regulation of the private sector.

In the early part of this century, governmental interference in the economy was relatively minor. The Great Depression changed the role of government because the private sector could not find ways of dealing with problems that were created by the misery of unemployment resulting from the economic situation.[24]

President Roosevelt was faced with almost insurmountable problems during the Great Depression because he needed to find a balance between saving the free-enterprise system and preventing the type of revolution that resulted in the rise of Hitler in Europe. To prevent a violent upheaval of society, Roosevelt implemented a large number of new programs which helped put people back to work.

In addition, the onset of the Depression revealed weaknesses in the free-enterprise system that needed to be corrected. Among other reasons, the Depression was caused by excesses in the free markets. Companies issued stocks with little or no value to investors. In addition, some people found ways to manipulate the stock market artificially to drive market prices up.[25] They would then sell the shares to the public, who would find them to be worthless.

The rapid rise of stocks tempted financial institutions such as banks to invest in the market. When the market crashed, the financial institutions went down with them. Congress enacted the Glass–Steagall Act[26] to prevent banks from engaging in activities related to the stock market. In addition, Congress enacted the Securities Act of 1933[27] to regulate the sale of securities and the Securities Exchange Act of 1934[28] to regulate the purchase and sale of investment securities.

One of the costs of producing goods and services is damage to the environment. The need to protect the air, waterways, and land has gained attention in a modern society. The regulation of pollution created by the society's industries is a responsibility of the federal and state governments.

Throughout the country there are toxic waste sites that pose a danger to nearby residents and to the area's drinking water. One problem associated with these toxic waste dumps is that the companies which created them are often no longer in business. It is difficult to obtain money from organizations that no longer conduct business.

The decisions as to how these matters are pursued and financed is left to the political process in the United States. This means that these decisions are made by politicians, lobbying groups, and a few interested citizens. This often results in policies that can swing from one direction to another, and means that no intelligent process exists that can deal with these problems.

WHO MAKES THE LAWS; WHICH LAWS?

As noted above, premodern rulers were able to issue laws with little public involvement. Few countries still have such rulers. Citizens in many parts of the world question their authoritarian governments. In the United States, people question their own "democratic" institutions.[29] Each type of government has its own strengths and weaknesses. It is often difficult to determine which system works best.

There has been a reaction against the consequences of crime, and many citizens believe that the government has become powerless to prevent it. On the other side, a number of people point to the danger that increased emphasis on the rights of victims could lead to pressure on the police and prosecutors to find perpetrators of crimes in order to satisfy the desires of victims for resolution of a criminal matter.

The victims of crime have asked that their rights be included in a new constitutional amendment. This amendment would give standing to participate at various stages of the criminal trial process. This would represent a radical shift in the process of conducting a criminal trial.[30]

The basic purpose of a criminal trial has been to determine if a crime has been committed and if the defendant was the person who did it. The entire process could be changed if there is an assumption that there are victims. At what stage should the court allow victims to testify? How would one go about defining what *victim* means? Does *victim* include just the person directly injured, or does it also include family members of the injured person?

In the U.S. system of government, decisions regarding the final wording and passage or rejection of the amendment depend on the political process. The defense attorneys are lining up to oppose it, whereas prosecutors generally favor it. Some groups representing battered women favor the amendment, and some oppose it. The final version will probably reflect a compromise among competing views.

In a more authoritarian system, the ruler might consult with advisers and then announce a decision. If the ruler is wise, he or she will find a decision that balances the interest of both the defendant and the victims. This might also be the result in a democracy that is working well. An authoritarian government needs to be less concerned with the input of the public. The leaders of such governments are more likely to be concerned with maintaining order and a sense of stability. Individual rights are of far less importace in such societies.[31]

In the United States, laws against criminal conduct are determined by elected officials under the watchful eye of judicial officials who are mindful of the protections provided in the Constitution. Much of U.S. criminal law is based on English law that resulted from court decisions handed down by judges. The criminal law concepts of substantive and procedural due process also have resulted from legal rulings throughout many years.

More Laws in a Complex Society

As society becomes more complex, traditional legal concepts may become less relevant and newer concepts, more important. The erosion of trust in the nation's institutions adds to the belief among many that they are alone and must

BOX 4.5 Second Amendment Rights

There is renewed debate about the role of guns in our society. While the Second Amendment provides support for the right of individuals to own guns, it was written in a far less complex society than the United States is today. The Second Amendment was passed shortly after the American Revolution. The War of Independence had been fought and won by a volunteer militia. The country was predominantly rural and was sparsely populated.

The United States is no longer rural and sparsely populated. Use of firearms in our major cities can result in multiple deaths in seconds. Gun control supporters point to these deaths involving guns as justification for tighter controls. Opponents note that the use of guns by criminals in urban areas makes the right to private ownership of guns even more important because of the need to protect oneself. They argue that because criminals have guns, individual citizens need guns.

The actions of the Federal Bureau of Investigation at Waco and in other operations have created a belief among some that law enforcement agencies represent "the enemy" rather than an agency that will help defend them. Activities of local police departments have added to the sense among many citizens that law enforcement agencies have become entities with their own agendas and are answerable to no one. The minority community looks at police departments as the enemy, and some call for the arming of citizens as a way to protect themselves.

be prepared to protect their own lives from society's predators. The debate over the use of guns is likely to increase. A more complex society has more complex problems and deserves more thoughtful and creative solutions. Unfortunately, what we often see are "knee-jerk" solutions to many problems.

The framers of the Constitution had no concept of automobiles or their effect on society. In 1999, several states were considering asking for the death penalty if a defendant is convicted of causing a death by driving while intoxicated.

Little in the Constitution or the writings of its drafters gives people guidance for dealing with this issue. The framers could not have foreseen the benefits and risks associated with use of the automobile. Although the automobile provides Americans with enormous freedom of transportation, there are risks associated with people speeding around in 3000-pound hunks of metal.

As use of the automobile grew, it became necessary to enact laws to regulate its use to reduce the likelihood of property damage, personal injury, and death. Although driving is not a right guaranteed under the Constitution, it is a privilege which has become so important in our society that it cannot be taken away unless the driver has been given some protections.

As a result, there is now an entire bureaucratic and legal structure built around granting and taking away the privilege to drive. Furthermore, there are lawyers who prosecute individuals who may have broken traffic laws as well as those who specialize in defending alleged traffic violators. Making these decisions can be difficult for both society and the individual. One could make a good argument that there are too many bad drivers on the road. They create all sorts of problems for good drivers and tend to create more than their share of accidents.

However, people build much of their lives around being able to drive their automobiles. They plan residential locations around the ability to get to work by automobile.[32] Depriving someone of the right to drive is a severe punishment in

---

■ ■ ■ **BOX 4.6   Highway Safety** ■ ■ ■

Almost everyone in the United States over the age of 18 drives an automobile. This means that the nation's roads and highways are clogged with many drivers who have a variety of poor skills and bad habits. This creates a great deal of stress and tension.

As this book is being written, there has been a sharp upsurge of violent acts on the country's thoroughfares. People are reacting to real and imagined slights by becoming increasingly aggressive. This has resulted in hostile verbal and physical actions in response to these "threats." Road rage is a response to situations that reflects anger rather than rational thought. It includes profane gestures, physical violence, aggressive driving, and use of weapons. Road rage has resulted in an increasing number of injuries and deaths.

An ethical person finds ways of coping with the actions of other drivers without overreacting to situations. An ethical person is able to "laugh off" situations and does not try to "get even" with other drivers. An ethical person recognizes that all of his or her fellow drivers face difficult situations and are often unprepared for problems.

People are going to make mistakes, and an ethical person understands that. An ethical person follows the rules of the road that society demands of each driver and shows respect for the needs of other drivers. An ethical driver follows principles that will promote a high level of harmony on the roads. An ethical person recognizes the need to find common ground that can meet the needs of all parties.

U.S. society. If a person's license is suspended or revoked, the individual's entire lifestyle will be changed. Therefore, the legal system provides that in a matter involving traffic violations, a defendant is also entitled to procedural and substantive due process protections.

Generally, such violations have been punished by monetary fines or suspension of the driver's driving privileges. Given the potential damage that can be inflicted on others, driving an automobile may be compared with using a firearm. If one uses either with care, there can be a productive result. If one abuses the privilege of driving an automobile, one can cause damage to others and one's own privilege will be revoked.

One issue that is seldom addressed carefully relates to the process of determining who will be permitted to drive. The United States is a country that values equality, individual freedom, and democracy. As a result, the tendency was to extend the privilege of driving to as many people as possible. Is this an ethical solution?

The written and physical tests necessary to become a driver are relatively easy. The state is unlikely to know if one's driving skills have improved or become worse since one took the test. There are people driving who should be off the road. These drivers constitute an inconvenience and danger to safer drivers. At what point do their interests outweigh the interest of the individual driver? At what point do the interests of society to have safe roads outweigh the interests of individual drivers?

The crash landings of aircraft and the consequent loss of life raise the issue of the role of government as necessary to protect citizens from poorly run private-sector operators. The appropriate level of the regulation of private-sector activities is one that has concerned ethical decision makers since the industrial revolution.

A major function of government has been to regulate the private sector to reduce or prevent its excesses. The flying public expects its government to protect them from unsafe airlines. Similar situations arise with respect to the making and sale of products. People may hate paying taxes, but they want to be protected from goods that could cause them harm. In addition, citizens expect government to do these things for them.

In a complex society, products and services become more complex. As a result, regulation of these goods and services requires the abilities of specialists. However, it is often difficult for government to attract qualified persons who have the ability to effectively monitor the complex activities of private-sector organizations.

Cleaning up our environment has become more important since citizens have discovered the damage that chemicals and other toxic substances have caused. Michael Diamond[33] points out that it is difficult for regulatory scientists to cope with the complexity of the manufacture and distribution of chemicals since the end of World War II. Diamond argues that these chemicals enter our system before we are born and remain within our bodies our entire lives. The consequences of ingesting these toxins are not fully known, but could be very negative.

The historian Barbara Tuchman has argued that we are descending toward a more brutish society and that the United States has lost its honor, truthfulness, discipline, love of justice, and perseverance. She noted in 1987 that the United States was characterized by "deteriorating ethics, poor performance, poor thinking and lawlessness," saying that "it does seem that the knowledge of a difference between right and wrong is absent from our society, as if it had floated away on a shadowy night after the last World War."[34]

As this section is being written, Tuchman's fears seem to have been justified. Our political system reels from scandal after scandal, prominent corporations are regularly found guilty of fraudulent practices, our public school students achieve only mediocre results in comparative test scores among industrialized societies, and many Americans seem prepared to engage in violence to vent their anger at various institutions or perceived injustices.

Diamond argues further that the consequences of our toxic-driven society are hidden from view by legal and regulatory systems. He argues that the regulators cannot cope with the complexity of such issues and are incapable of advising citizens of the dangers to the environment.[35] Americans have tended to distrust the federal government except in times of war. Diamond argues that we should look at our environmental crisis as similar to a state of war. That is, the country is in a severe state of danger and only the intervention of the federal government can cope with it.[36] If Diamond is correct, the ultimate safety of the country is at stake, and drastic measures are required. However, in a country that dislikes governmental intervention, it is unlikely that citizens will give the federal government the powers that are necessary to deal with an environmental crisis of fundamental importance.

Diamond argues that constitutional provisions which require the federal government to guarantee a "republican" form of government to the states and to protect them from domestic violence means that the federal government must take action to solve the environmental problems. He contends that we have made ourselves a sick and impaired society and now face the possibility of leaving the Earth uninhabitable for our children.[37]

The complexity of this problem is similar to others faced by society. We are left with an enigma. If only governmental action on a massive scale such as that required by World War II can solve such a problem, how do we do so when the country's citizens seem opposed to large government? Much of the opposition to governmental action is based on the fear that it will interfere with the entrepreneurial activities of the nation's large and small business owners. The United States has been built partially on the activities of the nation's business-people. They have developed new products, created jobs, and built an economy that has been the envy of much of the world.

Businesses are built because people are willing to invest their resources, time, and energy in order to earn profits by meeting customer needs. Taxes and governmental regulations take time and resources away from the production and sales of the business's products or services. Although government intervention was necessary to solve the problems of the Great Depression and to win World War II, many people object to what they see as excessive taxes or regulation when there is no national crisis. It is difficult to succeed in the fiercely competitive international business world, and taxes divert resources away from a business. New businesses have a difficult time thriving in almost any climate. The world's economic situation allows businesses in one part of the world to compete very quickly with domestic companies. If our business organizations are at a disadvantage, the United States will lose jobs and our economy will suffer.[38] Most new businesses fail.[39] Small differences in taxes or regulations can mean the difference between failure and success.

If the role of government in a modern society is to carry out those very large tasks that the private sector is unable to perform, we need to find a balance between asking more of government and asking the private sector to pay for it. Unfortunately, our institutions do not seem to be equipped to find that balance. Currently, many decisions are reached by the tug and pull of various groups. This may not be a process that is likely to achieve a just result for the entire society.

BOX 4.7 Business Costs

Jones decides to open a new business in order to continue the family's tradition of home building. Jones hires one carpenter. He places weekly advertisements in the local newspaper to solicit new business.

Jones discovers that he must pay Social Security and unemployment taxes based on his employee's wages. When he starts to acquire land, he discovers that he must appear before the local planning appeal board with an application and plan. This costs Jones several hundred dollars.

Jones works on a close profit margin, and these additional taxes and charges make it more difficult to earn a profit. If Jones considers the purposes of the programs, he might not object to paying the taxes and fees. Social Security provides a reasonable supplement to the standard of living for the elderly. Unemployment insurance is designed to do the same for those who are out of work. Planning fees permit the orderly development of the community where Jones will build the homes.

Regardless of the valuable purposes of these governmental programs, the owner of a small business is likely to find that these costs make it more difficult to earn a profit. As a result, business-people tend to be opposed to more governmental programs.

Often, a society becomes so confident about its institutions that its citizens fail to examine whether they should continue to exist in their current form. Although Americans complain about their government and politicians, there have been few calls for a total change of our system of government. The movement for term limits[40] seemed to represent a meaningful call for change. However, the movement seemed to have lost steam in the 1996 elections. The split between the presidential and congressional results, as well as the high turnover in Congress, seemed to make term limits less important.

The problems of our society have become more complex as our society and economy become more complex. Can a system of government that is a mix between what our framers intended and various accretions grafted on during the past two centuries cope with these new problems? This will be the challenge for the United States at the beginning of a new millennium.

BOX 4.8 "Political Depression" May Cripple U.S. Democracy If It Isn't Corrected

Pardon us, but do you see the dinosaur in the living room? It is standing there in the middle of the carpet and nobody wants to talk about it. We all just tiptoe around it, year after year, pretending it's not there and hoping it will go away.

After the recent elections, commentators generally ignored the glaring fact that, once again, voter turnout decreased. It is typical for reports of elections overseas to mention voter turnout on a near-equal basis with election results, but you had to work hard to find references to turnout in the latest round of voting—or rather nonvoting.

Let's take Virginia. Turnout in the 1997 governor's race among registered voters was 48 percent—as opposed to 67 percent and 61 percent in the state's last two gubernatorial elections. And that doesn't even count eligible voters who never registered. Turnout among eligible adult Virginians was an abysmal 34 percent.

But Virginians can take heart. Their turnout was better than Broward County, Florida, where a mere 7 percent of registered voters made their way to the polls. Such shockingly low numbers were found in numerous localities.

Detroit's mayoral primary turnout was 17 percent of registered voters; in Charlotte's primary, it was 6 percent. General election turnout was under 40 percent of registered voters in Miami and New York City and under 30 percent in Boston and San Francisco. And, of course, 25 percent of the eligible voters typically remain unregistered.

The United States now has on average the lowest voter turnout in the world among mature democracies. The long-term implications of our plunging voter turnout surely are as serious as fluctuations in the stock market. But because it is like a crippling disease, creeping up slowly, the crisis of our "political depression" generally goes unrecognized.

At what point does a democracy cease to be democratically governed? Bill Clinton was re-elected with the support of fewer than one in four eligible voters. Republicans won control of the House of Representatives with even fewer votes. We maintain the corner posts of representative democracy, but with the active consent of fewer and fewer citizens.

It is time for prominent national and state discussions about the roots of our political depression. Thomas Jefferson wrote in his twilight years that "laws and institutions must go hand in hand with the progress of the human mind. As that becomes more developed, more enlightened, as new discoveries are made, new truths disclosed, institutions must advance also, and keep pace with the times."

BOX 4.8 *(continued)*

Our political leaders and concerned citizens must be as bold as Jefferson and his contemporaries, and consider changes that will allow voters to see a real connection between their votes and policy. Here are some proposals to consider:

- *Nonpartisan redistricting.* One-seat legislative districts give incumbents the opportunity to gerrymander district lines using sophisticated computers and census data. They quite literally choose their constituents before their constituents choose them. This consigns most Americans to "no-choice" legislative races.

- *Election holidays, weekend voting, and mail-in-balloting.* Making the practice of voting more convenient will have a beneficial effect on voter turnout.

- *Campaign finance reform.* Most voters have lost all faith in current campaign finance practices. Without concrete changes, cynicism will only grow.

- *Unicameral state legislatures.* Two houses in a state legislature undercut accountability and increase costs; bicameralism is simply redundant in state government, since both houses represent overlapping geographic areas.

- *Increased size of legislatures.* The U.S. House of Representatives has remained at 435 representatives since 1910, despite our population nearly tripling. Many state legislatures also are small; California's state senate districts now are larger than its congressional districts.

- *Instant runoff voting.* As more important races are won by a simple plurality like the Clinton presidency, or the recent New Jersey governor's race, it becomes more important to use this Australian system that ensures a majority winner in a single round of voting. It also should replace current two-round runoffs or primaries, thereby maximizing turnout and saving candidates and taxpayers the cost of the second election.

- *Proportional representation voting systems.* Used in nearly all mature democracies, proportional systems mirror a free market economy. Voters have the multiplicity of choices they treasure so highly as consumers.

- *A political force winning 51 percent of votes earns a majority, but not all; winning 10 percent wins 10 percent of representation, not nothing.* Proportional systems increase voter turnout substantially because voters have more choices and a greater chance to elect their favorite candidates.

Debating such rule changes is only the beginning. Pulling us out of our political depression will not be easy, but we must not wait. If President Clinton seeks a place in history, calling for a national campaign to address our political depression would be a lasting legacy.

Call it a new deal for democracy. It's time to talk in earnest about that dinosaur standing in the middle of the living room.

Source: Rob Richie and Steven Hill, Knight-Ridder/Tribune Information Services, *Kansas City Star,* November 16, 1997. Reprinted with permission of Knight-Ridder/Tribune Information Services. (Richie is executive director of the Center for Voting and Democracy in Washington. Hill is its West Coast director.)

SUMMARY

One of the tasks of any government is the determination of which laws will be made and who will make them. In the early past, this function was performed by the king and today is performed by legislatures and congresses. The role of the courts is also important, especially in English common law, where the concept of legal precedent (prior decisions of other courts) plays an important role.

The industrial revolution and the era that followed played an important role in the development of government and the role it would play in society. The advent of large corporations, and the power these organizations possessed, forced the government to step in and take a more active role in the society, if for no other reason than to protect the members of that society from the abuses of this new form of organization, the industrial corporation.

Government was not the only force in society to attempt to protect the individual. Socialism and communism were born as a direct response to the excesses of industry. Government was faced with a new central problem of balancing society's interests with the interests of the individual and resolving disputes among those interests. This problem has been addressed by government taking an active role in the society in the form of regulations for business and industry. Essentially, industry is free to do many things as long as it stays within the regulations of the government. When the excesses of industry outweigh the natural tendency of government not to get involved in regulation, the government, historically, steps in reluctantly. Indeed, the history of active government involvement in U.S. society could be told as a series of incidents where industry failed to act or where it was incapable of acting and the government was forced to step in.

With the end of the Cold War, the private sector in the United States, as well as the government, will face new challenges. The questions of who will produce the goods and service has generally been answered, with private industry producing the majority and the not-for-profit sector, including the government, producing those goods and services that are deemed necessary to the society but not necessarily profitable enough to interest profit-making corporations.

The nation would now seem to be divided into two camps: those that want more government involvement in the society and the economy and those that want no more involvement and possibly less. But the involvement of government in society is certainly going to remain. The lesson of the Great Depression was that left to its own devices, the market would spiral into a situation that was simply not acceptable to the nation as a whole and could lead to a situation similar to that which developed in Fascist Italy and Nazi Germany.

Problems abound for government attention. Toxic waste and other forms of pollution are only a part of the challenge that faces government. Cleaning up past pollution and preventing future problems are primary concerns of the state and federal governments. Crime is yet another aspect of the society that requires government attention. Victims are demanding that their rights be considered when sentencing convicted criminals. The society is becoming more complex and decisions regarding the law, punishment, and the rights of victims and the society are more complicated than they have been in the past.

The erosion of trust in the nation is a by-product of the Vietnam War, the Watergate affair, and other aspects of society. There has been a disconnection that could endanger society and the American way of life. People have become disconnected from their neighbors and from the society. The news seems to be only a list of who killed whom and what store or bank was robbed that day. Road rage seems to be just a car length away, and the difference between right and wrong seems to be less and less clear. Society must refocus its attention on what is important and what is necessary to survive as a society or the results may be only what the society deserves.

Questions

1. What do you see as the role of government in a complex society?

2. How should government officials decide to what extent business should be regulated?

3. How might you establish a decision-making process to resolve societal problems?

4. How does an increase in the complexity of society relate to the problems faced by government?

5. Can the current system of government cope with the complex problems of the future?

6. Explain how the Great Depression affected government's role in the United States.

7. Explain how World War II affected the role of government in American society.

8. The last several Presidents of the United States have urged citizens to give something back to their country by volunteering for various activities. What are the advantages and disadvantages of people volunteering to engage in community activities?

9. Some argue that volunteer activities take jobs away from lower-skilled people and are a poor substitute for government programs. Do you agree with this position?

10. Would you engage in volunteer activities?

11. In which activities would you be willing to participate?

12. Explain why you would be willing to perform these activities.

13. What would you want to accomplish?

14. Do you believe that you would be taking jobs away from others?

15. Is this a job you believe government should be performing? Why or why not?

16. If you had the power to implement more government programs, which ones would youimplement? Why?

17. How would you provide structure to these programs? What would you want to accomplish?

18. How would you pay for these programs?

19. In general, how do you think that governmental programs should be paid for?

20. How would you change existing methods of paying for governmental programs?

CASE I

You have recently been named the head of the Division of Family Services for a large urban state. The division's problems with respect to providing adequate services for an appropriate level of financing have recently appeared in the state's largest newspaper. You also have just met with your staff, who advise you that there are insufficient human and other resources to meet the needs of clients serviced by your division. The governor, who is up for reelection, has pledged that there will be no increase in taxes. You have also been informed that it is not likely that your division will receive additional resources in the future beyond those the division currently receives. This is a position you have wanted to achieve for years. However, after your initial analysis, you are not certain that it is one you want to occupy.

You have asked your staff to make suggestions as to how to perform their mission with the current level of resources. However, your staff has advised you that it does not seem possible to find ways to cut costs. You are concerned that your unit will not be able to serve adequately the needs of your clients and their families. If your workers are unable to do their job fully, there will probably be an increase in the number of child abuse cases as well as an increase in the deaths of children abused by their parents.

1. What do you do?

CASE 2

In the United States, one of the primary roles of government is to act as a balance to the private sector and as a check on its excesses. It is accepted that government has an adversary role to play with respect to the activities of the private sector. As a result, some businesspeople see the government as "the enemy" because of its regulatory role.

In Japan, the role of the government is seen differently. It is understood that one of the purposes of government is to help Japanese businesses succeed in the international economy. After World War II, Japanese business made a decision that its future depended on its ability to export its products to other countries. As a result, the Japanese government has enacted policies that promoted Japanese exports of products to other countries. This has resulted in complaints by other nations that the Japanese government is unfairly subsidizing the export of Japanese products.

It is difficult to decide the role of government with respect to business.

1. Is the role of government to act as an adversary or as a friend of business?
2. What actions do you think government should take to regulate or support business?
3. How would you decide such matters?

CASE 3

You are the director of a state agency that regulates the activities of certain private-sector businesses that perform activities involving the welfare of the general public. Your agency has the authority to level fines against businesses that violate the agency's rules and regulations. As the director, you have the authority to determine the level of the fines, although your decisions are subject to judicial review. The fines are meant to punish violations and to deter similar conduct in the future.

1. What are your ethical responsibilities to the public?
2. What are your ethical responsibilities to the businesses your agency regulates?
3. How do you find the proper ethical balance between responsibilities to the public and to the businesses you regulate?

CASE 4

You are the governor of a large southwestern state. A person convicted of a serious felony, has applied to you for a pardon. The evidence indicates that DNA results point to the applicant's innocence despite the victim's testimony to the contrary.

You are aware that the public is very concerned about the crime. In addition, you know that your state's voters will not support political candidates who appear to be "soft" on criminals.

1. What is your ethical duty as governor to the applicant?
2. What is your ethical duty as governor to the citizens of your state?
3. What is your ethical duty to your office?
4. What is your ethical duty to yourself?

CASE 5

You recently became the manager of the environmental department of a large manufacturing company. It is your job to ensure that the company complies with all federal, state, and local laws relating to the environment. You review the current policies and procedures of the company. You also go out into the field and examine the actual activities of the company. You discover that some of the company's practices violate local ordinances, relating to the use of the land on which the company is located. You review this situation with the plant manager, who admits that the company has added onto the plant without complying with local law. He implies that the company has been "paying off" the local zoning office and building inspector in order to continue its operations. To comply with all local ordinances would cost the company thousands of dollars.

1. What process do you go through to make a decision?
2. What do you do?
3. Who would you talk to for advice?

References

1. Drucker, Peter, *The five most important questions you will ever ask about your non-profit organization*, Jossey-Bass, San Francisco, 1993.
2. Blackstone, William, *Commentaries on the laws of England*, G. W. Childs, Philadelphia, 1868.
3. *The Federalist papers*, Arlington House, New Rochelle, NY, 1966.
4. Nye, Roger H., *The challenge of command: readings for military excellence*, Avery Publishing, New York, 1986.
5. Toffler, Alvin, *The third wave*, William Morrow, New York, 1980.
6. Ibid.
7. Ibid.
8. Marx, Karl, *The communist manifesto*, H. Regnery Co., Chicago, 1955.
9. Ibid.
10. Maidment, Fred (ed.), *Annual editions: international business, 1997–1998*, Dushkin/McGraw-Hill, Guilford, CT, 1997.
11. Blackstone, *Commentaries*.
12. Eldridge, William, *Contracts*, Prentice Hall, Upper Saddle River, NJ, 1998.
13. Blackstone, *Commentaries*.
14. Ibid.
15. Toffler, *The third wave*.
16. Ibid.

17. Marx, *The communist manifesto*.

18. Fussell, Paul, *The great war and modern memory*, Oxford University Press, New York, 1975.

19. Keynes, John Meynard, *The economic consequences of the peace*, Macmillan, 1919.

20. Keynes, John Meynard, *The general theory of employment, interest and money*, Harcourt, Brace, 1935.

21. Waller, Willard, *The veteran comes back*, Dryden Press, New York, 1944.

22. Drucker, *The five most important questions*.

23. Adams, Henry Carter, *Relation of the state to industrial action and economics and jurisprudence: two essays*, Columbia University Press, New York, 1954.

24. Keynes, *The general theory*.

25. De Bedts, Ralph F., *The new deal's SEC: the formative years*, Columbia University Press, New York, 1964.

26. Ibid.

27. Ibid.

28. Ibid.

29. Longworth, R. C., "U.S. prosperity hasn't spred to everyone," *Chicago Tribune* (published in the *Kansas City Star*, October 26, 1997).

30. Krohn, M., and R. Akers, *Crime, law, and caution: theoretical perspectives*, Sage Publications, Beverly Hills, CA, 1978.

31. Ibid.

32. Clark, S. D., *The suburban society*, University of Toronto Press, Toronto, 1966.

33. Diamond, M., *If you can keep it*, Brass Ring Press, Westfield, NJ, 1996.

34. Tuchman, B., "A nation in decline," *New York Times*, August 20, 1987.

35. Diamond, *If you can keep it*.

36. Ibid.

37. Ibid.

38. Maidment, *Annual editions*.

39. Jenkins, M., *Starting and operating a business in Pennsylvania*, Oasis Press, Grant's Pass, OR, 1993.

40. "Americans to limit congressional terms," *Kick the bums out!* National Press Books, Washington, DC, 1992.

THE ORIGINS OF MODERN SOCIETY

Concepts : You Will Learn ■ ■ ■

the origins of Western society
the origins of societies in Asia and other parts of the non-Western world
about societies in emerging nations

WESTERN EUROPEAN SOCIETY AND CULTURE ■ ■ ■

The Greeks ■ ■ ■

The traditional beginning of Western society has always been with the ancient Greeks.[1] It should be noted, however, that there were civilizations in various parts of the world prior to the Golden Age of ancient Greece. Egypt and Babylon, as well as India and China, were present long before Homer. But it is with ancient Greece that the story of Western culture and civilization, as a distinct idea, really begins.

The importance of ancient Greece in Western civilization is that it represented the first distinct flowering of civilization among a European people and that it originated many of the ideas that have characterized Western society since that time.[2]

The importance of the individual is one of the key Western ideas to come out of this civilization. The history of Western civilization can be viewed as a struggle of individualism with the other idea of the group. Much of what is known of ancient Greece is based on the individual. The gods looked like human beings, not like the Egyptian gods, which were half human and half something else. The arts glorified the human form,[3] taking it to new heights and a kind of idealized realism that is valued even today.

The literature of the ancient Greeks were stories about people, and although the gods often played a role in the stories, the central figure was a human being. Homer had his Ulysses, and Euripides had his heroes and heroines. The stories, the plays, and the poems are about people. Even the *Iliad*,[4] which is about the Trojan War, focuses on the roles of individuals in the war: Achilles, Paris, Agamemnon, Hector, Ulysses. The guiding principle of the stories is that they are about the works of individual people.

Ancient Greece was also one of the locales of the birth of the idea of *demos cratia*, democracy.[5] Although only a relatively small percentage of the population could participate in the democratic process, it was certainly far more than were able to participate in other societies. The secret of the flowering of ancient Greece was that this idealized society of artists, orators, and scientists was, as all the great flowerings of civilization were, based on the enslavement of a large portion of the population. To have art, literature, and science, people have to have time for art, literature, and science, and that means not having to worry about eating. Slaves provided the labor necessary for Euripides to be able to eat while he wrote his plays. This was the situation in all great civilizations prior to the industrial revolution, when machines took over many of the tasks that had been done by human beings, who were often slaves, serfs, or peons. In Western society, slavery did not end so much because of its inherent immorality, but because it became unprofitable.

The Greeks were also one of the first societies to attempt to explain the natural world in rational terms.[6] Other societies had attributed much of what went on around them to the work of whatever god they worshipped. The Greeks were different, in that they attempted to think things through. Aristotle was one of the first scientists, and although many, if not most, of his conclusions were simply wrong, he did attempt to make some sort of rational sense out of the world around him: in a sense, to systematize his surroundings into a logical, coherent whole. In the *Republic*,[7] Plato attempted to do something very similar with regard to government and organization. The *Republic* is Plato's answer to the question, "What would be the best form of government for the city-state?"

BOX 5.1   Homer

The first great poet of Western civilization was Homer. Homer was the author of two great epic poems, the *Iliad*, about the war and eventual sack of Troy, and the *Odyssey*, about the return voyage of the Greek hero, Odysseus, from Troy. Many scholars doubt whether Homer, as an individual person, really existed, and no one is sure where, or for that matter, when he lived. There are several points of agreement: (1) if he did live, it was 400 to 500 years after the actual Trojan War; and (2) according to tradition, he was blind.

Homer is important because he represents the very beginnings of Western literature. All literature in Western society starts with Homer. In all likelihood, Homer's two great poems represent the distillation of an oral tradition of bards, who sang their songs for anyone who would listen. They also represent some of the earliest Greek writings and are believed to have been written down shortly after the introduction of writing to Greece. Whether Homer was a single person, two people, or a committee is not really important. What is important is that Homer is the foundation, the start of the great Western literary tradition that includes Shakespeare, Mark Twain, Geothe, and Dante.

Plato was attempting to devise a plan for a government of individuals. Other Greeks, including Euclid, became well known for their scientific contributions and accomplishments. The Greeks are important because they provided the basis for the successful questioning of authority. The gods were not an adequate answer. The Greeks knew that there had to be more because they recognized and celebrated the importance of the individual. The power and rulers of the society could silence Socrates with hemlock,[8] but they could not extinguish his ideas. Ideas and the individual became important in ancient Greece and have remained the hallmark of Western civilization ever since.

One final important aspect of Greek civilization was its spread throughout much of the ancient world. Alexander the Great, a Macedonian and student of Aristotle, first conquered Greece and then united it.[9] He then went on to conquer most of the known civilized world, including Egypt, Persia, and India. Alexander brought the ideals of Greek civilization with him and spread them throughout his dominions. He ensured that Greek ideals would not become part of the dust of history and in the process became one of the great figures in the history of the ancient world, not because of his conquests and great leadership but because of his adherence, devotion, and practice of many of the ideals of ancient Greece.

The Romans

After the death of Alexander the Great, his empire was split up among several of his generals.[10] This, of course, included Greece itself, where fighting soon began among the various city-states. Finally, the Greeks, so weakened by their wars, were dominated by a non-Greek state—Rome. By this time the Romans had conquered most of Italy, including Greek colonies that had been established along the coast and in Sicily. At this point the Romans were a fairly rough-and-ready group, and in an effort to become a more civilized society, adopted many Greek ideas. Greek scholars were often taken to Rome, sometimes as slaves, sometimes not, to teach the children of wealthy Roman families.[11] Through this educational process, many Romans adopted Greek ideas. Many of these ideas survived through the Roman republican period and into the empire.

While the Western Roman Empire lasted into the 400s and the Eastern Roman Empire as long as 1456,[12] they kept two very important ideas alive, ideas that have had a great impact on modern society. The first idea was the principal informing idea of the ancient Greeks: the importance of individuality, of questioning the world and attempting to develop a systematized view of what the world is like. This was the legacy of Aristotle, Socrates, and Plato. The second important idea that was preserved, spread, and developed by both the Eastern and Western Roman Empires was Christianity. It is, perhaps, one of the great ironies of history that the Roman Empire, in particular Constantine the Great, a Roman emperor, did more to establish Christianity as the religion of European civilization than was done by any other single force.[13] Christianity and Christians had been persecuted since the very beginning as a religious movement and a sect of Judaism. The spiritual founder and prophet of the faith, Jesus of Nazareth, was himself crucified by the people of Jerusalem, and that crucifixion is an important article of faith among Christians. Although Christ was said to have died for the sins of his followers, the religious movement that was founded as a result of his teachings has lived on to be one of the most important religions of the world and certainly one of the most important institutions of European civilization.

Under Constantine the Great, the Roman Empire did away with the old pagan gods and established Christianity as the state religion.[14] That faith was then adopted by the entire empire, so that by the time the Western Roman Empire had fallen to the barbarian hordes that had come across the borders to conquer and sack the once imperial city of Rome, the Church remained as a separate, indeed the only surviving institution in what had been the Western Roman Empire. The Church was to provide the necessary glue to hold Western European civilization together for the next 500 to 1000 years.

The Eastern Roman Empire was centered in Constantinople (the city of Constantine), now Istanbul.[15] The Eastern Empire survived for 1000 years after the fall of its Western brother. The fortunes of the empire ebbed and flowed over that period of time, during much of which it was the most important city in Europe. Finally, in 1456, the city fell to Süleyman the Magnificent, of the Ottoman Turks.[16] It was not the first time the city had fallen or been sacked, but it was the last. The Eastern Empire's legacy was the establishment of Orthodox Christianity in much of Eastern Europe. It had served as a bulwark against the advancing Islamic tide that had swept over Africa and the Middle East and had

---

BOX 5.2 Constantine the Great

Constantine the Great was an Emperor of Rome responsible for many changes in the later part of the empire's history.

1. He consolidated the role of the empire under one emperor, thus bringing an end to the system of shared rule between two senior and two junior emperors begun by Emperor Diocletian in A.D. 293.
2. He moved the capital of the Roman Empire from Rome to Constantinople, thus laying the foundation for the Byzantine or Eastern Roman Empire, which would survive until the fifteenth century.
3. He recognized Christianity as legal, and the Church was allowed to own property and even had property returned that had been seized from it.
4. Although not a Christian, he presided over the Nicene Council, which repudiated the Arian heresy that Christ was of a different substance than God and established a statement of essential beliefs called the Nicene Creed:

   > We believe in one God, the Father Almighty, maker of all things, both visible and invisible, and in one Lord, Jesus Christ, the Son of God. Only begotten of the Father, that is to say, of the substance of the Father, God of God and Light of Light, very God of very God, begotten, not made, being of one substance with the Father, by whom all things were made, both things in heaven and things on earth, who for us men and for our salvation, came down and was made flesh, was made man, suffered, and rose again on the third day, went up into the heavens, and is to come again to judge both the quick and the dead, and in the Holy Ghost.

5. He greatly supported the spread of Christianity by establishing churches in various parts of the empire, building the first great Christian cathedral, the Lateran Basilica in Rome.
6. He became the first Christian emperor of Rome by being baptized on his deathbed.

spread as far east as the Philippines and as far west as Spain. Islam and the civilization it represented could be said to have reached its peak in 1456, when cannons were used for the first time in Europe to literally batter down the walls of Constantinople.[17] But the tide was already receding in Spain, where Islamic culture and civilization were left with only a foothold in Grenada, and by 1491, the Moors would be completely out of Spain.[18]

The Greeks and the Romans formed the bedrock of what was to become Western civilization. They developed and/or spread the two important and sometimes contradictory ideas of individuality and Christianity and maintained a solid defense against the encroachment of Islam into Western Europe. People perish, empires die, but ideas live on.

The Middle Ages

While the Eastern Roman Empire was flourishing and holding back the tide of Islam, civilization in Western Europe was in serious difficulty. The old order of the Roman Empire had been overthrown and replaced with something that was far from order. Nomadic tribes conquered the native populations and imposed their own form of order, only soon to be threatened and sometimes conquered by other nomadic groups. Whether they were called Huns, Vikings, or Vandals, they all struck fear into the more civilized peoples, who seemed powerless against them. In Britain, the native Romanized Celts were pushed back to Wales, Cornwall, Scotland, and Brittany by the advancing hordes of Germanic Angles, Saxons, and Jutes.[19] The resistance of the Celts has been memorialized in the legends of King Arthur and the Round Table.[20] The Germanic tribes were in turn subjugated by Vikings, Danes, and other Northmen. Indeed, one of the prayers to come out of Anglo-Saxon England was: "Lord, protect us from the fury of the Northmen, and things that go bump in the night."[21]

For nearly 500 years after the fall of Rome, Western Europe was in a "dark age."[22] The weak were subjugated by the strong, and the strong were always vulnerable to the stronger still. Although there were momentary glimpses of order during this time and many of the institutions of Western civilization, especially in England, have there roots in this era, it was, on the whole, a violent and dangerous period. Charlemagne ruled briefly in France[23] and much of Germany, and Alfred the Great started the Doomsday Book and English common law,[24] but these were only brief, shining moments in what was, on the whole, a fairly dark and miserable time.

The one continuous bright spot during the Dark Ages in Western Europe was the Church. The Church was a haven for learning and knowledge.[25] One of the essential tasks performed by the Church was the copying and preservation of manuscripts written originally by the ancient Greeks and Romans. Many monasteries engaged in the practice of copying these manuscripts, and although many monasteries and their libraries were destroyed by fire or war or some other tragedy, many survived and became part of the Renaissance. During the Dark Ages, the Church performed the important function of providing a certain kind of order in society and the hope of better times—if not in this life, then in the next—as well as preservation of the knowledge acquired by the ancients. Without the Church and its activities, ranging from copying

---

■ ■ ■   **BOX 5.3   The Crusades**   ■ ■ ■

One of the major reasons for the end of the Middle Ages and the beginning of the Renaissance
was the Crusades. The Crusades consisted of eight major military expeditions, mostly by Christian
knights, raised by calls from the Church to free the Holy Land from the Muslims. The Crusades went
on from A.D. 1096 to 1270 and represent a general expansion of Western European economies, philosophy, militarism, and Christianity. Although the Crusades failed to accomplish their main goal of
retrieving the Holy Land for the Christians and the Muslims remained in power (Christian kingdoms
in the Holy Land were short-lived), the Crusades were important for a number of reasons:

1. The divide between Eastern and Western Christianity, especially after the Fourth Crusade, became
   even wider.
2. Trade between Europe and the Middle East was encouraged, thus leading to economic growth in
   both Europe and the Middle East.
3. New ideas and knowledge were brought from the East to Europe, leading to the end of the Middle Ages.
4. New and better technology became available in Western Europe, leading to better ships, better
   tools, and better ways of doing things.

---

manuscripts to calling for Crusades against the Islamic usurpers of the Holy
Land, the great awakening that would begin in Italy would have been far more
difficult to achieve.

The Renaissance

The Renaissance, or "awakening," began in Italy.[26] The importance of the Renaissance is that it represents the beginning of what is called modern civilization in Western Europe. Starting around 1100, new ideas, new practices, and
new objects started to become available on the Italian peninsula. Some of this
can be traced to the Crusades and some to the trading activities of the great Italian merchant cities of Genoa and Venice.[27] The only thing that is certain is that
Western civilization became reborn. The Church, which had preserved the ideas
of the ancient Greeks and Romans, was now confronted by ideas that were contrary to its own regarding life, nature, and the general order of things. Copernicus, Galileo, and Leonardo da Vinci all experimented with new ideas and
challenged the authority of the Church. Books were being written, and perhaps
the most important invention in Western Europe during this time was the
movable-type printing press, the personal computer of its day.[28] Average, common people now had something to read. When they read, they formed their
own conclusions about what they were reading, and this led to dissent: dissent
in politics, religion, and all manner of things. The idea of the individual once
more began to play a role in society, an idea that descended from the ancient
Greeks and Romans, backed up by their rediscovered writings. People could
now make up their own minds—and Western Europe would never be the same.
    An immediate result of this was religious dissent in the form of the Re-
formation, with Calvin, Luther, and Knox[29] being leading figures in this field.
They were followed by such people as Locke and Rousseau,[30] who explored the
political aspects of this new era of individualism. Their work culminated in

Adam Smith's *Wealth of Nations*,[31] Thomas Jefferson's Declaration of Independence, and France's Declaration of the Rights of Man.

The individual became an idea—an idea that has remained a constant in Western civilization for over 500 years. Although there have been other ideas and philosophies that have sought to limit the role of the individual, notably socialism, fascism, and communism, none have survived against the power of the importance of the individual as an idea in Western thought. Great issues of today, such as human rights, democracy, and economic and political freedom, are all traced to the concept of the individual human being as the center of what is important in the society. If the individual has life, the society has life; if the individual has liberty, the society has liberty; if the individual can pursue happiness, the society can pursue happiness and become whatever it chooses in the aggregate to be.[32] These are the ideals of a free society, and the ideal of Western society is a free society.

Modern Western Society

Today, much of Western civilization extends beyond Europe and North America. As the dominant society since the start of the Age of Discovery over 500 years ago, Western society and the institutions of Western society have been planted in other parts of the world.[33] Succeeding waves of colonial expansion have all helped to spread Western ideals and institutions. The first institution to be spread was the Church. Certainly, the most resilient legacy of the conquistadors in Latin America has been the Church, along with the Spanish language.[34] In North America the English became the dominant European power after long struggles with both the French and the Spanish. Although French culture and influence remains in Quebec and to a lesser degree in Louisiana, the growth of French influence was certainly curtailed after the purchase of Louisiana by the United States from Napoleon.

Spanish influence came to an end for the most part when the various nations of Latin America revolted against Spain and Florida was purchased by the United States. With the exception of a few islands in the Caribbean and off the coast of Canada, and some isolated colonies in Guinea and Belize (British Honduras), all direct European involvement in the Americas had come to an end by 1900. The end of colonization did not mean the end of Western institutions in the Americas; it simply meant the end of formal ties to the various mother countries. The revolutionaries were the descendants of the colonists who had come to these countries seeking a better life, not the indigenous population, and they kept, in somewhat modified form, the customs, institutions, and culture

---

BOX 5.4 Manifest Destiny

Traditional expansion for the United States seemed inevitable in the 1840s and became known as Manifest Destiny. It was believed by many people in the United States that the country was destined to govern all of North America and was a major rationale for the Mexican War and later the Spanish-American War. People believed that it was God's will that the United States should expand across the continent because of American economic and political superiority and the rapidly growing population. People who stood in the way of Manifest Destiny, notably Mexico and Native Americans, would simply have to be brushed aside so that the United States could fulfill its destiny.

they had brought with them.[35] European civilization had been transferred from Europe to the Americas and then modified to fit local conditions. Some countries, such as Argentina, Canada, and the United States, evolved into very European societies; others did so to a lesser degree.

During the time that the Americas were in the process of discarding their European ties, other parts of the world were in the process of being assaulted by the Europeans. If the nineteenth century marked, for all practical purposes, the end of European colonialism in the Americas, it marked the beginning of extensive European activity in Africa and Asia. Starting with the French and Indian War in the American colonies, the British then pushed the French completely out of India and began a rule that would last 200 years.[36] The British often led the way in colonization in the nineteenth century, in Australia, New Zealand, and parts of Africa. Other European powers followed, including the Germans in Tanganyika, the French in North Africa, the Belgians in the Congo, the Italians in Libya, and the Russians in Siberia.

Wherever the Europeans went, they attempted to transplant their ideas and institutions.[37] In India, the British attempted to unite the country and plant the seeds of democracy, which they did with some success. France and other European powers did much the same thing in their colonies, but this colonization was remarkably different from prior waves of colonization. In the first place, not as many people immigrated from Europe to the frontier. Life was more difficult on the frontier than in Europe. Not only that, but there were alternatives to immigrating to a colony. North and Latin America offered attractive alternatives in often more hospitable environments. For perspective British colonists, Australia, New Zealand, and even South Africa offered possibilities. Colonization of India meant supplanting an established civilization that was thousands of years old, and the African climate and tropical diseases often meant the European colonists were at a risk that many of them found unacceptable.[38]

In the rest of Asia, the French and British vied for various possessions in Southeast Asia and the Middle East, but while they could threaten and intimidate China, none could truly dominate the vast Chinese Empire or culture. The French could succeed in Indo-China, the British in Burma and Malaya, but China and Japan remained unyielding to European expansion.

Wherever the Europeans went in their attempt to colonize Asia and Africa, they planted the seeds of Western institutions and culture. These institutions are rather like the icing on a huge cake of indigenous culture. These countries may have many of the official institutions of European-based societies, such as courts, parliaments, and some sort of desire, at least, for representative government, but once one gets past the icing, the "cake" of the real culture is to be found.[39]

NON-WESTERN SOCIETIES

Asian Society

Asia has been the home of a number of great civilizations. The Fertile Crescent, India, and China have all been the home of highly unique and diverse societies.[40] Because of the vast landmass of Asia, these societies developed largely independent of each other, although there was obviously some contact between them.

Civilization may have begun in Babylon and the river valleys of the Tigris and Euphrates Rivers. This ancient civilization has produced a varied and rich legacy for humanity. Three of the world's great religions were founded by societies that trace their beginnings to Mesopotamia. Today, the dominant religion of the region is Islam, but Christianity and Judaism are also practiced there, and religion has been one of the reasons for the great conflicts that have plagued this region for many years.[41] This part of the world has been subjected to European onslaughts since the Crusades, and European ideas have taken root to a modest degree in some of these countries, but Middle Eastern civilization has been unique in its own development and has produced great art, literature, and architecture. It is a civilization that has produced unique societies, ranging from the theocracy of Iran to the dictatorship of Iraq and the democracy of Israel: all highly different and diverse, with their own way of doing things and their own unique outlook on society, humanity, and the world.

India also provides a unique civilization that can be traced back for thousands of years.[42] Conquered, reconquered, and conquered again, Indian civilization has remained and survived. Perhaps the core of Indian civilization can be found in the Hindu faith. The languages of the subcontinent vary tremendously and the ethnic backgrounds of the people may differ, but the religion of Hinduism remains the unifying structure of India, as well as one of the lasting legacies of the British colonial period, the English language, which is the official language of the entire country, rather than Hindi or Bengali or Pashto. This may be a source of irritation to the government of India, but it remains one of the unifying forces in the country. India today is in the process of slowly coming out of its reaction to British colonialism and starting to loosen government rules and regulations for business and foreign investment.[43] But there are problems. Most of India's population remains in abject poverty, and while there is a significant and growing middle class, the birth rate is at such a high level that the population of India is expected to exceed China's sometime during the twenty-first century.[44] Right now, India can feed itself, but for how long? If it were to reach the point where it could no longer feed itself, then what? The problems as well as potential opportunities in India are huge. The question is: What is going to happen?

India has a long history and its society has developed some unique characteristics. Although it is now illegal, the caste system still has great weight in Indian society. Essentially, in the caste system people are born into a particular group, whether merchants, warriors, or farmers, and they live their lives in that group no matter what their particular talents may be. Someone may be born with the ability to become the world's greatest heart surgeon but if the person was born into the merchant caste, he or she will spend his or her life buying and selling goods.[45] This has obviously created problems in the society.

India's problems are not just its own but are likely to become a problem for India's neighbors as well as the rest of the world. What would happen if India were to run out of food? If it were to run out of space? If it were to run out of resources? India's neighbors would be most directly affected by this, but so would everyone else. Added to this is the fact that India has atomic capabilities and the prospect of a destabilized subcontinent in the next 25 to 50 years becomes a real threat.

BOX 5.5   Buddha

The given name of Buddha, the founder of Buddhism, one of the world's great religions, was Siddhartha Gautama, and he was born in northern India around 500 B.C. At the age of 29, Buddha had a religious experience that led him from a life of worldly pursuits to the life of a holy man. Buddha taught a continuing cycle of death and rebirth. The dharma, Buddha's teachings, preaches the theory that each person's position in life is determined by behavior in a prior life; that the way to nirvana, a state of peace and happiness, could be achieved by people ridding themselves of worldly possessions. Buddha's teaching is that those who are willing to follow the Middle Way which avoids uncontrolled satisfaction of human desires and extreme forms of self-denial and self-torture, will find Nirvana. Buddha also taught that the Noble Eightfold Path will also lead to Nirvana:

1. Knowledge of truth
2. The intention to resist evil
3. Saying nothing to hurt others
4. Respecting life, morality, and property
5. Holding a job that does not injure others
6. Striving to free one's mind of evil
7. Controlling one's feelings and thoughts
8. Practicing proper forms of concentration

By any standard, China is also a great and unique culture. It should be noted that while Westerners tend to view China as a single culture and country, it is made up of a great many diverse groups and even has two major dialects that are nearly languages, Mandarin and Cantonese. It would, perhaps, be more accurate to view China as a kind of long-term united Europe with dialects of Cantonese and Mandarin being akin to Spanish, French, Italian, and Rumanian for Latin-based languages, and German, English, Norwegian, and Swedish as dialects of German-based languages.

China is an old society and civilization.[46] When Europeans were running around in animal skins and living in caves, China was experiencing art and poetry. One of the unique aspects of China is that although Europeans attempted to dominate China, especially during the nineteenth century, they never succeeded, even briefly. China's society has survived without strong European influence and, as such, is unique among nations.

China represents what might be the biggest question mark of the next century. The country is so large and represents such a large portion of the human race that it simply cannot be ignored. The country is coming out of its period of socialism and is starting to experience capitalism. It should be mentioned that Chinese capitalism is nothing new and that the Chinese have engaged in commerce for centuries. If anything, the imposition of a planned economy on China by the communists was a new and unique experience. Capitalism in one form or another has always been the Chinese approach. The question in China is how the power structure will maintain itself as various forms and levels of free markets are introduced into the country. If the people of China are going to experience choice in the marketplace, they will soon expect the same kind of choice in politics. The South Korean example is useful. Once the country experienced choice in economic terms, the people expected choice in political terms. In China, once the population experiences choice in economic terms, won't they expect it in political terms? How long can the current political order in China hang on? What will happen when it is challenged, as it surely will be? The way in which political and economic power evolves in China will be a major concern for the rest of the world. If China should develop in a peaceful way, the rest of the world will certainly benefit. If, on the other hand, the development is violent, there are certain to be problems not only for China, but for everyone else.

China has the potential to turn, if not the twenty-first century into the Chinese century, then certainly the twenty-second century. Today, the United States dominates the world as the leading military and economic superpower. The twentieth century has been called the American century, and while the United States may have dominated the world scene during this time, there is no guarantee that it will continue to do so. China, a united Europe, Japan, India, and even a reborn Soviet Union could potentially supplant the United States as the dominant power on the world stage, but all of them need to make significant changes in order to do so. China's, as well as India's, potential is immense, but there is no guarantee that both will not self-destruct in some way before they are able to assume greater power and prestige. However, the potential is certainly there.

Japan is another country with a unique and highly developed history and culture; Japan was a closed country for hundreds of years until it was opened by Admiral Perry and the U.S. Navy in 1854.[47] Recognizing its relative weakness compared to Perry's flotilla, the Japanese set about attaining technological and military parity with the European powers. It developed many European institutions by examining the best Europe had to offer and then basing its new industry, military, and government on those models. Japan forced itself into the modern era and within 60 years was able to defeat a major European military power in the Russo-Japanese War. Japan would continue to expand into China and other parts of Asia until the end of World War II, when it was defeated by the United States and its allies in its attempt at military expansion.

After the war, Japan had to rebuild its economy and political system completely because both had been destroyed during the war. The rebirth of Japan is one of the economic and political miracles of the late twentieth century. Twenty-five years after the end of World War II, Japan and Japanese products

---

■ ■ ■   **BOX 5.6   Chinese Capitalism**   ■ ■ ■

There are at least two countries in mainland China today, if not more. One is the old communist state founded by Mao, and the other is the emerging capitalist state, with roots in Hong Kong, Shanghai, and Quong Dong Province. Quong Dong, the province next to Hong Kong, has served as the workshop annex for the former British Crown Colony. Many goods manufactured in China come from this province. Today, capitalism of all sorts may be found here, right next to an old poster extolling the virtues of communism. The people of the province are living better lives than their cousins farther inland, and the dynamic of capitalism may be seen everywhere. Quong Dong, Hong Kong, and Shanghai represent only the beginning of what is sure to be an economic and political revolution in China.

were able to compete successfully all over the world, even in the home markets of the victors of World War II. In the 1950s, Japanese products were considered junk, but in the 1970s, many Japanese products became the standard by which the products of the rest of the world were judged.[48]

Japan has had many advantages in attaining the economic and political miracle of the post–World War II era. One advantage has been the recognition on the part of Japan that its only real advantage is the Japanese people. Japan has little in the way of natural resources and other assets.[49] Nature was not generous when the Japanese islands were made. The result has been that Japan has a highly developed and trained workforce and a recognition that it must aggressively engage in selling its products to the rest of the world. This workforce is very homogeneous, as there are few non-Japanese in Japan and the culture solidly supports the development of the people as a group, not just individuals.

Unfortunately, Japan's strength in a highly skilled but very homogeneous workforce has the potential to be a long-term weakness.[50] Seven of the 10 largest organizations in the world are Japanese, but the Japanese have a problem.[51] They are used to dealing with Japanese, and seldom with other groups in the world society, other than to try to sell them something or make war on them (in Japan there is a saying that "Business is war!"). Japanese organizations are almost entirely Japanese, especially at the senior level. This creates a long-term self-limiting situation for the Japanese and the future of their economy and industries. Put simply, if one restricts oneself to a pool of managerial talent of 120 million people, and the rest of the world is able to draw on a talent pool of potential senior managers 4 to 5 billion people in size, the group drawing on the smaller pool is going to have more problems in senior management than organizations that can select people from a base 40 to 50 times larger. Talented, highly motivated people can be found everywhere. Not to consider these people simply because they are not from the same homogeneous group is to impose a self-limitation on the organization that, in the long run, can be very damaging. Japanese firms are going to have to learn to accept non-Japanese in senior positions if these organizations are going to continue to enjoy the success they have had. This is not to say that Mitsubishi or Hitachi are in danger of going out of business, but that a highly significant cultural change is going to have to take place for these companies to continue for the next 50 years the success they have enjoyed over the past 50 years. If they do not, they are going to start to experience a slow decline, relative to the rest of the world, because the talent that they have chosen to ignore is going to be competing against them and is bound to experience at least some success.

Indo-China, Hong Kong, Korea, Burma, Singapore, Malaysia, Taiwan, Thailand, the Philippines, and Indonesia, some of them known as the "tigers" of the Pacific rim, also represent an area of Asia that is rapidly expanding. Although they fell on hard times in the late 1990s and their economies may still be suffering, this will end when the appropriate reforms take effect. These societies have been developing for a very long period of time, and while heavily influenced by both India and China for hundreds of years, they have developed their own distinct languages and cultures.

Indonesia, formerly known as the Dutch East Indies, has many diverse cultures and ethnic groups within its borders.[52] A developing nation as are the other countries in this group, Indonesia is one of the world's five largest countries in terms of population. About the size of the United States, Indonesia is currently ruled by a dictatorship and the country has many problems with frequent ethnic unrest. Economically, the country is growing rapidly, but a question remains as to how long the current political environment can continue. Indonesia has the potential to become the Yugoslavia of Asia, complete with "ethnic cleansing" and religious persecution.

Thailand is another country in Asia that is under political dictatorship. While the economy continues to grow and some U.S. firms are staking their future on the country,[53] the transition from a monarchy to a democracy has been a rocky one at best. Both Thailand and Burma would certainly be considered developing countries. Both have long histories, unique cultures, and distinct languages, and both offer exciting potential for foreign investment by foreign organizations, but they are a long way from developing into the kind of democratic industrialized democracy that can be seen developing in other parts of the developing world.

Singapore is a kind of anachronism in the modern world. A city-state and one of the great economic success stories in Asia,[54] Singapore is an extremely productive and law-abiding society. Small in area but sitting on one of the most important trade routes in the world, Singapore represents almost a shining city in Asia—prosperous and growing in wealth.

Malaysia is another country that has adopted its own unique form of capitalism. Malaysia was a British colony that almost fell to a communist insurrection in the 1950s.[55] It may sound almost unbelievable given the aggressive capitalism that now exists in the country, but the communists almost won the war. Today, Malaysia is a growing country that continues to increase its prosperity and trade with the rest of the world.

Taiwan represents one of the most perplexing situations facing the world economy in that it is the remnant of what is left of precommunist China.[56] A kind of outcast in many ways, yet a prosperous and somewhat democratic nation, Taiwan produces a great many goods that are consumed throughout the world. The mainland Chinese claim it as a runaway province, but the Taiwanese do not see it that way. Although during the 1940s and 1950s, they may have had dreams of returning to the mainland to take back China, those days are long gone. Taiwan has become its own nation, and although the mainland Chinese may not agree with that assessment, as long as the U.S. Seventh Fleet patrols the waters of the Formosa Strait, there is little that China can do about it.

Hong Kong also represents a unique situation in the world. Returned to China by the British in 1997,[57] Hong Kong has been one of the great Asian tigers of the Pacific rim. Banking, finance, manufacturing, and all manner of commercial activity have found a home in Hong Kong. The basic, and really only important question for Hong Kong is what is going to happen now that China has taken over. Is China going to be able to tolerate the raw capitalism in Hong Kong? Can China develop as a two-system society—one capitalist, the other socialist—with all that means in terms of political power in Beijing? No country has ever tried to tolerate two different economic systems while maintaining a political system that so obviously favors one or the other. The best that can be hoped for is that capitalism will eventually spread through the entire country in addition to the areas along the coast, with Hong Kong and probably, Shanghai as the major commercial centers. Or China may contain and eventually, perhaps, be forced to destroy what Hong Kong stands for. Although Hong Kong and China may seek a middle ground, in the long run (and in

China that can mean a very long time) there can be only one system. Capitalism is eventually going to end communist rule in China or be destroyed in the attempt to do so, because capitalism represents choice whereas communism does not, and the two have great difficulty coexisting.

Perhaps the most difficult situation to understand in all of the Pacific rim countries is the Philippines.[58] The Philippines have many advantages over their neighbors when it comes to potential economic development. These include a history of special ties to the United States as a former U.S. possession, a history of U.S. and Filipino blood being spilled together in World War II, similar institutions as a result of the historic U.S. presence, and a large number of English-speaking citizens. Yet the Philippines have remained an economic backwater in this part of the world. The reasons became obvious when the Marcos government was deposed. Political corruption had become so outrageous that no major country or company was going to bother with Manila, especially when there were so many other opportunities available in the region. The Philippines lost out because of the demand for bribes and other forms of corruption on the part of the government. The situation is not as bad today as it was then, but there are still problems and the Philippines has a long way to go to catch up.

The Korean peninsula offers one of the great contrasts of the modern world.[59] At the end of the Korean War, both North and South Korea had been completely destroyed. There was nothing left and the people on both sides of the demilitarized zone were starving. Both Koreas had the same people, the same traditions, the same culture, but were about to embark upon a future using different systems. In the south, capitalism, with help from the United States, would be allowed to grow and expand, while in the north, a fairly puritanical form of communism would be instituted.

The results of this experiment after 45 years have not been lost on the rest of the world. South Korea is one of the economic tigers of Asia. Simply stated, things are better today for the average South Korean than they have ever been in the entire history of the country, despite the recent economic problems brought on largely by what would be considered corrupt practices in the United States, but were legal in Korea. Not that they are nearly as prosperous as the average American or Japanese or Western European, but they are far better off than they were at the end of the Korean conflict, far better off than they have ever been in the history of the society, and they have the hope of even better things to come.

North Korea, on the other hand, is not much better off than it was nearly half a century ago. The country is falling apart and is begging the international community for food, using an implied threat to restart the Korean War if it does not receive the food and other items it needs. Although it is unlikely that the North Korean military could sustain a protracted conflict, it could inflict great damage on South Korea and would draw the United States into the conflict due to the number of U.S. troops stationed there. Nobody wants this. So the United States, South Korea, and other interested countries have the paradox of trying to sustain a communist regime in North Korea so as to keep it from self-destructing and in the process damaging all those involved. How long this can be maintained remains to be seen, but the process cannot be open ended. Eventually, even the North Koreans will grow tired of it and want to change and move on.

Perhaps the most difficult situation for Americans to deal with is the issue of Vietnam. It has been over 20 years since the fall of Saigon to the North Vietnamese,[60] but the wounds are still there and are likely to be there until every member of the Vietnam generation is gone. Vietnam does, however, offer much in the way of potential. Although communism is still the official line of the government, the reality is that Vietnam is eager for foreign and especially U.S. investment.[61] Only recently has the U.S. government lifted the official policy of embargo against Vietnam, but that policy has not prevented the Europeans and Japanese from entering the country and doing business. For the United States the war is over, or should be, and Americans are now starting to take an active role in Vietnam. The Vietnamese people have many outstanding qualities: obvious determination to succeed, no matter the cost; rich natural resources; a U.S.-made infrastructure in the South, that although in disrepair, can be fixed. Vietnam may well be the next tiger of the Pacific rim; although it may take some time for it to achieve this status, it certainly has the ability to do it.

There is one additional group that needs to be addressed in Asia. It is not a country but an ethnic group that has extensive business interests throughout this part of the world and growing activities in the United States, Europe, Latin America—indeed, the entire rest of the world.[62] The primary members of this group, known as "Greater China," are ethnic Chinese not living in China but often with investments there. Many family-operated enterprises controlled by the members of Chinese families that have lived outside China for generations, perhaps hundreds of years, have maintained some kind of a link to China even during the most difficult days of World War II, the Communist Revolution, and the Cultural Revolution. Greater China, combining mainland China, Taiwan, and various Chinese-controlled enterprises outside China, may be one of the major economies in the world. It is hard to say, because there is no central reporting system and the Chinese are notoriously closed mouthed on these issues.

There is, however, one important limitation on these businesses that the offshore Chinese are going to have to overcome if they are going to continue to grow and expand—and that is the family orientation. Historically, these organizations have grown through marriage and children, in the belief that there is no closer bond than using family members as means of expansion. Unfortunately, while ensuring loyalty, this practice is self-limiting. There can be only so many daughters, sons, nephews, and nieces in any family, and while traditional Chinese families have tended to be rather large, there are limits. How these family businesses handle their growth and development over the next 50 years is probably going to determine their success. Greater China has the potential to be a significant economic force in the twenty-first century, but it is probably going to have to change some of its business practices to do so.

Societies in Emerging Nations

In addition to the Pacific rim nations, the nations of Africa and Latin America are an increasingly important segment of the world. Most anthropologists believe that Africa is the home of the human race. If that is so, the human race is not taking very good care of it. Africa is plagued by many problems.[63] Much of the continent, especially in the north, is simply not suitable for human beings.

The Sahara takes up vast reaches of the continent and is one of the most hostile places on Earth to live. These countries, many of them former French colonies, have large areas of essentially useless land. The area on the coast, where many of the nations of Africa are clustered, are small, with a varied history dating back to their days as colonies of the various European empires. Many of the same things can be said of the continent farther south. Clans and tribes still make up much of the social fabric of these countries, and the concept of nationhood is, in many areas, still remarkably weak. Many of the conflicts in Africa are based on this idea of clan or tribe, and vicious civil wars are being fought, often destroying any pretense of a national identity.

In Somalia, the United States attempted to intervene when conditions became so desperate that the country was on the verge of mass starvation, only to withdraw when U.S. servicemen were killed by local terrorists.[64] People are faced with not dissimilar situations in Burundi and Uganda, and the former Belgian Congo has recently finished a revolution that deposed the Mobutu dictatorship of some 30 years.[65]

The most modern, richest, and powerful nation in Africa for many years has been the Republic of South Africa.[66] A nation with a truly unique history and situation, South Africa is the only nation in Africa with a truly substantial European population, which traces its roots to the founding of Cape Town about 500 years ago. The Dutch settlers of South Africa were significantly augmented by the British about 100 years ago as a result of the Boer War, when Queen Victoria's empire imposed itself on much of Africa. The British brought with them to South Africa a large number of other ethnic groups, notably Indians, from the rest of the Empire. These peoples were all imposed on the native African population, creating an additional group of mixed-race people. The fact is that South Africa is a nation with many racial tensions within a wide variety of groups, whose diversity of origin is rivaled only by the United States. With the exception of the native African population, all of the various citizens of South Africa can trace their roots elsewhere, just as in the United States all the citizens, with the exception of the Native Americans, are the children of immigrants. South Africa has had a history of racial tensions.[67] The leading policy that created these tensions—apartheid—resulted in the country being shunned by most of the rest of the world. Today, those policies have been overturned and the country is ruled by an African majority government. But South Africa

---

■ ■ ■   BOX 5.7 Nelson Mandela   ■ ■ ■

Nelson Mandela is the father of black South Africa. Imprisoned for long periods of time by the then-ruling white minority, he became a *cause célèbre* of the African freedom movement in South Africa. Long a member of the African National Congress and originally an advocate of nonviolent resistance, he changed his stance in 1960 and began advocating acts of sabotage against the South African regime. Tried and convicted of these activities, he remained imprisoned until his release in 1990. In an effort to avoid violent revolution, he joined with white South African president F. W. de Klerk in a joint government of whites and blacks. After winning election as president of South Africa in April 1994 in the country's first all-race elections, he introduced a number of measures to improve housing, education, and economic development to improve the standard of living of the black population.

remains a collection of diverse societies with little in the way of true social integration. There remains a white society and native African society, and within these societies there are distinct boundaries between the Boers on the one hand and the British on the other, just as in the native African population the Zulus continue to separate themselves from the other native peoples. Indians and mixed-race people also play roles in South African society and government.

How South Africa is able to deal with this mix of people is going to be a very important development on the world stage. South Africa, just as the United States, has a long history of racial subjugation and abuse. Combining these divergent groups into a nation will be a very difficult task. The country does have certain advantages, however, as it is the richest, best educated, and most technologically advanced nation in Africa. But the success or failure of South Africa in creating a nation will have great impact on what will happen in the rest of sub-Saharan Africa. South Africa is in a position to lead the way into the modern era or to hold the rest of the continent back in the mire in which it currently finds itself.

The nations of Latin America are the other large group of emergent nations. Most of these countries have been independent from Europe for 200 years, or about the same amount of time as the United States, but their histories and development have followed a much different path both from the United States and often from each other.

European in outlook in many ways, they have, nonetheless, fallen behind Europe in an economic and political sense. Almost all of Latin America has gone through periods of dictatorship, usually military, in the period since World War II, and for the most part, these dictatorships have been a disaster for those countries in the long run.[68] They have also been marked by anti-Americanism, often not without cause, that has taken the form of nationalization of U.S. assets in Chile, Cuba, and Mexico,[69] communist dictatorships in Cuba and Nicaragua, and riots in Colombia and Peru. Today, some of these countries have started to develop democratic and capitalistic systems, and Mexico's Institutional Revolutionary Party (PRE) is being challenged in various parts of the country.[70] The repressive governmental control that so marked much of the economy and society of these countries is being lifted, and in many small ways, private enterprise is starting to take hold.

These changes in the economy and in politics have meant significant changes in the society as a whole. The black market, which flourished in many of the countries of Latin America, is starting to be cut back—not because the government has been successful in prosecuting it and the people involved, but because the need for it has declined.

For the United States, Mexico is the most important Latin country.[71] The amount of trade with Mexico is greater than that with any other country in the region, and it is part of the North American Free Trade Agreement (NAFTA). But Mexico has problems:

1. Political and economic corruption are a way of life for many Mexicans.
2. The single-party democracy contributes to many of the problems.
3. Like much of Latin America, Mexico is a society with distinct social classes, with "pure-blooded" Castilians on top and the indigenous people on the bottom.
4. For many in Mexico, grinding poverty is the only reality.

Things are changing for the Mexican people, but only slowly. The dominance of the PRE party is being challenged in many parts of the country, and the eventual establishment of some form of multiparty democracy seems almost inevitable. Political reform in Mexico is long overdue, but it is coming, and with its coming should end at least some of the graft and corruption that permeate the government and society.

Mexico's class system can be traced back to the conquistadors. The Spanish conquerors of Mexico superimposed their own set of cultural orientations on the country and its native people.[72] One of the most lasting is the Catholic Church, but the social order imposed on Mexico, with the Spaniards on the top and the native people on the bottom, is still very much alive in Mexico. This is a social class structure, bordering on a caste system, that is very hard for a person to break. There is no such thing as equal opportunity for many of the people in Mexico, or for that matter, in most of Latin America.

As in much of Latin America, most of the population in Mexico lives in what can only be described as grinding poverty. For these people on the bottom of the economic scale there is little in terms of real hope for any kind of true economic improvement. This is a major factor explaining the flow of illegal immigrants from Mexico and much of the rest of Latin America into the United States. Working for subminimum wages in the United States is better than trying to find work in their native country. The fact of the matter is that people vote with their "feet." As long as conditions in Latin America remain as they are with no real chance of substantive change in the foreseeable future, people will attempt to enter the United States to seek a better life. As long as these conditions exist, the problem of illegal immigration into the United States will continue.

There is one school of thought on the issue of illegal immigration which suggests that neither the United States nor the home countries of these illegal aliens are particularly interested in stemming the tide. From the U.S. perspective, illegal immigrants provide a useful source of subminimum-wage labor. In addition, it provides a useful safety valve for the neighboring countries because if these people were to stay home, they would surely promote political and economic unrest. For the home countries, they get rid of potential troublemakers and often receive much needed foreign currency from people in the United States who are sending money back home to their families.

The emerging nations of Africa and Latin America are only now beginning to become involved in the world economic equation. These countries have been politically unstable for many years and have had economic problems arising from a history of colonialism as well as an embrace of socialism almost immediately after independence. They now represent a new area of potential economic development, assuming they can maintain a favorable political environment that does not frighten potential investors.

NORTH AMERICA: THE SEMI-MELTING POT   ■ ■ ■

For years, historians, sociologists, and anthropologists described North America, particularly the United States, as a "melting pot."[73] By this they meant that people of various ethnic cultures and backgrounds have immigrated into the country and eventually merged sufficiently so as to become indistinguishable from the rest of the society. This may, in fact, have been the case with certain northern and western European groups, but certainly not completely and certainly not without a period of prejudice and unacceptance on the part of the remainder of the citizenry. The Irish and Italians have struggled for years to be accepted by and brought into the mainstream of society. The Irish suffered in part because of their historic animosity with the original English and Scottish settlers. This animosity was based on historic conflicts over land and religion, the English and Scots being primarily Protestant and the Irish, overwhelmingly Catholic. Battles and wars involving these differences were still being fought in the British Isles while Protestant England was colonizing America.

Italians started coming to North America in large numbers about 100 years ago. They found themselves at odds with much of the established order in the New World. Their church, an institution which in Italy had always been uniquely Italian, was controlled by Irish, German, and some English clergy, who found the somewhat different ways of these new immigrants offensive. They received little help from the church, and the political systems of most cities on the east coast were controlled by political machines such as those led by the Irish of Tammany Hall in New York and by "Honey Fitz" Fitzgerald in Boston. The result was that they turned to their own people for help and justice. The Italians had a ready-made organization in the form of the Mafia to provide them with the kind of help that the church or a political machine might provide the Irish. At least for a while, until Italians could work their way into the established institutions of church and state, the Mafia provided a focus. This probably contributed to the rather slow pace of Italian assimilation into the rest of the society. Certainly, the vast majority of Italians were repulsed by the workings of the Mafia, but the unique circumstances of the development of organized crime, helped by Prohibition during the 1920s,[74] did little to help in the general acceptance of Italians into the mainstream of U.S. society. All the great Italian-American artists, entrepreneurs, and educators, whether they were immigrants or native Americans, seemed to be battling against the image of the Italian gangster, an image that became part of the folklore of the United States. Somehow a Capone seemed to cancel out a Caruso, a Toscanini, or a Marconi. Today, Italians are far more accepted in society than they were just a few decades ago, but it has been a long and hard road, and the shadow of the Mafia can sometimes still be perceived in the background.

Asian Americans first came to the United States to work on the railroads in the western part of the country. Although their ways may have seemed strange to Americans of Western European background, they have been remarkably successful in the United States. These immigrants are composed of very divergent groups, including Japanese, Chinese, and Vietnamese, who generally have done well even though experiencing a great deal of discrimination in society, such as the internment of Japanese Americans during World War II.[75] Asian Americans have brought a certain spice to the semi-melting pot of American society.

People from Latin America have been emigrating to the United States for a long period of time. During continental expansion in the nineteenth century, Hispanic families in Texas, New Mexico, Arizona, and California were incorporated into the United States. Today, Hispanics represent a large portion of new immigrants into the United States, some of them legal and some not. They are a growing presence in the society, and their presence can be felt, not only in the Southwest but throughout the country.

■ ■ ■   **BOX 5.8   Internment of "Enemy Aliens"**   ■ ■ ■

During World War II, the government of the United States classified over 1 million immigrants from Italy, Japan, and Germany as enemy aliens. After the Battle of Pearl Harbor, some Americans looked upon all Japanese Americans as possible enemy agents. Anti-Japanese hysteria in 1942 led the U.S. government to move over 100,000 Japanese Americans living on the West Coast to relocation camps. Approximately two-thirds of these people were U.S. citizens who lost their homes and their jobs as a result of this action. It should be mentioned that the Canadian government relocated over 20,000 people of Japanese ancestry.

Of all the groups that have come to the United States, the one with the largest history of immigration are the Jews.[76] With their unique culture and religious heritage, the Jewish people have been able to maintain themselves and frequently, to prosper, while other religions and cultures have risen and fallen into history's dustbin. The Jews in the United States have prospered and, as a group, have done very well. That is not to say that there has not been anti-Semitism in the United States, but compared to the experience of the Jews in the Holocaust and the Inquisition, anti-Semitism in the United States has been very mild. There are essentially two reasons for this. The first is that the United States has had a policy since the founding of the republic of freedom of religion, and short of human sacrifice, the society tolerates a wide range of religious orientations. The second is the very Western and American belief in the importance of the individual. Most people in American society feel that if you mind your own business and don't bother them, they will do the same. This has been the attitude extended by the vast majority of Americans toward the Jewish people, who have, as a result, folded into American society perhaps better than they have anywhere else in the world. This is so evident that some Orthodox rabbis have charged that the United States represents the greatest single threat to the survival of Judaism as a distinct religion and culture. Because there is no persecution, no external threat keeping the people together, no immediate external enemy, there is less reason to maintain a separate identity.[77]

Finally, there are two groups of people who have defied almost all attempts to fold them into the larger society in the United States: Native Americans and African Americans. The Native Americans lived in the Western Hemisphere before Columbus and Cortez and before Jamestown and Plymouth. They are the people against whom the United States, first as a colony of Great Britain, and then as a nation, fought a protracted series of wars that drove the native people back from the shores of the Atlantic Ocean into what are now called Indian reservations.[78] Few people in the sordid history of people's inhumanity toward one another have been treated with greater disdain than Native Americans by immigrant Americans. This relationship remains one of the great sores in the human fabric, as the United States pursues the obviously failed policy of maintaining reservations. If and how this situation will eventually be resolved is one of the great challenges facing U.S. society in the years ahead.

Of all the immigrant groups to come to the United States, the one with the most unique history, and, in the end, the one that may be the most difficult to bring into the mainstream of society is the African American group.[79] African Americans were brought to the United States against their will. Whereas many immigrant Americans fled to the United States to escape some form of religious, political, or economic persecution, African Americans came against their will. The history of slavery in America is not a story of which to be proud. Rather, it is a story of hate, brutality, ignorance, and greed. African Americans have been the most victimized by racism and the group for whom many U.S. civil rights laws were passed. But racism is certainly not dead nor is it likely to die soon. The fact is that after almost 400 years of being in the United States, African Americans are still apart from the rest of the society. How the country deals with this minority is going to determine much of what is going to happen in terms of race relations. The United States must find a way to bring all its citizens into the mainstream to ensure prosperity and peace.

The United States continues to be a nation of immigrants. New people are seeking both legal and illegal entry into the United States. They do not come from Western Europe as often any more, but from Eastern Europe, Latin America, and Asia. These new immigrants bring new ideas, new customs and beliefs,

BOX 5.9   Money Income of U.S. Households: Percent Distribution by Income Level, Race, and Hispanic Origin, in Constant (1994) Dollars

Year	Number of Households	Under 10	10– 14.9	15– 24.9	25– 34.9	35– 49.9	50– 74.9	75 and Over	Median Income ($000)
				Percent Distribution for Income of ($000):					
All households									
1980	82.3	13.8	8.8	16.8	15.2	19.1	16.6	7.5	31.1
1990	94.3	12.9	8.4	16.1	14.5	17.6	17.2	13.3	33.9
1994	98.9	13.6	9.1	16.7	14.2	16.3	16.5	13.6	32.2
White									
1980	71.8	12.1	8.3	16.4	15.4	19.9	17.8	10.2	33.6
1990	80.9	10.9	8.1	15.9	14.7	18.0	18.1	14.2	35.4
1994	83.7	11.7	8.7	16.4	14.4	16.7	17.3	14.7	34.0
Black									
1980	8.8	27.7	13.2	20.0	13.4	13.4	10.2	4.0	20.4
1990	10.6	27.4	11.5	18.0	13.0	14.1	10.1	5.8	21.1
1994	11.6	26.3	11.5	18.9	12.8	13.3	10.8	6.3	21.0
Hispanic									
1980	3.9	17.8	11.7	21.2	16.8	16.1	11.7	4.6	24.5
1990	6.2	17.9	12.8	18.7	16.3	16.2	11.5	5.5	25.3
1994	7.7	20.5	12.2	20.4	14.9	14.4	10.9	6.7	23.4

Source: Statistical Abstract of the United States, 1996, table 709.

and new energy to the country. It is no accident or secret that so many outstanding students, doctors, lawyers, and writers are either themselves immigrants or are the children of immigrants. For them, the United States represents a promised land where the only measure of a person's worth is his or her achievements, not the person's ancestry or social position. For them, the United States is a land of opportunity, a land of the free, and the home of those brave enough to seize the opportunities before them.

SUMMARY ■ ■ ■

Western civilization began with the ancient Greeks, who developed several important ideas that were new to the world. The first was the idea of democracy and the second was the concept of the individual. The word *democracy* comes from the Greek *demos cratia*, the idea that a king or prince was not necessary to rule a people, but that people could rule themselves. The second was the concept of the individual, who was the center of Greek society. These ideas were reflected in their art and their system of government and religion.

Next came the Romans, who spread many of the ideas of the Greeks, whose religion they adopted and whose ideas they admired. Rome was responsible for many things, but perhaps its most important contribution was the spread of Greek ideas and the establishment of the Christian Church, Catholic in the West and Orthodox in the East.

During the Middle Ages, the Church served as the guardian of the Greek ideals that had been spread by the Roman Empire, and the Eastern Roman Empire served as a shield against the rising tide of Islam. In the West, the Church became the haven of civilization during the Dark Ages until the great awakening: the Renaissance.

During the Renaissance, Western Europe once again found the ideals of the Greeks and the importance of the individual. The hallmark of the awakening was a new questioning and search for knowledge. This period was marked by a revival of science and learning and led eventually to the age of discovery and the modern age.

Classics of Western literature and art evolved during the Age of Discovery. Although today, this period is often looked upon primarily as an era of colonial expansion, it was also a period of the spread of Western ideas and the development of Western society as we know it. The United States is a direct result of this age of what some would call imperialism and others would call expansion of Western civilization. Certainly, it was an age of colonialism, small and large wars, and subjugation, but it was also an era of enlightenment and great progress, both technological and intellectual. It represents one of the great leaps in the history of the world.

Many of the institutions of Western society have found themselves transplanted into other societies. Democracy has taken hold in Africa, Asia, and South America. Protection for and the involvement of the individual have made this ancient Greek ideal the basis of our evaluation of governments, societies, and nations. The cause of human rights, a very Western idea, is about the individual. Joined at the hip with individualism are the concepts of freedom and democracy. These are, and will undoubtedly remain, the legacy of Western society to the world.

The societies in Asia also represent unique cultures that have their own contributions to make to the modern world. China can never be ignored in any discussion of the development of society, no matter how Western the view. The sheer size of the Chinese population makes the case for importance. China is a unique and ancient society that will have a great impact on the course of humanity over the foreseeable future. It represents perhaps the only true rival to Western culture, perhaps, because it has remained relatively free of Western influence. All non-Western societies, except China, have Western institutions. How the Asian societies, including India, Korea, Vietnam, Thailand, Indonesia, and the Philippines, play out their fates is going to have a great impact on the rest of the world.

Emergent nations also need to be considered when viewing the world scene. These are countries that have not yet joined the rest of the world in true economic expansion, or, often, in political stability. Africa has many of these countries, but they may also be found in Asia and Latin America. These are societies with great potential and promise—but less than what one could hope for in results. If the global society is going to be successful, these countries must also be successful. Many of them are considered backwaters, desperately in need of an inflow of new capital and new ideas. If nothing is done to help and promote these societies, they will have a detrimental effect on the overall health of the world. These societies must be helped to the level of stability and prosperity enjoyed by the rest of the world if the planet is to have prosperity and peace in the next millennium.

Questions _____

1. Where was the beginning of Western society?

2. What is the importance of the concept of the individual in Western society?

3. How were the Greeks involved in the development of the idea of democracy?

4. Why was slavery important to the flowering of societies prior to the industrial revolution?

5. How was Greek civilization spread throughout the ancient world?

6. How did the Eastern Roman Empire preserve the spread of Christianity?

7. What role did Constantine the Great play in the establishment of Christianity?

8. Why was the Church so important to the preservation of civilization during the Middle Ages?

9. Why is the Renaissance important to the development of Western society?

10. How are the printing press, the Renaissance, and the Reformation linked?

11. What country led the way in European colonization in the nineteenth century?

12. How was European colonization in Africa and Asia different from what it had been in America?

13. What is the language of government in India?

14. China was never colonized by European countries. How and in what ways does this make the Chinese experience different from that of much of the rest of the world?

15. What are some likely areas of conflict in Chinese society in the next century?

16. In what ways does Japan differ from the rest of Asia?

17. Why are the "tigers" of the Pacific rim so important to the U.S. economy?

18. What is the importance of "Greater China" and its impact on the rest of Asia?

19. Why is it important for lesser and least developed nations to participate fully in the world economy?

20. How can the United States deal with all the immigrants that have come to its shore?

CASE 1

He is your very good friend, a brilliant mind, and one of the great scientists of the age. But how can you reconcile his obvious support of the Copernican doctrine with the teachings of the Church? As Pope, you are sworn to protect the Church from all manner of threats, and this could be even more serious than the threat of the heretics Luther and Calvin. This doctrine of the Earth moving around the sun challenges everything. If the Earth is not the center of the universe, it calls into question all else that the doctrine of the Church is based on. Genesis can be removed from the Bible, and if Genesis is no longer relevant, everything else can be questioned.

The real problem is that both Galileo and Copernicus may very well be right, and if they are right, how can it be heresy? As Pope, you have to find a way somehow to reconcile these factors. If they are right, and you strongly suspect they may be, it is a sin to execute Galileo simply for speaking the truth, no matter what Church doctrine may be. Besides, if he is right, surely others will discover it too, and this will be only the beginning of a long series of trials eventually vindicating Copernicus and Galileo. That letter from Cardinal Bellermine enjoining Galileo from teaching or professing the Copernican system is a forgery, but it could be used to convict Galileo, or simply ignored, or branded as the forgery it is. Tomorrow the trial ends and you will have to make a decision.

1. What should the Pope do?
2. If you were Pope, how would your treat Galileo?

CASE 2

He is coming back. That reformer who wants to institute real political change in the society. The problem is that real political change in the Philippines means getting rid of you, Ferdinand Marcos. Benigno Aquino is scheduled to return to Manila tomorrow, and you are not sure what to do about it. He has been in exile for years, but with his return he will surely become a rallying point for all opposition that has built up toward your regime. If you allow him to roam the country freely, he will stir up support against you. If you throw him in jail, he will become a focal point of protest, much the same as Mandella has become in South Africa. If you simply kill him when he arrives, he will become a martyr. The question is: What will do the least amount of damage both to your government and yourself?

1. If you were Marcos, what would you do about Aquino?
2. What would be the ethical thing to do?

CASE 3

Time was never really on his side, and de Klerk knew it. As president of the Republic of South Africa, he knew that he represented only a relatively shrinking minority in his own country. Sooner or later, the whites were going to have to come to grip with the fact that they were hopelessly outnumbered in their own country and were going to have to let the black majority participate fully in the economy, the government, and the society as a whole. De Klerk knew that this would not be easy. The Afrikaners had been in South Africa since the founding of Cape Town some 500 years ago and had established themselves there before most of the black tribes of modern South Africa had entered the country. It was really a simple choice that he faced. He could try to end apartheid and start the process of bringing the black majority into the mainstream of the society. He could continue to stonewall the desires of the blacks of South Africa, leading to the eventual violent revolution that was sure to come, led by the African National Congress (ANC), perhaps before, perhaps after, his death—but certainly during the lives of his children.

The international community was against apartheid and, while the economic sanctions taken against South Africa hurt, they could be endured. His own political party was totally committed to the status quo, and he would receive great opposition from most Afrikaners if he tried to end apartheid. The most powerful member of the ANC had been in a South African jail for almost 30 years. A convicted terrorist, Nelson Mandela had the respect of most of the black community as well as a respected reputation outside South Africa. Perhaps Mandela had mellowed and de Klerk might be able to work with him.

1. What is the ethically correct course for de Klerk to follow?
2. If you were Mandella, would you talk to de Klerk?

References

1. *Empires ascendant*, Time-Life Books, Alexandria, VA, 1987.
2. Ibid.
3. *Age of the god-kings*, Time-Life Books, Alexandria, VA, 1988.
4. Homer, *The iliad* (Robert Fitzgerald, ed.), Alfred A. Knopf, New York, 1992.
5. Bowra, C. M., *The Greek experience*, World Publishing, Cleveland, OH, 1958.
6. Ibid.
7. Plato, *The republic* (B. Jowett, ed.), Modern Library, New York, 1982.
8. Bowra, *The Greek experience*.
9. *Empires ascendant*.
10. Ibid.
11. Gibbon, E., *Decline and fall of the Roman empire*, T.F. Collier, New York, 1899.
12. Wells, H. G., *The outline of history*, Garden City Publishing, Garden City, NY, 1938.
13. Ibid.
14. Baker, C. P. *Constantine the Great and the Christian revolution*, Barnes & Noble, New York, 1967.
15. Maclagan, Michael, *The city of Constantinople*, Praeger, New York, 1968.
16. Wells, *The outline of history*.
17. Walden, William, *The cross and the crescent: Bysantium and the Turks*, Boston Publishing Co., Boston, 1987.

18. Wells, *The outline of history.*

19. Brown, R. Allen, *Origins of English feudalism*, Allen & Unwin, London, 1973.

20. Sabuda, Robert, *Arthur and the sword*, Atheneum, New York, 1995.

21. Arbman, Holger, *The Vikings*, Praeger, New York, 1961.

22. Wells, *The outline of history.*

23. Biel, Timothy, L. *Charlemagne*, Lucent Books, San Diego, CA, 1997.

24. Asser, John, *Alfred the great*, Penguin Books, New York, 1983.

25. Storey, R. L., *Chronology of the medieval world, 800–1491*, Simon & Schuster, New York, 1994.

26. *The European emergence: time frame 1500–1600*, Time-Life Books, Alexandria, VA, 1989.

27. Ibid.

28. Myers, R., and M. Harris, *Aspects of printing from 1600*, Oxford Polytechnic Press, Oxford, 1987.

29. Borakamm, H., *The heart of reformation faith, the fundamental axioms of evangelical belief*, Harper & Row, New York, 1965.

30. Locke, John, *An essay concerning human understanding*, Dent, London, 1976.

31. Smith, Adam, *An inquiry into the nature and causes of the wealth of nations*, A.A. Strahon, London, 1802.

32. Locke, *An essay.*

33. Wells, *The outline of hisotry.*

34. Dussel, Enrique, *The church in Latin America, 1492–1992*, Orbis Books, Maryknoll, NY, 1992.

35. Liss, Peggy, *Atlantic empires: the network of trade and revolution, 1713–1823*, Johns Hopkins University Press, Baltimore, 1983.

36. Cifarelli, Megan, *India: One nation—many traditions*, Benchmark Books, Tarrytown, NY, 1996.

37. Ibid.

38. Penrose, E. F., *European imperialism and the partition of Africa*, F. Cass, London, 1975.

39. Ibid.

40. Wells, *The outline of history.*

41. Ibid.

42. Cifarelli, *India.*

43. Ibid.

44. Kinsella, Kevin, *Population and health transitions*, U.S. Department of Commerce, Washington, DC, 1992.

45. Inden, Ronald, *Marriage and rank in Bengali culture: a history of caste and clan in middle period Bengal*, University of California Press, Berkeley, CA, 1976.

46. Worden, Robert (ed.), *China: a country study*, Federal Research Division, Library of Congress, Washington, DC, 1988.

47. Bowring, Richard, and Peter Kornicki, *The Cambridge encyclopedia of Japan*, Cambridge University Press, New York, 1993.

48. Ibid.

49. Ibid.

50. Maidment, Fred (ed.), *Annual editions: international business, 1997–1998*, Dushkin/McGraw-Hill, Guilford, CT, 1997.

51. "The international 500," *Fortune*, August 4, 1997.

52. *Indonesia: a country briefing book*, Senoyer Miller Consulting, Republic of Indonesia, May 1997.

53. "A company without a country," *Business Week*, May 5, 1997.

54. Huff, W. G., *The economic growth of Singapore: trade and development in the twentieth century,* Cambridge University Press, New York, 1994.

55. Holstein, Steven, *Asia's new little dragons: the dynamic emergence of Indonesia, Thailand, and Malaysia,* Contemporary Books, Chicago, 1991.

56. Lin, Zhiling, W. Thomas, *The Chinese and their future: Beijing, Taipei and Hong Kong,* AEI Press, Washington, DC, 1993.

57. Ibid.

58. Baldwin, Robert, E., *The Philippines,* National Bureau of Economic Research, Columbia, University Press, New York, 1975.

59. Cherry, Judith, *Cassell business briefings: Republic of Korea,* Cassell, New York, 1993.

60. Esper, George, *The eyewitness history of the Vietnam War, 1961–1975,* Balantine Books, New York, 1983.

61. Shultz, Clifford, William Ardry, and Anthony Pecotich, "American involvement in Vietnam: II. Prospects for U.S. business in a new era," *Business Horizons,* March–April 1995.

62. Krnar, Lonis, "The new power in Asia," *Fortune,* October 31, 1994.

63. Barret Richard, "But what about Africa?" *Harper's,* May 1990.

64. Prusher, Ilene, "Post-U.S. Somalia finds many cash in on chaos," *Christian Science Monitor,* October 20, 1997.

65. Baillou, Charles, "Now that the journalists have left is there still want in Congo?" *Amsterdam News,* October 2, 1997.

66. Duke, Lynne, "South Africans look north, invest in neighbors," *Washington Post,* November 6, 1997.

67. *South Africa: a country study,* Federal Research Division, Library of Congress, Washington, DC, 1997.

68. "Argentina starts to count again," *Fortune,* February 22, 1993.

69. Arriagada, Genaro, *Pinochet: the politics of power,* Westview Press, Boulder, CO, 1991.

70. Rudolph, James, *Mexico: a country study,* Headquarters, Department of the Army, Washington, DC, 1985.

71. Ibid.

72. Ibid.

73. Brinkley, Alan, *American history: a survey,* McGraw-Hill, New York, 1991.

74. Mass, Peter, *Underboss: Sammy the Bull Gravano's story of life in the Mafia,* HarperCollins, New York, 1997.

75. Smith, Page, *Democracy on trial: the Japanese—American evacuation and relocation in World War II,* Simon & Schuster, New York, 1995.

76. Klein, Emma, *Lost Jews: the struggle for identity today,* St. Martin's Press, New York, 1996.

77. Ibid.

78. DiBacco, Thomas, Lorna Mason, et al., *History of the United States,* Houghton Mifflin, Boston, 1991.

79. Ibid.

6

■ ■ ■

CURRENT ISSUES IN THE MODERN GLOBAL ENVIRONMENT

Concepts ⦂ You Will Learn ■ ■ ■

major trends facing the modern global environment

future issues facing organizations in the global environment

why diversity and multiculturalism are becoming more important issues

INTRODUCTION   ■ ■ ■

The development of the modern global environment was discussed in Chapter 2. Today's global environment is the result of a combination of forces that have conspired to develop the world we live in today. These forces include the social/cultural environment, the political/legal environment, the economic environment, and the technological environment. All of these factors have combined to produce the world as it is today. The issues that are faced by society today are the ones that are going to shape the world we live in tomorrow.

MEGATRENDS   ■ ■ ■

In 1982, John Naisbitt published a book called *Megatrends*[1] which dealt with the great trends in society both in the United States and in the world. He distilled these into 10 major trends.

Industrial Society ⟶ Information Society

The first trend that Naisbitt spotted was the change among developed countries from an industrialized society to an information society. Alvin Toffler has called this the *third wave*,[2] the first wave of change in civilized society being from the hunter/gatherers to an agrarian society, and the second from an agrarian society to the industrial age. This change started soon after World War II, when more Americans began working in offices than in factories, and has accelerated ever since.[3] In today's society, information workers are the ones in demand: people who either have information and/or manipulate information. Organizations have discovered that manufacturing can be done almost anywhere on the planet, and jobs that do not require much in the way of training are going to the lowest bidder. Information is the industry of the present and is likely to be for some time in the future.

Forced Technology ⟶ High Technology/High Touch ■ ■ ■

The second megatrend is from forced technology to high technology/high touch (user friendly). Perhaps the best example of this developing trend is computers. When computers first became available after World War II, they were imposing machines that required highly trained and well-paid specialists to operate them. They were "fussy," often needing special rooms and climate control to operate effectively. This all changed with the advent of the personal computer.[4] Now computers do not need special rooms and climate control, and they can be operated by anyone willing to take the time to learn how to do it.

Even within the personal computer field, there has been a movement toward higher tech and higher touch. The original operating systems were difficult to use and required that the operator essentially memorize a variety of options for the system to be operated effectively. Now, with the advent of the computer mouse, it is a simple matter to point and click to do a task. Even easier approaches, in the experimental phase of development, will make computer operation even more user friendly.

National Economy ⟶ World Economy ■ ■ ■

The third megatrend is the development of an integrated world economy. Because of improvements in transportation and communication, the world is a smaller place than it was just a few decades ago. As Robert Reich has written,[5] the traditional factors of land, labor, capital, and entrepreneurship have grown legs and can now move all over the world with little in the way to prevent them.

Through the use of modern communication technology, the international banking system has made the movement of financial assets around the world simple and essentially instantaneous. Simply by touching a few buttons on a computer keyboard, it is possible to move millions of dollars, franks, or yen almost anywhere in the world. Banking and financial assets in the modern, postindustrial age know no boundaries; they go where they will produce the best return.

Raw materials (land) represents another factor of production whose importance used to be tied to a particular geographic location, but that is no longer the case. Modern, reliable transportation systems, starting with railroads and leading to today's superfreighters and superjets, have changed the importance of the location of natural resources. Commodities can be moved around easily from place to place. For example, two very American products, pipe tobacco and bourbon, are shipped separately to Sweden, where they are combined into a particular brand of pipe tobacco. This brand sells very well in the United States when it comes back to the country. The raw materials come from the United States, processing takes place in Sweden, and the market is all over the world.

Entrepreneurship is the distillation of capitalism. Now that the Cold War is over, capitalism is the economic system of choice for most countries of the world,[6] and entrepreneurship is the heart and soul of capitalism: the ability to start and own one's own business, the promise of economic independence, and a life with no boss other than the customer. Not everyone becomes an entrepreneur, nor should they. Entrepreneurs take great financial and other risks; they work long, hard hours. But they are necessary because they represent the continual renewal of an economy. Where one business fails, two more rise to take its place. Entrepreneurship and freedom go hand in hand. Entrepreneurs take their fate in their own hands; they do not depend on a boss, an office, or a government ministry. They try to become the masters of their own fate, and many of them succeed.

The United States has always had an advantage in terms of entrepreneurship because going into business for oneself has always been encouraged. Jefferson's citizen/farmer was, among other things, a small businessman.[7] The government of the United States has established the Small Business Administration to help people start their own companies. But perhaps the most interesting facet of entrepreneurship in the United States has been the number of new immigrants that come to this country and start their own businesses.[8] These people often come from countries where starting a business is an impossible dream, but one that can become a reality here. Other societies also have long traditions of shopkeepers and small businesspeople. China, India, and the Arab World all have great commercial traditions based on small businesses. For now, regions of the world may be somewhat behind the West in the development of their economics, but one thing is certain—that as the people of these countries are granted more economic freedom, they will experience greater economic gain not through the central government, but through the development of new businesses and enterprises established by entrepreneurs.

Labor has been called the factor of production that has the least ability to travel.[9] This may be true, to some degree, but the history of the planet refutes this. Labor in the past has moved slowly. In the past, historians have tended to look upon these immigrations as the movement of people, not the labor they represent. But labor continues to move to where the work is. This history of the Western Hemisphere since Columbus has been a history of immigration, especially from Europe to the New World. Today, there continues to be movement, and although it may not be as fast as the movement of capital around the world, it still represents a movement of labor. People from Latin America, Asia, and Africa are still trying to get into the United States. Turks live for years in Germany, working to support their families back home, and executives (who are, after all, part of the hired help) travel all over the world, representing the interests of their firms. Labor may be the most sedentary of all the factors of production, but it is certainly mobile and involved in the world economy.

Short Term ⟶ Long Term

One of the most severe criticisms of U.S. corporations has been their continued focus on the short term.[10] Short-term profits, short-term investments, and short-term thinking have all characterized many U.S. firms. This is not, however, the way of the future: Organizations must take the long view if they are going to survive in the marketplace. They must be willing to make the kind of investment required to ensure the future of the organization for the long term. Over the years, U.S. firms have tended not to do that, whereas many others, particularly Japanese firms, have. Taking the long view means being willing to take a little less now so as to guarantee much more later. It means investing, not spending: in seeing the workforce as an asset, not as a cost.[11] Long-term strategic thinking is the way of the future, short term is the way of the past. Short-term thinking will only serve to shorten the life and viability of an organization for the future.

Centralization ⟶ Decentralization

One of the more interesting hallmarks of the end of the Cold War era has been the movement from a highly centralized form of structure to a more decentralized approach to organizing the activities of human beings. The beginning of this movement could probably be traced to the advent of the first personal computer. PCs made it unnecessary to have to go back to the home office to manipulate data for decision making.[12] Much of that data "crunching" can be done at the local level and then those results are forwarded to the home office to be compiled with the rest of the data from the other branches. Decentralization of data and information meant that the organization did not have to depend on the center for direction and leadership. Personal computers meant that local managers could act on their own information and respond much more quickly to local situations. Although it was possible to communicate with the home office for help and support, decentralized organizations found themselves much more responsive to the needs of local customers and clients, often getting ahead of the competition, which still depended on a centralized system of command and authority.

Institutional Help ⟶ Self-Help

As societies move away from socialism or systems that mix socialism and capitalism, the institutions established by the government to provide basic services to those who had difficulty in obtaining those services will decline. Whether it is called *welfare reform* or *workfare* or some other name, these agencies are going to have less in the way of government funding and are simply not going to be able to do as much as they had been able to do in the past. Unless there is some overwhelming reason why these services must be provided to individuals, they will not be. The social safety net[13] may not have disappeared completely, but it is certainly much more porous than it once was. The fact is that taxpayers and others in the society are tired of paying taxes for people who do not contribute to the society. As the economy has become more global it has also become more competitive. People who are not making their own contribution to the society will find themselves faced with a society far more reluctant to support them than has been the case in the past 50 years.

This is not to say that society is not prepared to help the truly needy and unfortunate, but rather, that to get help from the society, you must now be truly needy and unfortunate. American society, in particular, has always stood ready to help those in need, and has a history of generosity and philanthropy that is the envy of the rest of the world. But Americans have generally come to object to paying for the fifth and sixth generations of families on welfare. In those cases, institutionalized help obviously has not worked, and the alternative of self-help is now being tried on a wide scale.[14]

Representative Democracy ⟶ Participatory Democracy

Most democracies are republican forms of government. Most people simply do not have the time or the ability to travel to the seat of government and spend many days involved with legislation and the proposed laws of the land. So they send representatives. However, in today's era of instant communication, this may no longer be the case. States with voter initiatives are primary examples.[15] In these states, voters can petition to have an issue put on the ballot at a general election. The people then vote on the issue, and if it is passed, it will have the same effect as a bill passed by a state legislature and signed by the governor. Many controversial issues that would never have been passed by the state legislature have made it onto the ballots of these states, and some have actually been passed. California propositions 13 and 209 are cases in point. Both, it would be fair to say, would never have passed the state legislature, but both

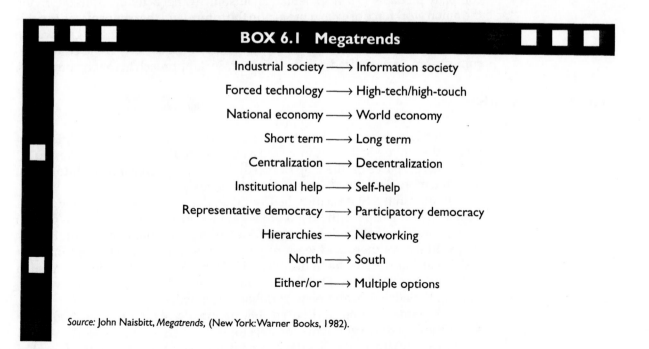

BOX 6.1   Megatrends

Industrial society ⟶ Information society

Forced technology ⟶ High-tech/high-touch

National economy ⟶ World economy

Short term ⟶ Long term

Centralization ⟶ Decentralization

Institutional help ⟶ Self-help

Representative democracy ⟶ Participatory democracy

Hierarchies ⟶ Networking

North ⟶ South

Either/or ⟶ Multiple options

Source: John Naisbitt, *Megatrends*, (New York: Warner Books, 1982).

were passed by the people of California in a general election. As societies and institutions decentralized, so does power, and the people of California, as well as those of other states, have chosen to exercise that power by bypassing the state's elected officials to enact the laws they wanted.

Hierarchies ⟶ Networking

Traditional industrial society has always been hierarchal in nature. Ever since Max Weber devised the first organization chart and established the bureaucratic method of organization, society has tended to have a hierarchal view of itself.[16] This, of course, could be traced back even further to the Church and to the military, which always depended on some form of hierarchal control and command. Society, however, does not have to be hierarchal in nature, because as people are finding out, a hierarchy is imposed on people as a way of organizing activity, and there are alternatives.

One of the alternatives that has become very popular is networking. Networking depends on communication among and between equals, all of whom share a common goal.[17] A hierarchy is based on command; a network is based on cooperation. As large organizations continue to downsize and decentralize, networking will become more important. An example is the use of outsourcing, which many large organizations are attempting to do over the objections of their unions. Outsourcing means getting something from someone else that you once produced yourself. It means a smaller operation producing the same number of products, but without a large investment in plant and equipment. The unions object because it means fewer jobs for their members and less clout in their negotiations with the company. There are several other consequences for the union: The new supplier may not be unionized or may be affiliated with another union. The company probably has the potential to outsource other activities, thus depriving the union workforce of even more jobs in the future, and the company can use this as a bargaining tool in future negotiations. Hierarchies are starting to give way to networks as alternative forms of organization in the society as the culture becomes more decentralized and participatory in its approach to solving problems.

North ⟶ South

Migration has always been an ongoing activity throughout the world. The history of the United States has involved a culture moving from east to west to fill in the blank spaces on the map of North America,[18] then from north to south, from the more developed areas to the less developed.

In the United States, after the Civil War, the South was devastated, and it took over 100 years for the region to regain the lost ground. Over the past 30 years, however, the South has risen. Much of recent economic growth has occurred in the southern and western parts of the country, while the Northeast and Great Lake States have declined. The new centers of business are such cities as Atlanta, Dallas–Ft. Worth, Houston, and Phoenix, while Cleveland, Buffalo, Philadelphia, and New York have declined.

The same may be said on an international scale. North and South are sometimes used as synonyms for developed and lesser and least developed countries, as many of the less developed countries tend to be south of most of the developed countries. As these less developed countries begin to emerge economically, their people are taking many of the jobs once held by workers in developed countries. Although these jobs tend to be low-paying labor-intensive positions, they are jobs, nonetheless. The manufacture of TV sets in Mexico, Nike shoes in Indonesia, and rocking chairs in Malaysia all involve jobs once done in industrialized nations, now being used as a springboard for further economic development in these poorer countries. The hope is that the developed countries will not decline but will actually continue to grow while the less developed countries expand and flourish.

Either/Or ⟶ Multiple Options

Much of the history of the world has involved an either/or choice, a yes/no set of alternatives that limited the opportunities of individuals and their ability to grow and prosper.[19] That kind of approach to life is starting to change. Rather than saying "You can have this or that," the options are now multiple, and the question is: "What do you want?" The choice of futures is staggering. People can be just about whatever they want to be. Societies have choices as to what they want to become, which is what the "great debate" in Japan, the United States, Europe, and China is all about. Given the various megatrends outlined and discussed above, what kind of countries do Americans, Europeans, Japanese, Chinese, and others want to be in the next 10, 25, 50, or 100 years? Countries, organizations, and individuals now have the possibility of contemplating that question. It is the essence of freedom. Only free people can determine their own fate, and freedom is perhaps the single largest megatrend in the world today. Economic and political freedom are moving together because they both embody options and choice. If a people has economic freedom, it will soon expect political freedom, as the leaders of China may soon find out and as the leaders of the Soviet Union discovered when they attempted economic reforms.

OTHER TRENDS IN SOCIETY

In addition to the trends identified by Nesbitt, there are several other major trends in the society.

Aging Population

The first trend is that the population in the developed world is aging.[20] While populations continue to explode in the less developed world, population growth in the developed countries is leveling off and the population is aging. This has certain consequences for these countries. In the United States, the baby-boom generation is now well into middle age and in a few decades will be drawing Social Security. Unfortunately, Social Security may not be fully prepared for the influx of boomers. Unless firm, perhaps politically unacceptable steps are taken, Social Security may go bankrupt. But there seems to be little political will to take the steps necessary to prevent a crisis. The result may be draconian measures once a crisis hits. This is also the case to varying degrees in most of the industrialized world. As the demographics of society shift, problems tend to shift with it.

BOX 6.2   Age of U.S. Population (Percent)

Ages (years)	1970	1980	1990	1995
Under 5	8.4	7.2	7.5	7.5
5–9	9.8	7.4	7.3	7.3
10–14	10.2	8.1	6.9	7.2
15–19	9.4	9.3	7.2	6.9
20–24	8.1	9.4	7.7	6.8
25–29	6.6	8.6	8.6	7.2
30–34	5.6	7.8	8.8	8.3
35–39	5.5	6.2	8.0	8.5
40–44	5.9	5.2	7.1	7.7
45–49	6.0	4.9	5.5	6.6
50–54	5.5	5.2	4.5	5.2
55–59	4.9	5.1	4.2	4.2
60–64	4.2	4.5	4.3	3.6
65–74	6.1	6.9	7.3	7.1
75–84	3.0	3.4	4.0	4.2
85 and over	0.7	1.0	1.2	1.4

Source: *Statistical Abstract of the United States, 1996.*

Advances in Technology

Another major trend in society has been the advancement of technology.[21] With the advent of the industrial revolution just over 200 years ago, the pace of technological change accelerated until today, it seems to be going along at breakneck speed. Virtually all of the machines and equipment in use today were invented in the past 200 years, most in the past 50 or 100 years. In 66 years, the span of a lifetime, human beings went from being glued to the ground to flying a few feet, then to traveling to the moon. The advancement of technology in one area has led to further advances in other areas. Biotechnology is a case in point. Fifty years ago biotechnology consisted essentially of producing better types of corn. Today, sheep and monkeys have been cloned. Aside from the obvious moral questions this raises, it does indicate an ability to do things that were once the stuff of science fiction. Just as Jules Verne's *Nautilus*[22] became reality in the 1950s, so the stories of Arthur C. Clark and Isaac Asimov[23] are starting to come true. The future is upon us, and there is no telling where it might lead.

Revival of Religion

Another great trend in the world has been the revival of religion. This is not just something that has occurred among fundamentalist Christians in the United States, but also in the Muslim world. Islam, often in its most fundamentalist form, is on the march,[24] frequently, fueled with money from oil deposits. Islamic countries are becoming more militant in their pursuit of fundamentalist Islamic principles. Countries such as Iran and Afghanistan are simply the most obvious examples. Other secular Islamic countries are desperately trying to control and contain the fundamentalist. These countries include Turkey, Algeria, and Egypt.[25] In the United States, organizations such as the Christian Coalition are flexing their political muscle.[26] These organizations mix christianity with patriotism and a unique view of the United States and its place in the world. They have been successful, partially because they, unlike "mainline" denominations, have a very clear idea as to who they are, what they are about, and where they are headed.

There are many reasons for the advent of fundamentalism both in Christianity in the United States and in Islam, and although it may not be appropriate to speculate, one of the things that religion promises is stability, a belief in an everlasting God. On the other hand, the only other thing that is not changing is change. Life today is full of change. Religion, on the other hand, promises stability, at the very least, comfort in a world full of instability and change.

BOX 6.3 Adherents of All Religions Throughout the World, Mid-1994

Christians	
Roman Catholic	1,058,069,000
Protestants	391,143,000
Orthodox	174,184,000
Anglicans	78,038,000
Other Christians	199,707,000
	1,900,174,000
Muslims	1,033,435,000
Hindus	764,000,000
Buddhists	338,621,000
Chinese folk religions	149,336,000
New religionists	128,975,000
Tribal religions	99,150,000
Sikhs	20,204,000
Jews	13,145,000
Shamanists	11,010,000
Confucians	6,334,000
Baha'is	5,835,000
Jains	3,937,000
Shintoists	3,387,000
Other religions	20,419,000
Nonreligious	924,078,000
Atheists	239,111,000
Total	5,661,525,000

Source: Encyclopaedia Britannica.

Diversity and Multiculturalism

Another major change in society is going to be in the area of diversity and multiculturalism.[27] As the world shrinks and cultures come into closer contact with each other, the ability to work with people of different backgrounds and different countries will become a key to the success of any organization. In the United States these two words have become buzz words for the changing demographics of the workforce and the society. It is absolutely true that the workforce is changing and that the workforce is a reflection of society. White males no longer make up 80 percent of the workforce. Rather, they account for about 40 percent.[28] Women and minorities, especially women, have now taken jobs that would have gone to men had there been enough men to take the jobs. Today, almost half the workforce is made up of women, many of whom have young children. "Father Knows Best" is a thing of the past.[29]

Minorities represent another large influx of workers. Most immigrants into the United States are from other than the traditional European countries. They come from Asia, Latin America, and other parts of the less developed world. These people have different cultures and different ways of doing things than those of many European immigrants. The key to success for organizations in the United States will be how they are able to take advantage of these differences.[30]

The same can be said on the international level. As the world becomes a smaller place, cultures and societies, long separated by distance and time, are now closely linked, and they do things differently from one to another. Learning how to deal successfully with these differences is going to be the key to success for many organizations.[31] To be successful, it is necessary to know one's customers and the employees who are going to serve the customer. Recognizing the diversity of both customers and employees is critical to success in the modern global economy. Failure to recognize the multicultural nature of the various societies of the world will lead to failure in the international market.

Societal Bifurcation

A problem facing the United States and some other developed countries of the world is that of societies divided into rich and poor.[32] In 1970 the distribution of family income more or less represented a bell-shaped curve, with most families in the middle and declining numbers on either side of the peak. Today, that situation has changed. Now there are more wealthy Americans than at any time in history, but the problem is that there are more poor Americans, and the center has been weakened. This represents a serious problem for the United States because it means that the society is separating into two distinct groups based on income and the things that go with that income, such as education. The problem facing the United States is that it is becoming a society of haves and have nots; of educated and uneducated; of hope and hopelessness.

The same situation may be seen on the international level. There have always been wealthy nations and there have always been poor nations, but the gulf has widened.[33] With the exception of the Pacific rim nations, there has been little movement in terms of less developed nations joining the ranks of the developed. This may be due, in part, to the relatively early adoption of capitalism

■ ■ ■ BOX 6.4   U.S. Prosperity Hasn't Spread to Everyone ■ ■ ■

Americans don't think of their country as being divided by wealth and class like a Latin American oligarchy. But that's the way the United States has been going for nearly 25 years, and the situation is getting worse.

After five years of the Clinton administration and six years of the longest boom in postwar American history, the rich still are getting richer and the poor are getting poorer. As a result, the United States, which wrote the idea of equality into its Declaration of Independence, is now by far the most unequal society in the industrialized world. Nowhere is the gap between rich and poor growing faster. Nowhere else is the cause not only rising wealth at the top, but falling income at the bottom. And nowhere is the middle class shrinking as fast as in the country that once proclaimed itself a middle-class nation.

This is the subtext of a dry stack of statistics that the Census Bureau issued recently. The figures included some good news—median household income is going up, as are wages for women and minorities. Administration spin doctors claimed that these figures, all of which are adjusted for inflation, prove that President Clinton's policies are working. But a few reporters caught the contradictions.

Women—at least those with full-time jobs—indeed made more overall in 1996 than in 1995, although they still aren't back to the wages they enjoyed in the three years before Clinton became president. Women now make 74 percent of what men do, which is the highest percentage ever. But that percentage is up mostly because men's wages are down. The median full-time male worker's wages peaked way back in 1973, and has been falling more or less steadily for 24 years, under six presidents from both major parties and many ideologies.

Again, median household wages indeed rose from 1995 to 1996, from $35,082 to $35,492. This is about a 1.2 percent gain and that's good. But don't break out the champagne yet. The increase in household wages is fully accounted for by the gain in women's wages, which offset the loss in men's pay. And virtually all of the gain took place in the South, the nation's poorest region, where household income went up 1.8 percent. In other regions, household income barely budged. In the Midwest, it actually fell.

This stagnation might not be a disaster but it's a pretty poor result of the longest recovery in the nation's postwar history, a mammoth boom that has sent stock prices, corporate profits, and executive pay through the roof. Real wealth is being created, but six years into the boom, the median worker is still 5 percent worse off than when it began.

That wealth, like grease, is rising to the top. Fully 99 percent of the increase has gone to the top 20 percent of all wage-earners: the top 1 percent, all by itself, has claimed 62 percent of the growing pie.

All this added up to a widening of the gap between the rich and poor. Inequality has become an end-of-century blight on American life. It wasn't always this way. In 1950, the top 1 percent of Americans owned 28 percent of the wealth. In class-ridden Britain, the figure was 44 percent. This picture has reversed. In Britain, the top 1 percent now controls only 18 percent of the wealth. In America, the top 1 percent owns no less than 38 percent of the nation's stocks, bonds, property, art, savings, and other forms of wealth.

Meanwhile, the poor have less. Thirty years ago, the bottom 20 percent of American society got 4 percent of the nation's income. That wasn't much, but it was better than last year, when that figure fell to only 3.7 percent.

And the middle class—the middle 60 percent of the society, the national bungalow belt of the non-rich and not-poor—is shrinking. Thirty years ago, this middle 60 percent brought home 52.3 percent of the national income. Now that's down to 47.4 percent.

BOX 6.4 (continued)

In other words, this middle class two-thirds of the American work force now earns less, collectively, than the one-fifth at the top. A 5 percent shift might not sound like much, but with a $5 trillion national pie, it means that $250 billion has been taken from the many and given to the few.

It's true, as Wall Street likes to boast, that 40 percent of all Americans now own stocks. But 90 percent of all stocks still are owned by 10 percent of the population.

This sort of thing just isn't happening anywhere else. In the United States, the richest 20 percent is 13 times richer than the poorest 20 percent. The factor in France is about 6. In Japan, the most egalitarian rich nation, it is only 4.

The gap is growing in Britain, but even there, the poor are gaining, although not as fast as the rich. Everywhere else, the gap between rich and poor is mostly steady. Much of this gap is blamed on the ravages of globalization, with American workers in competition with Third World workers who earn one-tenth as much. Technology also is blamed for stealing jobs and forcing white-collar workers to compete with the unskilled for worse jobs that pay less.

But globalization is, by definition, a global force that hits all countries equally. In other countries, minimum-wage laws, more social protection, and still vigorous trade unions have blunted its impact. Other countries are paying the price of globalization with higher rates of unemployment. U.S. unemployment is about as low as it can go, which should be sending wages up as employers scramble for scarce workers. The new income figures show this isn't happening.

Although few executives in Europe and Japan go hungry, American executives are the only ones to cash in big with seven-figure salaries and eight-figure stock options that have put run-of-the-mill CEOs in the kind of financial stratosphere usually reserved for pop stars.

The U.S. standard of living remains the world's highest—some 20 percent higher on average than that in Finland, the Netherlands, or Italy. But the poorest Americans live at levels 20 percent below those of the poorest Finn, Dutch, or Italian.

Ah yes, say Americans, but someone born poor in the United States has a greater chance to end up rich than he would if he was born in countries such as France or Japan, with less social mobility. Ah no, says the Organization for Economic Cooperation and Development, which found that people in other developed nations move up and down the social ladder at about the same pace as Americans do.

This inequality is having results. Politics in America is becoming more ideological and less centrist. Liberals and conservatives flay each other the way tories and socialists used to in Britain. The middle class, society's ballast, is eroding.

In the suburbs, the wealthy are building gated communities to keep the rabble at bay. Giant stores still are being built but increasingly, they are high-end stores like Bloomingdale's or low-end stores like Kmart, with not a lot in between. Nieman-Marcus is prospering and so, appallingly, are shops selling secondhand clothing.

If the ideal of democracy is equality, the ideal of capitalism is inequality. In America, it seems, capitalism has won.

Source: R. C. Longworth of the *Chicago Tribune.* Modified from the *Kansas City Star,* October 26, 1997. Reprinted with permission of Knight-Ridder/Tribune Information Services.

on the part of the Pacific rim countries as the method of economic development, but much of the rest of the less developed world is having difficulties. Africa is a case in point. If anything, Africa is less important today in terms of world trade than it was at the end of the colonial era.[34] Wars, corruption, and socialism have taken their toll on the economies of these countries. Parts of Africa that are fabulously rich in resources remain remarkably poor. Corruption is everywhere; wars seem to start over the slightest cause,[35] either real or imagined; and foreign investment, which is needed to develop the resources, has been frightened away because of the real chance of nationalization. The problem is that as the world develops, Africa must be included or it will remain a festering sore on the global economy.[36] But finding ways to develop many of the nations of Africa is a serious problem with no easy solutions.

These problems do not end in Africa but include most of the developing world. Two countries in Latin America are cases in point. Prior to World War II, Argentina was a model for the rest of Latin America. With the advent of Peron, Argentina started a slow but determined decline that featured military coups, death squads, and world-class political corruption and incompetence.[37] It was finally halted only when the Argentine military decided to take on the British in the Falklands. Meeting a competent enemy for the first time in over 100 years proved to be the undoing of the generals.[38] The British made short work of the dug-in Argentine army, and the Argentine navy was soon neutralized with the capture of a submarine at St. George Island and the sinking of a cruiser. Argentina's aircraft carrier never left port. Because of the blunders in the Falklands, the government of Argentina fell and eventually, the reform forces in Argentina were able to take over the government, but it will take time for Argentina to make up for 40 years of decline.

Mexico is another case in point. During the first 100 years of Mexico's existence, the country was plagued with political unrest. A series of dictators and invasions marked this period of Mexican history. Texas broke away to form its own country and eventually joined the United States. Later the United States invaded Mexico and took most of what now represents the southwestern United States. France invaded Mexico in the 1860s in an attempt to set up an empire in the Napoleonic tradition with the emperor Maximilian, but was repulsed. Later, the United States invaded Mexico again, chasing the bandit Pancho Villa in and out of the country.[39]

Today, Mexico is a one-party democracy and may be one of the most corrupt countries in Latin America.[40] The drug trade is rampant, with high government officials being bribed by the traffickers.[41] People are leaving the country in droves, seeking a better life and coming illegally to the United States. This immigration may be exactly what the Mexican government needs to stay in power. If these illegals were to stay in Mexico, they could easily become the basis of a revolution that would certainly destabilize the government, throwing the Institutional Revolutionary Party (PRE) out of power. For its part, the U.S. government is not interested in having a politically unstable neighbor immediately to the south, and the illegals provide a cheap source of labor for the United States. Certainly, if the United States wanted to stop illegal immigration into the country from Mexico, it could do it. But perhaps the price is too high in both direct and indirect costs.

Mexico has been on the verge of joining the developed nations for decades, but it has not been able to do it. For years, the United States has tried to find ways to bolster the Mexican economy and government, but each new step has only led to further problems. First the Maquelladora companies were designed to help Mexican workers develop skills to compete in the world economy, but all they seem to have done is to take away American jobs and provided cheap labor to produce goods for sale in the United States.[42] Working and living conditions in these communities are a scandal that both the American and Mexican governments seem unwilling to address. The North American Free Trade Agreement (NAFTA) seems only to have resulted in the collapse of the Mexican economy, an effort by the United States to try to save the Mexican economy and a huge American balance of payments deficit that before NAFTA had been a comfortable surplus.[43] The real problems in Mexico are corruption; a genuine class system where the closer one's background is to the native, non-European population, the lower the person's social standing; and a single party rule that continues to rule the country in any way that it sees fit. Mexico will not start to join the developed world until these problems are addressed and genuine political, economic, and social reforms are instituted.

Family Change   ■ ■ ■

The basic family unit has been the foundation of most of society since antiquity. With few exceptions, the family unit of mother, father, and children has been the basis of society. In biblical times it was not uncommon for a king or patriarch to have many wives and concubines. This was because it was not uncommon for babies and women to die from disease or childbirth, and life was otherwise very hazardous, so there was an imperative to have as many children as possible, to increase the chances of survival of the race. A biological fact of life is that a woman can only give birth about every nine months, whereas a man can father many children in nine months.

Today, the family unit is in a state of flux, as various alternative family units are being developed. Society is in the process of attempting to redefine the family. The extended family of aunts, uncles, and grandparents has been declining since the start of the industrial revolution.[44] Given the mobility of people in modern industrialized societies, extended families are very difficult to maintain, and as the demands of the industrial society continue to change, so will the family. The first and probably the most common alternative family unit is the single-parent family. This may be caused by a death of one of the marriage partners, divorce, abandonment by one of the partners, or having a child out of wedlock. Statistics demonstrate that this type of family situation has generally had a less than positive influence on the fate of the children. There is a higher incidence of crime among children from single-parent families, and poverty rates among this group tend to be much higher than when both parents are present.[45] The reason for the problems of the single-parent family are obvious. There is only one parent, and parenting is a difficult and exhausting job. An added task often is sole responsibility for the family's financial well-being. The job is tough and something often gets left undone in the process. Single-parent families need help, and society has not been prepared to deal adequately with this type of family group.

The welfare system has largely failed and has resulted in many fathers being driven from their children so as to maximize the benefits families receive from the system. The net result is more single-parent families and a spiral of welfare, poverty, and hopelessness that is difficult to break.[46]

Alternative lifestyles also offer alternative definitions of the family. Do two adults living together constitute a family? What if they are of the same sex? What if they are of different sexes? The state of Hawaii may recognize same-sex marriages with all of the appropriate obligations and rights associated with marriage.[47] Does this mean that other states, especially those with sodomy statutes, are obliged to recognize these marriages? Does one state have the power to negate the laws of another state by sanctioning certain arrangements as lawful that may not be considered lawful in other states? This is a question that has an impact in other areas of the law. For example, if a resident of a state where abortion is illegal goes to another state where abortion is legal and has an abortion, can that person be tried for murder in her home state? Can physicians who have performed legal abortions in their home state for people who are from states where abortion is illegal be arrested for murder if they set foot in a state where abortions are illegal?

This may seem a somewhat foolish argument, but it should be noted that the federal government of the United States has already done something similar to this under the Corrupt Foreign Practices Act.[48] Essentially, under the act, if a U.S. corporation does something that is illegal in the United States but is perfectly legal where the act is committed, it can be held liable for those actions in the United States. Similar logic has been extended by the Helms–Burton Act concerning trade with Cuba. Under this act, a foreign corporation that does business in both the United States and Cuba can be sued and have its U.S. assets jeopardized if it uses assets that belonged to U.S. firms prior to nationalization by the Castro government. In other words, a foreign firm is being held accountable under U.S. law for actions that took place in another country.

Many corporations have chosen to recognize same-sex cohabitation in their benefits packages. Disney, Microsoft, and Time Warner have all extended health insurance benefits and other employment benefits to same-sex partners of their employees.[49] Are they simply recognizing what has already happened in the society and, in particular, in the family? Perhaps, the law and legal institutions have not caught up with the reality of the situation, a not unusual circumstance in history.

Whatever the reason, the family is certainly experiencing change, and it is difficult to tell where that change is going to lead and where it may or may not end. It is fairly certain that there will continue to be family units. Human beings have a desire and a need to procreate, and some form of family seems to be the time-tested method of doing that. The question is: How many kinds of families will there be and how many of them?

Future Shock

Alvin Toffler has speculated on the effect of all the many waves of change on the average person in society. His initial speculation came in the book *Future Shock*,[50] where Toffler speculated that a new disease would develop to plague society. The disease would not be based on an infection or a biological condition; rather, it would be based on the inability of people to accept reality, a reality based on the development of scientific achievements that people had not

■ ■ ■   **BOX 6.5   She Just Didn't Believe It**   ■ ■ ■

She was born in Harlem, New York, around the turn of the century. When Harlem was an upper-middle-class suburb of New York City—a far cry from the changes that would overtake it after World War I, when it would become the center of African-American culture in the United States.

She grew up in New York and saw the horse and wagons slowly disappear from the streets, to be replaced by trucks and cars. She saw the advent of radio and then television; two world wars; the airplane, including jet transportation between the continents. The world had changed drastically since her days as a child, but there was one thing that she just could not accept.

On television she had seen men actually walk on the moon. She could deal with radio, television, even jet airplanes, but men walking on the moon was just too much. It couldn't be real. When she was a small girl, it had been the stuff of wild speculation. People laughed at the possibility of men walking on the moon. But now, nearer the end of her life than the beginning, she was being told just that and seeing them do it on TV. It couldn't be! It had to be a hoax from Hollywood. Just like back in the 1930s when the Mercury Theater ran that broadcast with Orson Wells about Martians invading the earth. That made a lot more sense than human beings actually walking around up there, and she would never believe it.

expected to happen in their lifetimes. People seem to forget that it took only 66 years to go from Kitty Hawk to the moon. Those living most of their lives during the twentieth century have seen more change than any group of human beings in the history of the planet. Change accelerated at a rate unknown in previous times, and it took some getting used to. A person born around 1900 was placed in a world of horses and buggies. Wooden sailing ships still plied the seas, although they were being replaced by steel steamships at a reasonably steady pace, and flying machines were the stuff of wild imagination and pulp science fiction. By the end of the twentieth century a great deal had happened: Horse and buggies were curiosities, sailing ships had become recreational vehicles, and human beings flew through the skies on regularly scheduled routes. For some people this was too much. They simply did not believe that men had landed on the moon; they thought it was a put-up job from Hollywood, an early sign, perhaps, of the disease of Future Shock, the inability to accept changes.

TRENDS IN THE DEVELOPED WORLD   ■ ■ ■

All the trends noted above are going on in the developed world, but there are several that need to be addressed more directly because of their connection to the less developed world. These trends are related to those discussed previously, but require further exploration.

The first trend is the development of what would appear to be a permanent underclass. This may be created in a number of ways. In Europe, immigrants from former colonial possessions have moved in to take many of the lower-paying, less desirable jobs in the economy. Many native Europeans are also on welfare, as the economies of the countries have not kept up with the changes in the society. In the United States, the welfare population seems to be particularly entrenched, and it is from this population that much of the violent crime in the United States arises. Added to this is the stubborn fact that 15 percent of those people who start high school in the United States will not finish. This is an average; in some states it is much higher.[51] This represents a permanent underclass in U.S. society, people who have never learned how to learn. It is difficult for people to pull themselves out of poverty if they do not know how to learn to use the tools to do that. The rest of the society is becoming progressively more impatient with such people and are calling for reforms that represent a cutback in the amount of money available to this group. This has important implications for society. The fact is that few societies can afford to have 15 percent of the population of able-bodied working-age adults not contributing. Add to this those who graduated from high school but do not have the necessary skills and abilities to function in society, such as the ability to read.

Illiteracy in the postindustrial age does not mean simply the inability to read the printed word. It means other types of illiteracy as well, the most common of which is computer illiteracy but includes math, cultural, historical, and science illiteracy—in fact, a whole host of illiteracies. Any of these problems will make it difficult for people to function in society; several of them will make it impossible.

Another situation facing the industrialized world is the reinvestment of capital in these countries. Now that the Cold War is over and many former socialist or communist countries are looking for investment monies, that is going to be more difficult.[52] The developed societies, especially the United States and Europe, need to replace their aging plant and infrastructure. Many railroads, highways, bridges, and sewer systems are approaching the end of the original useful life and need to be replaced, but the money to do that must now be found in competition with the needs of the awakening economies of central Europe and the Pacific rim. The need is particularly critical in the United States, where many facilities still currently in use were constructed before World War II. Unlike Europe, Japan, and much of East Asia, U.S. facilities were essentially untouched by the war. The rest of the world had to rebuild, so their plant and infrastructure are newer and more efficient than those in the United States. But from where is the money going to come? There is, it should be noted, plenty of money available for investment in the U.S. economy. The new heights achieved by the Dow Jones Industrial Averages and other indexes of stock prices are proof of that.[53] But for the most part, this represents money being invested in already established operations, not new ones or their replacements. What is needed is a way of investing money in new infrastructure, equipment, and technologies—all relatively high risk in nature, but necessary to maintain society.

TRENDS IN THE LESS DEVELOPED WORLD　■ ■ ■

As with the developed world, all the trends discussed above apply to the less developed parts of the world, but these societies have some particular problems. The first is the lack of education on the part of their workers.[54] Although historically, some developing countries had excellent school systems for their people, those systems are now reserved for the elite or have fallen into despair. Some countries have chosen to emphasize the university system, as has been the case in many African nations, while neglecting the primary and secondary systems. For a workforce to grow and prosper, it must have the tools to do that.

Just as in the United States, a workforce that does not have the tools to learn is a workforce that will be employed in menial jobs forever. Many less developed countries need schools so that they can compete for the more advanced type of industry.

The second issue is the creation, not the replacement, of the necessary infrastructure to be able to compete in a modern global economy.[55] A country that still depends on a crocodile-infested waterway as its main source of transportation is a nation with a serious transportation problem. Many of these countries have untapped natural resources on the same scale as the United States did over 100 years ago. But they do not know where they are; there are only a few organized attempts to find them; and there is no way to get them out, even if they are found. For these countries to become major players on the world scene, they are going to have to make real foreign investment attractive. Real foreign investment is not a shoe factory in Indonesia making Nike shoes and paying workers a few dollars a day.[56] Real foreign investment is developing local resources, establishing the necessary infrastructure, and paying appropriate wages to local workers, who can then purchase some of the products they make, and perhaps, even save a little and invest the money back in their economy.

FUTURE ISSUES IN THE GLOBAL ENVIRONMENT   ■ ■ ■

World Cooperation   ■ ■ ■

As the world begins to shrink even further than it already has, the importance of world cooperation and world competition increases. People on the planet must cooperate if they are to address successfully the problems that face them. Famine, disease, pollution, and ignorance know no national boundary. War has become far too expensive both in terms of human life and in terms of the destruction of the society. Human beings have become far too efficient at killing each other. A single bomb dropped from a single airplane on New York, Los Angeles, Tokyo, London, or any other major city has the potential to kill instantly more people than all of the Americans that have been killed in all of the wars fought by the United States. Atomic war is simply out of the question. Conventional warfare may still be fought, but only as a throwback by leaders whose reality is still in an earlier time. Societies, nations, and peoples must cooperate because the ultimate breakdown of cooperation is too terrible to imagine.

World cooperation is taking many forms. Since the end of World War II there have been a variety of efforts in the area of world cooperation, especially when enlightened self-interest plays a role. It should be noted that the first attempt at world cooperation, the League of Nations, failed,[57] because President Woodrow Wilson, the father of the League, failed to gain its acceptance in the United States. The purpose of the League was to prevent another world war— a purpose at which it failed spectacularly. But World War II ended with a greater determination on the part of the victors to avoid another world conflict and resulted in the founding of the United Nations. Although it is certainly possible to argue the effectiveness of the UN and the various peacekeeping missions it has assumed over the years, it should be remembered that although there have been many small wars and revolutions, there has been no great world war for over 50 years. The other aspect of the UN that is not particularly obvious has been the success of the various relief efforts among the various agencies of its member states.[58] The UN has played a role, often a key role, in combating hunger and disease, in addition to its military role of peacekeeping.

An agency that has experienced great success over the years has been the World Health Organization. It is in this area where the greatest degree of world cooperation has probably taken place. People recognize that disease plays no national favorites. In addition to the World Health Organization, other agencies have cooperated in the human struggle against disease, including the Pasteur Institute in France and the Centers for Disease Control in the United States. These agencies and the physicians, nurses, and other health professionals who make up these organizations have been the front line in the human race's struggle against its oldest and most determined enemies. They have learned that cooperation is the only way to defend successfully against these deadly diseases, whether it is AIDS, tuberculosis, small pox, or Ebola virus. Health and medicine have probably been the most successful arena of world cooperation over the past 50 years.

Competition remains, however. Competition is not necessarily a bad thing and can often be a good thing. Competition can bring out the best in people, and if properly channeled, can result in great advances for the society. Admittedly, if overdone, it can result in negatives that far outweigh the positives, such as war, the ultimate form of competition, but healthy competition can be a good thing.

The primary area of competition today is in the economic area.[59] People compete for jobs; corporations compete for customers and the factors of production; societies compete for increased standards of living. Yes, minor world conflicts remain, but the focus has shifted to the economic arena. The Japanese have a saying that "business is war," and they are right. Corporations, individuals, and countries are all in competition, but the paradox is that for them to succeed, they must cooperate.[60]

This cooperation takes many forms. For individuals, it may be networking, inside or outside their organizations. For companies, it may be in the form of mergers, partnerships, or joint ventures. The Japanese model of the Keirtsu is a case in point.[61] These are gigantic organizations that cooperate with each other in an effort to compete against other businesses throughout the world. They have such names as Mitsubishi, Hitachi, and Mitsui, and they are large and powerful organizations that are able to influence the role and actions of their government. In the United States there are similar organizations, perhaps not as large, but ones that the government will simply not allow to fail because of the critical role they play in some aspect of the economy. This would include the automakers, especially Chrysler,[62] which the federal government bailed out of its crisis, a crisis that was caused by woefully incompetent management. It would also include First National City Bank of New York, Citibank, which was quietly assisted by the Federal Reserve in an effort to prevent a banking crisis brought on by incompetent managers giving loans around the world to less than creditworthy applicants, especially Brazil. Simply stated, if the average person with Brazil's credit history showed up at Citibank, they would be laughed out of the bank. Citibank loaned Brazil and countries with similar histories billions of dollars, and there is no real hope that the money will be repaid. Citibank, Chrysler, and other large corporations will simply not be allowed to fail, no matter how much they may desire to do so. They and the government have become partners, and Citibank's president during its problems remains at the helm and is one of the highest-paid executives in the world.[63]

Governments themselves are entering into partnerships with each other. Some of these partnerships are along traditional military lines, such as NATO, but many of the new ones are along economic lines. Most major trading nations of the globe have entered into the World Trade Organization,[64] and other types of trade organizations are developing on a regional basis, with the European Economic Community (EEC) and the North American Free Trade Association the most prominent.[65] The strategic objectives of these two organizations are

---

■ ■ ■ BOX 6.6 Regulators Lift Order on Citicorp ■ ■ ■

Citicorp, the nation's largest banking company, said yesterday that federal regulators had released it from the strict supervision under which it had operated for two years. In February 1992, after mounting losses from bad real estate loans and other operational problems, Citicorp was forced to sign a memorandum of understanding with the Federal Reserve and the Office of the Comptroller of the Currency, the agency that regulates national banks. "This is a demonstration that Citicorp has come a long way and will have a greater flexibility to shape its future," Judah Kraushaar, a Merrill Lynch analyst said.

Needed Approval of Acquisitions

Memorandums of understanding are informal agreements with regulators and the mildest form of written regulatory supervision. In its memorandum, the banking company committed itself to raise capital, cut costs, and build a reserve for potential loan losses. Moreover, Citicorp was prohibited from making acquisitions or otherwise expanding without getting approval from regulators.

The importance of the lifting of restrictions is mostly symbolic because Citicorp is now shunning acquisitions in favor of building existing businesses. "Acquisitions have not figured in as part of our own strategy, John Morris, a spokesman for Citicorp, said. "We look upon our business as one of enhancing the value of our existing global core franchises." Still, the removal of what has been a stigma may make it easier for Citicorp to apply to regulators for new powers, such as the right to underwrite stock offerings.

Dividend Reinstatement Seen

The company is also expected to reinstate its dividend this year, perhaps at the annual shareholders' meeting in April. Mr. Kraushaar estimated that Citicorp's initial dividend might be about 20 cents a quarter, or roughly 17 percent of his estimate of Citicorp's 1994 earnings of $4.65 a share. Most money-center banks pay dividends equal to 35 to 40 percent of their earnings, he said.

In the last two years, Citicorp has made a remarkable recovery, reducing loan losses and slashing expenses. Last year, it earned $2.2 billion, a record for a U.S. bank. As of September 1993, Citicorp's capital, as measured by the tier 1 ratio, the main standard used by regulators, was 6 percent of risk-related assets. It was the first time since its troubles began that the company's capital had been more than 6 percent, the level at which the government defines a well-capitalized bank.

Source: Modified from Saul Hansel, *The New York Times*, Feb. 16, 1994. Copyright © 1994 by The New York Times. Reprinted by permission.

Author's note: Citicorp recently merged with Transamerica to form Citigroup.

very different. NAFTA is essentially a trade and customs union between the United States, Canada, and Mexico, and although it has gotten off to a somewhat rocky start with the collapse of the Mexican economy, the views of the organization remain essentially economic in nature.

The EEC, however, has a different aim, and that is to unite Europe in what is not only a single trade bloc, but a political union as well. Political union in Europe will be much more difficult to achieve than commercial union. These countries have a long history of war and hatred against each other and the wounds from World War II have not completely healed and have occasionally been reopened.

These regional trade blocs may represent the way the world will eventually be knit together: a region at a time and then the regions themselves. Political union may be far more difficult to achieve, but then political union may not be necessary, and in fact, not relevant as the arena of conflict moves from the military and political to the economic. Governments may simply become the avenues of power for the corporate organizations with which the governments are in partnership. This was the Ziabatsu model in prewar Japan,[66] where the government policy was a reflection of the needs of these large trading organizations. The results were not good and, in fact, ended in the destruction of Japan and the Ziabatsus, but that does not mean that the model was necessarily flawed, only that the people who attempted to use it were flawed. Who is to say that the nation-state is the ultimate form for the organization of human society or that even a worldwide nation-state would provide the most efficient form of organization? Corporations are far more efficient than nation-states. General Motors, with about 250,000 employees, has as much income in sales as the nation of Indonesia, with over 200 million people, has in gross domestic product.

■ ■ ■ BOX 6.7 The World's 50 Largest Organizations ■ ■ □

United States of America	$6727 billion GDP	1994
Japan	$4630 billion GDP	1994
China	$2214 billion GDP	1994
Germany	$2045 billion GDP	1994
U.S. government, all levels	$1836 billion taxes	1993
France	$1316 billion GDP	1994
Japanese government, all levels	$1228 billion taxes	1993
United Kingdom	$1027 billion GDP	1994
Italy	$1008 billion GDP	1994
Russia	$780 billion GDP	1994
German government, all levels	$745 billion taxes	1993
Brazil	$580 billion GDP	1994
French government, all levels	$548 billion taxes	1993
Canada	$523 billion GDP	1994
Spain	$478 billion GDP	1994
Italian government, all levels	$470 billion taxes	1993

BOX 6.7 *(continued)*

Mexico	$363 billion GDP	1994
South Korea	$356 billion GDP	1994
Netherlands	$331 billion GDP	1994
Australia	$320 billion GDP	1994
U.K. government, all levels	$316 billion taxes	1993
India	$287 billion GDP	1994
Argentina	$278 billion GDP	1994
Switzerland	$267 billion GDP	1994
Taiwan	$238 billion GDP	1994
Belgium	$229 billion GDP	1994
Poland	$206 billion GDP	1994
Canadian government, all levels	$198 billion taxes	1993
Austria	$196 billion GDP	1994
Sweden	$189 billion GDP	1994
Mitsubishi	$184 billion sales	1994
Mitsui	$181 billion sales	1994
Itochu	$169 billion sales	1994
General Motors	$168 billion sales	1994
Indonesia	$168 billion GDP	1994
Spanish government, all levels	$167 billion taxes	1993
Sumitomo	$167 billion sales	1994
Marubeni	$161 billion sales	1994
Netherlands government, all levels	$148 billion taxes	1993
Thailand	$142 billion GDP	1994
Denmark	$141 billion GDP	1994
Ford Motor Company	$137 billion sales	1994
Turkey	$129 billion GDP	1994
Iran	$125 billion GDP	1994
Saudi Arabia	$121 billion GDP	1994
South Africa	$120 billion GDP	1994
State of California	$115 billion total revenue	1994
Toyota Motor	$111 billion sales	1994
Exxon	$110 billion sales	1994
Royal Dutch Petroleum	$109 billion sales	1994
Norway	$108 billion GDP	1994
Nissho Iwai	$97 billion sales	1994

Adapted from: *The Fortune 500,* Fortune, April 29, 1996; *The Fortune Global 500,* Fortune, August 5, 1996;
Statistical Abstract of the United States 1996, U.S. Gov't Printing Office.

The New World Order

At the end of the Cold War, President Bush called for a "new world order." At this point, it is very unclear what that is likely to be. There are, however, certain things that can be detected:

1. There is currently only one superpower, the United States, and no significant political act, especially by the western democracies, can take place without U.S. involvement. Bosnia is only the most obvious example, a European problem that must be settled by the United States.[67]

2. There are only a few other potential superpowers in the world: China, a united Europe, and a revived Russian empire, all of which are years, if not decades away from challenging the United States.

3. The power and influence of the United States are likely to decline, especially if it is unable to get its economic and educational system in order. When you are on the top of the mountain, the only place to go is down: the only question being how far and how fast.

4. Economic considerations are going to carry more weight than political and military ones. The U.S. relationship with China is a case in point. Human rights seem to mean little in the face of greater trade and profits.[68]

5. Changes in the political landscape have not finished. The situation in the former Yugoslavia is only the most obvious example, but there are active separatist movements in Brittany, Spain, Belgium, Scotland, Hawaii, Sri Lanka, Quebec, India, Iraq, Turkey, Israel, and of course, Ireland.[69]

Food, Population, and the Environment

The problems of food, population, and the environment are so interconnected that it is virtually impossible to discuss one without the other. People eat food and food is grown in the environment. To endanger the food supply is to endanger the population with starvation.

Pollution does not recognize national boundaries. Pollution happens from both natural and human-made causes. The eruption of Mt. Pinitubo in the Philippines resulted in a tremendous amount of ash and other pollutants being thrown into the atmosphere.[70] This has coated the world with a layer of

---

BOX 6.8 Malthus and the Dismal Science

Economics is called the dismal science largely because in *An Essay on the Principles of Population,* Thomas Robert Malthus predicted that world population would outpace the food supply, depressing wages and living standards to bare subsistence levels. He theorized that even if some innovation were to stimulate food production, the rate of growth of the population would also be stimulated, resulting in no net gain.

This dismal assessment of humanity's future led people to refer to economics as the dismal science: a discipline that held no hope in the long run. As John Maynard Keynes would later comment, "In the long run, we are all dead!"

dust and resulted in spectacular sunsets for the past several years. But nature is not the only source of pollution. Modern civilization has also resulted in great amounts of pollutants being spewed into the air and water. Societies have paid terrible prices for this. Rivers have died, the air in many cities is simply not fit to breath, and even the oceans have suffered, along with marine life. Rachel Carson first brought this to national attention with her book *Silent Spring*,[71] but it had been going on for a very long time prior to her book and continues today. The Chesapeake Bay is a case in point. For many years, pollutants flowed into the bay from the Susquehanna, Potomac, and James rivers. They destroyed wildlife with their pollution, vastly decreasing the numbers of stripped bass, blue crabs, and oysters. Added to the situation was the over-fishing that occurred as the fishermen became more mechanized and better at their tasks. But the bay was fortunate in that it was close to Washington, DC, one of the major polluters of the Potomac, and the national media in Washington, who could focus attention on the plight of the bay. Today, the bay is being cleaned up, but it will probably never return to its former splendor, and the struggle to maintain the bay is likely to continue for the foreseeable future.

So far, science and technology have won the war against hunger and starvation, but there is no guarantee that the victories will continue. Changes in the climate caused by pollution or simply the natural course of events could change crop yields in just a few years. Some of the most productive farmland in the world is slowly being worn away, and a dustbowl future may await some of the world's most productive farmland. Prime agricultural land is also being used in other ways: for housing, shopping centers, and office buildings. In Lancaster County, Pennsylvania, some of the most productive farms in the United States are being sold for housing developments, and this same process is going on in other parts of the United States and the world.

Although growing food has not been a problem for the past several decades, getting the food to people has been. Many societies lack the appropriate infrastructure to get food from the farm to the consumer. This has been a problem in the former Soviet Union, where crops have been allowed to rot in the fields while people in other parts of the country have gone hungry.

In other parts of the world, despite efforts by many organizations to slow the growth of world population, the population continues to grow. In India, the second-largest country in the world, in terms of population, the number of people is expected to exceed those in China sometime in the twenty-first century. India, which for decades has been a food exporter, may once again have to become a food importer to feed its people. There are other countries, especially in the less developed world, whose population continues to explode, and for them, food is already subject to the whims of nature. Somalia, Ethiopia, and Sudan in Africa have experienced recent famines as a result of drought and war, and the rest of the sub-Sahara continues to experience an encroachment of the desert as it moves ever southward in its expansion. Only time will tell if this will continue or reverse itself as a natural cyclical movement of the environment.

SUMMARY   ■ ■ ■

There are many trends facing the modern global environment. John Nesbitt in his book *Megatrends* outlined 10 specific trends in modern society. In addition to Nesbitt's trends, several others have been occurring on both a global and a national level. Changes are occurring all over the planet in both developed and developing countries. Changes in each area are going to have an impact on changes in the other. World competition and world cooperation are going to grow. Although this may seem contradictory, it is not. Cooperation helps to achieve goals for which people, organizations, and nations strive. These same entities compete with everyone in an effort to achieve their goals. Both competition and cooperation are necessary for success.

Because of the end of the Cold War, it is uncertain what the "new world order" is likely to be in the future. Right now, the United States is the only superpower, but there are candidates as rivals or replacements. Because of the destruction and uncertainty of atomic or conventional war, these types of conflicts will probably be avoided in the future except for the most direct threats to society, and then only in a limited format, similar to Desert Storm. Economics, business, and trade will be the arenas of conflict for the foreseeable future. The Japanese saying that "business is war" is about to be played out on a global scale.

Finally, the problems of the environment are going to have to be addressed. If not, the consequences may be just as bad as atomic war, if not worse. Population growth and food, although not a problem at this point, have the potential to return as major considerations. Changes in the environment, whether caused by nature or war, also loom on the horizon. How much trash and pollutants can a system take before it breaks? How far can the limits of the earth's ecological system be pushed before the system starts to push back? How and when will human beings know that they have gone beyond the river's, lake's, ocean's, or sky's ability to absorb abuse and continue to provide the human race with the sustenance and protection it so desperately needs?

Questions _____

1. What did John Naisbitt mean when he wrote about "megatrends"?
2. Alvin Toffler called the change from an industrial to an information society the "third wave." Why?
3. Explain how the economy is changing from a national economy to a world economy. Give an example.
4. Why is entrepreneurship such an important part of capitalism?
5. What part has the personal computer played in the decentralization of society?
6. In the face of downsizing, networking has become the new watchword in organizations. Explain why this has happened.
7. Explain why going from either/or options to multiple options allows for greater creativity and better productivity.
8. Why is the trend of the aging populace in the society so important?
9. The religious revival has been important in the United States. How has it been important in other countries?
10. Why are diversity and multiculturalism in the workforce so important?
11. Why is NAFTA so important to the economy of North America?
12. How is the family changing?
13. The society is changing very rapidly. Do you think Alvin Toffler has a point in his book *Future Shock?*

14. Why is it important for a society to have as many members of the society making as positive a contribution as possible?

15. Why is it important for less developed countries to concentrate on developing their infrastructure?

16. What are some of the ways that there is world cooperation?

17. Why would the government of the United States seek to prop up and bail out major corporations while leaving the small ones to fend for themselves?

18. Why do you think that there are independence movements in so many parts of the world?

19. Was Malthus right?

20. What are some of the long-term problems facing the United States and other major political, economic, and social organizations?

CASE 1

Technological change was something the NCR Corporation was not counting on in the mid-1970s but technological change was happening nonetheless. For years the company had produced the finest line of cash registers and business machines in the world, but the world had changed. Electronics had taken over and was the wave of the future. However, NCR was woefully unprepared for it. The company had a huge investment in the old electromechanical technology, and the sales force was simply not prepared to sell these new products.

NCR had always prided itself on having the best sales force in the world, coupled with the best service. Unfortunately, most of the sales force did not understand the new electronic products, and the new electronic devices were so inexpensive that a customer could purchase a piece of new equipment for a fraction of what he had paid as many as 10 years before. In addition, the new equipment would be able to do even more than the old, at a much faster rate.

NCR had new products, but it needed a sales force that could sell those products in a very different market. Although it had great salespeople and a long tradition of corporate education, it needed a sales force that could sell its products in this new market and did not have it. The technology had changed, and as a result, the market had changed but the sales force hadn't.

1. If you were head of sales for NCR, what would you do?
2. Is there some way that NCR could salvage its current sales force?
3. Does it have an ethical obligation to do so?

CASE 2

Juan is certainly a good-looking man, thought Stella. Very suave, very Latin, he had been very attentive to her at the office. Only this afternoon he had suggested that they have dinner at his hotel, where he was staying until he returned to Argentina. She knew that such contact between employees was against company rules and had heard that Juan had a family back in Argentina, but he had been persistent. Several times she had to tell him no, but each time it had been with less conviction. She knew that if an American employee had been as persistent as Juan, he would have been a candidate for a charge of sexual harassment. But Juan was not from the United States, so didn't that make it different? In Juan's culture the roles of men and women were different than in the United States. Just then, Stella saw Juan walking into the office with a bouquet of long-stemmed roses that had a large "To Stella" on a note in the flowers.

1. What should Stella do?
2. Is Juan engaging in sexual harassment or just trying to get a date with Stella?
3. If Juan's name were John and he came from Akron, would this be different?
4. How should the company respond to this situation?

CASE 3

In another sign that the nation's ethical standards continue to decline, a Rutgers professor reports that the level of cheating on college campuses continues to rise. An Associated Press article noted that one reason for the rise is that cheating no longer carries the same level of social stigma.

> "Donald McCabe, who has done extensive research on the subject of cheating on college campuses, reported that the number of respondents who admitted cheating in 1993 was 64%, which was up from 39% in a similar survey in 1962. Professor McCabe reported similar findings among colleges which had honor codes." (Associated Press release, August 28, 1997)

1. What are the ethical considerations for the faculty, students, and colleges?
2. How would you tackle this problem?

References

1. Nesbitt, John, *Megatrends: ten new directions transforming our lives,* Warner Books, New York, 1982.
2. Toffler, Alvin, *Future shock,* Random House, New York, 1970.
3. Toffler, Alvin, *The third wave,* William Morrow, New York, 1980.
4. Maidment, Fred (ed.), *Annual editions: international business, 1997–1998,* Dushkin/McGraw-Hill, Guilford, CT, 1997.
5. Reich, Robert, "Who is them?" *Harvard Business Review,* March–April 1991.
6. Hill, Kenneth L., "Cold war chronology: Soviet–American relations, 1945–1991," *Congressional Quarterly,* 1993.
7. *The Federalist papers,* Arlington House, New Rochelle, NY, 1966.
8. Farrell, Larry C., *Searching for the spirit of enterprise,* Dutton, New York, 1993.
9. Reich, "Who is them?"
10. Peters, Thomas, *In search of excellence: lessons from America's best run companies,* Harper & Row, New York, 1982.
11. Ibid.
12. Maidment, *Annual editions.*
13. Nesbitt, *Megatrends.*
14. Ibid.
15. Kahn, Matthew E., "Demand for environmental goods: evidence from voting patterns in California initiatives," *Journal of Law and Economics,* April 1997,
16. Weber, Max, *Max Weber on capitalism, bureaucracy, and religion: a selection of texts,* Allen & Unwin, London, 1983.
17. Waugh, Troy A., "A marketing moment: big hat, no cattle," *CPA Journal,* September 1997.
18. Adams, Charles Kendall, *A history of the United States of America,* Allyn & Bacon, Boston, 1903.

19. Nesbitt, *Megatrends*.

20. Kim Young, J., and Robert Schoen, "Population momentum expresses population aging," *Demography*, August 1997, v. 34, n. 3.

21. *Innovation: a cross-disciplinary perspective*, ed. Kjell Grønhaug & Geir Kaufmann, Norwegian University Press, Oslo, 1988.

22. Verne, Jules, *Twenty-thousand leagues under the sea*, Naval Institute Press, Annapolis, MD, 1993.

23. Clarke, Arthur C., *2001: a space odyssey*, New American Library, New York, 1968.

24. Amanpour, Christiane, "Tyranny of the Taliban," *Time*, October 13, 1997.

25. Kinzer, Stephen, "Ataturk the icon is about to take a bit of a hit," *New York Times*, October 3, 1997.

26. "Not quite apolitical," *Denver Post*, September 20, 1997.

27. Price, Fay, "How to make diversity pay," *Fortune*, August 8, 1994.

28. Johnston, William B., and Arnold E. Packer, *Work force 2000: work and workers for the 21st century*, Hudson Institute, Indianapolis, 1987.

29. Fram, Eugene H., and Francena L. Miller, "Family or work: a matter of priorities," *USA Today Magazine*, May 1995.

30. Kutscher, Ronald E., "Outlook 1990–2005: major trends and issues," *Occupational Outlook Quarterly*, Spring 1992.

31. Brandt, Ellen, "Global HR," *Personnel Journal*, July–August 1992.

32. Longworth, R. C., "U.S. prosperity hasn't spread to everyone," *Chicago Tribune* (from the *Kansas City Star*) October 26, 1997.

33. Greenberger, Robert, "North–South split: with cold war over, poorer nations face neglect by rich," *Wall Street Jounal*, May 14, 1992.

34. Barnet, Richard, "What about Africa?" *Harper's*, May 1990.

35. Ibid.

36. Ibid.

37. Alexander, Robert Jackson, *Juan Domingo Peron: a history*, Westview Press, Boulder CO, 1979.

38. *War in the Falklands: the full story*, The Sunday Times of London Insight Team. Harper & Row, New York, 1982.

39. Call, Tomme Clark, *The Mexican venture: from political to industrial revolution in Mexico*, Oxford University Press, New York, 1953.

40. Dillon, Sam, "Mexican government plans to work with congress," *New York Times*, September 2, 1997.

41. Grayson, George, "Mexico's power crisis: President Ernesto Zedillo needs all the authority he can muster to fight narcotics corruption," *Christian Science Monitor*, August 29, 1997.

42. Darlin, Damon, "Maquilladora-ville," *Forbes*, May 6, 1996.

43. Coone, Tim, "Mexico on the mend," *Business Latin America*, April 3, 1995.

44. Bianchi, Susan, *Family disruption and economic hardship: the short-run picture for children*, U.S. Department of Commerce, Washington, DC, 1991.

45. Ibid.

46. Ibid.

47. Price, Deb, "Hawaii's top court appears willing to legalize same sex marriages," *Detroit News*, September 5, 1997.

48. Martin, Keith, and Sheila Walsh, "Beware the corrupt foreign practices act," *International Commercial Litigation*, October 1996, n. 13.

49. Nozier, Robert, "Boycott effort faults Disney compassion," *Hotel and Motel Management,* July 21, 1997.

50. Toffler, *Future shock.*

51. *Statistical abstract of the United States, 1996,* U.S. Department of Commerce, Washington, DC, 1996.

52. Maidment, *Annual editions.*

53. Barr, Paul, "Mix a cup of nerve, a dash of luck," *Pensions and Investments,* September 29, 1997.

54. Barnet, "What about Africa?"

55. Quelch, John A., and James E. Austin, "Should multinationals invest in Africa?" *Sloan Management Review,* Spring 1993.

56. Kim Sun, Bae, "Foreign direct investment: gift horse or Trojan horse," *Weekly Letter,* Federal Reserve Bank of San Francisco, March 20, 1992.

57. Armstrong, George G., *Why another world war? How we missed collective security,* Allen & Unwin, London, 1941.

58. *Basic facts about the United Nations,* Department of Public Information, United Nations, New York, 1995.

59. Maidment, *Annual editions.*

60. Rakstis, Ted, "Going global," *Kiwanis Magazine,* October 1991.

61. Tsurumi, Yoshi, *The Japanese are coming: a multinational interaction of firms and politics,* Ballinger, Cambridge, MA, 1976.

62. Iacocca, Lee, *Iacocca: an autobiography,* Bantam Books, New York, 1984.

63. Reingold, J., "Executive pay," *Business Week,* April 21, 1997.

64. Pitroda, Salil S., "From GATT to WTO: the institutionalization of world trade," *Harvard International Review,* Spring 1995.

65. Werther, William B., "Toward global convergence," *Business Horizons,* January–February 1996.

66. Tsurumi. *The Japanese are coming.*

67. "Aid groups want U.S. to remain in Bosnia," *Christian Century,* September 24, 1997.

68. Evans, Robert, "China policy and church partnership," *Christian Century,* September 24, 1997.

69. Turner, Craig, "Separation anxiety," *Los Angeles Times,* October 24, 1995.

70. Harlin, John, "The cataclysm and beyond," *Backpacker,* June 1991.

71. Carson, Rachael, *Silent spring,* Houghton Mifflin, Boston, 1962.

CURRENT ISSUES FOR THE MODERN BUSINESS ENTERPRISE

Concepts : You Will Learn ■ ■ ■

the nature of capitalism, especially with regard to private property, economic incentive, and economic and political freedom

modern forms of business organization, especially sole proprietorships, partnerships, and corporations

the role of small business and multinational corporations in the local, regional, national, and international setting

how one sector of the society deals with other parts of the society, and the importance of strategic management in planning for the organization

future issues for the modern business enterprise

THE NATURE OF CAPITALISM ■ ■ ■

Capitalism is the economic system under which most of the world now operates since the end of the Cold War. There are a few exceptions, notably Cuba and North Korea, and it is uncertain at this point exactly what is happening in China. Capitalism as an economic system has been the prevailing system the majority of the time since ancient days.[1] Although it may not have been called *capitalism*, merchants, farmers, and artisans certainly worked for a profit. But it was Adam Smith and the utilitarian school of economics that gave capitalism the initial substance and form that is known today.[2]

One of the key concepts of capitalism is the idea of private property. Private property gives the owner of the property certain rights, including the right to buy and sell the property.[3] Without this concept of ownership, it would be very difficult for exchange to take place and for capitalism to exist. In other economic systems, everything belongs either to the state or to the king or to whatever gods may be in favor. Capitalism is different because it allows people to own things, and when people own things they are in charge of them, responsible for them, and at least to a certain degree, in charge of their own destinies.

A second concept of capitalism is economic incentive, the profit motive.[4] Karl Marx wrote that the essence of communism is "from each according to his abilities and to each according to his needs."[5] In the same vain, capitalism could be described as "from each according to his ability, to each according to what he has earned." Although in capitalism, people may not always get what they deserve, they certainly have a hope that they will. In communism it really does not matter what you do; you will get only what you need, and that is likely to be determined by someone else. The key dynamic in capitalism is the profit motive: the opportunity to get rich and to gain power over your own destiny as much as one person can. This is the reason why so many immigrants to the United States go into business for themselves. They have the opportunity to control their own fate. They do not have to answer to a bureaucrat or a commissar. They only have to pay their taxes, which by world standards are fairly low, pay their bills, and keep their customers happy.

Private property and economic incentive are only a part of capitalism. A third important aspect is a relatively free market.[6] By *relatively free,* we mean that certain rules and regulations are needed to form the basis of a free market. These regulations should be designed to help the flow of goods and services, not to hinder them or become so onerous as to discourage people in the marketplace. A free market means that anyone can buy or sell any legal good or service within the context of the law. Black markets, on the other hand, are free markets, which may or may not sell legal goods but are outside the context of the law. Examples of black markets would include the market for illegal drugs in the United States, as well as a market for perfectly legal items that can often be found in societies that are economically stressed, such as war-torn countries or where rationing and shortages are common. Free markets are another basis for capitalism—they are what capitalism is based on.

One of the results of a free market for goods and services is the expectation of a free market for ideas. Capitalism and democracy are usually found together in most countries, and those countries that have a free market but do not have democracy are on their way to democracy. Free markets mean choice, and this expectation of choice soon flows over into the political arena. If one has a choice of goods and services, why shouldn't there be a choice in the area of government, politics, and ideas? A people cannot be half free to determine their fate: rather, they must be all free. This is why capitalism and free markets leads to democracy and political pluralism. Once a people has freedom in one area, they will come to demand it in another, and economics and political freedom need each other to survive.

THE MODERN CORPORATION: FORMS OF BUSINESS ORGANIZATION ■ ■ ■

Sole Proprietorships   ■ ■ ■

Sole proprietorships are the most common form of legal organization,[7] accounting for well over half of the businesses in the United States. Most sole proprietorships tend to be very small businesses, employing perhaps only the entrepreneur, but they can also be large organizations employing a number of people.

Sole proprietorships have a number of advantages over other forms of organization. The first is the simplicity of formation. One can simply go into business for oneself. This lack of a complex procedure is very appealing. Another factor in favor of the sole proprietorship is a very low startup cost. Legal fees are minimal. A third advantage of the sole proprietorship is that they are taxed as part of the entrepreneur's regular income. During the initial startup phase of an organization, revenues tend to be lower and costs tend to be higher. Entrepreneurs can treat this probable loss as part of their regular taxes, thereby lowering their total tax burden. But probably the most important advantage of the sole proprietorship is freedom. Entrepreneurs answer to no boss; and their only constraints are keeping the customer, the bank, and the government happy. The responsibility for the success or failure of the business lies squarely on their shoulders. The business is their responsibility alone, and the success or failure of that business belongs to them.

There are certain disadvantages to the sole proprietorship. The chief disadvantage is unlimited liability.[8] Anything that goes wrong with the company or its activities is the responsibility of the entrepreneur. The entrepreneur is responsible for all debts incurred in the venture. The second disadvantage is the difficulty in raising money for the enterprise.[9] Sole proprietorships are limited in that they are dependent on the ability of the entrepreneur to raise money. His credit and resources are the credit and resources of the business. Unless the entrepreneur is very wealthy, this can prove to be a very sizable obstacle to obtaining the necessary financial resources to grow and prosper.

Sole proprietorships also suffer from an image of instability. Essentially, they are dependent on one person, and should something happen to that person, the business may dissolve.[10] This plays into the fourth disadvantage of the sole proprietorship, which is that the business comes to an end on the death of the entrepreneur. This can cause the business to end or, at the very least, cause a severe reorganization of the business. The functions the business performs may not end, and the assets and other aspects of the business may be taken over by, or sold to, another business, but certainly, those functions that were performed in the name of that business are no longer done under that name. That business is over.

Partnerships

A second form of organization is a general partnership. Partnerships are defined by the Uniform Partnership Act as "a voluntary association of two or more persons to carry-on as co-owners a business for profit." This act was approved by the National Conference of Commissioners on Uniform State Laws in 1914 and is now the law in essentially all states.

General partnerships are really sole proprietorships multiplied by the number of people in the partnership. The best thing about a partnership is that it is able to grow by adding the talent and money of the partners to the enterprise. Because of this, partnerships are able to overcome one of the most severe drawbacks of the sole proprietorship—the dependence for the success of the enterprise on a single person.

Partnerships always include an agreement of some type and should always be in writing. The agreement should include the following:

1. Who gets what percentage of the partnership's profits
2. How much each partner invests in the business

3. Each partner's area of responsibility and who reports to whom

4. If necessary, how the partnership can be dissolved and how the assets would be divided among the partners

5. In the event of the death of one of the partners, how the surviving partners would be protected from the estate of the deceased

As mentioned above, the chief advantage of a partnership over a proprietorship is that they can draw on a larger pool of resources. Like proprietorships, they are easy to organize. There can be as few as two partners or several hundred, who can invest equal or unequal sums of money, and the profit they earn may or may not bear a relationship to their investment. Another advantage of a partnership is that the partner's profits are taxed as part of their individual income. They can also claim losses on their individual tax returns, thereby lowering their taxes.

Partnerships also have certain disadvantages. Chief among these disadvantages is the unlimited liability to which each partner is subject. If one of the partners does something as a part of the business and is sued, all of the partners are fully liable for those actions. In practice, this means that the partner with the greatest assets is the one most subject to a lawsuit if something happens. This is why general partnerships are the least common form of organization. Another problem is the difficulty in transferring ownership. No partner can sell his or her stake in the business without the consent of the other partners. So a partner who wished to transfer ownership, or to retire, must get the consent of the other partners involved. Finally, surviving partners may be faced with liquidating when one of the partners dies; however, the surviving partners may quickly form a new partnership and continue the business.

Limited partnerships can overcome some of the disadvantages of a general partnership. In this form of organization, the limited partners simply invest their money but do not take an active role in the partnership's operations and cannot be held liable for debts incurred by the active partners.[11] Limited partnerships usually require legal help when they are being formed, and if a limited partner starts to take an active role in the business, the person may lose his or her limited status. Another form of partnership is a real estate investment trust (REIT).[12] This type of partnership is managed by a trustee, often a bank or other financial institution. Ownership may be transferred easily and if one of the partners dies, will continue. Another form of partnership organization that has evolved to overcome the disadvantages of partnerships is the family partnership. The advantage of this type of partnership is that it allows partners to divide the income of the venture among members of their families, thus avoiding higher tax rates on the profits.

There are several types of partners:

1. *Ostensible partner:* both active and known as a partner

2. *Dormant partner:* neither known nor active

3. *Secret partner:* involved in the daily operations of the partnership but is not known

4. *Silent partner:* known but not active

5. *Limited partner:* risks only his or her investment in the partnership

6. *Nominal partner:* may pass himself or herself off as a partner, or others may say that he or she is a partner but is not an active partner in any sense

Regular Corporations

The dominant form of business organization is the corporation.[13] Although corporations account for only about one-fifth of business organizations in number, they make up a little less than 90 percent of sales. Although the word *corporation* implies a large business, this is not necessarily the case. Any business of any size may incorporate.

When a business decides to incorporate, it may do so under the laws of one of the 50 states or the District of Columbia. Outside the United States similar organizations are formed under the central government. John Marshall, a renowned Chief Justice of the Supreme Court of the United States, defined a corporation as "an artificial being, invisible, intangible, and existing only in the contemplation of the law."[14] A corporation can, therefore:

1. Make and sell products to customers
2. Buy, hold, and sell property
3. Sue and be sued
4. Commit and be tried and punished for crimes

The major reason why lawyers often recommend the corporate form of organization is limited liability. Investors in the corporation are obligated only for their investment in the corporation.[15] Their homes, other investments, and property are not held legally liable for any debt of the corporation. Another aspect of the corporate form of organization is continuity. Should the corporation prosper, it may outlive its founders. This is because the corporation is a legal person. A corporation is independent of the lives of the founders and may, in theory, go on forever.

Transfer of ownership is another advantage of the corporation. Stock may be purchased or sold. Many corporations are publicly held and traded on organized stock exchanges. There is a market for these shares of stock and a person can buy or sell stock in the company. Owning shares of stock in a company gives the stockholder certain rights. Some of these rights are:[16]

1. To caste one vote per share at stockholder meetings
2. To elect members of the board of directors of the corporation
3. To receive dividends according to the number of shares owned
4. To sell the stock to anyone

Another advantage of the corporate form of organization is the ability to raise money. The corporation raises money by selling stock in the enterprise, or bonds. It can use this money for investment and other activities of the corporation. Corporations are not limited by the assets of partners or the sole entrepreneur. Corporations can raise money from anyone.

There are, however, certain disadvantages in being a corporation. The first is double taxation. The corporation pays taxes on its income and shareholders pay taxes on their dividends as a part of their personal income, so the income of the corporation is taxed twice. The second disadvantage is that corporations are highly regulated by both state and national law. This is because they are a legal fiction, a creation of the law and a person only under the law.

A third disadvantage is the legal complexity of corporations. Legal help is often needed to be sure that the organization is in compliance with the law. This is part of the reason why corporations are far more expensive to form than sole proprietorships or partnerships. Almost all states have requirements that corporations keep extensive records, including financial records, minutes of board meetings, and documentation of business activities.

Owning stock in the corporation does not give shareholders the right to participate in the management of the organization. The only way that shareholders have any influence over the operation of the corporation is through casting their ballots for directors on a yearly basis. Unfortunately, the elections are often meaningless, as management seldom offers an alternative slate of directors to stockholders. Only very large shareholders have any real influence on the corporation, and often, they already have representation on the board of directors.[17]

Subchapter S Corporations

The Subchapter S corporation first appeared in 1958 as a part of the U.S. Internal Revenue Code.[18] Subchapter S corporations avoid double taxation and have the advantage of limited liability. However, there are some very specific legal requirements that must be met by Subchapter S Corporations:

1. Nonresident aliens cannot be shareholders.
2. Corporations cannot be shareholders.
3. Only individuals and estates can be shareholders.
4. There can be no more than 35 shareholders.
5. It must be owned and managed independently and not part of another corporation.
6. No more than 25 percent of the operating sales revenues can come from dividends, royalties, annuities, interest, rents, or stock sales.
7. Revenue from foreign nations is limited to 80 percent.

1244 Corporations

Congress passed the 1244 section of the U.S. Internal Revenue Code to encourage investment in small businesses. Under this legislation, should a small business go bankrupt, the investment in the company can be treated as an ordinary loss for tax purposes, up to $50,000 a year. Among the many stipulations for a 1244 corporation are:

1. Only $1 million can be raised for the new venture through common stock sales.
2. Stock must be issued for cash or property.
3. Stock cannot be issued in exchange for services.
4. Tax breaks apply only to individuals.

THE ROLE OF SMALL BUSINESS ■ ■ ■

Small business is where every large business starts. IBM, Exxon, and Ford all started as small businesses. An entrepreneur had an idea, a concept, that he or she was able to turn into a profitable business. Small businesses have been around a very long time, since ancient times.

During the 1980s small businesses began to be recognized as a remarkable engine of innovation and employment. Unburdened by the bureaucracy of large organizations, although often underfunded, small businesses have been able to invent and develop new ideas for products and services that larger corporations often seem unable to do. In addition, as the Fortune 500 actually decreased in size in terms of number of people employed during the 1980s,[19] small businesses have increased and flourished in number and more than made up for the difference. The growth of U.S. industry has always been in the area of small business.

The United States is unique among Western industrialized countries in its attempt to help and assist entrepreneurs. The Small Business Administration was established with the idea of helping entrepreneurs enter into business and remain in business.[20] The grim fact is that most small businesses fail in the first year, but entrepreneurs keep trying, despite the odds for success being against them.

Small businesses have many strengths:

1. Nearly all of the businesses in the United States could be defined as small businesses—over 20 million.
2. Small businesses usually outearn big businesses.
3. Small businesses can usually respond more rapidly than big businesses.
4. Small businesses allow innovation.
5. Small businesses create jobs.
6. Big businesses are dependent on small businesses for products and services.

On the other hand, small businesses do have certain weaknesses in addition to their high failure rate. Often, they are undercapitalized, which can easily

■ ■ ■ **BOX 7.1   The DeLorean Motor Company** ■ ■ ■

John DeLorean was president of the Pontiac Division of General Motors Corporation when he left GM to found the DeLorean Motor Company. The company eventually produced a two-seater sports car at its factory in Northern Ireland, but even while the car was being produced, the company was in trouble. Underfinanced and often suffering from a certain amount of inattention from its founder, the company was in financial trouble from the start. Also, the car had many problems and suffered from a number of manufacturing defects that were expensive to fix.

DeLorean needed new financing but the banks were very reluctant to extend the new automaker additional credit and DeLorean was desperate. DeLorean tried to solve his problems by dealing in cocaine. Unfortunately, the people he was dealing with were not drug dealers but federal law enforcement officers engaged in a sting operation. DeLorean was caught on videotape buying drugs, and although he did not go to jail as a result of his appeal, his company fell apart and the jobs, products, and hope that he had helped to bring to Northern Ireland came to an end.

lead to failure. They are also subject to bad management. Just because someone has been a successful manager in a corporate environment does not mean that they will be successful in operating their own firm. John DeLorean, who was the president of the Pontiac Division of General Motors, discovered a very different world when he started his own automobile manufacturing company.

In the future, small businesses are going to have to be international in scope. Given the fact that over 30 percent of the gross national product is tied directly to international trade,[21] it will be almost impossible for any organization to stay out of the international arena as either a buyer or seller of goods and services or perhaps both. As communication and transportation become better, so will the web of international commerce, and small businesses and entrepreneurs are going to be a part of that growth.

BOX 7.2   Small Business Ethics

Historical Perspective

While dominating the business news, the issue of ethics in business is certainly not new. The ethical performance of business owners is a very old concern. Warnings of local merchants who cheated their patrons have been found scribbled on Egyptian pyramids. Rigged scales robbing buyers of the full measure of their purchase were such a pervasive problem throughout history among all cultures that they came to symbolize the problem. (Today, the "scales of justice" represent our country's judicial system and symbolize the fairness and impartiality with which justice is meted out.) Although small businesses flourished globally throughout most of history, consumers were often cheated and defrauded. The warning "caveat emptor" became a universally acknowledged standard of business transactions.

Over time, laws were increasingly developed to protect consumers. Hammurabi, King of Babylon, issued a group of 300 laws that governed the proper conduct of both small business owners and patrons. The code is perhaps best known for the severity of punishment involved in violating these laws—often, death.

Small Business as Economic Driver

Frequently objects of suspicion and scorn throughout history, small businesses are viewed very differently in today's world. Results of a poll conducted for *Business Week* by Harris and Associates in 1995 reveal that Americans have considerably more faith in the people running small businesses than they do in those running major institutions, including big business, religious institutions, news media, and all levels of government.

Due to major restructuring in our economy during the past several decades, small businesses have taken on new importance. The amazing pace of technology has engendered numerous new industries and altered the foundations of established businesses, both creating new jobs and eliminating old jobs and procedures. Global competition has had a similar effect on jobs, especially in the field of manufacturing. Furthermore, with the merger mania and corporate restructuring of the 1980s and 1990s and the devastating shakeout of jobs that ensued, small business became the engine that drove the economy.

In many cases, the "downsized" employees were hired by small businesses; in others, they formed their own businesses, sometimes partnering with former co-workers. Many of these new business owners pioneered developments in technology (such as in software and drug development) and in business structure (such as in franchising systems and "virtual company" configurations). In

BOX 7.2   *(continued)*

any case, small businesses (which we define as those with 500 or fewer employees, according to the U.S. Small Business Administration definition) provided the jobs for those previously in the corporate world. According to the SBA, small business created 45 percent of the nation's new jobs between 1986 and 1988. Of the new jobs generated from 1970 to 1990, small business created 66 percent. This trend continued in 1993, with small businesses creating 71 percent of total new jobs. With over 99 percent of the nation's 21.5 million nonfarm businesses considered small, yet generating 54 percent of the sales revenue and 40 percent of the GNP and employing approximately half of the nation's work-force, the importance of this industry sector to the nation's economy cannot be overstated.

Defining Ethics in Small Business

Ethics is concerned with "doing the right thing." The ethical conduct of a business and its employees is sometimes written into the company's mission statement or business plan, a guideline to strive for in all its dealings. Sometimes a code of ethics is incorporated into a company's employee handbook, explaining the kinds of behavior that will not be tolerated and instructing employees in procedures to follow should they witness or be the victims of unacceptable workplace behavior. Indeed, as employees of all sizes of businesses increasingly take their employers to court, employers are taking increasing pains to document the standards of proper conduct that they expect on the part of their employees. They also specify the limits and measures of their own obligations to their employees.

Ethics in the small business workplace, then, is a two-way street. Both employees and employers have obligations to each other in fulfilling their respective roles. The employee is obligated to perform the work that he or she was hired to do in a manner acceptable to the employer. The employer is responsible for providing the employee with safe and adequate means with which to perform the work, and to compensate the employee according to the work performed.

Although the employee's obligations to the employer are limited to that relationship, the employer or small business owner operates within a wider context in which he or she is ethically responsible. What responsibilities must all small business owners fulfill?

1. *Economic responsibility:* obligation to maintain the health of the business itself, not to fail, to be profitable
2. *Employee responsibility:* obligation to provide employees with a safe working environment, adequate resources to perform the work, fair compensation, rewards based on merit
3. *Social responsibility:* obligation to the community within which the business operates not to pollute the environment, to pay taxes, to provide the product or service advertised, not to cheat customers or the government

Source: Modified from Myra Kostick.

THE ROLE OF THE MULTINATIONAL FIRM   ■ ■ ■

Not all large companies are multinational organizations, but many are. In today's economy it is almost impossible to be in business and not be involved to some degree outside the home country. Even electrical power companies are involved in power grids that cross national borders. Once an organization engages in foreign direct investment (FDI) it becomes a multinational enterprise.

This investment can be in as few as two countries or as many countries as there are on the Earth. FDI occurs when a company invests directly in new plant and equipment to produce a good in a foreign country.[22] This is more than renting space in an office building for a sales office to sell goods made in the home country. It involves a real commitment on the part of the organization to the country and to the market.

In the world economy, the role of the multinational firm is to bring the blessings of a technologically advanced society to other parts of the world. Successful multinational firms are ones that think globally but act locally. They have businesses in a number of countries, and each society is unique. This brings with it certain risks and rewards.

One of the first rewards for multinational firms is the ability to increase sales to a greater degree than they would be able to in Japan or even in a united Europe, which although they represent very large markets in and of themselves, are still rather small compared to the entire world market. Competing on a global basis simply offers more opportunity for sales than does competing only domestically.

A second advantage of the multinational corporation is the opportunity to learn from a broader base of employees and customers than is possible domestically. These customers can provide the organization with new markets, and in filling those needs, the employees can develop new ideas for products and services, which may then be transferred to other areas of the corporation.

A third opportunity is that the organization may actually grow faster outside the home market than it will grow domestically. Once an organization is close to reaching market saturation, growth can only come from outside the home country or with a different segment of the market. McDonald's is a classic example of this situation. Although there may be a few places in the United States that could support a McDonald's that do not already have one, there are not as many as there used to be. This leaves McDonald's with one of several choices: It can either find some other type of business to go into that may or may not be related to fast food, or it can expand its fast-food operations outside North America. McDonald's has chosen to establish fast-food restaurants in a variety of countries while trying experiments with different food items and different locations for its restaurants. The real growth prospects for McDonald's are outside the United States.

It is only fair to mention that multinational firms face greater risks in doing business outside the United States or Japan or Western Europe than they do in their home country. One major risk is the foreign exchange rate. The value of currencies is allowed to float against other currencies in the foreign exchange markets. An American dollar may buy 100 Japanese yen one day and three days later may buy only 90 Japanese yen. This means that the value of the American dollar has declined relative to the Japanese yen. Conversely, if after three days the American dollar can purchase 110 yen, the Japanese yen has declined in value relative to the American dollar. For Japanese or American organizations doing business in each other's countries, this is a serious consideration. Currency fluctuations can wipe out hard-earned profits. American firms do not pay their bills with Japanese yen in the United States, and vice versa—they use their home currency. There are techniques, such as hedging, that can be used to guarantee a particular exchange rate at a future time, but the situation remains risky.

BOX 7.3 Big MacCurrencies

For the past several years, *The Economist* has published an article on "Big MacCurrencies" as an indication of how well a particular country is doing versus the rest of the world. Although currencies may fluctuate over a period of time, this does not indicate very much about how a country may be doing, and what the cost and standard of living may be. A Big Mac, however, is the same "two all-beef patties, special sauce, lettuce, cheese, pickles, and onion on a sesame seed bun" anywhere in the world. The concept is based on the idea of purchasing power parity (PPP). The question is: How much of a person's purchasing power in a particular country does it take to purchase a Big Mac?

Country	Price in Local Currency	Implied PPP of the U.S. Dollar	Actual Exchange Rate, 10/4/92	Percent over (+) or under (−) Valuation of U.S. Dollar
Argentina	Peso3.30	1.51	0.99	−34
Australia	A$2.54	1.16	1.31	+13
Belgium	BFr1.08	49.32	33.55	−32
Brazil	Cr3,800	1735	2153	+24
Britain	£1.74	0.79	0.57	−28
Canada	C$2.76	1.26	1.19	−6
China Yuan	6.30	2.88	5.44	+89
Denmark	DKr27.25	12.44	6.32	−49
France	FFr18.10	8.26	5.55	−33
Germany	DM4.50	2.05	1.64	−20
Holland	Fl5.35	2.44	1.84	−24
Hong Kong	HK$8.90	4.06	7.73	+91
Hungary	Forint1.33	60.73	79.70	+31
Ireland	IL1.45	0.66	0.61	−8
Italy	Ure4,100	1872	1233	−34
Japan	Y380	174	133	−24
Russia	Rouble58	26.48	98.95	+253
Singapore	S$4.75	2.17	1.65	−24
South Korea	Won2,300	1050	778	−26
Spain	Ptas315	114	102	−29
Sweden	Skr25.50	11.64	5.93	−49
United States	$2.19	—	—	—
Venezuela	BS170	77.63	60.63	−22

Source: "Big MacCurrencies," *The Economist,* April 18, 1992. Reprinted with permission.

A second consideration in international business is the laws of the country.[23] The legal systems are highly advanced in both the United States and most Western European countries, but that does not mean that they are the same. The basis of U.S. law is English common law, while most non-English-speaking countries subscribe to other schools of law. An example of the difference between English common law and the Napoleonic Code, which is used in most of Europe and most former non-English or non-U.S. colonies, in that under the

English system the accused is considered innocent until proven guilty. Under the Napoleonic Code the accused is considered guilty until able to prove his or her innocence. The burden of proof is on the accused.

A third problem in international business is the problem of political risk,[24] although this aspect of international trade has probably been reduced with the end of the Cold War and the outbreak of capitalism in former socialist and communist countries. The risk remains and could increase in the future. Changes in the political environment can bring on changes in the attitude of the local government toward multinational firms. The assets of U.S. firms, as well as firms from other countries, have been nationalized in the past with little or no recourse on the part of the companies. U.S. assets have been nationalized in Mexico, Cuba, and Vietnam, to name a few. The Helms–Burton bill is an attempt to punish Cuba and non-U.S. companies using nationalized U.S. assets in Cuba, but the legality of such legislation remains in doubt. Nations are sovereign and can do whatever they want inside their own country short of crimes against humanity and genocide, but other countries need to have the political will to stop crimes against humanity and genocide: something that did not happen in Turkey with the Armenians, in Cambodia, in China with the Tibetans, in Nazi Germany, and most recently in Serbia, Kosovo, and a number of nations in Africa.

The multinational enterprise (MNE) is certainly going to be a form of business for the future. Large MNEs are going to continue to seek markets in which to expand and grow. The search for these opportunities will be enhanced as markets in the developed world become saturated and growth becomes tied more and more to the growth of the society.

THE SCOPE OF BUSINESS RESPONSIBILITY ■ ■ ■

Just exactly how much responsibility does an organization have to its various stakeholders, and who are the stakeholders of an organization? The easy answer, of course, is that everyone is a stakeholder of an organization, but that is too simple and too imprecise. To discuss the scope of business responsibility rationally, it is first necessary to ask the question, "Responsible to whom?"

The first and most obvious responsibility of any business organization is to its stockholders. This is a legal requirement of the business. The stockholders own the business. They have invested their hard-earned money in the business, and management has the responsibility and legal obligation to try to protect and enhance that investment through profits, dividends, and growth of the company. Management has the primary obligation of ensuring the survival of the company and protecting the assets of the shareholders. Management's failure to do so will result in the death, bankruptcy, or dissolution of the organization. It is through the board of directors that the shareholders, in theory, make their influence felt. But unfortunately, the reality is that oversight by the board of directors over the firm's managers is often only theoretical at best.[25]

A second area of responsibility for a corporation is to its customers. A company has a variety of obligations to customers. First, if a customer is not satisfied with your product, he or she can go down the street to your competitor. This represents one of the wonderful aspects of capitalism: If one does not like a product or service, he or she can always go to the next company and buy its product instead. It is the obligation of a corporation to fulfill the needs of customers in the best possible way that it can. The customer, on the other hand, has the right to expect that a company's products or services will meet his or her needs in an appropriate and cost-effective manner while allowing the business to make a reasonable profit for stockholders. In the free marketplace, prices are kept down by competition, and companies are constantly at war with one another to convince the customer that their product is best.

A third stakeholder in an organization are its employees. All employees have an interest in the success of a firm because if the company goes out of business, the employees will lose their jobs, their source of income, and perhaps even their homes. This lesson has been brought home by the empty factories that fill once-prosperous industrial towns and cities not only in the United States but in other developed countries. When the means of production in these plants became sufficiently obsolete that the plants were no longer competitive, even in their home market, the plants closed and the employees were put out of work.

Organizations do have an obligation to their employees to try to remain competitive in the marketplace. This ties directly into the interests of the stockholders, and although this may not be a particularly popular fact for management in this current atmosphere of antiunion and antilabor sentiment, it remains a fact. One of the things that Henry Ford understood intuitively when he went into the business of mass producing automobiles was that the person who made the model T was the person who was probably going to buy the model T. His customers and his workers were one and the same. Some companies, even entire industries, have lost sight of that, and in the search for greater profits and cheaper labor have moved production offshore in an effort to maximize profit and minimize costs. The result has been the removal of low-skilled, relatively high-paying jobs from industrialized countries to the less industrialized countries.

One of the problems that has plagued American industry over the past 20 years has been this disconnect in the minds of managers between customers and employees. Management often sees them as two distinct groups, and although the employees may, in fact, be a subset of the customer base, all the customers are the employees of all the corporations.

A fourth group of stakeholders in the organization are the suppliers. For the supplier of raw materials and component parts, the organization represents the customer, and like all organizations, suppliers' have a vested interest in the

---

■ ■ ■   **BOX 7.4   Nike Shoes**   ■ ■ ■

Nike, the maker of athletic footwear, had been highly criticized for its production methods outside the United States. Nike had subcontracted most of its production to companies located outside the United States, mostly in Asia. Workers were paid starvation wages and the working conditions were terrible. Nike was criticized for this, but explained that it had little control over its subcontractors and that many of them were operating within the law of a particular country.

Although privately held, Nike is estimated to have very high profits. The fact is that a pair of shoes that sells at retail for over $100 costs about $10 to produce. The rest is profit, advertising, and distribution costs. Nike has finally responded to the waves of criticism by canceling its contracts with the most flagrant suppliers and shifting production to other firms.

stability, fate, and future of their customers, as do the suppliers' employees, stockholders, and suppliers. The arrangement is reciprocal. The organization has an interest in the stability, fate, and future of their suppliers. This is something the Japanese realized some time ago with the development of the Keirtsu, which represents a reciprocal relationship between the companies in a group.[26] Suppliers have a stake in the fate of their customers, and their customers have a stake in the fate of their suppliers.

An additional responsibility of the organization is to the community at large. This can be done on the local, regional, national, or international level. Organizations have an obligation to the community in which they reside. If nothing else, they have the responsibility of being a good citizen in that community. It means helping when they can and not being on the receiving end of governmental largess. This is, of course, a very unpopular position with many businesspeople, who have their hands out to the government looking for one tax break after another. Corporations routinely demand tax abatements and other concessions from communities to locate or keep facilities in their towns, states, or regions, and they often get them. Sewer lines are laid to be able to hookup to the sewer system without cost to the company. Traffic interchanges are built on the interstate at no cost to the corporation. It is not unknown for companies to obtain financing through government-guaranteed bonds and when the situation changes, to leave a municipality with the debt and no business or jobs to show for it.

Managers need to be responsible citizens in both their private and their organizational lives. If they refuse to exercise this responsibility, it weakens the social contract that binds everyone in the society, the organization, and the managers who make those decisions.

Business also has an obligation to the environment and to keep the environment clean whenever possible.[27] Pollution is a problem that plagues the industrialized world, and much of that pollution is a result of the industrial

BOX 7.5   Henry Cisneros and San Antonio

Many companies and organizations hold themselves and the jobs they bring with them out for the highest bidder. They are often looking for tax abatements and other forms of free support from the cities, counties, and towns in which they are considering locating. For example, the NCAA recently decided to move from near Kansas City to Indianapolis, Indiana. The state of Indiana and the city of Indianapolis put together a package that was worth $10 million more than the people in Kansas City offered, and that was enough to convince the NCAA to move to Indiana.

Henry Cisneros did not play that game. As mayor of San Antonio, he went looking for organizations that wanted to be a part of the city and the community, who were interested in what they could contribute to the community and to be a part of the community, not in what the community and the city would give them in terms of special tax breaks and other considerations.

Cisneros refused to get involved in bidding wars for companies and jobs, and the strategy worked. During Cisnero's terms as mayor, San Antonio was one of the fastest-growing cities in the United States and became one of the largest cities in the country—in fact, one of the largest cities in the country without an NFL football team or a major league baseball team. Cisneros and San Antonio succeeded in attracting organizations that wanted to be a part of the community and to assume their own responsibilities to the community.

BOX 7.6   The Housatonic River

One of the most beautiful rivers in all of New England, the Housatonic River, flows south out of the Berkshires of Massachusetts, through the rural areas of Connecticut, and eventually empties into Long Island Sound. Along the way, parts of the Appalachian Trail wander along its banks and cross over the river just a few miles north of Candlewood Lake. The scenery and the river are beautiful, but don't drink the water, and especially, don't eat the fish. The Housatonic is polluted. Among the many unpleasant things floating in the water is an incredible concentration of PCBs, among the deadliest substances known. The PCBs are a legacy from an electrical manufacturing plant in Pittsfield that dumped the chemical into the river for decades, long before it was known how deadly it was. The plant was closed years ago, but its legacy remains, and it will be thousands of years before campers along the Appalachian Trail will be able to drink the water or eat the fish.

process. Pollution is a worldwide problem and is not limited to industry. There are natural sources of pollution, including volcanos and animal by-products, but much of the pollution that can be prevented or at least significantly reduced is human-made. Making things is a messy process and often results in waste and other by-products. Cleaning this waste up is a necessary and important function of the society.

One example of this situation is polychlorinated biphenyls (PCBs).[28] PCBs are inert chemicals and one of the most deadly substances known. For years they were manufactured and used in the electrical industry. During much of this time their deadly properties were unknown, and PCBs became an important pollutant of several rivers in the Northeast. General Electric and other companies that manufactured PCBs did not know that they were dangerous until much of the damage had been done, and there are surely substances currently being discharged into the water and air that are also harmful, but still unknown. On the other hand, Johns-Manville knew in the 1920s that asbestos was dangerous and not only did they do nothing about it but promoted laws requiring that asbestos be used as a fire retardant to coat the insides of many public buildings, especially schools. Executives at Johns-Manville knew that constant exposure to their product was harmful to human life, yet continued to promote the product until it became obvious from known cases of illness among their own employees that something was wrong. The company did not admit anything until the people involved in the decision to hush up the problems were dead.

The cigarette companies are another case in point.[29] For years they have denied the link between smoking and a variety of diseases as well as attempts to market directly to young people. But this case may soon be unraveling, as Liggett and Myers has recently settled with the government and turned over to the Justice Department many records outlining their research and marketing activities. Although the case is bound to be in the court system for years, there are several interesting aspects to this situation:

1. It is reasonable to suspect that the cigarette companies knew how harmful their product was.

2. It is reasonable to suspect that the cigarette companies did market directly to young people.

3. Executives who have made contrary statements to aspects 1 and 2 did so knowingly, before Congress and the courts, under oath, and may if nothing else, be guilty of perjury. It will be interesting to see if there will be any prosecution on this matter.

Corporations are members of the society. This is certainly true under the law, where they have the legal status of a person, but it is also true from the perspective of their role in society. Actions taken by managers of organizations in the name of those organizations have consequences for both the company and society. They affect stockholders; customers; employees; suppliers; communities in which they do business on the local, regional, national, and international levels; and the environment. Managers of organizations who do not recognize this fact are living in a fantasy world of their own creation. It is a dangerous world from the perspective of their organizations and the society because to deny accountability and responsibility is to invite other forces in the society to impose accountability and responsibility on them. It is an invitation to a set of circumstances that most organizations would find to be unpleasant, if not a threat to their very survival.

DEALING WITH GOVERNMENT AND SOCIETY ■ ■ ■

All organizations are a reflection of the leadership and the values of that leadership.[30] If the organization's leadership is honest and trustworthy, the organization will be honest and trustworthy; if not, the organization will not be honest or trustworthy. The leadership of any organization sets the tone and direction and can modify the culture of that organization.

A leader may attempt to lead through words and eloquence, and sometimes fear, but it is through their deeds that the rest of the organization will judge them. To paraphrase an old saying, leaders must not only be able to "talk the talk" but to be truly effective must also "walk the walk." Employees will soon spot a phoney and a hypocrite. Martin Luther King was a tremendously eloquent speaker, but a huge part of his ability to lead the civil rights movement stemmed from the fact that he was in the march and had gone to jail for his convictions. He "talked the talk" and "walked the walk," and the people in the movement knew it.

An example of leadership on the corporate level is Lee Iacocca, who took over as chairman of Chrysler Corporation[31] when Chrysler was in danger of going out of business. Things were so bad that Iacocca later admitted that if he had known the severity of the situation, he would not have taken the job.[32] But once in the job, he determined that he would do everything in his power to save the company. This meant cutting costs, people, and products; indeed everything had to be cut back. Once he realized how bad things were at Chrysler, he took a step that most CEOs would not dream of taking. He signed a contract as CEO for $1 per year. In addition, there were some incentives that were contingent on his success in saving the company, but only on his success in saving the company. In fairness, it should be mentioned that Iacocca was a wealthy man by most standards and could afford not to work, so the compensation of $1 per year posed no hardship for him or his family. What it did do, however, was to give Iacocca the moral authority to go to other members of the organization and ask them to take a 10 or 20 percent cut in pay. He could then go to the rank-and-file employees and their families and say that he was making a sacrifice far greater than he was asking of most of them, that they were all in this together, and that the important thing was to save the company and the jobs that went along with it. Martin Luther King, sitting in the Birmingham, Alabama jail and writing letters, and Lee Iacocca, taking a dollar a year in salary from the Chrysler Corporation during its darkest moment, were both equipped with moral authority as a result of their actions. They led by doing and showing others that they were willing to make sacrifices; that their values were not only the ones they preached, but the ones they were prepared to live by.

Leaders who have moral authority have the ability to institute change in an organization. An organization's leadership that lacks moral authority or has little of it will find it difficult to institute change or will be forced to resort to fear and threats to accomplish its goals. The accomplishment of these goals is likely to be highly transitory, as the employees are simply likely to try to wait out the current management. Sometimes this attitude is referred to as a "bunker mentality," "hunkering down," or being "passive aggressive." Whatever the name, the results are the same. Organizations that are poorly led are organizations that find change difficult, and poorly led organizations are those whose managements lack moral authority.

FRAMEWORK FOR STRATEGIC MANAGEMENT ■ ■ ■

Strategic management, a process by which management of an organization determines the future, takes place in an arena of uncertainty.[33] The idea behind strategic management is to determine the direction of an organization. If the organization does not do that, its competitors will, and it is unlikely that the firm will like what they have in mind.

The first step in the process is to determine the mission of the organization.[34] Another way to put this is to ask the question: "What business are we in?" The goals and objectives of the organization derive from the answer to this question.

Goals and objectives are similar but very different things. Goals are hopeful statements about the future. Objectives are also statements about the future but are observable and measurable. For example, a goal might be to "increase sales"; an objective would be to "increase sales, in terms of number of units, by 10 percent over the next year." The goal leaves the criteria for success unstated; the objective makes the criteria for success explicit. To know whether or not they are successful in accomplishing their mission, organizations need to have objectives.

To create the goals and objectives of an organization, it is first necessary to evaluate the internal strengths and weaknesses of the organization and then to compare those strengths and weaknesses to the opportunities and threats facing the company. This is often referred to as a SWOT (strengths, weaknesses, opportunities, and threats) analysis.[35] Every organization, indeed every human being, is good at something, just as every organization and human being is not so good at something. Knowledge of strengths and weaknesses is an important key to success. To be successful it is necessary to develop and implement those strategies that will build on the strengths of the organization while minimizing the importance of the weaknesses.

The opportunities and threats to an organization are generally outside the organization in the external environment. Identifying those threats and opportunities and then carefully matching them with the strengths of the organization so as to maximize results is the obligation, duty, and trust of senior management. The environment must be scanned and analyzed, and from these factors alternatives need to be selected.

The business of developing major alternative strategies is the purview of senior management. Senior managers are faced with the dilemma of not knowing what the "right" answer may be and not having anyone available to tell them it is the right answer, even if they should stumble upon it. There, in fact, may be no right answer, only answers that, in different ways, are more desirable than others. It is the management function of decision making—to choose—that becomes the next task in strategic management. A strategy has to be chosen, based on the best assessment of the strengths, weaknesses, opportunities, and threats to the organization, and then implemented by the organization.

Strategies are not implemented by senior management; they are implemented by middle- and lower-level employees. For this to happen, employees need to have an understanding of what their role is in the implementation of the plan. They must be able to take ownership of their roles and their part of the process. Failure to do so will lead to disaster for the strategic plan. This is where leadership comes in. Effective leaders are able to instill the members of the organization with the same vision and goals that they have. Dr. King called it a "dream."[36] They are able to take that vision and inspire their people to implement the strategy they have conceived to accomplish the dream. The people are motivated, and a motivated group is capable of accomplishing almost anything.

Finally, there is the issue of evaluation. There are many forms of evaluation. For corporations there is always the profit motive. Although it is a crude standard, profitability remains a useful guide, especially for profit-making organizations. The simple question "Did the company make any money?" is a form of evaluation. There are, however, other forms and standards of evaluation that need attention.[37] These may be in terms of employment, production, or any other accomplishment. The development of a drug that would cure AIDS or even the common cold would be a major accomplishment of any pharmaceutical company, but it is unlikely that this breakthrough would show up immediately in the profitability of the company. Still, no one would deny the importance of such a discovery, or the credit that would be due the organization and the people who made the discovery. By making such a contribution, the organization would have enhanced the quality of life of everyone on the planet. Strictly speaking, this may not add immediate dollars to the corporate bottom line, but society is far better off as a result and so is the organization.

FUTURE ISSUES FOR THE MODERN BUSINESS ENTERPRISE ■ ■ ■

In many ways the functions of the modern business enterprise will be the same in the future as they have been in the past. Businesses will create goods and services, employ people, be generally useful to society, and help to create wealth. In addition, however, business organizations will provide several other functions. The first is that they will serve to further integrate the global society and economy.[38] People from different places will be doing business together and will get to know each other better than they have in the past. Americans and Japanese, for example, will be doing even more business with each other than they are now, and although this may not lead to greater trust, it will certainly lead to less distrust and greater understanding on the part of both societies.

The second function that business is going to perform in the future is related to the first, but is internal to the organization. Industry in all its forms, the way people make their livelihood, will be a great force for integration of a society.[39] The common experience and common ground involved in the work environment will be shared by the vast majority of society. In prior generations, the armed forces provided such a common experience for society. Today, because the armed services are a volunteer force in most countries, they no longer provide a common ground of experience for all citizens. Industry—the art of making a living—does. It will be large and small businesses that will help to integrate the world's population: first, through doing business with each other on an international scale, and second, by having employees of diverse backgrounds working directly with each other in the organization itself. The business enterprise will become the common denominator of human society: the common experience and the common ground of society.

The impact of the organization on society, and vice versa, cannot be overemphasized. The capitalist system is the model that is being used or adapted in most of the world. Even in former communist bloc countries, many formerly state-owned industries are being privatized as fast as governments can do it. A reasonable prediction is that business organizations will be one of the primary forms of organization in society, if for no other reason because that is where the vast majority of the labor force spends its productive time.

Industry is the engine that drives all of the rest of society. It is the locomotive that pulls other institutions along, including government, not-for-profit, and others. Without industry, there is no production, profit, wages, or anything else to tax, and there is certainly no surplus to give away. Industry provides the means for everything else. Industry, particularly industry under capitalism, is a great dynamic wealth generator that makes the rest possible.

Today, in the United States at least, industry seems to be heading in two very different directions. The first is toward the multinational enterprise: huge corporations doing business all over the globe. In the United States, these firms include such companies as Ford, Exxon, and IBM. But this is not just an American phenomenon. Other economics have also spawned multinational organizations: Fiat (Italy), Shell (Royal Dutch Petroleum), and NEC (Nippon Electric Company), to name only a few.

The other direction is toward the small entrepreneurial organization. This is particularly true in the United States, but it is a growing part of economies all over the world. These small organizations employ most of the labor force and are absolute hotbeds of technological innovation and creativity. They are far more nimble than the multinationals when trying to compete in the marketplace, and they represent the future for most people entering the labor force.

Finally, one of the questions that is beginning to be raised about multinational organizations is whether or not these organizations have become a political power in and of themselves. Several large multinational organizations have gross sales greater than the gross domestic products of some fairly large Western European countries. They are subject to the conflicting laws of so

BOX 7.7 The Twenty Top Corporations in the Fortune International 500

Corporation	Country	Revenue (millions of dollars)
General Motors	United States	168,369.0
Ford Motor	United States	146,991.0
Mitsui	Japan	144,942.8
Mitsubishi	Japan	140,203.7
Itochu	Japan	135,542.1
Royal Dutch Petroleum	United Kingdom/Netherlands	128,174.5
Marubeni	Japan	124,026.9
Exxon	United States	119,434.0
Sumitomo	Japan	119,281.3
Toyota Motor	Japan	108,702.0
Wal-Mart	United States	106,147.0
General Electric	United States	79,179.0
Nissho Iwai	Japan	78,921.2
Nippon Telegraph and Telegraph	Japan	78,320.7
IBM	United States	75,947.0
Hitachi	Japan	75,665.0
AT&T	United States	74,525.0
Nippon Life Insurance	Japan	72,575.0
Mobil	United States	72,267.0
Daimler-Benz	Germany	71,589.3

Source: "Fortune's global five hundred," *Fortune*, August 4, 1997.

many legal jurisdictions that they are, in fact, subject to none of them. They have power in society that often far outweighs their true importance.

The problem is probably best illustrated by the oil companies and the conflict between the Arab states and the Western democracies in the form of the oil crisis in the early 1970s. Although most of the oil companies were either American or European in origin, the Organization of Petroleum Exporting Countries (OPEC) restricted the availability of oil to the West in an effort to get the Western democracies, particularly the United States, to change certain policies, especially the relationship with Israel. Although this effort failed in the United States, the situation did provide a useful illustration of the circumstances facing the oil companies as multinational enterprises. Essentially, the oil companies were caught between countries with very different interests. They had huge stakes in both camps. Although they were chartered as U.S. or European firms, their business interests had spread out so that they were now an important part of many societies and economics. The United States was frequently the largest market for their products but by no means the only market and usually represented less than half of their total sales. OPEC said "do not ship the oil" and for the most part, the oil companies complied with OPEC's demands, causing the price of oil to jump and Western economics to stall. Virtually all of these decisions were made by U.S. or European citizens, who put the interests of one group of countries ahead of those of their own countries. Although no one was prosecuted for this, the question remains: Why did the leaders of the oil companies accede to the demands of OPEC? Perhaps the answer is in the explanation that executives did what they thought would be best for their companies. If that is the case, given how large, powerful, and productive these multinational organizations are, are these executives citizens of the United States, the United Kingdom, or Japan, or are they now the citizens of General Motors, Unilever, or Hitachi?

SUMMARY

Capitalism is based on the idea of private property and economic incentive. In theory, at least, these two factors result in a free market, where goods and services can be bought and sold to the highest bidder. Capitalism and the free market system imply choice, and free markets for goods and services soon lead to free markets for ideas. Few capitalist systems have existed for long without some form of political choice. People who have become accustomed to choices in what they buy will soon expect to have choices in what they think, and that is what democracy is all about.

The modern corporation is an integral part of society. There are two main trends in business today. The first is toward the global, multinational enterprise, and the second is toward small business. Although one might view the multinational enterprise as the eventual flowering of capitalism, small business would certainly be the seed for that flower. Virtually all large organizations started as small ones. Small business is where it all begins, and while the multinational may be the engine for the global integration of the world's economy, small companies are where most people work and where technological innovation and creativity are most likely to occur.

Wherever they do business, organizations must learn to deal with the laws, government, and politics, as well as other aspects of the society. This means being able to accept change and to capitalize on it. A key to the success of any organization is going to be the leadership of the organization. Their values, honesty, integrity, and judgment will be reflected in how the company does business and the course of action the firm chooses to follow. That course of action is the strategic plan of the company. It involves the mission, the goals, and the objectives of the corporation. Top management's job is to analyze the strengths and weaknesses of the organization and to match them to the opportunities presented in the environment. At the same time, senior management is responsible for minimizing the potential threats to the company by choosing the strategy that is most likely to achieve the objectives of the organization. Making choices is the essence of what a manager does, and seeing to the implementation of those choices is how a manager spends much of his or her time.

Managers and their organizations do not operate in a vacuum, and there is more to the responsibility of the manager than simply attempting to make a profit for shareholders. Managers and their organizations have a responsibility to the society at large, but especially to their employees, customers, suppliers, and communities. They have an obligation to be good citizens in their communities in the widest possible sense of the term.

In addition to all the functions that corporations have traditionally performed in society of providing goods and services, jobs for employees, and a return on the investment of their stockholders, they now perform the additional function of integrating the global and domestic society. The global economy will be knit more closely together as world trade and the activities of multinational corporations increase in importance. Because of the ever-increasing competitive environment, organizations will be forced to take a more proactive role in integrating the social as well as economic aspects of the society. People will have to be judged on what they bring to and do for the company, not on their gender or color. The competitive environment will be the most demanding and in many ways unforgiving arbiter of what is right and wrong in society. To ignore one group on any level is to invite competitors to be successful and to encourage failure in the marketplace.

Organizations are going to have increasing impact on all societies, especially as more and more of them move to a capitalist form. Years ago, Calvin Coolidge said that "The business of America is business." He was right then; he is right today; and he is becoming more and more right on a worldwide basis. Industry is the primary form of organized human activity. It provides the basis of and capability for all other forms of human endeavor. It is where the labor force, which usually represents over half of the population, spends most of its time and where society is most likely to develop new forms and new combinations. These forms will be different from the ones currently in use and are likely to be more efficient and better suited for survival in the years ahead.

Questions

1. Explain why ownership is one of the key concepts of capitalism.
2. What is meant by "from each according to his ability; to each according to his need"?
3. Why are private property, economic incentive, and choice such important parts of capitalism?
4. Why do you think that most capitalistic countries are democratic?
5. What are the advantages and disadvantages of a sole proprietorship?
6. What are the advantages and disadvantages of a partnership?
7. What are the advantages and disadvantages of a corporation?
8. What is the role of small business in a modern technological society?
9. What is the role of a multinational corporation in a modern global society?
10. What are some of the problems facing multinational corporations in doing business outside their home markets?
11. Name at least three stakeholders in an organization.
12. How does organizational culture affect a strategic plan?
13. What is the importance of moral authority in leading an organization?
14. How will business organizations serve to further integrate the global society?
15. In what ways are organizations developing outside the current framework of the nation-state?

CASE 1

About a year ago, you and your family moved into a large metropolitan area in the Midwest. As part of furnishing your new home, you discovered that there were no stores selling unfinished furniture in this city. This struck you as strange because where you lived back east, there were seven such stores within 30 miles of your home.

You decided to look into this as a possible business opportunity and started investigating the market and the unfinished furniture industry. As a part of this process you visited stores in a nearby (200+ miles) major city and attended the annual unfinished-furniture show and convention. In addition, you contacted several major companies in the field and were directed by them to their manufacturer's representatives for information and advice.

During this time you developed a business plan and started the process of applying for a Small Business Administration (SBA) loan. You discussed your plans with various manufacturers' representatives in anticipation that you would be ordering inventory from them to stock your store. Some of the manufacturers' representatives were encouraging, and some were not. One manufacturer's representative was initially encouraging but became less so as the discussion progressed.

As soon as you received approval of your loan from the SBA, you telephoned the various companies and representatives you had contacted to tell them that the loan had been approved and you were planning on opening your doors in about eight weeks. When you telephoned the manufacturer's representative who had grown less encouraging, to tell him the good news, he informed you that he was now planning to open a store on the other side of town.

1. Should you have been less forthcoming in your discussions with vendors and manufacturers' representatives?
2. Don't you find it at least odd that the manufacturer's representative was less than enthusiastic about your entering a business that he was going into?
3. What are some lessons to be learned from this experience?

CASE 2

You have a part-time employee who you knew for several years prior to his employment with you. During that time he was the Scout master of your son's Boy Scout troop. Over the years, you have come to know him and his wife and family very well.

It has come to your attention that your employee is having an affair with the treasurer of the Scout troop. Your employee's wife has had enough and has told him to move out, as this is not the first time this sort of thing has happened. The Boy Scouts are quietly pressuring your employee to give up his position as Scout master, and as a member of the troop council, you have been approached by the district to help encourage his resignation.

This has made things very uncomfortable at the business. Your market and the overriding theme of all the advertising you do revolves around family. Family values are very important to your business and to you personally, and this action on the part of your employee has made you very uncomfortable in his presence.

1. How do you handle the situation?
2. Are there any legal consequences for you in this situation?

CASE 3

You are the head of a subsidiary in a foreign country of a major multinational corporation. While relations between the United States and the host country have always been friendly, there have been several issues on which both countries have never agreed: notably, the state of Israel.

Your company has recently appointed a new man as CEO. A highly respected businessman in the United States, the new Jewish CEO has also been very active in supporting the state of Israel through B'nai B'rith and other organizations.

The host country was at war with Israel 20 years ago and looks upon the Jewish state as the devil incarnate. The chief of security of the host country has recently called you in to ask what the new CEO plans for the company in his country and was obviously not pleased with the recent turn of events.

You know that your operation represents the largest non-U.S. division in the company and is very profitable. You also know that the host country is not a democracy and that the concept of "due process" is at best an abstraction.

1. What can you do about the situation?
2. What are some steps you could take to assure the host country?
3. What happens if Israel and the host country go to war again?

References

1. Marx, Karl, *The capital: a critique of political economy*, International Publishers, New York, 1967.
2. Smith, Adam, *An inquiry into the nature and causes of the wealth of nations*, R.R. Smith, New York, 1948.
3. Ibid.
4. Ibid.
5. Marx, *The capital*.
6. Smith, *An inquiry*.
7. Eldridge, William, *Business law: core concepts*, South-Western, Cincinnati, OH, 1995.
8. Ibid.
9. Ibid.
10. Beatty, Jeffrey F., and Susan Samuelson, *Business law for a new century*, Little, Brown, New York, 1996.
11. Ibid.
12. Ibid.
13. Eldridge, *Business law*.
14. Ibid.
15. Beatty, *Business law*.
16. Ibid.
17. Eldridge, *Business law*.
18. Ibid.
19. Comparison: "Fortune 500," *Fortune*, May 5, 1980, and "Fortune 500," *Fortune*, April 23, 1985. Fortune stopped listing total employees after this date. During the period above, employment declined by 2 million in the Fortune 500, or about 15 percent.
20. Willett, Shawn, "Small business no small change," *Computer Reseller News*, June 3, 1997, n. 743.

21. *Statistical Abstract of the United States, 1996,* U.S. Department of Commerce, Washington, DC, 1996.

22. Kim Sun Bac, "Foreign direct investment: gift horse or Trojan horse," *Weekly Letter,* Federal Reserve Bank of San Francisco, March 20, 1992.

23. Stapenhurst, Frederick, "Political risk analysis in North American multinationals: an empirical review and assessment," *International Executive,* March–April 1995.

24. Ibid.

25. Beatty, *Business law.*

26. Mori, Kiyoshi, "Industrial sea change: how changes in Keiretsu are opening the Japanese market," *Brookings Review,* Fall 1994.

27. "Best practice program update," *Safety and Health Practitioner,* September 1997, v. 15., n. 9.

28. Godfrey, Terry J., "Kalman filter method for estimating organic contaminant concentrations in major Chesapeake Bay tributaries," *Environmental Science and Technology,* July 1996.

29. "Selling cigarettes in Asia," *New York Times,* September 10, 1997.

30. Maidment, Fred (ed.), "Perspectives and trends," *Annual editions: management, 1997–1998,* Dushkin/McGraw-Hill, Guilford, CT, 1997.

31. Iacocca, Lee, *Iacocca; an autobiography,* Bantam Books, New York, 1984.

32. Ibid.

33. Eldridge, William, "Where angels fear to tread," in Jack Rubin, Gerald Miller, and W. Bartley Hildreth (eds.), *Handbook of strategic management,* Marcel Dekker, New York, 1989.

34. Ibid.

35. Ibid.

36. King, Martin, "I have a dream," *At testament of hope,* HarperCollins, San Francisco, 1991.

37. Seashore, Stanley, "Criteria of organizational effectiveness,"*Michigan Business Review,* July 1954; in Fred Maidment (ed.), *Annual editions: management, 1997–1998,* Dushkin/McGraw-Hill, Guilford, CT, 1997.

38. Bolt, James F., "Global competitors: some criteria for success," *Business Horizons,* January–February 1988.

39. Ibid.

CURRENT ISSUES FACING GOVERNMENT

8

Concepts : You Will Learn ■ ■ ■

the dilemmas facing government over centralization versus decentralization

traditional areas of U.S. governmental economic regulation and involvement

government regulation of conduct

future issues for government, including privatization, infrastructure, public education, health care, and others

ethical issues facing government

INTRODUCTION

Many of the current issues that affect the business community are similar to the issues that have affected the business community throughout the twentieth century. Government has been seen as necessary to protect the interests of the public since the age of the muckrackers, who exposed a series of wrong doings by businesses.[1] In addition, the ability of many firms to create large trusts that stifled competition to the detriment of the American public caused a flurry of antitrust regulation.[2]

Although it brought a higher degree of prosperity for many citizens, the industrial revolution also brought a host of problems, including severe accidents in the workplace, questionable products containing a variety of defects, foodstuffs of doubtful quality, and unethical practices regarding the sale of securities.

The Great Depression in the 1930s shook the U.S. economic system to its very foundations.[3] Indeed, it often appeared uncertain whether the American free-enterprise system would survive. The totalitarian philosophies that swept through Europe gained some adherents in the United States. The closing of many banks, massive unemployment, and the collapse of many industries necessitated an expanded role for government. Indeed, the federal government was legally charged with managing the economy following the Depression.

A variety of agencies were established to regulate the banks, the money supply, the stock markets, and management–labor relations. The government undertook the responsibility of providing financial assistance to a variety of groups. Many of these programs were expanded after World War II by both Republican and Democratic administrations at all levels of government.

Although these programs were of enormous help to many people, by 1980 many Americans had begun to raise questions about the costs of these government programs and their impact on the business community.[4] The election of President Reagan signaled a conservative shift in the United States toward the desire of a majority of the electorate to curtail or reduce the level of governmental activities. Similar election results occurred in congressional, state, and local elections, and by the early 1990s, a movement toward a more conservative approach to government was taking hold. By the beginning of the 1990s many states were experiencing significant revenue shortfalls. Thus was the stage set for the major government issue of the 1990s, that is, how does society accomplish necessary governmental tasks at a cost that does not overly burden the private sector?

PROBLEMS FACING GOVERNMENTS WORLDWIDE ■ ■ ■

Centralization versus Decentralization   ■ ■ ■

One of the major movements facing governments all over the world is the decentralization of governmental authority.[5] This is particularly the case in the former Soviet Union, but can also be seen in the various nationalist movements in Quebec, Scotland, and India. It means that the executive national center is weakening. As external threats have weakened, the glue that has forged countries made up of different religious and ethnic groups has also weakened in many places.

Yugoslavia is a case in point, being a conglomeration of several distinct ethnic groups that historically have never really gotten along with each other and have stopped fighting only when led by a strong government such as Austro-Hungarian Empire prior to World War I or by a strong leader such as Marshal Tito.[6] After Tito died the country disintegrated into its various ethnic parts. The same is happening in the former Soviet Union. All of the republics have declared some sort of political independence, including Russia herself,[7] and the Soviet Union has ceased to exist. The problem with the former Soviet Union is that like Yugoslavia, it could erupt into fighting, which could lead to civil war between the republics, and the Soviets have nuclear weapons. The dangers and temptations to use nuclear weapons in such a situation might best be understood in the context of the American Civil War, the bloodiest conflict in U.S. history, where no weapon or instrument of war was idle.

People in the world are also demanding and receiving greater political freedom. Although this may not be a problem for Americans or Western Europeans, it means a dramatic change in the way many countries conduct their business. At a recent meeting of heads of state of Latin America, there was only one person in a military uniform—Fidel Castro. All the other military strongmen, whether from the political right or left, were gone—a notable change from the situation a few years ago.

Along with political freedom comes economic freedom. Gorbachev recognized this with his programs of perestroika and glasnost. True economic freedom cannot exist without true political freedom, and vice versa. Each is dependent on and complements the other, because at the heart of each is the same principle: freedom for the individual to choose among products, services, or political candidates and issues. Economic and political freedom cannot be separated. They are really the same.

This drive toward decentralization of authority, and the demand for an increase in political and economic freedom that goes with it, have led to the breakup of the Soviet Empire and pressures on China to reform. The Chinese leadership has resisted, but they have allowed the camel's nose into the tent with experiments in capitalism in Guangdong Province outside Hong Kong.[8] Capitalism, even the experimental Chinese variety, demands the right to choose, and it should not be long before Chinese consumers of products start demanding the same kinds of choices in their government as they will learn to expect in the marketplace.

Trade Blocs

One of the interesting aspects of decentralization in both the political and economic areas has been the movement toward regionalization in international trade. Recent agreements between Canada, Mexico, and the United States, and Europe's move toward economic integration have created great regional economic trading blocs.[9] These blocs should eventually eliminate trading barriers between member states, creating huge open markets for each other's goods and services. This, in turn, will provide consumers of all participating countries with a greater choice of goods and increased competition, making the markets and the participants in them more efficient. The hope is for a higher standard of living for all participants and the creation of critical masses so as to be able to compete with large organizations in other giant markets.

BOX 8.1 Maquiladoraville

All along the U.S.–Mexican border a host of corporations have set up manufacturing facilities on the Mexican side to produce goods for the U.S. market. These organizations are there to take advantage of the much lower Mexican wage rates that allow these companies to produce goods for a fraction of the cost they would have to pay in the United States. Mexican employees of these companies are paid only a fraction of the legal minimum wage in the United States and many manufacturing jobs have left the United States, only to resurface in Mexico.

Although these jobs may be fairly low paying by U.S. standards, they are at least competitive and sometimes better than average for Mexican workers. Unfortunately, this has caused a great strain on the communities along the border because so many Mexicans have moved to this area and the infrastructure of water, roads, sewers, schools, and various government services simply has not been able to keep up with the new arrivals. As a result, Mexican environmental laws, which are usually not as strict as U.S. environmental laws, are observed more by omission than by commission. Add to that the general problem of corruption in the Mexican government, and the environmental picture becomes very difficult. The result of this is that these Mexican workers, who are employed in low-wage jobs, are often living in squalid conditions with no benefits from their employer and no services from their government.

Impact of Multinationals

Movement toward economic regionalization by governments may already be a classic example of "too little, too late." Multinational corporations have already crossed over national boundaries and established themselves in a host of markets. These organizations which at this point may have mostly American, European, or Japanese roots, operate under the laws of each country in which they do business. The decisions they make which involve where to produce, sell, and finance goods and services are made from the perspective of what will be most beneficial to the company, not necessarily the home or host country.

Robert Reich, a former Secretary of Labor, has argued that multinationals owe no national allegiance and that they really are responsible to no one except, perhaps, senior management itself.[10] Because they are regulated by so many different governments with so many different laws and contradictory regulations, they are, in fact, regulated by no one. If a multinational wants to do something that is against the law in one country in which it does business, it simply does it in the country next door. The recent scandals involving BCCI are a case in point. Not everything with which BCCI is charged in the United States is illegal in all the countries where it does business, and some of its business practices that are not illegal in the United States are illegal elsewhere. As Robert Morganthau, the New York District Attorney, whose office brought the first major criminal indictment, has indicated, the biggest single problem in the BCCI case was piecing it all together because the pieces were literally scattered all over the world and there was no general facility that could bring it all together. The illegal practices of BCCI were so complex that the chairman of the Federal Reserve Bank of New York has stated that "on a scale of 1 to 10, 10 being the most complex, it rates about a 15."[11]

TRADITIONAL AREAS OF U.S. GOVERNMENTAL ECONOMIC REGULATION AND INVOLVEMENT ■ ■ ■

Laws and Regulations

In a complex society, there is a need for government to do a variety of tasks. First, government regulation is needed to oversee the activities of sectors of the private economy that are critical to the welfare of the nation. The recent savings and loan debacle is illustrative of what can happen if there is a failure by regulatory authorities. Similarly, the health of the nation's banks and insurance companies is vital to the nation's economy and to the financial well-being of every citizen.[12] As a result, a host of federal and state agencies, including the Federal Reserve, Comptroller of the Currency, state banking boards, insurance commissions, and other entities, have been developed to regulate the well-being of the financial system. Although one can argue about individual regulations or the level of constraint, it is hard to imagine the system surviving without a salutary dose of financial regulation. Indeed, without the protection of depositors' money by MEDIC, the recent savings and loan collapse could have thrown the country into a deep depression similar to that which occurred in the 1930s.

BOX 8.2   The Great Depression

In October 1929, the greatest financial disaster ever to hit the United States happened in the great stock market crash. The crash started the Great Depression of the 1930s, perhaps the toughest economic times in the history of the nation. Other parts of the country had been suffering through bad times prior to 1929, notably the agricultural sector, and many other parts of the world were also having difficult economic times, but the crash was what put everyone in the same situation.

The Great Depression marked the end of the laissez-faire economy, and the actions taken by the federal government in an effort to try to revive the economy mark the beginning of big government in the United States. The alphabet soup of federal agencies that developed in an effort to try to do something about the economy and get it restarted was only one result of the effort. Social Security and many of our most important labor laws were passed during this time. But it was not until World War II, with its demand for armaments and other tools and supplies of war, that the Great Depression finally ended, although the era of big government has continued to the present day.

Similarly, the laws and regulation developed by Congress and the Securities and Exchange Commission have safeguarded the securities markets from many of the unscrupulous practices that plagued the nation during the 1920s and 1930s.[13] Without these safeguards, block trading and the actions of Boesky and Milken may have led to a total collapse of the financial markets. In addition, regulations requiring the filing of prospectuses and audited financial statements have allowed small companies to go public and assisted in generating the entrepreneurial boom of the 1980s and 1990s. Without the public confidence that the SEC regulations have generated in the basic soundness of the securities markets and in individual companies, millions of jobs would not have been created.

Bankruptcy

Bankruptcy is another area that has been left to federal jurisdiction since the writing of the U.S. Constitution. Essentially, bankruptcy statutes give people who have gotten themselves into financial difficulty a fresh start by allowing them to payoff a portion of their debts and to be discharged from the remainder. This is a classic trade-off between the interests of the debtor and those of creditors and the remainder of society who pay their debts.

Corporations may also file for bankruptcy either to liquidate assets and pay off creditors, or to reorganize so as to gain a fresh start at their business. Some corporations have gotten themselves into difficulty because of business downturns, onerous labor contracts, or from a large number of lawsuits relating to product defects. Johns-Manville, which was sued by many people who alleged that they had suffered injuries from asbestos made by the company, is an example of a corporation that filed for bankruptcy in order to gain a fresh start and to sort out the various claims against it.[14]

Other corporations have filed for bankruptcy to cancel labor contracts they believed to be unduly burdensome. This was permitted by the Supreme Court but was later modified by Congress. A more general issue illustrated by these cases is the conflict between the interests of labor unions and management. This

■ ■ ■ BOX 8.3 The Johns-Manville Corporation and Asbestos ■ ■ ■

For decades the Johns-Manville Corporation promoted the use of asbestos in the construction of buildings, especially public buildings, as a fire retardant and aid to insulation. During much of this time the corporation knew that asbestos could become a major health hazard and that the use of this material and its production by Johns-Manville constituted a major potential health hazard, not only for its employees and other workers, but for the nation as a whole.

As evidence against the use of asbestos mounted, the company continued to deny any connection between asbestos and brown lung disease, in much the same way that the tobacco companies would deny any connection between smoking and lung cancer. Finally, with the evidence overwhelmingly against the company, and after the death of the people who had made the decision to promote the use of asbestos in the face of their own research that demonstrated the hazards associated with the product, the company acknowledged its complicity.

The company's actions resulted in two things being set in motion. The first was an effort to remove asbestos from where it had been installed, a terribly expensive process that would eventually cost the country billions of dollars. The second was a cascade of lawsuits against Johns-Manville for knowingly promoting, installing, and manufacturing a hazardous substance and telling its customers, employees, and the government that the product was absolutely safe. The charges against Johns-Manville and the potential claims in the lawsuits filed against the company were so great that the company filed for bankruptcy protection in federal court. This action effectively ended all claims against the company, and the people who filed the lawsuits were left essentially without recourse.

is an issue that permeates much of the legislation which has been passed, modified, and changed since the 1930s.

The entire bankruptcy process also raises the issue of the amount of debt that can safely be carried by individuals, businesses, and governments. A major issue for all three is the willingness of each to mortgage the future to obtain current benefits. Federal deficits in the $400 billion range and tax benefits that accrue for going into debt have offered interesting examples for businesses and individuals in terms of planning their own finances. The amount of debt by businesses and individuals is one that threatens to engulf the economy in the future.

Workers' Compensation

Another issue that arose during the growth of the industrial economy is how the United States dealt with worker injuries received on the job. As they began to accumulate, the legal system dealt with the consequences through the usual mechanisms. This led to an enormous number of lawsuits, complete with allegations of negligence, defenses relating to assumptions of risks, but few recoveries for injured workers. The establishment of a workers' compensation system established a schedule of amounts that allowed workers to gain some remedy for their injuries.

Protection from Faulty Products

A similar issue of increasing importance relates to the staggering number of lawsuits relating to product defects that cause injury to consumers or others. As more and more products are sold to millions of buyers, it is inevitable that some will malfunction and cause personal injury or damage to property. These claims have also been handled through the legal system in the traditional way. This has resulted in multimillion-dollar verdicts, large legal fees, and enormous costs for manufacturers and others, including consumers involved in the process. Many people have questioned whether the costs of all this litigation have hurt U.S. competitiveness in the world's economy.[15] Other means of resolving these disputes have been suggested, including arbitration, which would protect the rights of the injured while reducing the costs to the manufacturer of products.

Similar issues have been raised with respect to drugs and other health-related products. Although it has been a traditional role of government to ensure their safety, the costs of testing them and defending lawsuits has substantially increased the price to buyers. In addition, drug companies have argued that some beneficial products cannot be brought to market because of the cost involved. The issue for government, business, and society may be to provide the proper balance between safety, costs, and the beneficial aspects that such products have for the vast majority of users.

Antitrust Enforcement

Antitrust enforcement also remains an interesting governmental issue as we move into the next century. Many of these statutes were passed to prevent actions by private companies that might tend to lessen competition substantially. Although they are necessary to prevent overreaching by large companies, many have questioned whether they tend to reduce the economic efficiencies that come with size. Those analysts point to the enormous Japanese conglomerates and argue that American companies cannot compete if they are excessively limited by overzealous antitrust regulations. Again, this question represents an interesting trade-off between effective regulation and economic costs and efficiency.

Although the merger mania of the 1980s seems to have passed, the issue of the extent of enforcement of antitrust statutes is likely to remain important as companies seek to find economic efficiencies. An important area is the banking industry, where U.S. financial institutions have lost their ability to compete and need to reduce costs.[16] The merger of Chemical Bank and Chase Manhattan is likely to be a precursor of other mergers of financial institutions.

As noted above, the federal government has been given the task of fine-tuning our nation's economy to maintain prosperity. One issue is how to accomplish this task in a political environment. Often, leaders play with economic controls immediately prior to elections. Although this may lead to short-term prosperity, it can also lead to longer-term distortions such as the large federal deficits that threaten future economic growth.

Housing

A related issue is the nation's housing policy. Traditionally, the American Dream was for a family to own their own home. Although this applied to areas in both the cities and suburbs, this is now more likely to apply to suburban homes. The government has supported the dream through tax deductions for interest on mortgages. With the increased urban density and rising housing prices, the dream and governmental policy may need to be reconsidered to reflect different living conditions, family structure, and economic conditions.

GOVERNMENT REGULATION OF CONDUCT

Governments have always been charged with prohibiting and punishing certain conduct of which society disapproves or believes is harmful. This was normally accomplished through the criminal law, which prohibited certain activities and imposed certain penalties for violating these laws.

Criminal Law

Although most people tend to think of criminal law in terms of common law felonies, such as murder, rape, or robbery, it also applies to business-related crimes such as embezzlement, fraud, insider trading, and others. Indeed, many of the more famous cases in recent years have involved business conduct that violated criminal law. Insider trading, stock manipulation, and violations of pollution laws are also crimes.[17] Traditionally, criminal legislation tended to codify the morality standards as expressed by our Judeo-Christian tradition. As a result, people are aware that some of the Ten Commandments have become part of the law, such as the prohibitions against killing people or stealing money. Certain sexual conduct also violates the law, although these prohibitions are less likely to be enforced.

Controlled Substances

Restrictions against the use of drugs, alcohol, tobacco, or gambling also reflects this tradition. Similarly, taxes on these products as a source of revenues also reflects a sense of the public that certain conduct is sinful and, if permitted, at least ought to be expensive. Although certain conduct is permitted for adults, it has always been seen as the law's function to protect minors by proscribing similar conduct by or to them.

Abortion

The issue of abortion is also one of whether the law should prohibit conduct that some people believe unethical but others believe not. Related questions address issues of public funding or permissible counseling by public health professionals and are also tied into the tradition of codifying the nation's sense of morality.

The issue of abortion and the prohibition of certain drugs has many parallels in U.S. history. The most common example is the Thirteenth Amendment, prohibiting the manufacture and sale of alcohol in the United States during the 1920s. The experiment is widely regarded by historians as having been a failure. People drank alcohol despite the laws. Bootleggers made and sold alcohol despite attempts to stop them. Corruption was rampant. There were turf battles and killings among rival factions of organized crime and the public developed a general disrespect for law. After about a decade, the country had decided that it had made a mistake and repealed the experiment in the Twenty-first Amendment. It will be interesting to observe whether history will repeat itself.

Environmental Control   ■ ■ ■

More recently, the various levels of government have also begun to deal with the issue of environmental pollution. Previously, almost any type of manufacturing progress was welcomed in the United States. Even smokestack pollution was seen as creating wealth and jobs. Few people worried that the smoke might be disturbing the environment. Indeed, few people even thought about the environment.

The same point of view prevailed with respect to the development of land. For many years, government and the law favored the development of as much land as possible. Fallow land was regarded as inefficient land. Again, almost any development was seen to be creating economic growth and producing jobs. As a result, the use of the land was often haphazard and overdeveloped in some areas.

In this century, people became concerned that overdevelopment of the land and unregulated economic growth were harming the environment as well as the land. The states began to develop zoning powers that allowed local governments to formulate master plans for the development of their communities and to regulate the types and density of use of the land. This permitted a more orderly development of our nation's real estate within each of the states.

Similarly, the federal and state governments began to address the problems associated with pollution of the environment. A multitude of laws and regulations were passed to control emissions into the air and water. Although these tended to reduce the level of pollution, they also added to the cost of producing products. Many company executives argued that the costs of environmental protection had become excessive. With the discovery of a large number of toxic waste sites throughout the country, the federal and state governments were left with the task of trying to clean them up. Generally, the states have looked toward the federal government, which did not have enough funding to solve the problem. As a result, the states have had to find the funds by taxing companies as well as the general public. In addition, the states have enacted a multitude of new laws and regulations complete with criminal sanctions to reduce the chances of this occurring again.

The nuclear reactor industry has suffered much the same fate as the chemical industry.[18] Once hailed as the solution to the world's energy problem, the industry was beset by a variety of difficulties. The difficulties at Three Mile Island, the tragedy at Chernobyl[19] and the need to dispose of nuclear waste raised public questions about the safety of such plants. As a result, the various levels of government have enacted laws to regulate the industry which many industry representatives have argued has effectively shut down any chances for future growth.

Employment Issues

For many centuries, the courts were unwilling to interfere with private employment relationships. The common law was that an employer was able to hire and fire employees at will. In an economy in which people generally worked on farms or for a single employer, one could argue that this was appropriate legal policy. However, as the economy moved into the industrial age, the government steadily moved into the area of employer–employee relations.[20]

Congress recognized the existence of unions in a series of legislation in the early part of the twentieth century and then expanded into the areas of wage setting, working hours, discrimination, pension benefits protection, and working conditions. The courts opposed much of the early legislation on the grounds that it interfered with the freedom to contract. However, the courts reversed themselves when it became clear that they were standing against the tide of public opinion.

Health and Safety

Congress and state legislatures have also adopted a variety of criminal statutes to control health and safety conditions. This is accomplished under the government's inherent police powers to protect its citizens. Again, industry representatives, especially small business advocates, have argued that the panoply of regulations are unduly expensive and harmful to business expansion. It was objections like these which helped to foster "the government's not your friend, but the enemy" rhetoric that fueled President Reagan's election victories in 1980 and 1984.

Many of the classic governmental issues over the past several decades have been confrontations between those who want more government and people who want less. Although activists held the clear advantage in the middle of the century, by the end of the twentieth century, conservatives seemed to have increased the power of their position. One issue for the future is how a potentially divided government will handle the problems of the future.

FUTURE ISSUES FOR GOVERNMENT

Many future issues for government reflect unresolved issues from the past. Others represent new claims by people who want the government to take certain actions, as opposed to people who want the government to leave themselves, as well as others, alone. In short, the future is likely to be the past. One reason for this is that the American people have not reached a consensus as to the proper role of government in a democratic society driven by a free market economy. Although one might argue that this is inevitable in a diverse society, other countries, such as Japan and Switzerland, have a strong sense that the basic purpose of their government is to assist the private sector in a highly competitive world economy.[21] This has not been the American tradition, and this leads to interesting issues for the future as the United States struggles to cope with finding the proper roles for its various levels of government.

The long-term importance of some of these issues may relate to the actual survival of the concept of U.S. democracy. The public has become quite discouraged with the ability of governments to solve the nation's problems, and the idea of turning over more and more government functions to private enterprise is gaining supporters.

Privatization

The concept of turning government functions over to private enterprise, called *privatization*, represents one of the most important of the emerging new governmental issues. The federal government has an enormous debt, the state governments are struggling with financial difficulties, and some of the nation's largest cities are near bankruptcy.[22] The citizens and governmental leaders are searching for less expensive ways of delivering traditional governmental services, and farming them out to the private sector seems more and more attractive. In recent years, prisons, court systems, security forces, road departments, schools, and other services have been privatized in various parts of the nation.

Privatization is an issue that has not traditionally been faced by governments. It represents a severe threat to the traditional concepts of government services and to governmental workers. On the other hand, privatization represents an enormous opportunity for the private sector to expand their business ventures into areas that were previously governmental monopolies. If privatization continues to grow as a concept, it will radically change the nature of government.

It is conceivable that future governmental leaders, such as mayors and governors, will spend much of their future time negotiating contracts with private-sector companies to provide normal governmental services. This would be a sea change in the nature of government as well as a landmark change in the structure of our political system. If there are fewer "government" programs, there will be fewer government workers with a vested interest in maintaining government programs. Conversely, there will be more private-sector companies and workers competing for government contracts.

Privatization would also provide an added element of competition in the governmental sector. Some authorities on government management argue that if governments had been subject to competition, it would have been a useful step in encouraging better management of government services. In addition, competing private-sector companies will have an impact on how the various levels of our governments will interact. This will create competition among federal, state, and local governments for tax dollars and the right to perform various services.

BOX 8.4 Ethics in Local Government

Awarding of professional contracts for engineering and legal services at the local level involves a network of contacts, which smacks of political patronage. Professional services are exempt from the state bid law. The decision-making process begins typically with political alignment, that is, the political party that the engineering or legal firm supports financially.

It has been pointed out that the awarding of contracts is about money. One needs to look no further than the hospitality suites at state leagues of municipalities conventions to understand who the "players" are and where the allegiances are nurtured. Engineering firms, most notably, host lavish cocktail parties that are by invitation for local officials elected and hired for the sole purpose of currying favor.

It is doubtful that such events would be so conspicuous if engineering services were contracted for by the bid process. Given that this process could easily be served, as engineering services are shaped by the project or hourly rate, would give no incentive for questionable ethical favors to be given. Legal firms do not go to great lengths for hospitality, but rather, make contributions to local campaigns in both time and money. A significant number of fund-raisers are run by legal firms affiliated with the respective political parties solely for the purpose of getting their candidate elected or awarded lucrative government work.

The nature of the work is not contrived or manufactured. Defense work for liability suits, planning boards, boards of adjustment, personnel, labor, contract review or bid work, and zoning are but a few areas that require bona fide legal work. The process by which legal advice is contracted presents ethical questions. Similar to awarding of engineering contracts, the awarding of legal contracts seems to be the simple process of selling time for the lowest cost. Contracting for legal services in the state of New Jersey is exempt from the bid law. As a result, for any law firm, regardless of the area of expertise, acquisition of work is certainly hit or miss. To gain a government unit as part of the client base means a constant cash flow as long as the professional services contract exists. Such a process has to create, if not the process itself, ethical questions.

Gambling, wagering, betting; these words conjure up images of the more legendary events of the American experience. Images of racketeering, the Untouchables, and the Roaring Twenties flash in front of our mind's eye. Conventional ethics in our society has professed that such behavior should be punished for reasons of morality. Laws were passed making such activity illegal unless the activity is conducted by the government.

Gambling in Atlantic City and by means of a lottery were conceived in New Jersey 20 years ago based on addressing three issues: the funding of education, the improvement of the plight of urban centers, and the improvement of the plight of senior citizens. As of the summer of 1997, New Jersey ranked first in the country in per pupil cost for education but in the forties for average SAT scores. A recent survey conducted by the *Newark Star Ledger,* using a 0 to 100 scale for overall educational quality by state, gave Wisconsin a 98 and New Jersey a 3. Most recently, headlines blared that public education in New Jersey rates an "F." Conservative estimates now show that $10 billion is needed statewide for facilities repairs. Although having received structural improvements, urban centers remain dependent on state funding for existence. Urban schools have steadily worsened since the inception of gambling and the lottery. The very city that was supposed to be the greatest beneficiary of gaming, Atlantic City, has, to the naked eye, improved very little. Senior citizens, interestingly enough, are the largest group of clientele in Atlantic City. How much trickle down impact the proceeds from gambling and the lottery have had on seniors as a group is anyone's guess.

The question that seems clear is: Who is guarding the guardian? This may be the only time in the history of games of chance (with the exception of New York, which lost money running off-track betting) that the "house" has not made a profit large enough to fill its needs. The sacrifice of conventional morality in the name of fiscal balance, let alone the question of fiscal responsibility,

BOX 8.4 **(continued)**

presents an ethical question, to be sure. Why, given the level of construction activity in Atlantic City, is it of any interest to the state to attempt to attract yet another casino/resort/hotel? Such attempts spawned the idea of a government-funded project to build a tunnel to connect the north end of Atlantic City to Brigantine, where a new facility was proposed to be built. Such an idea seems more ludicrous when two things are recalled. Until the 1950s direct rail transportation between the urban centers of north Jersey and Atlantic City was functional and ongoing. This is no longer the case. Second, the new convention center is not within walking distance of the boardwalk, which is the location of all the major resort facilities and the hub of retail activity.

The question of ethics arises again regarding the hiring of a municipal audit firm, a process that is exempt from state bid laws. It is the express responsibility of such an audit to confirm that a given governmental unit is in compliance with acceptable municipal accounting practices such as the state bid law! What action can be expected when an audit report reveals that the bid law has been violated? What action is taken when the auditor discovers that a snowplow contractor ran up costs of $75,000 and was paid without a bid; when a vendor of two-way radios supplies $15,000 worth of equipment without a bid; when a contractor is given work in excess of the bid threshold in the aggregate but in multiple transactions each piece of which is under the bid threshold; or when a bid threshold is exceeded and the work is than declared an emergent condition by the governing body, thereby negating the bid regulations? Indeed, who is guarding the guardian?

Source: Modified from Bob Yunker.

Interaction of Governments

The interaction of the three levels of the national system is likely to be another important issue in the future. Traditionally, the national government was responsible for national defense and a number of functions that were vital to the flow of interstate commerce. In fact, the state governments were always rather jealous of their powers and resented interference from the federal government. This issue was one of several that precipitated the Civil War and had led to several state rebellions before that.[23]

By the Great Depression, it was apparant that state governments and private charities were unable to assist all the people who needed help. Without aid from the national government, the state governments would be unable to function. As noted above, the various social programs that were started during the Depression were continued after World War II. By the 1960s, the states were clamoring for more assistance to help themselves and their large cities. Revenue sharing under both Presidents Johnson and Nixon enabled the states to fund a number of new and expanded programs. By the 1980s the federal government was telling states, cities, and counties that the cupboard was bare and that they had to fend for themselves. In the early 1990s states had spent most of the money they had raised during the boom years of the late 1980s. They had run out of money and were asking the President and Congress to help them.

The nation's largest cities are in even worse financial shape. Philadelphia went into bankruptcy in 1991, and some of the nation's other large cities, including New York, were not far behind. Since the federal and state governments were in trouble themselves, it was not clear how their situations were going to be improved. Some people argued that the federal government ought to step in and help the cities, while others stated that the cities had created their own problems through profligate spending and did not deserve to be helped. Others have suggested that cities need to collapse so that market values of land will decrease to levels at which the private sector will find it attractive to reinvest in them. How these issues are resolved will be reflective of a new relationship among the various levels of governments in the United States.

Infrastructure

Another important issue for the future relates to the nation's decaying capital infrastructure, which consists of bridges, highways, sewer plants, prisons, school buildings, and other capital structures that undergrid the nation's economy and have a life expectancy of more than one year. Originally, government was designed primarily to build these structures that helped the economy but could not be built by the private sector. Although this was the trend for many years, the political leaders began to support more programs that benefited individuals to garner votes and ignored the nation's infrastructure. Now, these years of neglect are coming home to roost. The bridges, highways, sewer plants, and other capital projects are falling apart, and this is beginning to hurt our economy. The Japanese and other countries are spending a much higher percentage of their gross domestic product on their infrastructure than the United States is, and this places them in a better competitive position.

In recent years, a significant number of political and business leaders have begun to recognize and address this problem and the long-term negative consequences to the nation's economy. The costs of correcting these problems is enormous, running into many billions of dollars. Again, the issue is: From where will the money be derived? Although normally, these expenditures are expected to be part of a government's capital budget, they also represent an enormous opportunity for labor unions and the business community. Construction and rehabilitation of the nation's infrastructure will create thousands of jobs and greatly stimulate the nation's economy. Indeed, it is vital for our country's future that this be accomplished.

Public Education

Another major issue is the rapidly growing concern about our public education system. A variety of reports and evaluations of test scores indicate that students in the United States rank near the middle among students in industrialized nations in terms of knowledge of a variety of subjects.[24] This is particularly true in the areas of mathematics and science, which will be of special importance in a worldwide economy of rapidly changing technological and communications advances. Although the results of the decline in test scores and the consequences for the nation are well known, methods for reversing the trend are not all that clear.

The breakup of the nuclear American family, the popularity of television, the decline in the prestige of teaching as a profession, the lack of a meaningful work ethic, the absence of effective role models, and the lack of meaningful competition for the public school system have all been cited as reasons for the decline. It is not certain what steps will reverse the decline, but a significant number of ideas have been advanced.

One suggestion has been to eliminate or reduce summer vacation and to lengthen the school year substantially. The proponents argue that this would compel teachers to teach longer and that students would learn more. Advocates note that Japanese students seem to do better because they spend more time in school and study for longer periods of time. This suggestion has a number of problems. First, the federal, state, and local governments barely have the money to keep the schools going now. Where are they going to get the money to lengthen the school year? Even if teachers could be compelled to work longer hours for the same amount of pay, the schools would still have to bear the costs of maintaining the buildings (including air conditioning in some areas) and related costs. It is also not clear whether this would actually result in more learning or more chair filling.

Another suggestion is to return to the basic reading, writing, and arithmetic curriculums of previous years and to eliminate many of the special courses and functions that have been assigned to the school systems through the years. The schools have become the dumping ground for all sorts of issues that previously were within the responsibility of either the family or religious institutions. Health and sex education are examples that have been raised by some people. The arts, such as music and theater, have been raised by others.

One can agree with the purposes of many of these programs and still question whether they interfere with the basic mission of the school system. Strategic planning, a management technique derived from the private sector, suggests that most organizations can accomplish only a few key objectives.[25] If they try to do too many things outside their areas of expertise, they are often likely not to do any of them very well. If this lesson is applicable, it may explain why the educational system is having such difficulties.

Other people have suggested that the public school system could use a healthy dose of competition from the private sector. This is similar to the idea of privatization discussed above. Proponents of this approach suggest allowing parents to choose schools for their children by giving them vouchers or tax credits that will help them pay for the cost of private schools. Proponents argue that the public schools will improve only if they are forced to compete against other alternatives. Opponents argue that private schools do not face the same problems as public schools because they are able to select only the best students. They suggest further that if government funds are diverted to private schools, the public school system will be destroyed.

Public school advocates contend that they are able to compete effectively with private schools. They argue that they would be better able to do so if they had additional resources, smaller class sizes, and rehabilitated school buildings. Some advocates for the public schools offer suggestions such as alternative routes for teacher certification, merit pay for teachers, or goal setting that reflects a more quantitative approach for measuring student and teacher performance.

It is not clear in which direction the various levels of government will try to push public education. Regardless of the direction, it is likely to meet with

BOX 8.5   Headstart

Perhaps the most successful program to come out of the War on Poverty is Headstart. This program is aimed at the children of poor families and is designed to help prepare them for kindergarten so that they will be on at least an equal footing with their more affluent classmates. By most measures, Headstart has been a success. The children who have been in these programs have tested, generally, better than those who have not, especially during the first few years of school. Unfortunately, the program suffers from a general lack of funds and must fight for its money with each congressional budget. Headstart remains an experimental program on the part of the federal government, even though the "experiment" has been going on for 30 years and the results are in. This is more a question of politics than of results. On the Headstart side, nobody wants to be seen as being against children. Scrooge, especially before Christmas Eve, is not a very lovable character. On the other side, there are those who see Headstart and much of what went on in the War on Poverty as a huge political pork barrel. The result is that although Headstart is almost impossible to kill, it will be forced to continue to exist on a shoestring, never quite totally fulfilling its promise.

criticism and opposition from a variety of entrenched interest groups that want the system to remain the same. It is apparent that public education will need to change if it is going to maintain its traditional role in U.S. society.

Health Care

Another issue for government in the future is that of providing health care for its citizens. The fastest-growing population segment in the country is the old-old grouping of citizens, over the age of 75.[26] Although it used to be unusual for people to reach age 90; it is now quite commonplace. As people age, they tend to need more health care. Our society has not had to face the problems associated with providing this quantity and level of care until relatively recently.

But it is not only the very old who want health care services. Some surveys indicate that our nation's infant mortality rate is becoming much higher than that of other industrial countries.[27] The baby-boom generation, born between 1946 and 1960, is now reaching middle age and will begin to ask for more medical care as it gets older. In addition, Americans have come to expect a high level of medical care from society and, on the whole, expect someone else to pay for it.

As medical science advances, the technology, capabilities, and costs of providing medical care spirals at an ever-increasing rate. There are new methods of sustaining and prolonging life that were unknown and in some cases, unthinkable, years ago. Inevitably, people are raising the questions of how much health care can we afford.[28] When former Governor Lamb of Colorado raised issues about how many years people would expect society to help them live beyond age 70, he was roundly condemned by people as being uncaring. Still, in a more general and less controversial sense, it is an issue that is worth consideration.

Beyond these issues is the question of how to pay for all these health services. Although a large number of Americans have either private health insurance or insurance at work, many others do not have any means of paying for health care. The issue then becomes who, if anyone, should pay for it. Some of our political leaders, mostly on the Democratic side of the aisle, have argued that it is government's responsibility to ensure that everyone receives adequate health care. They argue, with some justification, that the long-term costs of not providing adequate health care are greater than the costs of providing it when needed. The issue, of course, is how governments pay for health care when they are already running significant deficits.

Poverty Programs

Another issue is the responsibility of the government to help the poor. As noted above, the Great Depression ushered in a new role for the various levels of government. Previously, society relied largely on private institutions such as churches to take care of the economically less fortunate. The Great Depression created a situation such that these charitable institutions were unable to take care of the millions of families whose breadwinners were out of work.

In the 1960s, President Johnson, an early advocate of the social programs of President Roosevelt, launched the War on Poverty in an effort to eliminate poverty. The federal government began a variety of new programs to help the poor. The success or failure of these programs has been hotly debated by a variety of people.

What cannot be denied is that poverty was not eliminated.[29] There is some evidence that poverty, particularly among the young, has actually increased since the 1960s. What also cannot be denied is that by the 1980s the public had also become rather bored with poverty as an issue. Many people had become tired of paying the taxes associated with the various programs and were annoyed with the apparent lack of results. This was one of the reasons for the conservative tide that swept the nation during the 1980s.

Although President Reagan discussed the importance of maintaining a "safety net" for the economically less fortunate, it is clear that many people have fallen through the net. The issue remains to what extent government should be utilized to help the poor. It is worth remembering that although helping the poor may be a worthwhile objective, every dollar that goes to the government in the form of taxation is one less dollar in the private sector. The issue for government is finding a proper balance between the two.

Although some people might contend that U.S. government is a pendulum swinging between liberal and conservative approaches to this issue, the pendulum tends to swing too far in each direction. This is not an effective way to run a government. In addition, it does not allow for a careful analysis of the utility of individual programs. Starting a host of new programs and then cutting them after a brief period of time does not usually permit sufficient time for them to work. Neither does it usually permit sufficient time to decide that they will not work. A more thoughtful approach could produce both more efficient and cost-effective programs.

Closely related to this issue is the growing "tax revolt" sentiment that seems to be sweeping the nation. President Bush was elected in 1988 for, among other reasons, stating: "Read my lips, no new taxes." In an era when state governments face large deficits,[30] voters are rebelling against attempts to reduce those deficits by raising taxes. This makes the maintenance of social programs quite difficult and makes the initiation of new programs nearly impossible. Closing the holes in the safety net will be quite difficult if this attitude continues to prevail.

Another issue that will continue to affect government is the controversy over to what extent the various levels of government ought to be in the business of legislating morality and/or fixing society's injustices. The entire issue of abortion falls into this category. One group of citizens clearly sees abortion as an issue of profound moral significance; the question involves the "sanctity of human life." For the opposing side, the issue is one of preventing government from interfering with the "right" of women to make their own choices about whether to have children.[31] This represents the classic conflict between the government's traditional willingness to legislate and an individual's desire to be left alone.

A similar problem relates to questions about discrimination against certain groups in our society and what "remedies" governments should adopt to assist them. Although there is no question that some groups have been treated less equally than others in our society, to what extent do people who took no part in that treatment have an obligation to help disadvantaged groups? To what extent do they have the responsibility of limiting their own chances for success in order to redress past wrongs? These are also questions that underline debates about civil rights or quota bills.[32]

Drugs

The drug problem is another question that relates to the issue of regulating private morality. Although it is clear that the cost of drug use to society is enormous in terms of the loss of human potential, productivity, and lives,[33] people from various points along the political spectrum are beginning to question the costs of enforcement against drug use. They point to the huge costs associated with keeping the price of drugs high by making them illegal.

Extremely high prices for illegal drugs tend to encourage users to commit crimes to raise the money to pay for the product. The costs associated with enforcing drug laws, including drug-related crimes, are huge. Included among them are salaries for police officers, district attorneys, public defenders, judges, and court-related personnel. Also included would be the costs of building and maintaining prisons, as well as the costs of prison guards, cooks, doctors, and others who provide services to prisoners.

Balanced against all these costs is society's desire to disapprove of drugs by making their use illegal. Like many issues, society will have to decide whether the costs of compliance and people's disrespect for laws which they are not willing to obey are worth the benefit of continuing such laws.

OTHER FUTURE ISSUES

Some final issues are worth discussing because they are all tied to the changes that are occurring outside the United States. No society or organization is likely to be successful unless it considers how changes in the world will affect it. Perhaps the most important change is the general collapse of the communist system throughout the world.[34]

Much of U.S. foreign policy and economy after World War II was built on the idea of containing communism. The country fought the Korean and Vietnam wars based on this premise. Now that the growth of communism is no longer a threat, the United States needs to reorient its economy to combat new threats and exploit new opportunities.

One threat is the growing economies of Japan, Europe, and the Pacific rim. Although the United States was winning the Cold War, these other areas of the globe were building their economies and taking away what had been U.S. markets. The textile industry left and soon the steel industry was gone. Much of the automobile market went to Japan,[35] and now U.S. advantages in high-technology areas are in danger.[36] Somehow, the United States must find a way to restore its competitive advantage.

There have been about as many suggested solutions as there are problems. Some point to the need to invigorate our education system, others suggest that our managers need to plan for long-term market exploitation instead of focusing on short-term (quarterly) results,[37] others suggest that we need to learn how to better market our products overseas,[38] and many experts point to the need to move quickly toward a high-technology, information-based economy. All of these approaches also imply the need for a leaner and more cost-efficient governmental system.

At the same time, there will be an increased need for retraining of managers and workers in both the private and public sectors of our economy.[39] Unfortunately, the need for retraining has not been one that has been supported by our government. Studies indicate that government is one of the least likely sectors of the economy to receive any additional training and an argument could be made that it has some of the greatest need.

SUMMARY

The current issues facing government are large and complex. On the international level, governments must deal with rapidly changing circumstances. They are faced with increasing decentralization in the face of larger and more complex problems. The world is changing and they are going to have to run as fast as they can just to stay in place.

On the domestic level, the government of the United States faces many challenges. Reindustrialization, education, and competitiveness are only a few of the issues that government needs to address. Unfortunately, it would seem that the political will necessary to address these issues is in even shorter supply than the money that will be needed to carry out any solution to any problem.

Government's task is huge. It faces virtually unlimited needs with woefully limited resources. The task may be daunting and the supply of skilled managers, politicians, and leaders is limited, but government has no choice other than to tackle the problems before it.

Questions

1. How do the primary objectives of government differ from the objectives of companies in the private sector?
2. Explain some of the trade-offs of governments attempting to legislate morality.

3. In a governmental system dominated by frequent elections, is long-term planning possible? Why or why not?

4. How would you define the mission of a local government unit (city or town)?

5. Explain why defining governmental missions might be more difficult than in the private sector.

6. If you were the U.S. president, which emerging issue would be your first priority?

7. What would be your second priority?

8. How does the emerging international economy affect the role of our national government?

9. Should government attempt to "fine-tune" our nation's economy?

10. Explain how the aging of our nation's population might affect governmental policy.

CASE 1

You were elected mayor of one of the nation's largest cities in November and sworn in on January 1. Much of your support came from the city's municipal labor unions. You are having your first meeting with your budget director one week after taking office. She has carefully reviewed current programs. If expenditures remain the same as last year, they will total $7 billion. Unfortunately, projected revenues will total only $6 billion.

1. What do you do?

CASE 2

You have just been named head of policy and planning for one of the nation's eight largest industrial states. The governor, your boss, asks your advice in setting the three most important priorities relating to economic policy for the state.

1. What advice do you give?

CASE 3

You run a major urban police department. You were appointed the new police commissioner following a series of major scandals involving the police officers in the city. A number of officers were convicted of various crimes, ranging from assault to murder. Your department has had a history of being out of control. There has been a succession of chiefs with short-term tenures before yours. Many people stated that you were crazy to take this new job. However, you saw it as a challenge. You are not certain how to move forward. You are aware that there are people who support your appointment as well as those who do not.

1. What do you do?
2. How do you decide what to do?
3. What are your ethical obligations in this case?
4. What are the ethical obligations of the police officers?

References _____

1. Sinclair, U., *The jungle*, Buccaneer Books, Cutchogue, NY, 1984.
2. Parks, H., *The United States of America: a history*, Alfred A. Knopf, New York 1968.
3. Ibid.
4. Black, R., D. Boroughs, S. Collins, and K. Sheets, "Heavy lifting," *U.S. News and World Report*, May 6, 1991.
5. Maidment, F. (ed.), *Annual editions: international business, 1994–1995*, Dushkin Publishing Group, Guilford, CT, 1994.
6. Ajami, F., "Tribal fantasies in Europe," *U.S. News and World Report*, July 8, 1991.
7. Olcott M. B., "The Soviet (dis)union," *Foreign Policy*, Spring 1991.
8. Tanzer, A., "The mountains are high and the emperor is far away," *Forbes*, August 5, 1991.
9. Lee, S., "Are we building new Berlin walls?" *Forbes*, January 7, 1991.
10. Reich, R., "Who is them?" *Harvard Business Review*, March–April 1991.
11. Interview, *The MacNeil/Leher report*, August 1991.
12. Gilman, H., "How safe are your savings?" *Working Mother*, May 1991.
13. Allen, M., "More white-collar criminals face jail under new sentencing rules," *Wall Street Journal*, November 24, 1991.
14. Sherrill, R., "Murder, Inc.: what happens to corporate criminals," *UNTE Reader*, March–April 1987.
15. Margolick, D., "A speech by Quayle on the legal system unsettles lawyers," *New York Times*, August 14, 1991.
16. "As competition rises in global banking, Europeans have edge," *Wall Street Journal*, March 25, 1991.
17. Kahn, J. P., "When bad management becomes criminal," *Inc.*, March 1, 1987.
18. Greenwald, J., "Time to choose," *Time*, April 29, 1991.
19. "Chernobyl fallout," *U.S. News and World Report*, June 3, 1991.
20. Licht, W. "How the workplace has changed in 75 years," *Monthly Labor Review*, February 1988.
21. Ratan, S., "The big split," *Fortune*, May 6, 1991.
22. Minebrook, S., "Declarative statements," *U.S. News and World Report,* June 24, 1991.
23. Parks, *The United States of America.*
24. Maidment, F., "American economy suffers from a lack of educated and trained workforce," *Atlanta Journal and Constitution*, August 10, 1987.
25. Eldridge, W., "Why angels fear to tread: a practitioner's guide to strategic management in government," in Jack Rubin, Gerald Miller, and W. Bartley Heldreth (eds.), *Handbook of strategic management*, Marcel Dekker, New York, 1989.
26. United Nations World Assembly on Aging, Vienna, 1982.
27. The World Bank, *World Development Report, 1985*, Oxford University Press, New York, 1985.
28. Paine, T. H., "Benefits in the 1990s," *Personnel Journal*, March 1988.
29. Littman, M. S., "Poverty areas and the 'underclass': untangling the web," *Monthly Labor Review*, March 1991.
30. Roberts, P. C., "Read my lips, George, don't raise taxes," *Business Week*, December 5, 1988.
31. "Abortion test cases," *Time*, July 1, 1991.
32. Gethmeann, B. R., "The job market, sex bias, and comparable worth," *Public Personnel Management*, Summer 1987.
33. Kinard, J., J. Turner, and P. Wright, "Controlling substance abuse in the workplace," *Business*, December 1987.

34. "Cautious capitalism," *U.S. News and World Report,* November 5, 1991.

35. Ingrassia, P., "Auto industry in U.S. is sliding relentlessly into Japanese hands," *Wall Street Journal,* February 16, 1991.

36. Spero, D., "Patent protection or piracy: a CEO views Japan," *Harvard Business Review,* September–October 1990.

37. Korth, C., "Managerial barriers to U.S. exports," *Business Horizons,* March–April 1990.

38. Bertrand, K., "The global spyglass," *Business Marketing,* September 1990.

39. Maidment, F., "University-based executive education programs," Doctoral dissertation, University of South Carolina, Columbia, SC, 1983.

CURRENT ISSUES FACING SOCIETY

Concepts ⁝ You Will Learn ■ ■ ■

major societal issues facing society in the areas of business, government, religion, the family, and other areas

how society is changing with regard to demographics and technology

likely future issues in society in the area of competitiveness, productivity, standard of living, and cost of living

WHAT CONSTITUTES MODERN SOCIETY? ■ ■ ■

Business ■ ■ ■

Calvin Coolidge said that "The business of America is business."[1] In this simple statement he summed up the importance of commercial activity for both the United States and for the world. People tend to forget that the United States was originally settled by the Virginia Company, a commercial venture whose main purpose was to make a profit for its investors.[2] Although the company was eventually taken over by the British Crown, and then became the state of Virginia, many other colonies followed this model. Although historians have tended to focus on the fact that many people came to the British colonies of North America to escape religious and political persecution, which is, of course, true, they also came to make their fortunes.[3] Even during the colonial era, people came to what would become the United States and Canada for a better life. Europe was beset by a class system that would remain in place until the Napoleonic Wars, the vestiges of which are still seen today.[4] Those who wanted more, who were dissatisfied with their position in life, who wanted to move up the socioeconomic ladder, had to move out. Business, commerce, and the acquisition of wealth were all primary motives for people to come to America.

Thomas Jefferson envisioned a society made up of small, independent farmers,[5] but he could not have been more wrong. Today farmers represent only a small fraction of the workforce. Most people in the United States work for someone else in organizations designed to produce, distribute, and sell products and services that Jefferson could not even have imagined. American industry developed as a direct result of the industrial revolution, with much of the financing coming from European bankers who recognized the great potential for growth and return on investment that existed in the United States and Canada. There was, essentially, an entire continent waiting to be developed, as opposed to Europe, an entire continent busy threatening each other with wars and dynastic struggles. Big business started to grow in the United States in the form of the railroads, which tied the country together and then helped to expand and develop it.[6] This was followed by steel, oil, and autos, as well as all the other major industries in the country. In the process, North America became home to many large and small organizations engaged in the production and distribution of goods and services.

The United States has always had a dichotomy in its industrial base. During the era of the robber barons, a few large organizations attempted to completely dominate various industries in the form of trusts and to put smaller competitors out of business. The heirs of many of these large organizations are still in business today. Small businesses represent the other half of the business equation. Most people are employed by small businesses. In the United States, small business enterprise is encouraged by the government through the Small Business Administration. From a regulatory viewpoint, it is relatively easy to get into business in the United States with a minimum of fees and taxes. For example, in Missouri it is possible for someone to obtain the necessary government permits, pay all the fees (about $500, including a bond for sales taxes), and complete the paperwork in about $1\frac{1}{2}$ days with no outside help or bribes. However, in some countries it may take as long as a year and cost thousands of dollars in fees, permits, and bribes to open a legitimate business.

Small business and entrepreneurship make an industry vibrant. It is from small businesses that large businesses are born. When Bill Gates started Microsoft, he could not have imagined what it would become; the same could be said of Steve Jobs, J. D. Rockefeller, and Henry Ford. Small business is the main creator of innovation.[7] Small businesses represent people with ideas who are willing to take the risks necessary to see those ideas fulfilled. Their dreams do not always come true and they often do not succeed in their efforts, but many keep on trying. The history of U.S. industry is full of people who tried and failed repeatedly, only eventually to succeed.[8] Most entrepreneurs have a belief in their eventual success that is often eventually justified.

U.S. industry faces many problems in the global economy. Competition is far greater than it was 10, 20, 30, or 50 years ago. The economy is truly global in nature, and that is something that will not go away. The regulatory environment among developed countries is far greater than in the less developed world. There are more laws about pollution, equal employment opportunity, and market regulations than there are in the less developed countries. Indeed, part of the attraction of setting up business in some of the less developed countries is that they do not have all of the laws that exist in the developed world. Some businesses have essentially left their home countries to take advantage of this lack of regulation and have transferred their operations and in some instances, even their headquarters, to the developing world.[9]

Business, the sector of society concerned with the development and distribution of goods and services, will continue to grow as more people demand more goods and services that can be provided most efficiently by industry. The failure of the communist system was not a failure of industrialism or workers but a failure of the system that attempted to use those factors of production to its greatest advantage.[10] Soviet communism/socialism could not meet the demands that society placed on it, and as a result, the greatest single challenge to capitalism failed. Today, more and more societies are adopting capitalism as their means of economic organization. Centralized planning does not appear to work well for an economy. Adam Smith's "invisible hand" has been demonstrated to be the most efficient allocator of resources for present-day societies.

Government

Along with open markets comes open government. The basis of both capitalism and democracy is choice. As more societies adopt capitalism as their primary form of economic organization they will find that the same people who are the consumers are also the electorate. People become used to choice in the marketplace for goods and services and come to expect choice in the marketplace of ideas, especially political ideas that affect them directly. One of the main movements affecting all aspects of society, from business to government to religion to the family, is the decentralization of those institutions. The role of government is being actively contested between those who want to reduce the role of the centralized government and those who wish to at least maintain, if not increase it.[11] This reduction in the role of the central government has been taken to the extreme in the former Soviet Union and Yugoslavia, resulting in ethnic cleansing and civil war.

In the United States, the role of the central government is under attack on a number of fronts. In the first place, the cost of the central government, indeed, of all government in the United States, has become a very real issue. To a degree, this was part of the cost associated with paying for the Cold War. There is much truth in the idea that the West won the Cold War because it bankrupted the Soviets, who simply ran out of money before the West did. However, the Cold War is now over and many citizens are wondering where their "peace dividend" went.

The second problem is that like the Soviet system of a highly centralized government, the U.S. federal government has become highly centralized and as a result, often far less efficient and responsive to the needs of the citizenry. Washington has become the central source of funds and the main bottleneck in attempting to address problems facing the society. This was not what the framers of the Constitution had in mind. For most of the country, Washington is a faraway place with little or no understanding of the particular problems of each city, town, or state. The result has been an attempt to take back the powers of the federal government and for states or cities to take the initiative on issues facing them.

The deal struck between the tobacco industry and the various state attorneys general is a case in point. It represents a massive power grab on the part of the states with regard to the federal government. To understand the implications of this development, it is first necessary to understand the size and dimensions of the health hazard poised by tobacco: (1) It is a national problem affecting the entire country and much of the world; (2) the states, through Medicare/Medicade, are paying much of the bill associated with the health hazards of tobacco; and (3) after repeated studies and attempts over the past 30 years to address this problem on the federal level, all of which have essentially failed, the states have been compelled to take action because the federal government was either unwilling or unable to do what needed to be done.

Although it is possible to argue about the details of the settlement and the fact that it may be voted on by Congress and signed by the President, the fact is that the federal government was simply not involved. This represents a major shift in the power equation between the states and the federal government in that the states finally addressed an issue that the federal government was unable to solve. It marks the impotency of Washington and the power of local government to address issues in concert with other states. Local and state governments were faced with a problem that they had to solve or go bankrupt and Washington was unable to help, so they did it themselves, making the federal government irrelevant. For people who believe in a strong national government, this could mark the end of an era. Decentralization and the devolution of power to lower levels of government will continue. The federal government may continue to increase in size but its impact on the average citizen has been curtailed and the importance of the states will continue to increase.

This also has implications for the importance of what is called "good government." The writers of the *Federalist Papers* pointed out that in the federal system there was a sharing of power on the part of the various levels of government.[12] But in sharing power, the levels of government also shared its opportunities for political corruption. State governments and capitals that have born the exposure of the national media are prime examples of some of these activities. For example, when Spiro Agnew, former Vice President of the United States, was convicted of taking bribes when he was governor of Maryland, the spotlight fell on Annapolis, and the next two governors were sent to jail. Bill Clinton's successor as governor of Arkansas has also been convicted of fraud in a Little Rock courtroom.[13]

Because government now represents such a huge sector of the U.S. society, the need for good, honest government is even greater today than it was years ago. Unfortunately, corruption has always been a part of local and state government.[14] As the resources for governmental activities become more restricted, this will have to change. With all the talk about tax cuts at the federal level, these will only be marginal at best, so all levels of government are going to be forced to do more with less in the future. This is not only going to be difficult, but it is going to change the way many levels of government do business.

Some large U.S. cities, such as Chicago or Kansas City, which have long traditions of political corruption, are going to find that kind of activity less tolerated than in the past. Reformers, promising good, honest government, are likely to be elected in the near future, and if they do not deliver, will be replaced by others promising similar kinds of government. Although government may not get smaller in terms of cost in the future, it is likely to grow at a slower pace than the rest of the society and therefore become less influential. What increases in power there will be will be at local and state levels, with the federal government grudgingly giving way.

Religion

Religious aspects of U.S. society have been a part of the heritage of the United States since early colonial days. Although Virginia may have been founded to make money, Plymouth, the second successful English colony, was founded by people fleeing religious persecution.[15] Religion has always played an important role in the history of the nation, and it continues to do so in a rapidly changing and sometimes hostile environment.

To understand the role of religion in today's society it is first necessary to understand the importance of the religious revival that is sweeping the world. Members of many faiths, including Jews, Muslims, and Christians, are experiencing a religious revival and awakening that has not been seen for centuries. Among the Jewish people, the founding of the state of Israel has marked a tremendous revival of the Jewish faith, especially after the Holocaust.[16] For the first time since the Roman Empire, the Jewish people have a homeland. Jews the world over have gone to great lengths to support the establishment of the Jewish state and to maintain it in the face of a hostile environment. This has led to a reawakening of Judaism and a greater interest in the traditional aspects of the faith.

The Muslim world has also been the site of a massive religious revival. Often fueled by oil money, this has most distinctively manifested itself in the governments of Iran and Afghanistan, where there was a massive revolt against the very secular governments of those countries that to a certain degree had been imposed by the United States in Iran and the Soviet Union in Afghanistan. Islam represents one of the fastest-growing faiths in the world and is also growing in the United States, with current membership greater than that of some of the mainline Protestant faiths.[17]

Christianity in the United States is experiencing another of its periodic revivals. Interest in religion is nothing new in this country. There have been periodic revivals of religious fervor that have resulted in the establishment of several mainline Protestant denominations, especially the Baptists and the Methodists, in addition to the Church of Latter-Day Saints, the Church of God, and the Church of the Nazarene.

A major reason for the revival of interest in religion on the part of Christians in the United States has been the increasing secularization of mainstream U.S. society. One of the founding principles of government in the United States has always been the separation of church and state. Until fairly recently this was taken to mean that church and state cohabitated in the country. Each acknowledged the other's importance but did not ignore or try to subvert the other to its wishes. That changed when the Supreme Court ruled that prayer was no longer permissible in the public schools (*Brown v. Topeka Board of Education*, 1954). This doctrine of almost total separation of church and state has been carried by the courts to almost extreme measures, including the prohibition of nativity scenes on public grounds and a ban on the display of the Ten Commandments in courtrooms.

It is also only fair to point out that this separation has protected non-Christian groups in the society and that the lawsuit involving prayer in the schools was brought by an atheist. Over the past nearly 50 years, the society has changed. There are now many more non-Christians and non-Jews in the society. Home-grown atheists and agnostics have been supplemented by a large number of Buddhists among the recent Asian immigrants, and native Muslims (many of them African Americans) as well as recent immigrants from the Middle East. People from India have also brought their faith in Hinduism with them as they have immigrated to the United States. The growth of these non-Judao-Christian faiths can be demonstrated by the fact that in the 1950s the only mosque in the United States was in Washington, DC, just down from the National Cathedral, where it also served as the Islamic Cultural Center. Today, there are virtually no major metropolitan areas in the United States without a mosque.

Christianity, especially the more fundamentalist version, has reacted strongly to these events. Realizing that they have been put on the defensive by a more secular society, coupled with new and often polytheistic worshipers, Christian denominations have sought to reassert themselves in the society by taking a more active role in politics and mass media.[18] This has often involved these faiths taking sometimes unpopular public stands on issues in which they strongly believe. Interestingly, it is the fundamentalist Christians who have experienced increased membership; the more middle-of-the-road and liberal denominations have experienced decline. Membership in the Southern Baptists, Church of God, and Church of the Nazarene is up; the numbers for the United Church of Christ (heirs of the Pilgrims and Puritans) and the Unitarians are down.

Part of the reason for this may be that while many of the stands taken by fundamentalists may be unpopular with the more secular aspects of the soci-

---

■ ■ ■   BOX 9.1   Religious Revival   ■ ■ ■

There is a religious revival in the United States just as there is worldwide. But it is not among the old traditional mainline Protestant churches. Rather, the fundamentalist churches are the ones experiencing new growth. These churches are where many people newly interested in religion are turning to experience their faith.

The fundamentalist churches are controversial in that they often take unpopular stands based on their religious beliefs. They tend to be politically conservative, with the Christian Coalition as their political arm. They are also generally pro-life and anti-gay. These stands have put them at odds with other groups in the society: notably gay-rights and pro-abortion groups. The religious conservatives are, indeed, in a struggle with these groups, and it is not much of an exaggeration to say that they are engaged in a battle for the soul of the society.

What is particularly interesting is that the religious conservatives continue to grow in membership. Their influence in the society, although often declared dead or in decline, seems to be at least holding steady, if not increasing.

The reasons for the continued growth of the religious right are obvious. In the first place, they represent an island of continuity in a vast sea of change. Members of the religious right believe in the same things that their predecessors believed in 100 years ago. The second reason is that at least the religious conservatives believe in something, and people are looking for that. So many of society's institutions seem to have lost their way and really do not know what they are about or even why they exist. Religious conservatives do not have that problem: They know who and what they are, and that makes them strong.

ety, even with the more liberal branches of Christianity, they remain stands and statements of faith and belief that other, less conservative denominations seem either unwilling or unable to make. Like it or not, they represent and stand for something. These denominations, in fact, feed on the derision and contempt of the society as a whole, aligning themselves with the early Christian martyrs who were so persecuted by the Roman Empire. Great Christian leaders and theologians have a long tradition of being persecuted by the leaders of the society dating back to the crucifixion. In the history of adherents to the true faith, suffering and sacrifice are the norm with which fundamentalists identify. Society's contempt only serves to strengthen that belief.

The result is that the more conservative denominations grow ever stronger in their membership, while the more liberal denominations grow weaker and become the objects of scorn and derision on the part of evangelicals. The attitude of some fundamentalist groups toward their more liberal brethren may be summed up in a rather bad joke about the very liberal United Church of Christ, often referred to as the UCC, which many fundamentalists say stands for Utterly Confused Christians.

It should be mentioned that the Catholic Church has experienced some of the same problems as those of the Protestant denominations. The Catholic Church has never been without dissent, but the current problem is that the church is changing. Once the bastion of Irish, Italian, German, French, and English Catholics, it has now taken on the role of a center for the influx of Hispanics, the vast majority of whom are Catholic. The church suffers from many problems, including its stand on divorce, contraception, abortion, women in the priesthood, marriage of priests, as well as the consolidation of parishes because there are not enough clergy to serve them. Many Catholics want change, but the Roman Catholic Church has never been quick to change.[19] Part of the problem is that while some wish for the church to become more liberal, others feel that the status quo or even more conservative stands are more appropriate. The church is caught in a world that is changing faster than it can change, and as a result, is facing many problems, all at the same time.

The involvement of religious organizations in the political life of the nation is very American and has a long history. Abolitionists first found their voice in the churches of the North. Opposition to slavery as well as stops along the underground railroad often involved churches and the ministers who served them. The temperance movement and many social welfare proposals first found their voice in the churches of the land, and of course, the black churches served as the incubator of the civil rights movement led by the Reverend Martin Luther King. The involvement of highly religious and spiritual people in the affairs of the government and the secular world is a long-held tradition in U.S. society.[20] Religious hermits have never had much of an impact, but committed religious people have put their stamp on society, often holding the high moral ground and insisting that the rest of the country confront its sins.

The Family

The essential basic unit of any society is the family. It represents the essential unit of the society and is the basis of organization upon which much of the society is constructed. The family provides for many of the essential functions of the society, including raising children; distribution of food, clothing, and shelter; care of the elderly; and the essential psychological needs of love, affection, and protection from the outside. Healthy families make for healthy societies.

However, the nature of the family is certainly changing and evolving. This change started with the industrial revolution.[21] In agrarian societies, extended families of uncles, aunts, cousins, and grandparents could often be seen. This ideal was not always followed as Americans moved west and left their extended families behind. So when the factories called for labor, it was a fairly easy thing for people to leave the farm and find work in the industrial portion of the economy. The result is that the American family has always been a nuclear family of the parents and children, whether off the boat from a foreign shore, seeking a new life heading west, or moving to the city to find work.

Today, there are many other changes affecting the family. First, the family has evolved from the nuclear family to even smaller units. Single-parent families, once a relatively rare occurrence as the result of a death of one of the parents, have become common.[22] Years ago, unattached, recently widowed, or (more rarely) divorced men and women would attempt to find a mate to help with the farm. George Washington married Martha, a widow, and Abraham Lincoln's mother died and his father remarried. Death by disease, accident, or hostile Indians was not an uncommon occurrence in frontier America, and somebody had to raise the children, put food on the table, and look after the farm. There were no social welfare agencies and people banded together and formed family units to provide what was needed.

Today, many single-parent families are headed by women.[23] The role of the man has been replaced by the state, which provides money for food, clothing, and shelter. Many of these families live in poverty. The typical single parent is not some Murphy Brown–like highly successful figure, but a poor, ill-educated, often teenaged young woman with a baby and little or no hope.

Single-parent families represent an increasing segment of the population, with over half of the African-American babies being born into these situations and over 25 percent of white babies experiencing a similar fate. They represent a long-term problem for society as fatherless children beget more fatherless children in an unending cycle of poverty and neglect, often leading to crime and other antisocial and undesirable acts.[24]

BOX 9.2   Babies Having Babies

One of the most serious problems facing American society is the problem of teenage, even pre-teenage girls, giving birth out of wedlock. The vast majority of these young women are in precarious economic situations. They have little in the way of marketable skills, little training, and less hope. They are bringing a baby into a world that is ill-prepared for its arrival.

The typical woman who has a baby out of wedlock is not Murphy Brown, the character played on the television series by Candice Bergen. Rather, she tends to be poor and ill educated. These women frequently represent hard-core welfare cases in the society. They already have a full-time job trying to be a mother to a baby and are simply not equipped to do more. The real tragedy is that many of these babies will repeat the same mistakes that their mothers made and find themselves in an iron circle of poverty, with each succeeding generation becoming more dependent on the largess of the state.

In addition to the nuclear and single-parent families, other types of family organization have started to appear in the society. One that has caused the greatest amount of controversy is the same-sex couple seeking to have and raise children. In the case of a female couple, the child may be conceived through artificial insemination or a brief sexual encounter with a male friend or acquaintance. In addition, there is always the option of adoption or surrogate motherhood, which could also be employed by male same-sex couples. For obvious reasons, same-sex couples have had greater difficulty in adopting than would more conventional couples, but that does not mean that they could not adopt. The objection that same-sex couples are not married and therefore do not have the stability of married couples is being challenged. For example, the state of Hawaii has granted many of the same benefits for same-sex couples as for legally married persons.[25]

Another aspect of the development of the family has been the increased reliance on grandparents to raise children. Over 1 million children are being raised by their grandparents for a whole variety of reasons.[26] These second families are often providing an additional and often unwelcome burden on the grandparents, who are spending their golden years changing diapers instead of tending a garden or fishing. This is certainly not the fault of the grandchildren being raised, and probably not of the grandparents, but it does represent a new development in society, the implications of which have yet to be determined.

The only thing that is certain is that the family is evolving into new and different arrangements than has been the case in the past. Where these arrangements will lead remains to be seen; the only thing that is certain is that in a democratic and free society, the family, of one sort or another, will remain. In the book *Brave New World*,[27] one of the first things that Big Brother did was to take away the children from the family and genetically engineer a new generation. Only in a totalitarian society would this kind of act be possible, a kind of hell on Earth where up is down and right is wrong.

Technology

The essence of a modern society in the world is the availability, use, and development of technology. The rapid development of technology started with the industrial revolution and has continued at an ever-increasing speed. Many inventions that are taken for granted in the modern world have only been in use for 100 years. Flying from New York to San Francisco is an everyday occurrence involving thousands of people, but during the 1849 California gold rush, it involved months of hard and often hazardous travel.

Three of the areas of technological advancement that are certain to provide real gains for the human race are biotechnology, electronics, and the space program. Biotechnology is truly an industry in the beginning stages of development. This industry has often been compared to where the field of computer technology was just after World War II. Biotechnology is only now starting to show some of its promised results. For many years advances have been made against diseases that have plagued all forms of life on Earth. Treatments and cures have been found for polio, smallpox, and rubella, but that represents only the beginning of the potential that may be achieved.[28] Various gene therapies are now being explored, with new discoveries being announced on a regular

■ ■ ■　　　**BOX 9.3　Sheep Cloning**　　　■ ■ ■

One of the latest scientific advances comes in the area of cloning. A sheep cloned in Europe raised all kinds of speculation as to the ethics and other considerations of such activity. The sheep, an apparently healthy ewe, was cloned from another ewe and has now grown to adulthood. Whether or not the cloned sheep will be able to reproduce in the conventional manner remains to be seen, or if this could be a possibility in the future.

Ethicists, scientists, and religious leaders have all had their say about cloning and many have been able to offer widely differing opinions on the efficacy of cloning. One thing is certain, however, and that is the fact that science has, once again, outrun the human capacity to deal with the consequences of cutting-edge, scientific research.

One other thing is also certain: We now have the capability to clone a reasonably complex animal, and there is no reason not to presume that human beings will not be far behind. The real challenge is what to do with this newfound capability. At one extreme is the horror of armies of clones enslaved in a surrealistic version of hell—a new source of cheap labor—while at the other extreme is the prospect of being able to grow vital organs for medical use. Instead of waiting for an appropriate heart for a transplant, scientists may be able to grow a heart from the patient's tissue. This would not involve the creation of a fully developed clone that would serve as a "parts bank" for the original but as a procedure to grow individual organs. This could conceivably cut down on the rejection of organs, which is the principal problem in transplant patients.

The possibilities are endless, but so are the potential abuses. Society has not yet figured out how to deal with these issues and is going to need some time to do so. The legend of Frankenstein still haunts our consciousness and the prospect of the monster walking off the movie screen is now more than just a Saturday matinee thrill.

basis. Genetic causes for a whole host of ailments have been discovered and more are certain to follow. In addition, the prospect of being able to clone body parts is a real possibility. This obviously causes certain moral and ethical dilemmas. Although various groups have come out against the cloning of human beings, it is obvious that at some point in the future, it is going to be done. Exactly what will be the rights and responsibilities of the clone and of the society toward the clone? What will be the relationship of the "original" and the copy? Does this mean immortality, or does it mean simply another way to reproduce? What is the impact on this for the family as a unit? There are many questions that arise from this aspect of biotechnology that are going to have to be answered, but certainly, society is not now prepared for these questions.

Other aspects of the biotechnology industry include the hope for an improved food supply and better crops and other agriculturally related products.[29] This is a hope that people will be able to continue to improve the food products that are raised on farms and other venues to support an increasing population.

Electronics represents a second obvious growth industry for the future.[30] Communication of all types is tied to this industry, and the World Wide Web is only the beginning. Other parts of people's lives will be affected by the electronics revolution that have not even been considered. Although Microsoft may seem to be in control, at least as much as it is possible to control something like this, others are sure to challenge and eventually succeed Microsoft, just as Microsoft succeeded IBM.

Nobody knows where the electronics industry is heading, but one direction is obviously the World Wide Web. This is a means of communication that is available to anyone with access to it for a very nominal fee. The control of this communication system is going to be one of the major questions facing society in the twenty-first century. The government of the United States has recognized this and has attempted to gain control via the issue of child pornography. There is no question that child pornography is available on the Web, and although it may be disgusting and repugnant, it is something that some people want. The other aspect is that the Web does not end at the border but is international, and people on the other side of the planet can talk to each other. Controlling this access is not something that national governments are going to be able to do. It is like radio. All you need is a receiver turned to the right frequency. But the Web is better because you can talk back. The real reason that governments want to control access is so that they can tax it and obtain money for their own purposes. The Web has become a seditious instrument over which there is little control, and so far no revenue is being generated for government. Most governments want to stop that, but unfortunately for them, they have yet to figure out how. This frustration can be tied directly to the decentralization of power and governments all over the world. Controlling the Web would be a big step in reestablishing central control, but it would be against the continued movement toward decentralization in the society.

The space industry is also going to have a remarkable future. In many ways, space is the future not only of society but of the entire human race. Many products have been spun off the space program, to the point where one justification for the program has been these products. The amounts of money involved have been huge and the payoffs have been incredible, but there is still a great deal to do. Humankind will continue to pursue a role in space if for no other reason than because that is its fate, and it must.

Technology is what makes modern society different from all previous civilizations. Technology is what supports the ability of the human race to survive and to prosper. It represents the chief area of societal development and the aspect of the society that is most likely to change and to have an immediate impact on each person.

Modern society is a highly complex and diverse organism. The major components of business, government, religion, the family, and technological change have combined to provide a major portion of the world's population with a better and more productive life than has ever been the case for so many before. Those who are not part of this advanced society are doing everything they can to achieve the same kind of life now enjoyed by many of the people in the industrialized Western world. The changes that will come in the reasonably near future are changes that will be demanded by these people who only want the same kind of life that is now enjoyed by those in the industrial countries. They will demand it, and, to some degree, they are going to get it, because they are willing to work for it.

HOW SOCIETY IS CHANGING

Besides technological change, there are other ways in which society is changing. Some of these have been made possible by technological change or at least assisted by technology. One of the primary changes that has occurred in the world has been the immigration of people. Immigration is not a new idea and people have moved elsewhere, seeking better lives for centuries. What is new and important is that many of the patterns of immigration have changed over the years and will certainly continue to change in the future.[31]

The United States is experiencing two separate and distinct forms of migration: one internal and one external. The internal migration is part of the long history of the westward movement of people in the country. This movement started in colonial times and has continued so that now the center of population in the United States is somewhere in southern Missouri.[32] But the movement of people is not only in a westward movement, but also in a slightly southern direction as well. This reflects the economic fortunes of the respective regions of the United States. During the 1970s and 1980s, many Americans journeyed to the southern part of the United States. The populations of Florida and Texas increased immensely, while the states of the Northeast either slightly increased their population or remained about even. New York lost its place as the state with the largest population to California, and numbers in many cities along the East Coast declined, while cities in the South, including Atlanta, Houston, and San Antonio, continued to grow. Americans started moving out of the rust-belt cities of Cleveland and Detroit and moving to the suburbs or the South. During this time, the economy of the Midwest suffered as a result of a decline in manufacturing and other economic activities in this region, while the South often prospered. This was a simple reflection of the political doctrine "People vote with their feet," the economic equivalent of which is: "People go where the jobs are."

Immigration from outside the United States is another factor. Although most Americans trace their roots back to Europe, the same cannot be said for most of the immigrants entering the United States today.[33] Some do come from Europe, but most are from other parts of the world, most notably from Latin America and Asia. These new immigrants are changing U.S. society and making their presence felt both politically and economically. In a political sense this has been particularly true of the Hispanic community, which has become a major organized and important force in many areas. Asians have tended to focus on the economic opportunities offered to them, to the point where they now have a higher per capita income than any other identifiable ethnic group, including whites.[34]

BOX 9.4 Money Income of Households by Race (1996 Dollars)

Year	All Households	White	Black	Asian Pacific Islander	Hispanic
1990	29,943	31,231	18,676	38,450	22,330
1991	30,126	31,569	18,807	36,449	22,691
1992	30,636	32,209	18,755	37,801	22,597
1993	31,241	32,960	19,533	38,347	22,886
1994	32,264	34,028	21,027	40,482	23,421

Source: *Statistical Abstract of the United States, 1996.*

Immigration is also occurring on a global basis. This, also, has been going on for many years but some of the trends are instructive. Developed countries generally have a lower birthrate than less developed countries, and as a result, many developed countries are experiencing an influx of these people, especially if they are from former colonies of now almost forgotten empires. Africans and Algerians certainly have a presence in France, as do Indians and Pakistanis in Britain. Turks, originally brought into the country to help in the development of Germany after the war, now represent a significant minority in Germany, as do Serbs and Croates. All these people are following work, and they go where the jobs are. Although labor may be the least transportable factor of production,[35] it is not completely stationary and never has been.

The one thing that there can be no doubt about is that the world is now a smaller place, and it is of the greatest importance that we all learn to accept and appreciate other peoples and cultures.[36] As little as just over 100 years ago, Jules Vern could write about an Englishman going around the world in 80 days as a tale of fiction. Today, astronauts go around the world in about 80 minutes, and flying from New York to London or Tokyo now takes hours, whereas 150 years ago, such a journey could take months.

Communication is worldwide and instantaneous. During the 1950s, to make a personal call from the East Coast of the United States to Hawaii required a reservation on the Pacific Cable and was limited in the amount of time one could take. Today, the only limit is on the size of the bill one is willing to pay, and it can be done simply by picking up a telephone from anywhere in the country. Radio, television, the Internet, and CNN have conspired to make communication as easy as it has ever been in the history of the planet.

There no longer is a grace period as there was when events could occur without any sort of outside judgment being placed on them while they were in progress. Events such as the people's uprising in China would not have received the worldwide condemnation that it did while it was in progress because word simply would not have filtered out to the rest of the world. In the old days, the incident would have been long over before the rest of the world knew about it and nothing could have been said or done about it. In fact, the Chinese communists would have been able to deny that it ever happened or at the very least, placed themselves in the most favorable light possible, given what happened. But the worldwide communication industry would not allow that to happen.

From a business perspective, this shrinking of the world community has had great impact on the way people do business. This includes simple things such as directions for a product being printed in at least two and often three different languages (English, Spanish, and French) so that the entire North American continent may be reached as a market. It also includes some of the more sophisticated aspects of the business world, such as advertising. While some firms try to stress the same message in their advertisements to their customers all over the world, it should be recognized that not everything works everywhere. A few years ago a Japanese auto firm tried to introduce an advertising campaign into the United States that had been highly successful in Japan. Unfortunately, the ads, which were done in English and featured only bits and pieces of the car, proved to be a disaster in the United States. The automaker ignored the fact that Americans like to see what they are buying and the ad never showed a complete shot of the entire car. A door here and a tire there, but not

BOX 9.5   E-Mail and the Internet

Weekly newspapers and journals, personal letters, and messages carried on horseback were the fastest means of communication into the nineteenth century. In the twentieth century, communication has changed. In the last ten years, communication has changed even more drastically. From weekly newspapers and journals, we moved to daily newspapers and daily television news. Now, we have moved to 24-hour news networks, and news on-line. From personal letters and messages carried on horseback, we moved to telegrams and telephone calls. Now we have moved to electronic mail (e-mail), discussion groups on-line, and real-time computer communications.

Today, e-mail and the Internet are the quickest methods of communication. They may also be the least expensive methods of communication. Although related, the Internet and e-mail are two separate functions. A third communication device (not discussed here)—computer on-line discussion groups—provides another variation of computer-based communication.

Electronic Mail

E-mail is a method of sending messages from one computer to another. This may occur within a business, agency, or organization. It may occur outside the business, agency, or organization. This works much like an answering machine. You call a phone number, but after a few rings, an answering machine clicks on, so you leave a message. With e-mail, your computer calls another computer and leaves the message you type.

To access your answering machine messages, on most machines you may do so in one of two ways: in person, pushing the Play button; or remotely, by calling your phone number and punching in a remote access code to access the answering machine messages. The same applies to e-mail messages. From your computer, your business, agency, or organization has probably established a quick connection to your e-mail message address, just like pushing the Play button on your answering machine. You may also access your e-mail from a different computer if you have a remote access code.

Let's examine e-mail in more detail. Your computer must have a modem connected to a phone line, or your computer must be connected to another computer by hard-wiring. With a modem, you must also have an Internet service provider (ISP) that authorizes an e-mail account for you, directly from your personal computer to the ISP's computer. With the hard-wired system, your personal computer is connected to your business's computer, which is usually connected to an ISP computer. The ISP authorizes e-mail accounts for your company, which then assigns them to you.

With the increasing use of computers at home for business purposes, the number of Internet service providers has increased at a rapid rate. Most telephone companies offer this service, as well as many local companies. America On-line is one of the largest ISPs in the United States, but telecommunications companies such as Sprint and Southwestern Bell are rapidly growing ISPs. A standard charge for most of these ISPs in 1997 was $19.95 per month, with unlimited access.

If your ISP does not provide e-mail for you, you may obtain an e-mail address without charge from one of a number of e-mail servers: <www.hotmail.com>, <www.rocketmail.com>, and <www.yahoo.com> are three popular servers. In using one of these e-mail servers, you will need to establish an account, with a user ID and password, which you will need to remember. It's easier to remember if you write both on a page in your planner, notebook, or briefcase. (The standard notation <> is used in this article. The text printed between < and > is the text as it should be typed in the Location or Address box.)

The reason there is no charge to you for this account is that the e-mail server sells advertising space and may sell your e-mail address to companies for them to send you junk e-mail (just like the junk mail you receive in your home mailbox). Once you have established one of these e-mail accounts, you may access it from any computer that is connected to an ISP.

BOX 9.5 (continued)

E-mail is easy to use. Take the time to examine the icon buttons and the pull-down menus on the e-mail opening page. A master menu for accessing messages is usually labeled "Messages" or "Composer" or "Communicator". In sending messages, it is very helpful to establish an Address book. This is a way of storing the e-mail addresses of those to whom you send messages regularly. An icon that normally represents the Address book often looks like a Rolodex file. By recording addresses in the Address book, you do not need to retype the address every time you send a message. You merely click on the Address book icon, then click or highlight the address (or name) of the person to whom you wish to send a message. This will automatically enter the person's e-mail address in the To box. Tab down to the message box. Type your message. Click the Send button. This message is then saved automatically in an Out or Sent folder and sent to the recipient. Periodically, you will need to purge old messages from your In, Out, and Trash folders.

A handy feature of most e-mail systems is the ability to send attachments. When you attach a file to an e-mail message, the recipient's computer will record the message and store the attachment in a directory on the recipient's computer. Be sure to prepare the attachment in a word processing format (such as Word or WordPerfect) that the recipient's computer can read. Unless you know what word processing format the recipient uses, it is best to include that information in the body of your e-mail message.

To read your incoming messages, check the "In" folder in your e-mail window. Your e-mail system will also allow you to print that message, reply to the message, forward the message to another e-mail address, and save the message. You may open any attachment, make changes or revisions, and send it back to the originator. This greatly improves the ability to circulate documents for comments, corrections, or revisions in a short period, without printing many drafts. Once everyone has contributed input to the document, it can then be printed and circulated.

The Internet

The Internet is a connection of many computers together, much as a volleyball net is a connection of many strands of string. You can move from one point to another on the Net in several different ways. The same applies to the Internet: You can move from one computer on the Internet to another computer on the Internet in several different ways. For more information on the Internet and the World Wide Web, see the resources at the end of this article.

Once you have established ISP service and can log-on to the Internet, a whole new world awaits you. You can use any number of search engines, such as: Yahoo, Excite, Lycos, and others, to explore the Net. Simply type the subject in the search box, click the Search button, and wait for the results. As you use these search engines, you will learn how to limit your searches, how to expand your searches, and how to jump from one search location to another to follow new leads.

The Internet pages are built around hyperlinks, which you can click to jump to a new address. Each address is a file on a computer that is linked to the Internet. To learn more about what each part of an address means, see the resources at the end of this article.

Using the Internet can shorten your research process by reducing your trips to the library. It is not a complete replacement for traditional library research, but is an additional method. Using the Internet can also provide you with access to the most current information. However, because the Internet is an unregulated, uncensored means of communication, the sources must be evaluated carefully for accuracy and completeness.

When examining an Internet source whose address ends in <.gov>, you may rely a great deal on that source, since it is a government source. If the address ends in <.com>, realize that the source is a commercial site, or provided through a commercial site, with all the potential inaccuracies that

BOX 9.5 *(continued)*

arise with any site that is not reviewed for accuracy. Addresses that end in <.edu> are educational sources, and these can be a significant source of information. Evaluating these sources is just like evaluating information you obtain from the *Wall Street Journal,* the *National Inquirer,* and Uncle Harry on your father's side. Be aware of the entity that sponsors the Internet site. Ask yourself whether anyone is reviewing the site for accuracy. Does the sponsor have a reputation for accuracy? Is there any requirement for academic rigor in the preparation of the information on the site? Does the site contain original information, or is it secondary? Is the site monitored by a known publisher? Is the writer of the site a person known in the community?

As you use the Internet, you will learn some sites that you find to be very reliable. You will want to remember the site address, so that you can return to it whenever you wish, without going through the search process. One way is to write in a notebook the complete address of the Internet site you want to remember. Because many Internet locations or addresses (URLs) can be quite long, it is better to develop a Bookmark file. You can store hundreds of URLs and you will not have to worry about accurately typing the full address.

If you do not share your computer, you may just save the bookmarks on the hard drive of your computer. However, if you share your computer, or you use more than one computer, you may want to save the bookmarks on a 3.5-inch diskette.

To save an Internet address or location as a bookmark, go to the address on your computer. Simply click on the Bookmark menu or icon; then click Add Bookmark. This will save that address in your Bookmark file. If you are saving to a diskette, under the File menu, click Save As and save it to your diskette. Some Internet browsers will automatically look for a bookmark in the A diskette drive when starting. Otherwise, you may need to open the <a:\bookmark.htm> file to access your diskette-saved file. When using bookmarks, you may click on the Bookmark menu or icon, then click Go to Bookmarks to edit your bookmarks. Regular Internet users will have hundreds of bookmarks, which they organize into file folders in the <bookmark.htm> file. You can use the edit function to name the file folders and arrange them in any hierarchy you wish. With an extensive bookmark file, your research will be shortened, just like your knowledge of where particular reference books are located in your favorite library.

Some government Internet addresses you may want to explore are:

1. <http://www.whitehouse.gov>
2. <http://www.house.gov>
3. <http://www.senate.gov>
4. <http://www.gao.gov>
5. <http://www.gpo.gov>
6. <http://www.irs.ustreas.gov>
7. <http://lcweb.loc.gov/homepage/lchp.html>

Some Internet addresses for business information are:

1. <http://www.sec.gov>   Securities & Exchange Commission
2. <http://www.dbisna.com>   Dun & Bradstreet
3. <http://www.wsj.com>   Wall Street Journal
4. <http://www.nyse.com>   New York Stock Exchange
5. <http://www.nasdaq.com>   NASDAQ
6. <http://www.cbot.com>   Chicago Board of Trade

BOX 9.5 *(continued)*

In addition, many colleges and universities have Internet sites with hyperlinks to many business and governmental sites. Begin by accessing the college's or university's home page (its primary Internet address), then clicking on any hyperlinks to other sites. Hyperlinks are shown as icons or as different-colored text (often underlined). If your mouse cursor becomes a hand with finger pointing when it is placed on an icon or differently colored text, it is a hyperlink. Simply click the mouse and wait as your Internet browser jumps to the new location.

The best way to learn how to use e-mail and the Internet for modern communications and research is to use it. You will make mistakes. Learn from them. Open your mind to the possibilities. The whole world is at your fingertips. Explore it!

Further Reading

Crump, Eric, and Nick Carbone, *Writing On-line: A Student's Guide to the Internet and World Wide Web,* 2nd ed., Houghton Mifflin, Boston, 1998.

Gilster, Paul, *The Internet Navigator,* John Wiley & Sons, New York, 1993.

Hacker, Diana, *A Pocket Style Manual,* 2nd ed., Bedford Books, Boston, 1997.

Hahn, Harley, *The Internet Complete Reference,* 2nd ed., Osborne/McGraw Hill, Berkeley, CA, 1996.

Harnack, Andrew, and Eugene Kleppinger, *On-line! A Reference Guide to Using Internet Sources,* St. Martin's Press, New York, 1997.

Lundsford, Andrea, and Robert Connors, *Easy Writer: A Pocket Guide,* St. Martin's Press, New York, 1997.

Pejsa, Jack, *Success in College Using the Internet,* Houghton Mifflin, Boston, 1998.

Reddick, Randy, and Elliot King, *The On-line Student,* Harcourt Brace, Orlando, FL, 1996.

Source: Greg Plumb.

the complete car. Ambiance and metaphor may work in the Japanese market, but the U.S. market wants to get a good look at what it is being asked to buy.

Another way that things are changing is the realization that everyone is a stakeholder in the society in different ways and that the public, the customers, the voters, and the employees are all one in the same. What affects the voters affects the employees because they are one and the same. Henry Ford realized this fact in a limited way when he started building the Model T and started paying his workers $5 per day.[37] Henry Ford built a car that he wanted his workers to be able to afford to buy and then paid them enough so that they could afford to buy it. This drove up the cost of wages for everyone, so Ford created a market for his products by making sure that his employees could purchase what he was making. Henry Ford realized that all of the economy is interconnected and that everyone depends on everyone else to survive and prosper.

FUTURE ISSUES FACING SOCIETY

Competitiveness and Productivity

One of the most important issues facing any society today is the issue of competitiveness. How can a society gain ground in providing a better life for its people, or for that matter, not lose ground in providing that better life, in an increasingly competitive global, economic environment? In a world where money flows around the world with a push of a button or the click of a mouse, where raw materials and finished goods can be transported anywhere, and where new business enterprises are springing up all over the world, how can a society remain competitive? The answer lies in the development of the one resource that every society has—its people. The Japanese have demonstrated that it is possible to develop a high standard of living with little in the way of natural resources, or even equipment, because at the end of World War II, the only thing that Japan had was a highly educated workforce. In 50 years, Japan became one of the world's top economies.

Given the mobility of the other factors of production, the ability of the workforce is rapidly becoming the determining factor in the increasingly competitive atmosphere of the global economy.[38] As jobs and skills become more sophisticated, and the need and ability to learn new jobs and new skills increases in importance, the educational level of the workforce becomes ever more important. Societies with highly educated workforces are going to have a competitive advantage over societies that do not have highly educated workforces, and the degree of education of that workforce is going to be a factor in the relative prosperity of the society to other educated workforces.[39] The portion of the workforce that is not educated or poorly educated will be a permanent drag on the competitiveness and productivity of the society.

In the United States, the high school dropout rate, on the national level, is about 15 percent and has remained at roughly that level for many years. This means that 15 percent of the population does not have a high school education, the basic minimum for entry into modern society. These people are the basis of a permanent underclass in U.S. society who will usually be less productive and less competitive than they need to be to be successful in the society. They will certainly need additional support, on the whole, from the society to support them, because, simply put, they will not be able to carry their own weight.

This lag on competitiveness and productivity is likely to take many forms. The first is the payment of welfare and other direct forms of support over extended periods of time. This is the chronic welfare state, where generation after generation remains on welfare and other forms of public assistance. This already exists in the form of public housing, Aid to Dependent Children, food stamps, and other programs. Nobody should begrudge the temporary use of these programs by people who are in relatively temporary need of assistance. This is part of the social safety net for the citizenry. The problem is with permanent users of these programs who have no real prospect of turning their situation around—the 15 percent that seems doomed always to be part of the social, economic, and educational underclass. The society needs to find ways to get such people off welfare and into productive and successful lives.

The other major expense in dealing with a permanent social, economic, and educational underclass is crime and the costs of dealing with crime in the society. For many years the United States has led the industrialized world in violent crime, especially murders. Although many of these crimes go officially unsolved, the perpetrators are often tried and convicted for other crimes.

The cost of crime to the society takes two forms. The first is the actual cost directly associated with the crime: the stolen goods, the pain and suffering of the victim, and the possible death of the victim. The second area of cost is the official cost of the police, the legal system, and the punishment of the convicted person. In a purely monetary sense, these expenses can be far greater than the cost of the crime, and society today is demanding that people stay in jail longer, thus increasing the cost of prison. Most prisoners are from the lower levels of the social, economic, and educational strata of society. This is not to say that educated and prosperous people do not go to jail or that they do not commit crimes, but if the same proportion of all people in jail was the same as the number of people with college degrees in jail, the prison system would not represent a major burden to the society.

Dealing with the social, educational, and economic underclass is going to be one of the major challenges facing society. Keeping people in school so that they can be educated enough to be trainable in a rapidly changing technological society is simply not happening often enough when 15 percent of the people in high school drop out. Ways must be found to make this portion of the workforce and the society at least complete high school, and to do so with real, marketable abilities, not just passing them through, based on social promotion. This portion of the society needs to be able to read, write, and do math to be trainable for other more sophisticated tasks.[40] Not to do so is to invite a permanent drag on the potential of all citizens in the society, something the society can ill afford.

Resources and the Cost and Standard of Living ■ ■ ■

One of the consequences of the success of modern technological society is that for the first time in the history of the human race, the limits of resources are starting to be questioned. For centuries, human beings treated the environment as though it was a limitless storehouse of resources. Farmers would clear the land, grow crops for a few years, and then move on when the land became less fruitful, to a new location a little distant. If the mines petered out on one mountain, the miners would simply move on to the next. Today, people have recognized that there is a limit on expansion and the continuous use of resources by a growing world population.

This is bound to have an impact on the standard of living and the cost of living. The essential principle of supply and demand is that as the demand for something increases and the supply remains relatively the same or may even decline, the cost goes up. What this means is that without new technologies, alternative resources, and reusable recyclable resources, the cost of living is likely to rise and the standard of living is likely to decline as people have to pay relatively more for the products and services they need.

The modern society that is enjoyed by the technologically advanced nations is the same as the society to which the less developed nations aspire. The problem is that as they all demand more, the cost of providing that sort of society goes up, as societies find themselves in a bidding war that cuts two ways.

The first is the cost of providing for the increased demand for products and services as those products and services become more expensive. The second is the effort to keep prices down as much as possible by finding the lowest possible production costs, often seeking wage rates of $5 per day or less in some of the least developed parts of the world.[41] It is a paradox that the nations with the greatest need for new capital and investment find themselves bidding for production work with the lowest possible wage rates they can supply. The population of these societies is growing at a much faster rate than that of the developed world and their demands in the future are going to be greater than they are today.

Modern society is a combination of conflicting demands on the government, business, family, and other institutions that constitute it. Stress and change mark modern society, and the technological advancement of society is, at the same time, one of the necessities for global advancement and one of the hallmarks. As the world grows smaller, so does the need for everyone to share in these advances and to have access to the opportunities necessary for their own fulfillment, as well as the promise of a unique contribution to the society. How many Einsteins, Mozarts, and Edisons could there have been if only people with the same kind of talent had the opportunities that these great contributors to society were able to take advantage of? How many will there be in the future to address the problems that face the new global economy? Certainly, all of the talents of the human race are going to be needed to address the current problems that face human beings today, as well as the problems that await in the future.

SUMMARY   ■ ■ ■

Modern society consists of a number of factions, including business, government, religion, the family, and technology. All of these factors are changing and interacting with each other. Business continues to become even more international while reengineering itself and attempting to deal with divergent groups and societies. Government is attempting to address issues while trying to learn to do more with less and less in the way of resources. Religious groups are attempting to reassert their influence and importance both in the United States and abroad. This rise in religion is not limited to Christians but also includes much of the Islamic world. The family is also evolving and changing. The traditional nuclear family of mom, dad, and the kids is giving way to other forms of families, made up of different combinations. Technology remains one of the foremost instruments of change, as it has during the last 200 years. Today's society is as different from the society of 200 years ago as it is from ancient Rome, and the pace of that change only seems to be getting faster.

Other factors are also influencing American society, including immigration and the changes that are occurring in those patterns. Today, most immigration to the United States is from Asia and Latin America, not Europe. Communication and transportation have all led to a shrinking world. CNN and other media are on the scene almost instantly for any major news story, so it is now almost impossible to hide any event from the rest of the world.

A restriction that is going to be placed on all people in the world is in the use of resources. The resources that were easy to obtain have been obtained, and resources are going to be more expensive to extract or produce in the future than they have been in the past. This will put limits on the ability of people to have things that they now take for granted unless substitutes can be found. When resources become more expensive, the cost of living goes up and the standard of living goes down.

Questions

1. People came to what is now the United States for many reasons. Why would improving their economic situation be one of them?

2. Why did American society develop very differently than Thomas Jefferson thought it would?

3. Small businesses employ most people in the United States. Why do you think this is so?

4. What do you see the role of government becoming in the next 10, 20, or 50 years?

5. How do you see the role of religion in society? Do you think religion will become a more or less important factor in society?

6. In what ways do you see the family developing in the United States and other postindustrial societies?

7. How do you think immigration will change American society?

8. How does the shrinking of the world in terms of communication and transportation affect the way people interact with each other?

9. Why is the ability of the workforce so important for the economic success of a society?

10. How do you think scarcer resources will affect the cost of living and the standard of living in the future? What are some things that can be done about this?

CASE 1

As the new plant manager for ACE Manufacturing, you have recently taken over one of the largest plants in the country for ACE. ACE is not, however, just a domestic U.S. firm; it has operations all over the world, including many countries that are predominantly Islamic in faith.

The company publishes an international corporate newsletter that is circulated throughout the organization. In the last issue, the lead article concerned the company practice of allowing overseas Islamic workers prayer breaks so that they can observe their religious responsibilities during work hours. Historically, in the United States, the company has always remained carefully neutral regarding religion, and the various faiths seemed to get along well.

Now, however, that would seem to be changing. You have just received a request from the five or six Islamic workers in the plant to allow prayer breaks similar to those which the company allows outside the United States. In addition, one of your supervisors, whom you know to be an active, born-again Christian, has sent you a memo inquiring whether the company would object to his holding a bible study class on the grounds of the factory after hours. Although you have never really practiced your Jewish faith or heritage overtly, you are uncomfortable with activation of the various religious faiths in the factory and the division that might cause. You can just imagine how your Aunt Sadie would react to reports of Islamic prayers being said at the factory you manage. After all, she lost her son, your cousin, to a terrorist attack in Israel just a year ago.

As you are sitting in your office, the receptionist buzzes you to let you know that a contingent from the Buddhist monastery has arrived and would like to speak to you about the coming Buddhist religious holidays and the participation of some of your Buddhist employees in those activities.

1. What do you do?
2. What are your ethical obligations?

CASE 2

Unical Corporation has moved most of its corporate offices and much of its senior management to Singapore, so that now it has essentially two corporate headquarters. The reason for this is that Unical has invested heavily in Thailand, which has been accused of various human rights violations and has thus become a kind of pariah nation. As a part of the move to Thailand, the company has sold off its once extensive network of gas stations and is now even more committed to Thailand than it once was.

Unical maintains that it has little control over what the government does in its new home and that it is simply trying to obtain the best possible return for its investors.

1. What are the firm's ethical obligations?

References

1. Evans, Bergen, *Dictionary of quotations,* Avenel Books, New York, 1978.
2. Beverley, Robert, *The history and present state of Virginia,* Institute of Early American History and Culture, Williamsburg, VA, 1947.
3. Ibid.
4. Marx, Karl, *The communist manifesto,* H. Regnery Co., Chicago, 1955.
5. Koch, Adrienne, *The philosophy of Thomas Jefferson,* Columbia University Press, New York, 1993.
6. Blumberg, Rhoda, *Full steam ahead: the race to build a transcontinental railroad,* National Geographic Society, Washington, DC, 1996.
7. Gartner, William B., "'Who's an entrepreneur?' is the wrong question," *Entrepreneurship: Theory and Practice,* Summer 1989.
8. Burford, Betty, *Chocolates by Hershey,* Carolrhoda Books, Minneapolis, MN, 1994.
9. Prasso, Sheri, and Larry Armstrong, "A company without a country," *Business Week,* May 5, 1997.
10. Frankel, Benjamin (ed.), *The Cold War, 1945–1991,* Gale Research, Detroit, MI, 1992.
11. Segal, Lydia, "The pitfalls of political decentralization and proposals for reform," *Public Administration Review,* March 1997, v. 57., n. 2.
12. *The Federalist papers,* Arlington House, New Rochelle, NY, 1966.
13. Scherer, Ron, "Arkansas has more than Whitewater," *Christian Science Monitor,* November 22, 1996.
14. Ibid.
15. Rhys, Ernest, *Chronicles of the Plymouth fathers,* J.M. Dent, New York, 1920.
16. Shindler, Colin, *Israel, Likud and the Zionist dream: power, politics and ideology from Begin to Netanyahu,* St. Martin's Press, New York, 1995.
17. *Statistical abstract of the United States, 1996,* U.S. Department of Commerce, Washington, DC, 1996.
18. Shribman, David, "The Christian right regroups," *Fortune,* September 8, 1996.
19. "Fidel, the church and capitalism," *The Economist,* August 16, 1997.
20. Shribman, "The Christian right regroups."
21. Golden, Richard (compiler), *Social history of western civilization,* St. Martin's Press, New York, 1988.
22. *Statistical abstract of the United States, 1996.*

23. Ibid.

24. Goldstein, Richard, and Stephen Sachs, *Applied poverty research*, Rowman & Allenheld, Totowa, NJ, 1984.

25. Zimmerman, Janet, "Hawaii OK's benefits to same sex couples, law does not legalize marriages for gays, lesbians," *USA Today*, July 8, 1997.

26. *Statistical abstract of the United States, 1996.*

27. Huxley, Aldous, *Brave new world*, Limited Editions Club, Avon, CT, 1974.

28. Thompson, Larry, *Correcting the code: inventing the genetic cure for the human body*, Simon & Schuster, New York, 1994.

29. Steyer, Robert, "Monsanto, Calgene in deal," *St. Louis Post Dispatch*, May 24, 1966.

30. Pereira, Pedro, "Assembling a global empire as it eyes $4.5 B," *Computer Reseller News*, August 4, 1997.

31. Wheeler, Sheba R., "Obstacles to 'open world' Korean-American struggle to learn U.S. laws, customs," *Denver Post*, July 27, 1997.

32. *Statistical abstract of the United States, 1996.*

33. *Historical atlas of the United States*, National Geographic Society, Washington, DC, 1988.

34. *Statistical abstract of the United States, 1996.*

35. Johnson, William, "Global work force 2000: the new world labor market," *Harvard Business Review*, March–April 1991.

36. Miller, William H., "A new perspective on tomorrow's workforce," *Industry Week*, May 6, 1991.

37. Cahill, Marie, *History of the Ford Motor Company*, Smithmark, New York, 1992.

38. Johnson, "Global work force 2000."

39. "Education and the wealth of nations," *The Economist*, March 29, 1997.

40. Ibid.

41. Gray, Charles, "Protection or protectionism," *Far Eastern Economic Review*, September 13, 1990.

10

ETHICS AND THE LAW

Concepts : You Will Learn ■ ■ ■

how criminal law relates to the concept of ethics

how law relating to public matters relates to ethics

how criminal procedures relate to ethics

the role of the lawyers and judges in the U.S. system of justice

how civil law relates to the concept of ethics

the role of appellate courts

INTRODUCTION

Certain celebrated cases during the 1990s have helped raise the level of public interest in the issue of the relationship between the law and ethics. It is clear that the public has less than a meaningful understanding of how the two relate. Although there is a relationship between law and ethics, the two are not the same. Although much of the law is based on ethics, other parts of the law are founded on concepts necessary for the establishment of an orderly society and the administration of justice.

Ethics relates primarily to the conduct of individual affairs.[1] Although the law also deals with the regulation of individual conduct, much of the law deals with public matters as well as relationships among people in various contexts. It is useful to take a look at each of the areas regulated by the law and see how the law relates to ethics.

Criminal Law and Ethics

When the public thinks about the law, it most often thinks about the criminal law. How do ethics relate to those laws that prohibit certain types of conduct?

One way to deal with this issue is to separate the criminal law into its substantive and procedural aspects.

Substantive criminal law relates to the imposition of penalties for engaging in certain types of conduct.[2] It is here that there is a relatively close link between ethics and the law. One ethical principle is that it is not ethical to take an action that would harm either a person or a person's property based on the use of physical force. It is also an ethical principle that one should not be able to profit from one's deceit or other manipulative conduct.[3]

Criminal law also deals with these types of issues. Criminal laws impose sanctions against people who engage in such conduct. Below are some examples of the merger between these ethical principles and criminal law sanctions.

Laws prohibiting the taking of another's life by use of force coincide with criminal laws that impose sanctions against taking a life deliberately, *murder*, or through conduct that is in wanton disregard of human life, *manslaughter*. The taking of another person's property through force is called *robbery*. Taking property by entering another's dwelling is called *burglary*. Taking another person's property without paying for it is called *theft*. If one acquires property through deceit, it is called *theft by deception*. If one lies in order to sell property, it is called *fraud*.

The criminal law implements these underlying ethical principles against the use of force, stealing, or use of dishonest tactics to deprive another of that person's life or property. The criminal law imposes sanctions on those who knowingly violate its provisions. More recently, the criminal law has extended into more public areas. The power of business is so extensive that it can have adverse impacts on society as a whole.[4] As a result, there are laws designed to protect society against investor fraud, pollution, or other actions that can cause damage to the public interest.

In recent years there has been renewed concern about protecting the land, sea, and air.[5] Companies which sell or produce products that may pollute the environment now are subject to cradle-to-grave liability for its products. The organization must clean up any pollution created by its products or pay for the government to have it cleaned up.

Public Criminal Law: Whose Ethics Count?

In the area of public criminal law, the relationship between the law and ethics becomes somewhat less clear because of the various interests involved. Although it is ethical for companies to clean up pollution and to provide accurate information to investors, the appropriate level of regulation is also a matter of

 BOX 10.1   Public Stock Offering

NBX Corporation wants to sell stock to raise money to construct a new plant. If it wants to sell stock to the public, it must comply with the 1933 Securities Act, which states that a company offering securities to the public must fill out a registration statement and a prospectus. These documents must comply with the requirements of the Securities and Exchange Commission, which are designed to protect investors from fraudulent or misleading claims of a company issuing stock.

ethical judgment. Too much regulation may be regarded as unethical because it leads to a waste of resources and stifles needed investment. Too little regulation could lead to an increase in the number of fraudulent stock issues and defrauded investors. Too little regulation of pollution could lead to a decline in the environment. Too much regulation could lead to an excessive squeeze on profits and a decline in jobs.

The various regulatory agencies established by Congress also have the power to enact regulations that have the force of law. In addition, these regulations allow the agency to impose sanctions for their violation. When the agencies enact these regulations they intend to benefit the public in some way. However, such regulations also have a cost to them. Businesses must pay to comply with them and they do restrict their ability to conduct their business. Job losses also have a multiple effect, so that a loss of jobs in one area will affect jobs in other areas.

The questions of how these conflicts are resolved is usually left to the U.S. political process. As a result, the law relating to such questions as the regulation of the stock markets, labor–management relations, the environment, and product safety are left to Congress and the executive branch. This can result in a swinging pendulum that bears little relationship to what is "ethical."

Ethics and Criminal Procedures

Recent criminal court cases have highlighted ethical issues relating to the process of determining a defendant's guilt or innocence. Some public concern results from a lack of understanding of the basic procedures relating to trying a defendant. Under U.S. law, a defendant is presumed innocent until proven guilty.[6] All Americans are also protected by certain rights, including the Fourth Amendment right against search of a person or person's property unless the government has probable cause to believe that a crime has been committed.

After a person has been charged with a crime, he or she has certain protections. A defendant has a right to an attorney who will represent his or her client in a zealous fashion. The defendant is also entitled to an impartial judge who will rule on the evidence that is to be admitted against the defendant. If the crime is serious enough, the defendant is also entitled to be tried by a jury. The members of the jury are to be impartial and drawn generally from the community.[7] Under a Supreme Court decision, the jury is supposed to be truly representative of the community. It is not lawful to exclude members based on racial, religious, ethnic, or other irrelevant factors.

The Roles of the Lawyer and Judge

The O. J. Simpson case and others have raised some fundamental questions about the roles of lawyers in a criminal case.[8] Although each is supposed to be an effective advocate for his or her side, each also has certain obligations to the court and to legal ethics. The prosecutor is in the most ambivalent position. It is his or her job to present the evidence on behalf of the government and to convict the defendant if there is sufficient evidence to do so. However, the prosecutor also is responsible for evaluating all the evidence and making a responsible judgment about whether a trial is in the interests of the entire community.

BOX 10.2   The Cost of Prosecution

In the O. J. Simpson case, the prosecutor had some difficult decisions to make. The defendant was a person with a great deal of money and was capable of hiring the best defense counsel in the nation. These factors meant that the criminal trial was going to cost taxpayers millions of dollars as well as tying up much of his office staff. In addition, the case would tie up the resources and personnel of the Los Angeles Police Department. Furthermore, the caliber of the prosecution witnesses raised serious doubts about their credibility. In short, the prosecutor could spend millions of taxpayer dollars and lose the case. It was a criminal case that cried out for a plea bargain. Conversely, many citizens would not have understood that such a decision was in their best interest and might have argued that the prosecutor was being too "soft on crime." Still, it is the responsibility of the prosecutor to make these difficult decisions.

The prosecutor also has the duty to turn over any evidence that may tend to show the defendant's innocence to the counsel for the defense. In addition, the prosecution has the obligation to inform the defense of any matters that may adversely affect the credibility of the prosecution's witnesses.

The defense counsel's role is much clearer. His or her job is to provide the best possible defense for the client within the confines of the law and legal ethics. If the defense counsel knows that the client will lie, he or she may not put the person on the witness stand. Similarly, the defense counsel may not put witnesses on the stand whom he or she knows will lie, nor may counsel knowingly lie to the court. However, the defense counsel also has the obligation to explore every option that may point to the defendant being found not guilty. This includes the obligation to point out flaws in the evidence or procedures of the prosecution. In the Simpson case, the defense spent considerable time exposing flaws in police procedures in collecting and analyzing the physical evidence.

The public may expect defense lawyers to consider the "public interest" when trying cases. If they do, they have misunderstood the role of the defense lawyer in our adversarial system of criminal justice. It is expressly not the role of the defense counsel to consider the public interest. To do so would violate the fundamental duty of the defense counsel to represent the interests of his or her client zealously. Protecting the public interest is someone else's duty.

The judge has a number of roles in our system of criminal justice.[9] Few positions in our society are more important than that of judge. More than anyone, it is the judge who decides how U.S. citizens will view our system of justice. If citizens believe that judges' decisions meet their conceptions of justice, they will have confidence in the process. If they do not, they will become cynical and lose faith.

The primary role of the judge is to apply the law that is found in federal and state constitutions, in the statutes enacted by Congress and the state legislatures, as well as the law as announced through various court decisions.[10] The judge is the necessary impartial arbiter between the government and the individual or between various parties to a civil lawsuit. Without such a person, the entire system of justice would break down.

Although having some discretion, the judge is bound by the principles of law that he or she finds in statutes and court decisions. Statutes are laws that are passed by the legislative body. Court rulings are judges' decisions that rule on the facts or decide the applicable law based on the facts that are presented to the court.

In a criminal case, the judge's main function is to ensure that the defendant receives the due process requirements provided in the U.S. Constitution.[11] It is the due process clause which requires that the defendant receive adequate notice of the charges so as to be able to prepare a defense. A hearing on the charges must be scheduled and the defendant must have the opportunity to defend against them. The defendant also has the right to have a licensed attorney represent him or her at the hearing. It is the judge's responsibility to ensure that these due process requirements are carried out. In addition, Supreme Court rulings designed to protect a person's rights against improper search and seizure and against self-incrimination have become controversial and need to be discussed to fully understand the role of a judge in a modern criminal trial.

In *Miranda*, the Supreme Court ruled that a person who has been placed into custody must be advised that he or she does not need to talk with law enforcement officials and that he or she has the right to have an attorney present. The purpose of the *Miranda* ruling was to protect accused persons from oppressive police tactics.[12] If police officers obtain statements without complying with *Miranda*, the statements will be thrown out. This may result in judgments that seem unfair. The courts are attempting to find a balance between allowing police officers to do their jobs and protecting citizens' constitutional rights against improper questioning.

Under *Gideon*, the Supreme Court ruled that a person who is facing prison has the right to the assistance of legal counsel.[13] The result of this decision was that the government needed to appoint public defenders to represent those who do not have the resources to defend themselves. This has had a significant impact on the criminal justice system. In both the *Miranda* and *Gideon* rulings, the Supreme Court was carrying out the ethical principles in the Constitution. Under any ethical system of criminal justice the accused should have the right to independent legal advice before being sent to jail. The more controversial rulings have related to the exclusion of evidence obtained in violation of the *Miranda* requirements or Fourth Amendment protections against unreasonable searches and seizures. In these cases, ethical principles collide.

It is ethical to admit evidence of crimes against guilty people. However, it is not ethical to invade people's privacy and take papers or other "evidence" without reasonable grounds to believe that a crime has been committed. When ethical principles are in conflict, judges have a difficult job. They try to strike a balance between the two ethical principles. If the police violate the protections provided by the Constitution, the judge must set aside any evidence obtained improperly.

This may result in guilty people being set free. This often angers members of the public who are justifiably concerned about crime. However, the courts have few other alternatives if they are to protect individual liberties. The usual remedy for people who have been injured by the acts of another is to bring action to recover money damages from the person who caused the injury. This is not a practical remedy with respect to police actions. Few policemen have a great deal of money or other resources. In addition, making them personally liable might tend to discourage good police work. As a result, the

---

BOX 10.3   Hearsay Evidence

Statements of others supposedly heard by a second party are called *hearsay*. Such "evidence" is generally regarded as unreliable, for several reasons. First, it is difficult to determine if the person hearing the statement heard it correctly and is telling the truth. In addition, one cannot question the person who allegedly made the statement. The courts believe that a jury could be unduly influenced by hearsay evidence. A layperson might listen to such a statement and give it far more weight than it deserves. Often, the average person does not understand the reasons that such evidence is excluded.

---

courts have few alternatives other than to refuse to admit evidence that was obtained improperly.

The judge also has important duties with respect to running the trial. One of the judge's responsibilities is to rule on the admissibility of evidence presented to the judge and the jury. In a trial by jury the rulings on the admissibility of evidence are extremely important. Juries are heavily influenced by the evidence which they hear. The rules of evidence are designed to prevent the jury from hearing evidence that is inherently unreliable.

All of these matters raise ethical issues that the law tries to resolve. Some evidence deserves to be admitted; other evidence does not. Although it is ethical to admit evidence that goes to show the truth of the case, there are other ethical issues that may be even more important.

Another function of the judge is to monitor the activities of the jury.[14] Members of the jury are taken from the general public. In addition, the members are often drawn from the least educated segment of our community. During the Simpson trials a number of jurors were dismissed because of various forms of misconduct. As a result of this atmosphere, it is important that the judge exercise firm control over the proceedings.

The judge must also instruct the jury about the law before presenting the case to them. Jurors are only triers of fact. They must apply the law as it is given to them by the judge. This is another important ethical issue. The Constitution clearly provides that a person has the right to be tried by a jury. However, the average juror has little understanding of the law. In addition, there are considerable indications that our jurors are not capable of understanding issues of high complexity. Therefore, it becomes especially important for the judge to provide clear legal instructions to the jury. This is the highest ethical responsibility of the judge in a criminal case. One of the major causes of appellate court reversal of jury verdicts is the failure of the judge to give adequate instructions to the jury.[15]

CIVIL LAW AND ETHICS

Much public attention has focused on criminal trials, but most of the law deals with civil law matters. Civil law involves legal questions relating to private matters between and among individuals.[16] The most commonly recognized civil law matter may be issues involving contracts.

A contract is an agreement between two or more people that the law will enforce. Normally, few ethical issues are involved with the performance of contractual duties. However, ethical issues do arise if a party fails to perform contractual duties. The first question is to what extent the courts should intervene. If they were totally uninvolved in contractual disputes, persons adversely affected would have little recourse except to take actions outside the law.

The same situation applies when a person or a person's private property is injured. If courts do not intervene, people would have to take some action on their own or forget the issue. The courts decided that they should intervene. Ethically, what should be the role of the courts? How should the injured party be compensated? How should the party who committed the act be affected?

The basic remedy in civil cases is to try to place the party injured in the same position that he or she would have been if the act causing the injury had not happened. The person causing the injury will be required to pay the amount of money necessary to place the injured party in the same position as if the injury had not happened. In an ethical society, a wrong to a person would be compensated by the person who did the wrong. This allows the injured party to stay within the law and be restored to his or her previous position.

One should note that the purpose of the civil law is not to punish but simply to restore the parties to their proper position. Punitive damages, which are designed to punish, are reserved for a defendant who committed deliberately wrongful acts.

In our system of adversary justice, the lawyers in cases are responsible for representing their client. The judge and the jury's role is to act as the impartial arbiter of the law and the facts. The burdens of proof in criminal and civil cases are different, and this can lead to different results. In a criminal case, the prosecution has the burden of proving the defendant's guilt beyond a reasonable doubt. This is a very high standard. A plaintiff in a civil case need only convince the jury by a preponderance of the evidence.

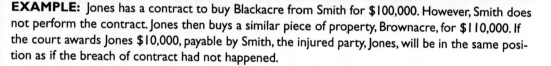

BOX 10.4   Civil Case Examples

EXAMPLE: Jones has a contract to buy Blackacre from Smith for $100,000. However, Smith does not perform the contract. Jones then buys a similar piece of property, Brownacre, for $110,000. If the court awards Jones $10,000, payable by Smith, the injured party, Jones, will be in the same position as if the breach of contract had not happened.

EXAMPLE: Wilson was driving his brand new Blast sports car at 75 miles an hour when the car jumped the curb and injured Small Sally. At the trial, Small Sally's attorney showed that the accident was Wilson's fault. She also showed through expert testimony that Sally's injuries will diminish by $100,000 Sally's ability to enjoy her life and to earn a living. Wilson should pay Small Sally this amount.

EXAMPLE: Halton writes a defamatory article about Marut's hotels. The article is proved to be deliberately false. Marut's attorney introduced various people who state that they decided not to stay at Marut's hotels as a result of Halton's article. Expert witnesses testify that the level of damages because of the article is $50,000. Halton should pay Marut this amount.

▪ ▪ ▪   BOX 10.5   The Legal Process   ▪ ▪ ▪

In the Simpson civil suit, the jury awarded punitive damages because it believed that the defendant had committed deliberately wrongful acts that caused injury to the Brown and Goldman families. In the Simpson criminal case, the defendant was found not guilty. In the civil trial, the defendant was found liable for wrongful death. Both verdicts can be justified based on the different burdens of proof. Both verdicts can be justified based on appropriate ethical standards.

Much of the controversy among the public about the Simpson and other widely publicized cases may result from two factors. First, there is a lack of understanding among many people about the purposes and mechanisms of the legal system. Second, discussions of the process sound like pit-bull fights. A more thoughtful approach that explained instead of debating would help the public understand the legal process.

The Role of the Appellate Courts   ▪ ▪ ▪

One aspect of the U.S. legal system is that people who are unhappy with the result in a lower court may appeal the decision to a higher court. For example, a defendant convicted of a crime has the automatic right to an appeal. Appeals are based on the premise that the trial court may have made a mistake in applying the law or instructing the jury as to how the law should be applied. In the specific case, many reversals are based on incorrect instructions from the judge to the jury. If the instructions are incorrect, the laypeople on the jury are unlikely to reach a correct verdict.

The role of appellate courts is to look at the law and how it is applied by the judge at the trial court level. Generally, appellate courts usually accept the decisions of the triers of facts with respect to the facts. Appellate courts see their role as interpreting the law as applied to the facts determined by the lower court.[17] Appellate courts have performed an extremely important role within the U.S. legal system. They have been the defenders of the Constitution and seem willing to expand individual freedoms. Their role is to protect one's rights even in the face of public opposition or indifference.

Many of the best known cases were brought by people with little or no influence. *Gideon* was brought by a prisoner who believed that he was denied a fair trial because he was not represented by an attorney. The result of this landmark case was that every person who could be sent to prison is entitled to be represented by an attorney. This has had an enormous impact on our system of criminal justice.

The judges of the appellate courts have the freedom to stake out new positions that change society. *Roe v. Wade* permitted women to obtain legal abortions. Such a ruling represented a major departure from previous legal and religious traditions. The political debate has continued to rage over abortion, but the principles of *Roe v. Wade* seem firmly entrenched in the law.[18]

The appellate courts have a vital role in our system of justice. They are the guardians of the ethical standards of fairness and equity, which are the foundation of our legal system. They protect the constitutional freedoms that form the basis of our legal system. In addition, they keep the other participants honest by reviewing individual cases as well as examining legal principles and procedures.

Legal Ethics

Lawyers play essential roles in the U.S. system of justice. Despite the many jokes about attorneys, the vast majority of lawyers conduct their activities in a highly ethical manner. Furthermore, the judiciary and the bar are concerned about the ethics of lawyers and regularly conduct disciplinary proceedings against lawyers who violate legal ethics.

The first duty of a lawyer is to represent the client faithfully. This includes the responsibility to take good care of the client's resources. Lawyers are required to place clients' assets into separate accounts. This protects the clients' assets from being commingled with the attorney's personal assets. An attorney will be severely disciplined if he or she does not faithfully safeguard clients' assets and maintain appropriate records regarding their use. Although some lawyers have misused their power to oversee clients' assets, a much higher percentage carry out their responsibilities in an ethical manner.

A client may disclose the most confidential matter to an attorney because a client's conversations with his or her attorney are protected by the attorney–client privilege. This means that no court can compel an attorney to disclose what a client told him or her. This also represents an ethical decision by society.

Although U.S. society might achieve certain benefits by requiring attorneys to disclose conversations with their clients, it has made a decision not to do so. Without the attorney–client privilege, a person might feel afraid to disclose important information to an attorney. This would have a detrimental impact on our system of justice because it would deprive people of effective legal representation.

Attorneys must also avoid any conflict of interest between the client's interests and their own or those of another person. Generally, the attorney should also try to avoid even the appearance of a conflict of interest. Some attorneys get themselves in difficulty by placing their interests above those of their clients. Again, they will be disciplined by the courts if they fail to act in an ethical manner.

Every licensed attorney is considered an officer of the court. That is, the attorney is presumed to be acting in the interests of justice and telling the truth. This allows attorneys to file papers and make representations to the court. Attorneys are disciplined if they make false statements to the court.

SUMMARY

The criminal law is an important area of ethical conduct. Society demands that it be protected from the less desirable elements, and in a civilized society, that is accomplished by the criminal law. But society must be careful about application of the criminal law. The last thing that the legal system wants to do is to let an innocent person be punished for a crime that he or she did not commit.

The criminal law has both substantive and procedural aspects. The substantive is the law itself and the procedural is the application of that law. Both these aspects of the law must be applied with due diligence if society is to accomplish the goals of protection from crimes as well as misapplication of the law.

To understand the criminal legal system and how it works, it is necessary to understand the role of the judge and the attorneys. The prosecutor's job is to present evidence on behalf of the government and to convict the defendant if there is sufficient evidence to do so. But the prosecutor is also responsible for evaluating all the evidence and making a responsible judgment as to whether a trial is in the interests of the entire community.

The defense counsel's job is to provide the best possible defense for the client. Counsel has the obligation to explore every possible option that may point to the defendant being found not guilty.

The judge's duty is to apply the appropriate federal or state statutes to the case. This also means that the judge is responsible for assuring that the defendant receives due process, for running the trial, for monitoring the activities of the jury, and for instructing the jury on the law.

Most of the law deals with civil matters between individuals, often involving contracts. Because contracts have not been fulfilled, people have suffered injury and the civil law is designed for them to redress that injury.

Lawyers play an important role in the U.S. legal system, whether as judges, prosecutors, or defense attorneys. The ethics and standards to which these people are held is the key to the viability of the U.S. legal system.

Questions

1. What is the link between public law and ethics in the United States?
2. How is this link decided in a democracy?
3. What is the link between the Fourth Amendment and ethical standards?
4. What is the link between the Fifth Amendment and ethical standards?
5. What is the link between the Sixth Amendment and ethical standards?
6. What is the link between due process and ethical standards?
7. What is the burden of the prosecution in a criminal case?
8. What is the burden of proof for the plaintiff in a civil case?
9. How could one reach different results depending on the standards of proof required in the case?
10. What are the ethical standards involved with the *Gideon* ruling? Do you agree with this ruling?
11. What ethical standards are involved with the *Miranda* ruling? Do you agree with the *Miranda* ruling?
12. Explain some civil law principles and how they relate to ethical principles.
13. What is the role of the appellate courts in the U.S. system of justice?
14. How does the role of appellate courts relate to ethical standards?
15. Name some ethical standards of lawyers and judges.

CASE I

John was a neighborhood bully who regularly terrorized the other citizens in the neighborhood. John would drive his car very close to his neighbors automobiles, scream at his neighbors, and throw rocks at them when they drove by. In addition, John would block his neighbors access to their property, assault them, chase them through the neighborhood, force their cars off the road, and engage in other activities that frightened his neighbors. Among the neighbors terrorized was Danny. Along with his neighbors, Danny asked local law enforcement officers to intervene. However, they said they could not take action unless they witnessed the events. For several months, the neighbors documented these events at the request of the police. One day, John and Danny were out on the street together. John yelled at Danny that "his family was as good as dead." Danny had a gun with him. He fired the gun and killed John. The prosecution charged Danny with murder. At the trial Danny testified that he was afraid of John. He also testified that he did not remember firing the nine shots that killed John. Before the case was sent to the jury, one of the jurors was dismissed from the jury for misconduct.

1. If you were a member of the jury, would you convict Danny of murder?
2. What are your ethical reasons?
3. What factors should the jury consider?
4. What alternative courses of action are available to society in cases such as this?

CASE 2

You have just passed the bar examination. You have been assigned to defend a person charged with murdering three prostitutes. The defendant is indigent and cannot afford a private attorney. You have tried two traffic ticket offenses previously. Your client was abused as a child and refuses to discuss the details of the case with you. The evidence provided to you by the prosecution indicates that there is little evidence of your client's guilt except for a "confession" that he gave to local police. The confession was obtained without the presence of an attorney. It is also clear that law enforcement personnel were in a hurry to find a suspect because of the intense media publicity surrounding the case. There is also evidence that the police had three other suspects before your client's confession. They stopped investigating the other suspects after your client's confession. Your client's files indicate that he has an IQ of 63 and finished fifth grade. He has been in and out of a variety of reform schools. He has also pleaded guilty to two small thefts for which he spent three months in a reformatory. You believe that he may be innocent of this crime because the confession is filled with inconsistent statements. In addition, there is some evidence that your client was out of town at the time of the murders.

1. What do you do?
2. What are your responsibilities as an attorney?
3. What are your ethical and legal responsibilities as a citizen?
4. Given the evidence above, how would you vote if you were a member of the jury?
5. If your client was found guilty, would you still want to be an attorney?
6. Why or why not?

CASE 3

Jeanine N. was a 10-year-old girl who had been left alone by her parents. Someone broke into her house and abducted her. A few days later, Jeanine's body was found in a wooded area. She had been raped, sodomized, and bludgeoned to death. The citizens of the area were outraged by the crime. The county police and district attorney's office indicted Jorge Cruz for these crimes. Later, Patrick Dugan confessed to the crimes. Despite the confession, the law enforcement authorities went forward with the prosecution. Cruz was later convicted by a jury of these crimes.

Later, it was determined that the police had made up their evidence and the prosecutors had encouraged them.

1. What are the ethical issues for the prosecutors, the police, defense attorneys, jurors, and the public?

CASE 4

At a middle-sized college located in an urban area, an African-American male student was driving his automobile at about midnight. He came to a stop at a red light next to a white pickup truck that was to his right. After the light turned green, the truck remained in place. The student waited about 5 seconds and then turned right in front of the truck, which was being driven by an off-duty campus police officer. When the car turned down the road, the police officer followed. The student continued in his car with the truck in pursuit. After a few minutes the campus police officer cut off the student. At this, both the officer and the student got out of their vehicles and began to run at each other. As they got closer, the police officer drew a gun.

1. What are the ethical issues for the officer?
2. What are the ethical issues for the student?
3. What are the ethical issues for the school?

CASE 5

You are a police officer in a large, urban police department. You have observed numerous acts of police corruption. In addition, your partners have offered you money to forget about the systemic corruption within the department. When you reported these actions of corruption to your superiors, nothing was done. In addition, you have been the subject of various threats from other members of the department. When you testified about this corruption, before a governmental agency, you received death threats over the telephone.

1. What are the ethical obligations of an honest police officer in a corrupt department?
2. Explain the role of corruption among the police.
3. How does culture affect these situations?
4. Why do these situations occur?

References

1. Flexner, Stuart Berg, and Leonare Crary Hauk, *The Random House dictionary of the English language*, 2nd ed., Random House, New York, 1987.
2. Shur, Edwin M., and Hugo, A. Bedau, *Victimless crimes: two sides of a controversy*, Prentice Hall, Englewood Cliffs, NJ, 1974.
3. Bird, Otto, *The idea of justice*, Praeger, New York, 1967.
4. Brooks, Theodore, *Accountability: it all depends on what you mean*, Clifton, NJ, Akkad Press, 1995.
5. Tyson, Peter, *Acid rain*, Chelsea House, New York, 1992.
6. Summer, Lila, and Samuel Woods, *The judiciary: laws we live by*, Raintree/Steck-Vaughn, Austin, TX, 1993.

7. Ibid.

8. Lange, Tome, *Evidence dismissed: the inside story of the police investigation of O.J. Simpson,* Pocket Books, New York, 1997.

9. Summer and Woods, *The judiciary.*

10. Ibid.

11. Ibid.

12. Riley, Gail Besser, *Miranda v. Arizona: rights of the accused,* Enslow Publishers, Hillsdale, NJ, 1994.

13. Wice, Paul B., *Gideon v. Wainwright and the right to legal counsel,* Franklin Watts, New York, 1995.

14. Summer and Woods, *The judiciary.*

15. Ibid.

16. Eldridge, William, *Business law,* South-Western, Cincinnatti, OH, 1995.

17. Summer and Woods, *The judiciary.*

18. Guernsey, Joann Bren, *Abortions: understanding the controversy,* Lerner Publications, Minneapolis, MN, 1993.

11

ETHICS AND
THE ENVIRONMENT

Concepts : You Will Learn ■ ■ ■

how concern for the status of the environment should affect ethical decision making

mechanisms that are in place to protect the environment

how the requirements for protecting the environment are balanced with the need for economic growth

mechanisms for protecting the environment with a view toward ethical balancing of the environment and economic interests

THE NEW ENVIRONMENT ■ ■ ■

Until the later part of the twentieth century, there was little concern about the environment.[1] The principal focus of the public, business, and government was to promote a growing economy that would create wealth and jobs. North America was a vast unexplored continent, and worrying about its environment seemed unimportant.

The main task of the settlers was to take the available natural resources and build an economy that would support the continent's new residents. The continent's original residents, the Indian tribes, had a reverence for the land, sea, and air. The new Europeans were more concerned with amassing vast quantities of wealth that would be derived, in part, from exploiting the continent's natural resources.

The vast majority of Americans made their living by working on farms. However, substantial wealth was more likely to be achieved through commercial enterprises. Exploiting logging and mining resources represented major opportunities to earn wealth, even vast fortunes. However, growth of these industries changed the relationship between employers and employees. It also changed the nature of the relationship between the residents and the land.

Although trees and ore are certainly suitable for human use, large industries initiated procedures that often did terrible damage to the environment.

Loggers destroyed miles of forest and miners initiated the practice of strip mining which had a terrible effect on the land. One of the tragedies of the Great Depression was the Dust Bowl conditions that prevailed in the Great Plains and drove many farmers from their land.[2]

During the Great Depression, the country was much more concerned with promoting economic growth than with protecting the environment. The disastrous economic conditions of the Great Depression were one cause of World War II. It was not until after the war that the economy revived.

The Effect of World War II

During World War II it became important to develop whatever weapons were necessary to save American lives and to defeat the axis powers, including atomic and chemical weapons. These weapons were improved by the U.S. military during the Cold War between the United States and the Soviet Union. As a result, tons of various forms of toxic materials were dumped into the environment during the last half of the twentieth century.

The chemical industry also mushroomed following World War II. Manufacturer's of a large number of items found that chemicals were useful in the production of their goods. Chemicals allowed manufacturers to better preserve perishable items and permitted them to vary their product offerings. U.S. consumers were promised that they would live better lives as a result of chemical advances. Although it is true that living standards are now higher than ever before, the increases often came at a considerable cost to the environment. Such large quantities of pollutants were dumped into the environment that by the late 1960s and early 1970s it was clear that actions had to be taken to protect the environment.

Both Congress and the executive branch saw the need for a federal agency that would have the responsibility of safeguarding the environment. The Environmental Protection Agency was created at the federal level, and similar agencies were created at the state level.[3]

Environmental Ethics

Protection of the environment remained a major concern of the nation's citizens and of the various levels of government. Public opinion polls taken throughout the 1990s indicate that safeguarding the nation's air, land, and water is an important concern of the voters. It has become an issue with which decision makers in all sectors of our economy must be concerned. Decisions must now include projections as to how they will affect the nation's environment.

Balancing Business and the Environment

The primary purpose of business is to maximize shareholder wealth by earning profits.[4] The role of governmental regulators is to enforce laws enacted to protect the environment. It can be difficult to find a balance between these two roles.[5] An ethical society attempts to find an appropriate balance between creating jobs and wealth and protecting the environment. This is a difficult job under any circumstances, but it is becoming more difficult as society, the economy, and technology become more complex. The mechanisms for resolving these issues may no longer be adequate. In some cases, they may no longer make much sense.[6]

Cellular phones have become very popular. Growth of the cellular phone business creates jobs and is helpful to the entire economy. But to allow people to have access to these phones, towers from which signals can be transferred must be built. The towers are often unsightly, and residents near them are often not only offended by the view but alarmed that the towers may be dangerous.

Traditionally, decisions regarding the construction of new developments are made by local planning boards or boards of adjustment. Such boards are composed of ordinary citizens who listen to cases presented to them. They are guided by local ordinances and statutes that control the state's right to regulate land use. The results of decisions of such boards are often influenced by local politics or by citizens who protest any new development located near their homes. The decisions often do not reflect a high level of rationality.

As a result, it often becomes necessary for developers to appeal unfavorable decisions to the courts. The judiciary has the power to reverse the decisions of local boards if the courts find them to have been made in an "arbitrary and capricious" manner. In addition, the courts have ruled that certain uses are "inherently beneficial" and may not be rejected by local planning authorities. Experience has demonstrated that communities will regularly reject certain uses because of community pressure. As a result, the courts have declared that municipalities may deny these uses only under certain limited circumstances.

It is expensive for developers to prepare applications and to appeal adverse decisions. One can legitimately question the mechanisms for making these decisions at the local level. The following questions could reasonably be raised:

1. *Should these decisions be made at the local level?* Although local officials and town residents are affected by developments, the development can have a much broader impact. It can affect surrounding areas and potentially affect many others, such as the environment, employees, customers, and other users. Local interests are likely to be too narrow and overly represented. At the same time, broader interests are likely to be underrepresented when such decisions are made by town residents.

2. *Should these decisions be made by citizens who are chosen through the political process?* In most towns the members of the planning and zoning boards are selected by the mayor or the governing body. There is no requirement that these appointees have any particular qualifications. Although the appointees have the guidance of trained professionals such as engineers and attorneys, they retain the discretion to decide cases based on their own best judgment. In addition, they are regularly exposed to pressure from neighbors and others who have opinions about the development. Furthermore, planning board members often do not follow the advice of their professional advisers if they feel strongly about the development. This process can lead to unusual results which have a negative impact on both the area and the economy. Poor developments may be approved and good applications may be rejected.

A better alternative might be to set up regions throughout the states. Applications could be heard before administrative law judges who have specialized

BOX 11.1   Voter Fraud

One issue that is regularly confronted in democratic elections relates to the pattern of voting in certain urban areas. It is an ethical problem that is encountered regularly during close elections in large urban states. Although our nation's civics teachers may instruct their students about the importance of voting one's beliefs, the leaders of the nation's political parties know that the votes of many citizens are for sale to the highest bidder, particularly in the nation's cities. Democrats may use "street money" to encourage certain people to go to the polls; Republicans, to encourage certain people not to vote.

In the election for governor of the state of New Jersey in 1993, both sides were concerned with the level of voter turnout in the state's urban areas. The Democratic candidate wanted a large turnout to provide the difference in a closely contested election; the Republican candidate wanted to make inroads into traditionally Democratic areas. On election night, the Republican candidate won by a margin of about 20,000 votes out of about 2 million votes cast. Reports indicated that voter turnout among traditionally Democratic urban voters was significantly lower than would be expected in a gubernatorial election. This lower turnout was cited by commentators as the reason for the loss by the Democratic incumbent.

A few days later, Ed Rollins, who was a campaign consultant for the winning Republican candidate, told a group of reporters that Republicans had paid money to African-American ministers so that they would urge their parishioners not to vote in the election. His statements caused an outcry among the press and in the African-American community. Rollins later retracted his statements. An investigation was completed by the U.S. Attorney's office into Rollins' statements. The office concluded that there was insufficient evidence to bring any criminal charges.

During this period, members of the Democratic party argued that the results of the election should be set aside. Members of the Republican party urged authorities to start an investigation of Democratic use of money to pay people to vote. Republicans also alleged that some of these payments went to persons who voted improperly by casting more than one vote and by casting fraudulent ballots.

There are a number of ethical issues involved with this situation and similar types of cases. Our democracy is based on the premise that citizens will take the time to understand the process of government and to vote based on their understanding of what is in society's best interests. Unfortunately, this is not what occurs in reality. It is well known among political leaders that citizens do not perform these activities. They have little time, inclination, ability, knowledge, or desire to determine what is good for the society. Instead, they vote their party affiliation, what's in their own interests, how someone tells them to vote, or decide not to vote at all. As a result, the votes of many Americans are up for sale to the highest bidder. There are many instances in which elections have been won or lost based on who had bought the most votes. Although the purchase of votes is not as common as earlier in our country's history, it still occurs. This means that we often have people being "elected" who are not chosen by a "rational" process. This means that we can have people making important decisions with few qualifications for the job. This is the ethical dilemma of a democracy. Such a form of government permits significant public input. This tends to prevent the rise of oppressive dictatorships. However, it can also result in the election of the incompetent and the unqualified.

Is such a system of government ethical? If public officials are selected by the exchange of money for votes, is their election ethical? Is a society that tolerates the selection of its public officials through such a process an ethical society? Should an ethical person owe allegiance to a society that selects its governing bodies through such processes? An ethical society would choose its officials among the most educated and ethical members of the society.

The system of election in the United States results in a society of people who may appeal to the lowest elements of a society rather than to its highest ethical principles. The electoral process encourages both parties to commit fraud. Both parties are encouraged to buy votes or discourage people from voting.

In the 1960 presidential election, Richard Nixon and his advisors believed that the Democrats had stolen the election by casting thousands of fraudulent votes in Chicago. The future President decided not to contest the election, for a number of reasons, including the possibility that Republicans had cast fraudulent votes in downstate Illinois. Similar considerations caused both political parties to drop calls for further investigations relating to the 1993 gubernatorial election in New Jersey.

How would you reform such a system?

knowledge in the area of planning and are supported by adequate professional staff. The applicant would submit his or her case, and local residents would be given the opportunity to voice their concerns. However, the administrative law judge would be less likely to be improperly influenced by political considerations. This would probably lead to better results for both the environment and the local economy.

In the case of cellular phones, an administrative law judge could balance concerns for the environment, the local residents, the developer, and product users. This alternative might be better than the current process.

Many areas of this country have land that contains large quantities of chemicals. Love Canal is one of the best known, but there are thousands of others. In some cases, the persons who dumped the chemicals on the site have died or vanished. In other cases, the persons responsible can still be held liable for the damage to the land.

However, the issue is how much responsibility the private and public sectors should bear for cleaning up these areas. One could argue that private parties responsible for the damage should bear the loss. Conversely, one could contend that the public sector should bear the responsibility because the public benefited from the use of the products.

Chemicals have been used in manufacturing many products purchased by the general public. Theoretically, all members of the public bear some of the responsibility for these dump sites. In addition, private companies often do not have the financial resources necessary to pay for the cleanup.

The general approach has been to require that both the private and public sectors bear some responsibility for cleaning up these sites. This approach provides some balance between the various interests and levels of responsibilities. In some cases, localities suspect that there may be a specific environmental cause for illnesses among residents but no one can find it specifically.

In his book, *If You Can Keep It,* Michael Diamond[7] observes that our entire society has been polluted by various toxins and that the United States is declining because of this pollution. He argues that we have reached a crisis point that requires massive national intervention. Diamond argues the following points:

1. There are dangerous amounts of toxic materials in the air, land, and water which expose the entire population to unhealthy conditions. In addition, the nation's consumers have made a variety of unhealthy nutritional choices and have been exposed to dangerous medicines. The result of these conditions is to bring about declines in human health and human potential.

■ ■ ■ BOX 11.2 Sam's Creek ■ ■ ■

The town of Sam's Creek has a cancer rate among children that is three times the national average. This fact bothers the parents in the town, who discuss this matter repeatedly with their appointed and elected officials at the local, county, and state levels. The officials listen to the parents as well as to their own internal specialists. There is no conclusive evidence that there is a specific reason why Sam's Creek has such a high rate of cancer among children. However, the state department of health has put together a series of proposals to study possible causes for the high cancer rate. After the studies have been completed, there are still no specific reasons for the high rate. There is some evidence that some of the children may have been exposed to secondhand cigarette smoke from the time they were born.

2. There are also global changes including increases in ultraviolet radiation and carbon dioxide, a decrease in oxygen, changes in the global climate, and destruction of the ecosystems on which the population depends for sustenance.

3. The decline in the ability of students to pay attention and to achieve an appropriate level of knowledge is related directly to the levels of toxic substances in the environment. The toxins in people's bodies increase their tendency toward violence, decrease their ability to comply with the law, and lead to increases in crime.

4. The level of pollutants in the environment has also led to an increase in the level of chronic illness despite the increasing amounts of money injected into the nation's health care system. In addition, emphasis on the use of drugs and other addictive substances has hurt the overall state of the nation's health.

5. The levels of employee motivation and abilities have actually declined in recent years and this is having a negative effect on our ability to compete in the world's economy.

6. The overall decline in our society will make it difficult for us to sustain our institutions or to be a positive force in the world.

In 1962, in her book *Silent Spring*,[8] Rachel Carson warned that the use of pesticides was dangerous and would not control insects. She was concerned about pesticides that are not washed off fruits and vegetables and wind up in

■ ■ ■ BOX 11.3 Workers Have Less Trust in Bosses ■ ■ ■

A survey by the Marlin Company of 1000 workers indicated that people are satisfied at work but have mixed feelings about top management. Another survey by consultant Watson Wyatt indicated that although 61 percent of workers are satisfied or very satisfied with their jobs, only 32 percent feel that management makes good and timely decisions. Only 35 percent of workers characterize the level of trust between senior management and employees as favorable, and only 36 percent said their companies actively sought workers' opinions. Only 38 percent said the information needed to accomplish their work was widely shared.

Source: Modified from an Associated Press release, September 1, 1997.

our bodies. Indeed, crop losses have not declined, and toxins have found their way into our bodies, along with various growth hormones given to farm animals. These materials may have an impact on the human nervous system and cellular structure.

Michael Diamond contends that our environment has been so polluted by chemical toxins, pesticides, and other substances that the intellectual, ethical, moral, and physical capacities of the U.S. population are being diminished.[9] Diamond argues that a clause in the U.S. Constitution must be employed to solve these environmental problems. Article IV, Section 4 of the Constitution provides: "The United States shall guarantee to every state in this union a republican form of government, and shall protect each of them against invasion; and on application of the legislature, or of the executive (when the legislature cannot be convened) against domestic violence."

Diamond argues that the actions of various people constitute domestic violence against the citizens of the various states and that the federal government must intervene to protect them. Diamond urges reallocation of resources away from military expenditures and toward cleaning the environment.[10]

CORPORATE AND PERSONAL ENVIRONMENTAL ETHICS   ■ ■ ■

If the state of the environment is as precarious as Diamond and others suggest, all of us have an ethical responsibility not to make the situation worse. Sellers of products have a particular obligation to make them as environmentally friendly as possible, even if this results in added costs to the seller.

If one believes that one's organization is not acting ethically toward the environment, one has to choose how one will react to this problem. A person could do nothing, or conversely, could take a variety of measures to cope with the problem. These could include one or more of the following.

1. Do nothing. It takes courage to confront ethical problems. Not everyone has this type of moral courage. Even people with physical courage may not have the moral courage to confront ethical issues. One must be willing to accept confrontation, personal difficulties, possible reprisals to induce disciplinary actions, and outright dismissal. If one if not willing to face these issues, it is better to do nothing.

2. Make certain that one has the facts. Often, "problems" become less imposing if one has taken the time to gather all the facts.

3. Define the problem carefully. Get some advice from people outside the organization. This may be a good time to consult with one's own attorney to obtain independent advice about one's course of action.

4. Consult with someone in the human resources section of your organization. These staff members are supposed to be in a position to help people who are having problems.

5. Discuss the problem with your superior. One of the jobs of bosses is to help subordinates with situations that they may not be able to resolve. The best bosses are good coaches who extend themselves in order to help subordinates with problems. They use their greater experience to help solve these problems.

6. If a person engaging in unethical behavior is the boss, one might want to write a memo to the person, asking him or her to change behavior. A copy of this

BOX 11.4 Boss Should Go

You have been in your new position for about seven months. Your job is at a senior level, but you report to the division head. You have come to the conclusion that although your boss is intelligent, she is not capable of managing the division effectively. You have reached this conclusion after considerable soul searching. The division has no plan, does not establish goals, and does not perform activities normally associated with effective management. You have discussed several ideas with your boss, but they were quickly rejected. You are aware of the importance that organizations give to loyalty and utilizing the chain of command. You believe that you have an ethical obligation to the organization and to others not to let this situation continue. What do you do?

memo should be kept. As much as possible, the memo should be written in a non-threatening manner. However, if the boss is unwilling to modify his or her behavior, one should make it clear that there will be negative consequences.

7. If one's boss refuses to modify unethical behavior, another step is to talk to the boss's superior. This is a dangerous career move and should never be done unless one is certain that he or she is correct and that every other possible remedy has been exhausted.

When ethical problems occur, one is supposed to be able to obtain the assistance of senior managers. However, some managers and organizations have adopted the unethical idea that one should be "loyal to principal rather than to principle."[11] This is a dangerous idea. However, many organizations place considerable importance on the concept of loyalty with little thought as to their responsibilities of loyalty to employees. The same problem exists with respect to many managers. They may begin to believe that their employees' highest duty is to them.

Although employees have some duty to show loyalty to their superior, their greater duty of loyalty is to the organization. In some cases, they have an even higher duty to society or to an ethical principle. The manager should understand these loyalties, but many do not understand them. Instead, they put loyalty above the employee's other obligations. This creates a very difficult situation for an employee if the boss is engaging in unethical behavior. Organizations have a duty to recognize that these problems can occur and to have mechanisms to deal with them.

One method of dealing with an unethical boss is to place his or her actions before a superior or before the organization in some other way. Well-run companies establish procedures that allow a subordinate to report a superior's unethical conduct safely, without being the victim of reprisals.

One possible method of dealing with ethical issues is to form a committee to deal with them.[12] An employee could present the problem to the committee, which could then decide if unethical behavior has occurred and on the appropriate remedy. The committee could also determine what the organization ought to do to correct the problems presented to them.

8. If an employee discovers that the senior management of an organization is engaging in unethical conduct, the employee is faced with an almost insurmountable problem: Should one simply "go along" with the unethical conduct in order to "get along"?

One should be aware that it is not a legal defense to claim that one was simply following the instructions of one's unethical superiors. As a result, one may

◼ ◼ ◼   **BOX 11.5   Situational Ethics**   ◼ ◼ ◼

While writing this book, the authors sought the advice of people who had experience and academic training in the field of ethics. A number of people stated that ethics depends on the specific situation and people involved. Often called situational ethics, this is the concept that there are no universal ethics and that each situation must be handled individually. Many people who are concerned about ethical issues find it difficult to explain concepts that would be applicable in all situations.

Obedience to the law in a just society is normally one of the first principles of an ethical human being. However, this principle is subject to a number of difficulties. First, how does one decide if one is operating within a just society? What are the elements of a just society? If one believes that a society is just, should one obey every law of the society? Which laws should one follow? What citizens have the "right" to decide which laws should be followed and what citizens do not have such a right?

In many totalitarian societies, it is clear that the government is brainwashing its young people. In other countries, the brainwashing techniques of society are much more subtle. As a result, these techniques can be much more effective than the more obvious ones in totalitarian countries. It becomes increasingly difficult to determine what a just society is when so many misleading statements are passed along to members of the public. The American public has become cynical because of the barrage of false and partially false messages that it hears on a regular basis.

have a legal responsibility as well as an ethical one. How does one deal with a situation when one is not able to obtain assistance from one's own organization?

In a pluralistic society, the balance of organizations prevents anyone from obtaining too much power. An employee should be able to find people and organizations that can offset another's unethical conduct.

Most private-sector organizations are regulated by at least one, and often more than one, governmental agency. As a result, an employee can go to various agencies if he or she believes that superiors are engaging in unethical behavior. One method of coping with these problems is to threaten to talk to people at such agencies.

Sometimes the mere threat of talking to governmental groups is sufficient to stop unethical conduct. If not, one could discuss the conduct of superiors with attorneys or with regulatory authorities. Another appropriate remedy is to bring a lawsuit.

If power corrupts, it is useful to have power that can be used to counteract unethical behavior by senior managers. The regulatory mechanisms and the legal system are available to people who believe that their superiors are engaged in unethical conduct.

9. One could threaten to go to the news media. Organizations do not like to have their internal matters become public. It may be sufficient to tell senior executives that one would expose unethical conduct by going to the media.

10. A lower-level employee could actually go to the media and expose the unethical behavior of senior managers. This is also an act that requires considerable courage because one may be fired if the managers discover who exposed the unethical conduct. One might try to expose the unethical conduct in secret, but the media are often reluctant to accept statements from employees unwilling to allow their names to be used. Media organizations must be concerned about libel suits. They may be unwilling to believe an employee who appears to be disgruntled.

It is helpful to have physical evidence if one decides to go to the media. This evidence could be written or might be some form of physical indicator of pollution or damage to the environment which violates the law or general ethical principles.

It takes an even greater level of courage to allow the media outlet to use one's name. One will become subject to intense media scrutiny, and one is likely to be treated as a pariah, at least within the organization. In addition, one may be dismissed by the organization, although it may be improper to do so.

11. The ethical problems may also constitute legal violations. In these cases one may want to contact law enforcement authorities who can investigate the actions of senior management. In the case of environmental violations, local, state, and federal authorities may have jurisdiction over the issues.

The employee may want to contact law enforcement authorities to report ethical violations. This act also requires courage. One will find oneself in the middle of legal controversies and will find one's motives, abilities, and performance questioned by a variety of sources. One could ethically decide that the effort of reporting the ethical violations of superiors is not in one's own best interest.

The methods of deciding the "justice" of various claims have become so confused that there is little "real" justice.[13] The various parties involved are active in "spinning" their positions. The media sees opportunities to earn money, and the people involved often find themselves thrust into a maelstrom for which they are unprepared.

One should recognize that it takes considerable fortitude to become involved in such controversies. One should seek the assistance of competent counsel to help guide him or her through the process. Power tends to support power and the person's problems[14] can become lost after a disclosure of the ethical considerations.

12. One could refuse to carry out instructions that one believes to be "unethical." Under U.S. law, one should refuse to carry out orders that one knows are unlawful or unethical. One might want to inform senior management that one will not perform unethical acts. This is particularly important with respect to issues affecting the environment. When damage is done to land, air, or water, it cannot be easily repaired. The act of refusing to perform improper acts may prompt others to examine their conduct.

13. One could also decide to sabotage the activities of an organization that is engaging in unethical conduct. One could pretend to perform improper actions. One could also gather evidence against an organization that is harming the environment.

One has a duty to be loyal to one's superiors and to one's organization. However, we all have a higher duty of loyalty to society and to the planet on which we live. It may be useful to write a memorandum that outlines the actions of everyone involved in particular activities.

Although it is useful to put things in writing, this should be done carefully.[15] One should recognize that many written materials belong to the organization rather than to the individual. It is much safer and better to use one's own resources to document unethical behavior of senior executives. Computer disks and related materials may also belong to the organization. If one uses

BOX 11.6   E-mail Ownership

Tom and Mary are concerned that the senior executives of their organization are permitting an excessive amount of pollution to enter the water table that surrounds the company's plant. The two of them regularly exchange e-mail messages in which they discuss their concerns. They also send e-mail to others outside the company.

Tom and Mary should understand that e-mail sent and received on organization premises belongs to the company. In this case the company could gain access to these messages. It would also be permissible for the company to punish Tom and Mary for misusing company resources. It was impermissible for Tom and Mary to use the company's resources except for business purposes.

them to document unethical behavior, one may find oneself being charged with unethical behavior.

Many organizations in the United States involve money and power more than they involve justice or fairness.[16] We should not expect institutions to be interested in issues of equity. They are more likely to be concerned with protecting their own advantages than to be helping individual employees.

One should expect that ethical questions will arise in many institutions and be prepared to handle them.[17] The level of competence and ethical behavior in the United States is so low that it is almost impossible to underestimate either one.[18] Before beginning employment one should develop a plan that provides a variety of mechanisms for planning how to cope with unethical or incompetent superiors, unprepared colleagues, and lazy subordinates.

The decline the U.S. educational system has resulted in a low level of academic achievement in many areas[19] and a rise in the number of diploma mill–generated graduates with degrees but little knowledge. The Vietnam and later conflicts have also shattered many of the ties that bound Americans together.[20]

The illusion of "American greatness" that existed after World War II was shattered by the country's loss in Vietnam and by the explosion of foreign imports in the 1960s and 1970s. The premature deaths of John Kennedy, Martin Luther King, Jr., and John Lennon further eroded the American belief that its heroes could save its citizens from themselves. The U.S. culture was compromised further by a series of scandals that revealed the underside of institutions such as medicine, government, the military, law enforcement, the clergy, and the legal profession.

If Diamond and others are correct, the United States will continue in decline because of the various chemicals that have been dumped into the environment. Their view is that we should recognize that the United States has become a country of high standards but low actual performance.[21] The environment continues to decline as we pursue our dreams of happiness while being relatively unconcerned with the problems or needs of our fellow citizens.

The artificial prosperity of the 1980s led to overexpansion in certain businesses. As a result, many organizations are trying to catch up with their competition. This can result in increased pressures to obtain profits and may also result in added pressure to cut corners and to engage in unethical conduct with respect to the environment and in other ways. We should expect to encounter a significant number of ethical problems and be prepared to deal with them.

SUMMARY

Historically, business, industry, and government gave little or no thought to the environment in the United States. The nation was so big and the land so vast that little consideration was given to the impact on the land of development. The land was there to be used and the pioneers intended to use it. As the nation developed, however, this began to change. The nation is no longer a nation of farmers seeking their living from the land. Rather, it is a nation of workers, employed by corporations that are in the business of producing goods and services for the society.

World War II and the emergence of the United States as the world's primary world power has changed much of the attitude of people toward the environment. The forced development of a variety of industries and the impact on the environment made people look at the cost of doing business in ways that had not been done prior to the war. Questions were asked about how much pollution the environment could stand without seriously injuring it and possibly injuring people in the process.

It became necessary for the society to balance the needs of the society in terms of goods and services with the needs of the environment. This was something the society had not had to consider in the past and one that would be difficult to administer. As industry expanded, industries vied for the right to use parts of the environment for their development. There were many proposals, projects, and attempts to use the environment, but only a few could be accommodated. Government regulation started to take hold, and of course, when hard choices are made, someone is always upset at the result.

Another aspect of the change in the environment was the realization that much of the mess that had been left before the advent of environmentalism would have to be cleaned up, and that it was going to be expensive. Love Canal is only the most notorious example of this situation. People died at Love Canal, but people also died elsewhere for many of the same reasons.

A third aspect of environmentalism was the realization that the environment did not stop at the national border. Wind and rain do not respect national borders, and pollution in one country often means pollution in that country's neighbors. To be effective, pollution control has to be on a global scale if it is to succeed.

Individuals can and must take appropriate action to protect the environment even if organizations with which they are involved choose not to. It is in the interest of every human being on the planet to make sure that the environment is protected from unnecessary pollution. However, saying that and putting it into practice are two very different things. There are many alternatives in trying to do something about pollution, but it is critical that people have their facts straight and that they are prepared for the consequences of their actions. Some of those consequences may not be favorable to the individual and some of them may not be favorable to the institution, but there will be consequences nonetheless.

Finally, if the effort to save the environment is going to be successful, it must be an effort of all concerned. Business, government, and the society as a whole are going to have to provide the necessary leadership to accomplish the job. Unfortunately, that is not nearly as easy as it sounds. People today are wary of their leaders. From the Vietnam war to Watergate to "White Water"-gate to soft political money to massive layoffs of workers while top managers collect millions of dollars in bonuses, most people in the United States simply do not trust their leaders, and they have good reason. Explanations of actions such as "no controlling legal authority" and "What's the big deal? Everybody does it!" simply add to the cynical attitudes of many members of the society. But that will not solve problems or contribute to the well-being of the country. Only full realization and a determination that something needs to be done and done in a hurry will continue the process of protecting not only the environment, but the entire society.

Questions

1. What do you believe is the responsibility to the environment of society in the United States?

2. What do you believe is the responsibility to the environment of business in the United States?

3. What do you believe is the responsibility to the environment of government in the United States?

4. How would you find a balance between economic growth and the environment?

5. Do you personally lean more toward the environment or toward economic growth?

6. What agency of the federal government has responsibility for protecting the environment?

7. What agency in your state has responsibility for protecting the environment?

8. What is a local planning board?

9. What are the functions of a local planning board?

10. How does a local planning board help protect the environment while permitting economic growth?

11. What is a local board of adjustment?

12. What are the functions of a local board of adjustment?

13. How does a local board of adjustment help protect the environment while permitting economic growth?

14. What was the effect of World War II on the environment in the United States?

15. What has been the effect of the use of chemicals on the environment?

16. What are the consequences of Michael Diamond's positions as they relate to appropriate governmental environmental actions?

17. Outline some steps you might take if your organization's senior executives were to violate their ethical obligation to the environment.

18. What would you do if you were placed in a position such as that described in Question 17?

19. How would you balance your obligations to your organization with your own beliefs and obligations to the environment?

20. What resources would you use to prevent unethical conduct by your organization?

CASE 1

You are the president of a large corporation that has been having financial problems. The company is subject to a significant number of environmental laws and regulations of the federal, state, and local governments. If all these regulations were enforced fully, the company would not be able to earn satisfactory profits. The local zoning official has been rather rigorous in enforcing local laws that protect the environment.

You check with some local businesspeople about the zoning official. They laugh and tell you that he is very strict except to those who take him out for very expensive dinners and entertainment. Your company has a policy of not engaging in expensive entertainment. However, you calculate that your company could save thousands of dollars if the zoning official eased off somewhat. You do not believe the environment would be severely damaged by this course of action.

1. What do you do?

CASE 2

You are a member of a local planning board. You became a member because you were concerned that overdevelopment of the community was spoiling the town's environment. During recent cases you have demanded that the board enforce strictly laws and regulations that govern the environment. You notice that the other board members have taken positions quite different than your own.

One day you meet the mayor of the community. He had appointed you to the planning board. The mayor informs you that he is concerned with bringing new ratables into the community. The mayor explains that he wants to keep the tax rate low to achieve this. He asks you not to be too strict in demanding enforcement of the town's environmental regulations.

1. What do you do?

CASE 3

NPZ Industries is considering building an addition to its plant in Springdale. The facility was built in 1962 when the local and state authorities were very concerned with obtaining tax ratables and providing jobs for people in the area. The plant was also built at a time when environmental concerns were less important. The plant was presented to the local planning board without an environmental impact statement, which is now required as a matter of law.

The plant's activities also are now subject to various laws that were enacted after the plant was approved by local authorities. New legislation requires that similar plants submit annual reports to the state and that the company file environmental impact statements which outline how the applicant's project affects the community from an environmental perspective.

You investigate the plant, which has been operating at full capacity for the past year. In your capacity as the company's environmental manager, you observe certain problems with its operations and relatively minor violations of current laws relating to the plant's operation. These violations relate to how the plant disposes of materials that are not used in the final product. Currently, this material is simply thrown into a dump site. The dumpster is picked up and emptied twice a week. Certain of the materials contain pollutants that could be harmful to the environment. The existing process means that these materials lay around outside for periods of three or four days. In addition, unauthorized people could simply pick them up and take them away. This could have negative consequences for the environment and for the persons involved.

You bring these concerns to the president of your company. He advises you that the company complies with all federal, state, and local laws. He states that the company's only responsibility is to comply with the law. You believe that it is the responsibility of decision makers to consider the effects on the environment of their decisions.

1. What do you do now?

CASE 4

You are the senior executive officer of the state's office of environmental protection. You have been in your position for about one year. This has given you the opportunity to review the major laws and regulations that govern how businesses may conduct themselves with respect to the environment. You believe that they are inadequate to protect the state's environment. You are particularly concerned with the laws and regulations controlling the level of pollutants that manufacturers are permitted to emit into the air.

The governor has indicated her support for effective environmental controls. However, she has also made a major commitment to bringing more business into the state. Your staff has urged you to propose to the governor laws that would regulate business more strictly. Conversely, corporate leaders with whom you meet regularly complain that the regulations are sufficient and already make it difficult to expand their operations.

1. What do you do?

CASE 5

Joe runs a series of fast-food franchises that serve hamburgers and hot dogs to "eat in" and "takeout" customers. They also serve a large number of ancillary products, such as French fries. Traditionally, Joe has served drinks and food products in Styrofoam cups and holders. He has recently read some articles about the environment and wonders if he should be using more "environmentally friendly" items. However, it will cost Joe a substantial amount of money to make a conversion. In addition, his current customers seem to like the existing containers. Joe runs his business on a very close profit margin and is concerned that he may lose business to larger fast-food establishments. If he shifts to other containers, he is concerned that he will reduce his profit margin.

1. What should Joe do?
2. What options would you suggest that Joe consider?

3. What are the advantages and disadvantages of each option?
4. What options would you suggest that Joe adopt?
5. Did you find a balance between economic growth and protecting the environment?

CASE 6

QZC Corporation wants to develop a parcel of land and build a supermarket. It is aware that the market will generate considerable traffic on a major street that is already characterized by backups, traffic jams, and high levels of pollution.

QZC wants to be a good corporate citizen. In addition, it is concerned that too much traffic will be harmful to its future business. It puts together a plan for the local authorities that would reduce traffic in the area nearby the new supermarket. The plan provides for QZC Corporation to build a bypass that will move traffic around a major bottleneck on the street in front of the supermarket. The plan proposed by QZC Corporation would cost the company about $1 million, and it will relieve many of the traffic problems on the street.

QZC Corporation submits its plan to the Maplefield planning board authorities. It encounters substantial objections from neighbors, who argue that the supermarket will generate too much traffic and are also concerned that the market will attract too many "undesirables" into the area. QZC Corporation argues that the property will be improved and that its new traffic design will result in enhanced traffic flow in the area. QZC Corporation also contends that its supermarket will generate jobs for young people and a large ratable for the community. QZC Corporation states that it has found a proper balance between the economy and the environment.

1. If you were a member of the planning board in this locality, how would you vote on the application of QZC Corporation?
2. How would you help QZC Corporation meet its obligations to the community and environment?
3. Have the neighbors met their obligations to the economy and the environment?
4. Given the close proximity of one town's economy and environment to other communities, what are the ethical obligations of QZC Corporation, the neighbors, and the Maplefield planning board?

References

1. Carson, Rachel, *Silent spring*, Houghton Mifflin, Boston, 1962.
2. Vexler, Robert I., *Chronology and documentary handbook of the state of Kansas*, Oceana Publications, Dobbs Ferry, NY, 1978.
3. *Protecting the environment: a research strategy for the 1990's*, Office of Research and Development, U.S. Environmental Protection Agency, Washington, DC, 1987.
4. Smith, Adam, *An inquiry into the nature and causes of the wealth of nations*, Great Books Foundation, Chicago, 1948.
5. Protecting the environment.
6. Ibid.
7. Diamond, Michael, *If you can keep it*, Brass Ring Press, Westfield, NJ, 1996.
8. Carson, *Silent spring*.
9. Diamond, *If you can keep it*.

10. Ibid.

11. Westin, Alan F., Henry I. Kurtz, Albert Robbins, *Whistle blowing: loyalty and dissent in the corporation,* McGraw-Hill, New York, 1981.

12. Southard, Samuel, *Ethics for executives,* Thomas Nelson, Nashville, TN, 1975.

13. Bedau, Hugo Adams (ed.), *Justice and equality,* Prentice Hall, Upper Saddle River, NJ, 1971.

14. French, Peter A., *Collective and corporate responsibility,* Columbia University Press, New York, 1984.

15. *Whistle blowing.*

16. Toury, Michael, and Albert K. Reiss (eds.), *Beyond the law: crime in complex organizations,* University of Chicago Press, Chicago, 1993.

17. Bradshaw, Thorton, and David Vogel, *Corporations and their critics: issues and answers to the problems of corporate responsibility,* McGraw-Hill, New York, 1981.

18. Ermann, M. David, and Richard J. Lundman (eds.), *Corporate and governmental deviance: problems of organizational behavior in contemporary society,* Oxford University Press, New York, 1982.

19. United States National Commission on Excellence in Education, *A Nation at risk: the imperative for educational reform, a report to the nation and the secretary,* The Commission, Washington, DC, 1993.

20. Prasher, Ivan (ed.), *Duty, honor, country: twelve men of west point,* Arbor House/William Morrow, New York, 1988.

21. Toury and Reiss, *Beyond the law.*

THE NOT-FOR-PROFIT SECTOR

Concepts : You Will Learn ■ ■ ■

what a not-for-profit organization is

the purpose of not-for-profit organizations in a capitalistic society

the difference between profit and not-for-profit organizations

conflicts facing not-for-profit organizations

strategies used by not-for-profit organizations to deal with those conflicts

ethical dilemmas facing not-for-profit organizations

WHAT A NOT-FOR-PROFIT ORGANIZATION IS　　　■ ■ ■

A not-for-profit organization is usually an organization established to perform a particular task in the society or to achieve a specific goal. Not-for-profits have specific missions that are the basis for their existence. As Peter Drucker has written: "[M]ission comes first. Nonprofit institutions exist for the sake of their mission. They exist to make a difference in society and in the life of the individual. They exist for the sake of their mission and this must never be forgotten."[1]

There are many types of not-for-profit organizations. Virtually all colleges and universities would be classified as not-for-profit organizations. Most hospitals and health organizations would be included, along with government, associations, religious groups, and charities. To appreciate the size of this sector of the U.S. economy, a few examples can be cited:

1. The government of the United States at all levels spent $2,374 billion in 1993; this was more than the individual gross national products of all the nations on Earth except the United States and Japan.[2]

2. The expenditures of the government of the State of California in 1994, $105,831 billion,[3] would make it the third-largest corporation in terms of sales in the United States in 1994[4] (number 2, Ford, $108,521 billion; number 3, Exxon, $97,825 billion).

3. There are approximately 85,000 government units in the United States with the power to tax.[5]

4. Nearly 30,000 associations are listed in *Gales Encyclopedia of Associations*.[6]

5. The revenue of the city of New York, $44,487 billion in fiscal 1992–1993,[7] would make it the seventh largest corporation in the United States in 1993[8] (number 8, Chrysler, $43,600 billion; number 7, Philip Morris, $50,621 billion).

A not-for-profit organization is an organization that has been established to accomplish some mission or task and not to make a profit.

WHY NOT-FOR-PROFITS EXIST   ■ ■ ■

Not-for-profit organizations exist to perform tasks that are deemed necessary by the society. Many of these tasks have to do with providing for the general welfare of the community. They involve the traditional governmental functions of police protection, fire protection, roads, water and sewer plants, and so on. This is not to say that many of these functions are not performed in the private sector. Trash collection is often cited as an example of profit and not-for-profit organizations working next to each other, but they seldom serve the same customers. For example, industrial disposal may be handled by a for-profit sanitation firm while neighborhood trash collection is performed by the city.

Not-for-profits provide those services deemed necessary for all and in which there may be an actual moral dilemma if the products and services are offered by a for-profit organization. Few people would deny the need for emergency care for people who have been injured in an auto accident, but who should provide it? Emergency medical technicians from the local hospital? the local fire department? the independent rescue squad? the for-profit ambulance service? the local mortician?

In most communities, but not all, assistance is provided without question. Early fire departments started out as a part of the fire insurance business. When a fire was reported, companies sponsored by various insurance firms would rush to the scene and then determine whether or not they had insured this particular property. If they had not, they would not fight the fire and would allow it to burn. The owner of the property either had to wait for his insurance company's fire brigade to arrive or strike a deal with the ones that were already there. Striking a deal with the fireman to put out the blaze in your house while it is burning in the background does not place the property owner in a particularly advantageous bargaining position.

The government is part of the not-for-profit sector, as are virtually all segments of the society that are concerned directly with the well-being of the society. In addition, organizations established for a particular purpose would fall into this category. Charities such as the Heart Fund or the American Cancer Society have been established for the specific purpose of conquering specific human ailments. Nonhuman ailments are also addressed in this sector, by organizations such as the American Society for the Prevention of Cruelty to Animals (ASPCA).

Not-for-profits often exist to augment governmental institutions. Private schools, hospitals, and even cemeteries are examples. They also sometimes provide additional services that the private sector traditionally provides. In sum, not-for-profit organizations provide products and services, often at subsidized rates, that the society needs but which would be difficult to provide on a for-profit basis.

How Not-for-Profit Organizations Differ from Profit-Making Organizations

Not-for-profit organizations are different from profit-making organizations in a variety of ways. The first and most obvious is that the profit motive is not a part of the rationale of the organization. Not-for-profits lack this gauge of easily measurable effectiveness.[9] In the profit-making sector, a consistent and easily understood measure of organizational effectiveness is whether or not the company made money. But not-for-profits are not supposed to make money. They do not even use the word *profit*; if they have any money left at the end of the year, it is called a *surplus*.

Although there are differences in the way a not-for-profit organization operates compared to a for-profit organization, there are also similarities: Each offers a particular product or service to clients or customers; each has stakeholders in the organization in the form of employees, suppliers, government, the general public, and so on; each has both direct and indirect effects on the community as a whole; and finally, each has goals and objectives, including the basic survival of the organization, which are certainly not as easy to measure as simple profit or loss.[10]

Domination by Professionals

Not-for-profits are different in a number of ways from other organizations. One of the first ways they differ is that they tend to be dominated by people other than professional managers.[11] Business organizations tend to have a class of employee whose main motivation is successful management of the enterprise. This cadre of professional managerial talent is primarily interested in and motivated by the success of the enterprise. They have frequently trained, either internally or in higher education, for managerial positions in industry, and their careers and values are usually tied to the firm. This is especially true among large, older companies where the founder is gone from the scene. The managerial class of employees operates the company, which is what it has been trained and educated to do. On the other hand, not-for-profits are often dominated by nonmanagerial professionals. Doctors, lawyers, psychologists, clergy, and other members of occupational professions frequently have a dominant role in the management of not-for-profits. They have been educated in their profession, and their values and ethics reflect that experience, but they frequently have not received instruction in business and managerial techniques. Their values and goals will frequently reflect their profession, and those attributes may not be the best possible set for the organization.

Importance of Resources

One of the primary differences between not-for-profit organizations and for-profit organizations is the source of the revenue.[12] As may be seen in Box 12.1, there is a direct one-for-one relationship between a firm and its customers in the

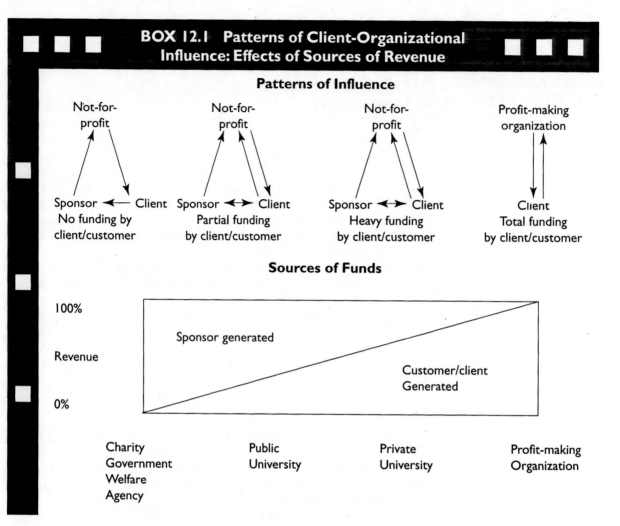

BOX 12.1   Patterns of Client-Organizational Influence: Effects of Sources of Revenue

Patterns of Influence

Sources of Funds

for-profit sector. The firm provides certain products or services to customers and the customers pay for them. It is a simple, straightforward relationship.

Not-for-profits, by contrast, can be divided into three basic subgroups: (1) heavy funding by recipients of services, (2) partial funding by recipients of services, and (3) no funding by recipient of services. The differences are important because of the power that the recipient of the services has in the relationship. In the for-profit model, the customer has the ultimate power, especially in a capitalistic economy, which encourages competition. Industries that are monopolistic in nature tend to compensate for this with heavy governmental regulation.[13] If customers do not like the products or services they are receiving from the firm, they can go to a competitor and take their money with them. It is the responsibility of the corporation to keep customers happy and returning to purchase more items so that the firm receives more funds.

Not-for-profit organizations that receive heavy but not complete funding from their clients are not in the same position as a for-profit company. Although they may rely on the client/customer for a large percentage of their funding, they are not completely dependent on the customer and have other clients whose needs, wants, and desires they must address. Private colleges and universities, which receive a large part of their funds from tuition, would be a prime example of this type of organization. Other sources of income may be in the form of grants, interest on the endowment, and other enterprises on the campus, such as the athletic department, bookstore, cultural events, and alumni donations—each with its own set of needs and wants that the organization must satisfy.

Organizations that receive only partial funding from the recipients of services are even less dependent on them for funding. Frequently, these nonclient/customer funds are from governmental sources: tax dollars. With each additional tax dollar received by a not-for-profit organization, the role of the client declines and the role of the government in setting the goals, objectives, and agenda of the organization increases. These organizations need to be even less receptive to their customers' needs to survive. Although the customer still has a degree of power in the relationship, it is vastly diminished compared to the customers' power in the private sector. The client usually still can go elsewhere for services, but the ability to effect change in the specific provider/recipient relationship is vastly reduced. Public colleges and universities are excellent examples of these types of organizations. The cost of a student's education is heavily subsidized by the state—to the point where public in-state tuition can be less than one-fifth of the tuition at a private college. For example, if for some reason, ten students paying $2000 each per year in tuition leave a public college, the school loses $20,000 in tuition. If those same ten students leave a private college where they pay $10,000 per year in tuition, the college loses $100,000. The difference, $80,000, will generally serve to gain the attention of a college administrator.

Organizations that receive no funding from their customers can become even further removed from the client. If the client pays nothing, the client has little or no influence on the specific provider–client relationship. Such agencies frequently include charities and government welfare departments. The services they provide are often for people who live in a particular area, and there are frequently no alternative sources for this type of service available to the recipients. The recipients have no power. The services are provided on a take-it-or-leave-it basis by the agency. There are no other choices. Not-for-profit organizations in this category are monopolies in their relationship with their clientele. The agenda is dictated not by the needs of the clients but by the desires of the funding sources. The political consequences associated with "welfare rights" and "welfare cheats" can be traced to this lack of power. The only avenue available to the clients of these types of agencies is in the political arena and their ability to draw the attention of the media to their complaints. If they want or need services provided by the not-for-profit agency, they have no choice but to take what the agency gives them, and it is almost impossible to effect change. The only alternative is to draw attention to the situation and hope that this will cause the agency to change.

Organizations respond to the needs, wants, and desires of the people providing the funds, and one of the primary differences between profit and not-for-profit organizations is that in the case of for-profit organizations, the funds come directly from the customer, whereas in not-for-profits, the relationship is not as direct.

BOX 12.2 Public Schools and Educational Vouchers

A proposal for reforming education in the public schools is the use of educational vouchers. Under the plan, parents would receive a voucher from the government for a sum of money roughly equal to the expense of educating their child. The voucher could then be used to pay for the child's education at a school of the parent's choosing, provided that the child was accepted by that school as a student.

Apart from the administrative and procedural problems of this approach, the voucher system makes a fundamental change in the public school system. Today, public schools receive no direct funding from their clients, the students. All of their funds come from the government. Although under the voucher system, the funds would still come from the government, parents of the students, the legal guardians of the children, would now have discretion as to exactly which school received those funds. This would force the schools to be more receptive to the needs of the students and their parents.

Although most educators would argue that the schools are receptive to the needs of students and their parents, there are those who would disagree. The dismal record of public education in producing high-quality students over the past 20 years compared to the results of competitive testing with other industrialized nations causes the success of public education to be called into question. Reports such as *A Nation at Risk* have supported the view that elementary and secondary education in the United States is not working as well as it needs to work in an increasingly competitive international environment. The voucher system would at least make the schools more accountable to clients and their guardians, which would change the very nature of the funding of these not-for-profit organizations.

If nothing else, it would give students and their parents the option of going elsewhere without the undue expense of a private or parochial school. Schools would be forced to compete not only on the athletic field, but for the very funds they need to keep operating. The power of the boards of education and administrators would be vastly reduced because people could vote with their feet and go elsewhere at little personal financial expense if they are unhappy with the services they are receiving from the school.

Schools that excel would find themselves, in theory at least, deluged with good students, while schools that did not excel might find themselves with empty classes, their teachers and administrators out on the street, looking for work.

Influence of Stakeholders and Publics

Not-for-profit organizations are subject to the influence of stakeholders and other publics to an even greater degree than the typical corporation is. This power grows in proportion to the degree to which the agency does *not* depend on the client for funding. Although the people who work in these organizations frequently entered into them because they believed in the mission, that ideal can be lost in the daily operation of these organizations. Not-for-profit organizations are caught in a paradox. On one hand, they are trying to perform a social good by meeting the needs of the recipients of their services; on the other hand, they must address the needs of their financial supporters, and the wider the division between the recipients and the supporters, the more difficult the task. The publics these agencies must address include, but are not limited to:

1. *Politicians.* This group is in a position of decision making that directly affects agencies receiving tax dollars. They frequently influence the budget directly.

2. *Clients.* This group receives the services of the agency and has varying degrees of influence, depending on the sources of funding for the agency.

3. *Media.* Good press can be a key in funding the agency.

4. *Experts.* Not-for-profit organizations are often involved in areas that include the social, economic, and political welfare of the society. Getting "expert" endorsement can be a key to success.

5. *General public.* This includes the voters, the ultimate authority and source of funds for organizations receiving tax or any other kinds of money.

The key to understanding the management of not-for-profit organization is in learning who pays for the services.[13]

MANAGING THE NOT-FOR-PROFIT ORGANIZATION: THE NEED FOR STRATEGIC MANAGEMENT

All organizations need to practice strategic management. This type of activity includes all the traditional functions of planning, including defining the mission, establishing goals and objectives, development and implementation of plans, and a review of the results of those efforts.[14]

Strategic management sets the tone and direction of the organization.[15] This is particularly important for not-for-profits because they do not have the profit motive as an indicator of success. Not-for-profit organizations must measure their success and effectiveness in other ways and they need to determine what those other ways are by establishing the objectives of the organization. Like all good organizational objectives, they must be observable, measurable, and obtainable.[16]

The process of strategic planning can be summed up by asking five very simple and straightforward questions:

1. *Where has the organization been?* All organizations have a history that influences their future course. Even organizations that are only recently established have a history, if only the history of the people involved.

2. *Where is the organization now?* What is the current situation in which the organization finds itself? This involves both an analysis of the internal strengths and weaknesses of the agency as well as the external situation. The organization needs to look at how it interacts with the external environment. The needs, wants, and desires of the various publics must be balanced with the internal capabilities of the agency.

3. *Where does the organization want to go?* Another way to ask this question is: "What do you want to do when you grow up?" These are the missions, objectives, and goals of the organization.

4. *How are you going to get there?* What is the organization's plan? Goals are wonderful things, but if they are going to be attained, the agency needs a plan to achieve them which is reasonable.

5. *How will you know when you have arrived?* What controls does the organization have in place? How will you measure your progress?

Every not-for-profit organization will develop its own unique strategy to achieve its goals and objectives. The key is that without a strategic plan or a measure of organizational effectiveness, such as profitability, the organization can flounder and lose its way.

PROBLEMS IN IMPLEMENTING STRATEGIC MANAGEMENT IN NOT-FOR-PROFIT ORGANIZATIONS

■ ■ ■

Because not-for-profit organizations generally lack a single measure of effectiveness as found in for-profit corporations, they will tend to adopt multiple and sometimes conflicting goals.[17] These goals usually reflect the desires of the constituent publics of the agency and, of course, the more stakeholders the agency has, the more objectives it is likely to try to achieve and the more likely it is that these goals are going to be in conflict. For example, in an era of government constraints, due to a decline in tax receipts because of an economic downturn, an agency that is at least partially funded by the government may receive fewer tax dollars in support of its mission. At the same time, the demand for the agency's services may skyrocket, due to people being out of work because of the downturn. Because of paradoxes such as this, the planning function often focuses on the problem of obtaining money for the organization and not on how best and most effectively to deliver services to clients. In the profit sector, the delivery of services is direct, tied to the compensation the organization receives, whereas in the not-for-profit sector, these two events may be linked only partially or not linked at all.

Ambiguous and conflicting objectives also create opportunities for goal displacement that tend to generate internal politics. As the competing stakeholders vie for limited resources to achieve their particular goals, the internal jockeying becomes even more active. Some not-for-profits have even gained a reputation for internal politics that would seem to be inversely proportional to the stakes involved. Woodrow Wilson, former president of the United States, governor of New Jersey, and president of Princeton University, said: "I learned my politics from the faculty at Princeton and then went to Washington to practice with the amateurs."[18]

Due to the dominance of professionals in the not-for-profit sector, the managers of the agency must balance their values and needs with the objectives and goals of the organization. Professional values may be in conflict with the values of the funding agency. This will usually result in one of several outcomes:

1. The professionals will leave the agency, often taking with them, or damaging, the organization's creditability.

2. The professionals and other staff members will subvert the funding source's demands, often simply ignoring them.

3. The professionals and other staff members will outwardly accept the demands of the funding source while undermining them covertly. The best example of this is passive aggressive behavior.

Whatever the eventual outcome, the difference in goals and values is bound to lead to conflict in the organization and the expenditure of energy on issues that do not contribute to the organization's achieving its objectives.

BOX 12.3   The Federal Government and Abortion

The government of the United States has recently ruled that family planning clinics that receive federal funds may not discuss abortion as a possible option in family planning. This ruling goes directly against good medical practice, which insists that the patient has the right to know all options for effective treatment. This has created a direct conflict between the U.S. government and the medical profession. The government is preventing the physician from practicing, in his or her view, sound medicine in these clinics. In response to this, doctors will either leave the clinics, ignore the ruling by discussing abortion with their patients, or covertly undermine the ruling by essentially asking their patients to step outside the clinic to discuss abortion.

It will be the patients who will suffer. It is not the needs of the patient that have been taken into account in this ruling, but the wants and desires of the funding agency. If the doctors in the clinics discuss abortion with their patients, the clinics can lose their federal funds. This money represents a significant source of revenue that these clinics can ill-afford to lose.

Unfortunately, this is not a medical but a political problem. The people of the United States have elected people to political office who owe their election to pro-life supporters who are antiabortion. This is the will of the people, the general public, the taxpayer—all one and the same. The government is acting on this issue in the manner in which the voters have indicated through the election of their representatives. It is representative democracy at work. The fact that it conflicts with the values and ethics of the medical profession, or the health and perhaps the very life of the expectant mother, is not relevant. The only thing that is relevant is that if the clinic wants the federal funds to help pay for the services it offers to people who cannot be reasonably expected to pay for those services, the clinic is going to have to accept the rules, find another source of funds, or go out of business.

Evaluation in the Not-for-Profit Sector

Managers in not-for-profit agencies often share problems in evaluating the success of their employees and organizations with their for-profit counterparts. Rewards may have little or nothing to do with performance.[19] In the corporate environment, this is particularly true in staff areas where success is not as easily measured, as in the line functions of sales or manufacturing, where revenue and production are relatively easy to determine. Among not-for-profits, lacking that single criterion of profitability, the agency must resort to other measures to determine the aggregate success of the organization. The questions, of course, frequently center around what types of measures, and compared to what? What ruler is going to be used to measure the success of the organization; who determines it; and how is it going to be used? Embedded in all objective measurements are subjective criteria, and the more difficult the objectives are to measure, the more subjective the objective results become.

Managers of not-for-profit organizations typically address this in several ways. The first is to try to quantify the objectives of the organization as much as possible. This is frequently difficult to do at best and is often resisted by the staff of the organization. The resistance is grounded in the fears of the employees, because if an employee's activity cannot be measured, it cannot be evaluated, and the employee cannot be fired for cause because the management cannot evaluate his or her work.

A second type of evaluation procedure is that of process indicators. This type of measure focuses on activity rather than results. It would include such things as the number of clients seen per week and the number of new clients added to the caseload. In the case of a hospital, this type of measure would count the number of beds occupied but not the number of patients cured.

The third type of evaluation that often reflects the mission of the not-for-profit organization most directly, while being the most difficult to actually determine, is the social indicator.[20] The answer to the question "Is this a better place because of the organization?" is the evaluative criterion. Although it is difficult to get an actual measure for this criterion, a way to ask it is to reverse the question to "What would this place be like without this not-for-profit organization?" If a hospital is removed from a community, what happens to the health care of people in that area? If a college closes its doors, what happens to the students, alumni, faculty, and the quality of life in the community? If a Headstart program closes its doors, what happens to the children who were and would be involved in that program and their families? How many of those families would then have to go on welfare? What would this place be like without this not-for-profit organization?

CONSTRAINTS ON THE MANAGEMENT OF NOT-FOR-PROFIT ORGANIZATIONS ■ ■ ■

Newman and Wallender have identified five constraints on the management of not-for-profit organizations:[21]

1. Service is often an intangible and difficult to measure.
2. Client influence may be weak.
3. There is strong employee commitment to a profession.
4. Resource contributors may intrude upon management.
5. There are restraints on the use of rewards and punishments.

Most not-for-profits are engaged in providing some sort of service to clientele. Services are not like products. A product can be seen, picked up, and weighed, whereas a service cannot. Many organizations sell services but measure their productivity in a product that is used to help provide that service. McDonald's is a primary example. McDonald's really sells service: fast, dependable, consistent, no-surprises food in a spotless restaurant anywhere in the United States and in many parts of the world. A Big Mac is "two all-beef patties, special sauce, lettuce, cheese, pickles, and onions, on a sesame seed bun" anywhere in the world. Unfortunately, not-for-profits do not have such a simple task. They do not have the luxury of making Big Macs. Not-for-profits are often engaged in long-term projects that are difficult to measure. Although most people do not think of police departments as being not-for-profit organizations, they are, and they provide an excellent example of the type of service provided by not-for-profits. Solving a crime can often take long, boring hours of basic police work. Figuring out who committed the crime does not mean that there is enough evidence to arrest the suspect, and an arrest certainly does not mean that there will be a conviction, with the criminal going to jail. A detective can "solve" a crime but not be able to arrest the perpetrator because of lack of evidence or because of the way in which the evidence was obtained, and the crime goes unpunished. As has already been discussed, client influence is directly proportional to the financial contributions made by the client. Clients that contribute little or nothing to an organization have little or no influence on the organization.

Not-for-profits are frequently staffed by people whose primary occupational loyalty is to the profession and not the organization. These professional organizations can be very powerful and exert a powerful influence on the not-for-profit. Contributors of resources also have a great deal of influence on the organization. As the expression says, "He who has the gold makes the rules." Not-for-profit organizations that are dependent on outside funding cannot expect to receive funding from those sources if they are not meeting the needs, wants, and desires of those sources. Given the current state of affairs, it is unlikely that a birth control clinic which provides abortions is going to receive funding from the Catholic Church.[22] Nor is it particularly surprising that a government consisting of elected officials who were strongly supported by antiabortion groups in their elections would seek to curtail the availability of abortions at tax-supported clinics. This is a simple case of voters exercising the power of the purse through their elected representatives.

Rewards and punishments are also difficult for not-for-profit organizations to administer. In the first place, rewards have little to do with performance. Second, many of the people involved with not-for-profit agencies are volunteers. How do you discipline a volunteer? Finally, the pay in not-for-profit organizations is often relatively low compared with pay in the private sector. The salary of the president of the United States is inadequate compared to the compensation programs of the CEOs of Fortune 500 companies. Yet the U.S. president has the power of life and death over the entire globe. Certainly, that makes it a more important position than being in charge of producing cars, but the salary does not say so.

Response to Constraints

Faced with many obstacles, not-for-profit organizations have developed a variety of responses to deal with these problems. Probably the first response to these situations is to select a dynamic leader—a task easier said than done. Potentially dynamic leaders are difficult to identify and have little in the way of identifiable characteristics. Experience is not a substitute for vision and determination. Probably the most qualified man to become president of the United States was James Buchanan, who had served well in nearly every office except president prior to his inauguration. James Buchanan is considered by historians to be perhaps the worst U.S. president in history. His successor, Abraham Lincoln, a backwoods, self-taught lawyer from Illinois whose "national" experience consisted of a few terms in the House of Representatives and was best known for losing an election to Stephen Douglas, may very well have been the greatest U.S. president. The failure of Buchanan is only amplified by Lincoln, the backwoods lawyer from Illinois, and Truman, the failed businessman from Missouri.

Organizations should be warned, however, that there will come a time when the dynamic leader is no longer on the scene, for whatever reason. When that happens, a vacuum usually results, with the various factions that had been kept in line by the leader vying for power and position. There usually tends to be a fairly rapid turnover in the leadership of the organization, going through several "leaders" prior to finding someone capable of dealing effectively with all factions.

A second method of dealing with constraints is to establish rules and procedures for the organization.[23] This serves to bureaucratize the organization and to institutionalize the cause of the not-for-profit. Although it is not necessarily a bad thing, it does tend to channel energy away from the mission and into the daily operations of the organization. The truly exciting time of the movement, when the organization was created, is over and has been replaced by a reactive mode of applying rules and regulations to a variety of circumstances. The civil rights movement was most effective when Martin Luther King and the Southern Christian Leadership Conference (SCLC) had little in the way of structure and rules. After his death, more structure and rules were added, but the SCLC was not as effective as it had been under Dr. King's dynamic leadership.

Other organizations seek to develop a certain aura or mystique about themselves so that, perhaps, they appear stronger, larger, and better organized than they really are. No one would argue that the aura surrounding the U.S. Marines has not had an impact on the corps or that the American Association of Retired Persons has sought to create a political mystique far in excess of anything that the number of members would indicate. This image can be very effective when dealing with an external hostile environment or an internal "friendly" environment. The Society of Jesus (Jesuits) would certainly be counted here.

Finally, another response to constraints would be to appoint a strong board of directors. An important consideration is for the board to be fully committed to the goals of the organization so that they will support it and resist any attempt to subvert the mission. This requires not only commitment to the cause, but the ability of individual board members to withstand attacks both inside and outside the organization. Strong boards need strong members who can indoctrinate future members of the board, as well as important factions of the community, on the need and mission of the organization, without dominating the agency and getting in the way of the achievement of its goals, a sometimes delicate balance.

COMMON STRATEGIES FOR TRYING TO SOLVE NOT-FOR-PROFIT PROBLEMS

In addressing the problems and constraints faced by not-for-profit organizations, several patterns have developed.

Establish a For-Profit Enterprise

One of the first strategies is to develop a for-profit business that is outside the general mission of the organization. In this instance, the not-for-profit enters into the profit-making sector the economy and assumes all of the risks normally involved with a regular business. To do this, not-for-profits need to address several questions:

1. Is there a need for the enterprise? Will this enterprise fulfill some need in the society?
2. Does the organization have something to sell? The organization will now enter into a one-to-one relationship with customers, and for some organizations, this will be a new experience.
3. Does the organization have the necessary management talent? Can they meet a payroll as a business owner would meet a payroll, and make a profit? This is a very different world from depending on subsidies from the government.
4. Do the trustees of the organization support the venture? The board may feel that such an enterprise is outside the mandate of the not-for-profit organization.
5. Is there sufficient entrepreneurial spirit in the organization to enter the market successfully?
6. Does the organization have sufficient funds to sustain it during the startup phase of the venture?

Not-for-profits that establish for-profit enterprises are certain to run into several constraints in the marketplace. The first is the cry of unfair competition, which is sure to be heard from businessmen who feel that the new enterprise will be competing with them directly. An example of this would be when a public hospital seeks to set up a hotel for relatives of patients, and perhaps, in some instances, for the patients themselves. The owners and managers of local hotels might protest this new, in their view, tax-subsidized venture. It is bad enough when someone new enters the market, but it adds insult to injury when your own tax dollars are being used to do it. This is exactly what happened in Hershey, Pennsylvania, home of the Penn State University Medical School and Hospital. The hospital sought to establish a hotel for this purpose in the town. It should be understood that there is no lack of hotel rooms in Hershey, the home of Hershey Foods, Hershey Park, and one of the leading vacation destinations in the United States.

Another restriction is that the Internal Revenue Service has rules and regulations regarding these types of ventures. Essentially, the IRS has ruled that no more than 20 percent of the funds can come from for-profit enterprises. There is always the risk that the for-profit enterprise will not make any money and that the organization will actually lose money. A new enterprise could also interfere with the organization addressing its primary mission. The for-profit aspect could take so much time that it would interfere with the primary mission.

Finally, the for-profit enterprise could change the general perception of the organization on the part of the public. Perhaps the best example of this was when American GIs had to pay for coffee supplied to them by the American Red Cross during World War II. Well aware that the Red Cross was receiving generous support from the people back home, many GIs resented the fact that they had to pay for these items. What they were not aware of was that the Red Cross was under orders from General Eisenhower to charge for the coffee and other items. The Red Cross groups from other countries were not as well supported by their civilian populations and often had to charge their soldiers. General Eisenhower felt that for the Americans to receive services without

---

BOX 12.4   Bovine Bingo

One of the recent ways to raise funds by holding a special event has been the development of a game called Cow-Chip Bingo or Bovine Bingo. Rather like a lottery, a grid is placed on a football or similar field with numbered rows across and alphabetized columns up and down the field. Then a cow, which has been well fed, is released in the center of the field and allowed to wander about until its digestive process is completed and it deposits the "chips" somewhere on the grid. Chances are sold and the squares on the grid are selected at random for the participants. Prizes are then awarded to the winner of the event, the person who received that particular square in which the cow made its deposit, in exchange for a donation. The prize could be merchandise (donated or purchased), a sum of money, or even the cow. In the case of an overlap of squares by the cow's chips, all decisions by the judges are final.

---

paying might create problems between the various national forces serving in the war, so he ordered the Red Cross to charge or not provide the services at all. Unfortunately for the Red Cross, most servicemen were not aware of this and the GIs went home after the war with a taste of bad Red Cross coffee. It is no exaggeration to say that it has taken decades for the American Red Cross to live this down.

Establish a Foundation

A not-for-profit organization, especially one that is heavily dependent on tax dollars, needs to establish a foundation that can receive gifts and other items for the use of the organization. Colleges, universities, and hospitals have been doing this for years. Foundation money is independent money that is not subject to the strings of tax dollars. An endowment can be developed to help the organization through difficult financial times and should be guarded carefully. Tax-deductible donations can be made to the foundation for the use of the not-for-profit organization.

Organize Fundraising Events

Bingo and bazaars have been a staple of many churches for generations, but there are other types of events that can be used, depending on what is legal. Raffles and lotteries have been used for years. Dances, parties, indeed any event can be turned into a fundraiser; all there has to be is a charge at the door.

ETHICS AND NOT-FOR-PROFIT ORGANIZATIONS

Ethical considerations for not-for-profit organizations often come down to two questions:

1. *Where does the money come from?* Although there are those who would say that money is money, certain considerations must be taken into account: (a) What strings come attached to the money? (for example, what do you have to do to

get it and keep it?), and (b) even if the arrangement has no strings, what does it look like? Not only must the arrangement be "at arm's length," but it is equally important that it look that way.

2. *Where does the money go?* In an era of tight budgets, who gets the services? the old? the young? These are difficult questions. One of the most difficult questions facing American society is health care. Who gets the limited supply of medical care, and to what degree? Some people call this rationing, and it is, but society is already rationing health care based on the ability to pay. Those who can pay, get it, those who cannot, do not. That is rationing. But is it moral or ethical? If society decides to change the criterion, what will be the new criterion? How will that affect the elderly, who vote, and the young, who do not? Is society prepared to let a 55-year-old man who needs a kidney machine die because society cannot afford to offer the device to people over that age, or to let a newborn die because its mother cannot afford to have appropriate prenatal care? In a world of limited resources, these are the kinds of questions that must be addressed.

NOT-FOR-PROFIT ORGANIZATIONS AS THE TOOLS OF SOCIETY ■ ■ ■

Not-for-profits need a mission if they are going to be successful. The single most important aspect of measuring a not-for-profit organization is to ask how far they may have come in the accomplishment of their mission.[24] Mission is everything.

Society has allowed not-for-profits to address those tasks that might be considered unseemly if placed in the profit sector or simply where it is almost impossible to make a profit. But these are good causes. Indeed, not-for-profits are almost universally set up to "do good," whether for the society, individuals, or specific organizations.

This is not to say that there has not been some abuse and that from time to time these agencies do not need to be reminded of their purpose. A case in point are corporate foundations, which frequently are established with the idea of helping a corporation dispense various sums of money to worthy causes. The corporation deposits the money in a foundation it establishes for this purpose, and then a separate board makes decisions concerning the money. Corporate officers and members of the corporate board sit on this group and there may be an occasional representative from the union or some other interested constituent. One of the common programs of foundations is a matching program for contributions made by employees to worthy causes. The foundation matches, doubles, perhaps even triples an employee's contribution. All the recipient has to do is notify the company of the employee's donation and they are sent a check.

The problem is that many of these foundations were not dispensing very much money: some less than 1 percent of their principal, and some even none during a given year. The foundation's funds were being used for the purchase of stock in the parent corporation so as to solidify management's hold on the firm. Foundations were also being used as a veil for the takeover of other organizations, and it was all tax free. The Internal Revenue Service has now put a stop to this practice and a corporate foundation must now donate a certain minimal percentage of the principal every year or lose their tax-exempt status.

There is one final problem that besets not-for-profit organizations: that of success. What happens to a not-for-profit organization when it has succeeded? when the disease is cured? The problem of success was effectively dealt with by the March of Dimes. Founded to find a cure for polio, the March of Dimes helped greatly in this almost holy war against a dreaded killer.

It is necessary to understand what polio was and what it meant prior to the development of the vaccine in the 1950s. Polio is a killer and a crippler. It struck down people of all ages, races, and creeds. One of the oldest scourges of the human race, pictures of its victims with withered legs can be seen on the walls of ancient Egyptian buildings. Every year thousands of people were crippled or died as a result of the disease. Franklin D. Roosevelt, perhaps the greatest president of the United States during the twentieth century, suffered from the disease and spent most of his term in a wheelchair. Roosevelt could lead the nation through the Great Depression and World War II, but he could not go across a room without help—and he was one of the lucky ones. Finally, after years of research, a vaccine was developed that stopped polio in its tracks. It is truly one of the great success stories in the history of medicine, but it left the March of Dimes without a cause.

The March of Dimes had developed an infrastructure with leaders doctors, hospitals, and other facilities. It found itself in its greatest moment of triumph "all dressed up with no place to go." It needed a cause, and an important one, but most of the important causes already had their own foundations. It was an ironic twist of fate that the success of the March of Dimes had led directly to a lack of other causes to which it could direct its attention. Other organizations addressed heart disease and cancer. Finally, the March of Dimes adopted birth defects as its cause, and today is campaigning actively to combat them. But with the discoveries being made in genetics, the March of Dimes may one day find itself looking for another mission, another cause.

SUMMARY ■ ■ ■

Not-for-profit organizations are established in a society to accomplish some goal of the society and to promote the general welfare. They differ from profit-making organizations in that they do not, by definition, seek to make a profit. Not-for-profits can be subdivided into three classifications based on the participation by clients in the funding of the organization:

1. Major funding by clients
2. Some funding by clients
3. No funding by clients

This distinction is important because the key to understanding the management of not-for-profit organizations is learning who pays for services. Various stakeholders and publics have an interest in these organizations, and their ability to influence them and direct their mission, goals, and objectives is proportional to the funding of the organization.

Not-for-profit agencies have an even greater need for strategic management than for-profit organizations because they lack a single easily understood measure of organizational effectiveness. These goals, objectives and criteria for evaluation must be compatible with the funding sources and the clients for the services. If they are not, then severe conflict can develop inside of the organization.

Money, and the strings that go with it, represents the heaviest constraints on the organization. In addition, professional and personal values of people involved in these organizations can create conflict. Not-for-profits have responded to these problems in a variety of ways, including the start of for-profit businesses, foundations, and fundraising events. They have sought strong leaders, strong boards of directors, and the establishment of rules and regulations to help them manage themselves.

These agencies are often placed in difficult ethical positions. Seemingly always pressed for funds, they must sometimes decide which qualified clients receive services and which do not. They must also be certain that the sources of their funding are beyond reproach. Conflicts of interest can destroy the greatest asset of these organizations by casting their good intentions into doubt.

Not-for-profit organizations are the tools of the society. They are used by society to accomplish goals that enhance and promote the general welfare of the society and its constitutent groups.

Questions

1. Not-for-profit organizations, by definition, do not make a profit. What are some of the ways that not-for-profits can measure their effectiveness?

2. Organizations in a capitalist society exist to make a profit. Why, then, does society allow not-for-profit organizations?

3. Three different types of not-for-profit organizations exist. What are they? What are examples of each?

4. Not-for-profits may have a large number of stakeholders. How could they influence the goals of the organization?

5. The text outlines five specific constraints faced by not-for-profit organizations. What are they? How do you think they influence not-for-profit organizations?

6. Many organizations seek a strong leader. What are some problems associated with this approach?

7. Often, strategies for addressing the needs of not-for-profit organizations focus on obtaining funds. What are some of the strategies?

8. Not-for-profits are in the business of "doing good." If that is so, why is the source of funding an important consideration?

9. According to Peter Drucker, not-for-profits "exist for the sake of their mission." What happens to a not-for-profit organization when it loses sight of its mission?

10. Paradoxically, success can be a disaster for a not-for-profit organization. How can this be?

CASE I

You are the administrator and chief operating officer of a large medical school. You have been informed by your board chair that he has been able to gain major funding from a single giver, a major distiller and brewer, for a center to study and treat alcohol and drug abuse. This would enable the medical school to become far and away the leader for such issues in your geographical location.

1. What do you do?
2. What are your reasons for doing that?
3. What values do those reasons reflect?

Source: Fred Maidment, *Annual Editions: Management 1999–2000.* ©1999 by Fred Maidment (Ed.). Guilford, CT: Dushkin/McGraw-Hill.

CASE 2

Things certainly have changed over the past six years for Cub Scout Pack 81. Six years ago, the pack was on the verge of disbanding. There were barely enough boys for an effective den, and they had been losing membership for as long as anyone could remember. The cub master was trying to pass his job on to any parent foolish enough to take the helm of a sinking ship, and the volunteer fire department that sponsored the pack was openly considering dropping it.

But that was six years ago. Today, the pack has one of the largest memberships of any in the Lancaster/Lebanon Council. It has started its own Boy Scout troop, into which the webelos can graduate, and it has received a presidential citation for its antidrug program. The pack consistently wins competitions with other packs in the council, and the fire department is very happy about its sponsorship. Membership in the pack is now around 60 cubs at all levels, and they have a new cub master.

"Parents want their boys to be in a successful program," says Cub Master Mike Murphy. "Look, I can't do everything. We depend on the parents and boys to get things done. Everybody understands that we want to have a successful program, and that means that we all have to participate to achieve that success. I can't do it all, but if we can unleash the energy these boys have, there isn't anything in the Cub Scout Program we can't do!"

It was not always like that. "About five years ago we placed fourth for our booth in the Scout Expo at the Mall," says Mike. "Everybody was shocked! Who was Pack 81? We were all elated! It was one of the best things to happen to this pack in years. Now, if we don't win at least something, we're disappointed. Our kids expect to win, and so do their parents." Fourth place at the Scout Expo eventually led to several first places. Success leads to success, and the community around Pack 81 knows it.

"Last year, we made our annual presentation to the boys and their parents at the elementary school. We were with several other packs, each one trying to drum up interest in their program. When everyone was finished, the boys and their parents went over to the table of the pack that most interested them. We must have had well over half of the people at our table. I was embarrassed! They were standing six or seven deep in front of our table, and there was virtually nobody in front of the others."

1. How do you explain the success of Pack 81?
2. If you were Mike, how would you propose to continue that success?

Source: Fred Maidment, *Annual Editions: Management 1999–2000.* ©1999 by Fred Maidment (Ed.). Guilford, CT: Dushkin/McGraw-Hill.

References _____

1. Drucker, P., *Managing the nonprofit organization: practices and principles*, HarperCollins, New York, 1990.

2. *Statistical abstract of the United States, 1996*, U.S. Department of Commerce, Washington, DC, 1996.

3. *Statistical abstract of the United States, 1996*.

4. "The Fortune 500," *Fortune*, April 14, 1994.

5. *Statistical abstract of the United States, 1996*.

6. *Gales Encyclopedia of associations*, 1997.

7. *Statistical abstract of the United States, 1996*.

8. "The Fortune 500."

9. Drucker, *Managing the nonprofit organization*.

10. Marguilies, W., "Make the most of your corporate identity," *Harvard Business Review*, July–August, 1977.

11. Drucker, *Managing the nonprofit organization*.

12. Herman, Robert D., & Heimovies, Richard D. *Executive leadership in nonprofit organizations*, Jossey-Bass, San Francisco, 1991.

13. Ibid.

14. Eldridge, W., "Why angels fear to tread: a practioner's guide to strategic management in government," in Jack Rabin, Gerald Miller, and W. Bartley Hildreth (eds.), *Handbook of strategic management*, Marcel Dekker, New York, 1989.

15. Drucker, Peter, *Management: tasks, responsibilities, practices*, Harper & Row, New York, 1974.

16. Ibid.

17. Drucker, *Managing the nonprofit organization*.

18. *Bartlett's familiar quotations*, 16th Ed., Boston, Little Brown, 1992.

19. Gaber, B. "The hidden agenda of performance appraisals," *Training*, June 1988.

20. Seashore, S., "Criteria for organizational effectiveness," *Michigan Business Review*, July 1965.

21. Newman, William H., and Wallender, Harvey W. "Managing the not for profit enterprise," *Academy of Management Review*, January 1978.

22. Morton, T., "Cardinals urge respect for life, defense against defections," *Christianity Today*, May 27, 1991.

23. Eldridge, W., "Private sector management practices can help government," *New Jersey Human Services Reporter*, New Jersey Department of Human Resources, Trenton, NJ, 1994.

24. Drucker, *Managing the nonprofit organization*.

ISSUES IN THE WORKPLACE

Concepts ⋮ You Will Learn ■ ■ ■

reasons for job specialization in the workplace

how the industrial era created the modern work environment

some current problems and challenges facing affirmative action

the causes and roots of gender discrimination

why age discrimination is so widely practiced in industry

the impact of the Americans with Disabilities Act

the mommy and daddy tracks

the "glass ceiling"

recent developments in child and elder care

the problems faced in the workplace with AIDS and other conditions

education and training for business and industry

challenges to compensation and benefits for employees

worker safety and unions

international human resource management

HISTORICAL DEVELOPMENT OF THE MODERN WORKPLACE ■ ■ ■

The Preindustrial Era ■ ■ ■

Even before the dawn of history, tribal groups assigned different tasks to various members of the band. Often, these roles evolved traditional patterns, frequently along gender lines. The men would go out and hunt game and protect the family group from other bands, while the women would remain with the children, gathering whatever crops they could and seeing to the domestic needs of the group. People would specialize according to their particular talents. If one member of the tribe seemed particularly good at tracking and hunting game, he would often lead the hunt; if another always seemed to be able to catch fish, that person would lead fishing expeditions. As talents became useful, the tribe put them to work so as to achieve the maximum benefit for the group. Occupational specialization was born even before recorded history.

Recorded history started with the advent of the great agricultural civilizations of the Nile, Indus, Yangtze, Tigris, and Euphrates river valleys.[1] Human beings settled in one place and were able to produce an agricultural surplus, which they were then able to trade with their neighbors. Cities arose because people could produce more food than they needed. This gave rise to government, craft-based manufacturing, music, art, literature—indeed, what is commonly accepted as civilization.[2] Because people no longer had to be concerned primarily with the gathering of food so that they could survive, they now had time for further specialization in both their occupations and their leisure pursuits. Most of the time that is known as recorded history took place during this era. It was not until about 250 years ago that the industrial revolution started what Alvin Toffler has called the second wave of human development.[3]

The Industrial Era   ■ ■ ■

The industrial revolution started in Great Britain in the mid-eighteenth century.[4] Beginning in the textile industry, it soon replaced many of the crafts that had been the basis of the production process for centuries. With the industrial revolution came the factory system, which brought workers together in a single place for the purpose of creating goods to be sold. Generally, the workers operated machines that produced goods at a much faster and more uniform rate than could the craftsmen they displaced, and those craftsmen soon found themselves either out of work or serving a much smaller group of customers who could afford their products.

During the early days of the industrial revolution it was not uncommon for tests between machines and flesh and blood to end with the man or beast of burden winning the contest. Horses racing locomotives and the legend of John Henry are cases in point. But the mechanical machines got better, while the men and beasts remained the same. Eventually, machines displaced the men and beasts entirely in most areas.

Probably the most dramatic change took place in the United States. Whether it is called the Civil War, the War Between the States, or even the Late Unpleasantness, the conflict in the United States between 1861 and 1865 was really a conflict between two different civilizations: the agrarian South and the industrialized North.[5] The economy of the South was based on agriculture and at the core of the system was slavery. Slavery was the dirty little secret of civilized societies. Virtually all "flowerings" of civilization prior to the industrial revolution occurred among a very small elite who were supported either by slaves, serfs, or peasants or some other group of oppressed people.[6] Slavery, under various guises, exists even today in different parts of the less developed world. The industrial revolution made slavery obsolete because machines are more productive in terms of investment than people. The South was going against the march of history and the tide of economic development. There are those who have postulated that even if the North had lost the war, for the South could not have won, the South would have been forced, through economic necessity, to abandon slavery by the end of the century. In short, the Southern cause and the "peculiar institution" of slavery were doomed from the beginning. The North could lose the war, but the South, despite all the effort, could only briefly preserve a cause that was already lost.

The industrial revolution changed the human condition as no other force had done since the settling of the Nile Valley by the ancestors of the ancient Egyptians.[7] Unfortunately, not all of the changes were positive. There were many abuses in the factory system. Wages were often at starvation levels, child labor was common,[8] and working conditions were sometimes deadly. Conditions in some Northern factories in the United States were so bad that they were used in the debates on the floor of the U.S. Congress as a justification *for* slavery.[9]

In the United States, industry continued to expand, along with the general expansion of the country. Indeed, during the period 1865 to 1917, U.S. industry expanded at an almost geometric rate of growth. Money from all over the world was invested in the United States to help to finance the growth of U.S. industry. Immigrants such as Andrew Carnegie became millionaires, well-to-do bankers such as J. P. Morgan became fabulously wealthy, and railroad tycoons such as Cornelius Vanderbilt spun their ribbons of steel across the continent.

However, this expansion was not without cost in human terms or a reaction to that cost. In Europe, as early as 1848, Karl Marx had written "Workers of the world, unite! You have nothing to lose but your chains!"[10] In the United States the first labor strike occurred among printers in Philadelphia in the eighteenth century, drawing the first lines between labor and management.[11] Other conflicts followed in the evolution of the labor movement with the establishment of the International Workers of the World, Homestead strike, Pullman strike, and Triangle fire.

The conflict continues to this day, and although there are those who would argue that the labor movement has lost its usefulness, the recent fire in a plant in North Carolina which resulted in the deaths of many workers as they piled up in front of the locked exits should not be dismissed.[12]

WORKPLACE ISSUES IN HUMAN RESOURCES   ■ ■ ■

If there is one message that has been brought home to managers over the past decade, it is that people get things done—not plans, not buildings, but people—and if an organization is going to be successful, people have to be considered in the firm's plans.[13]

The common thread that runs through all the research of Deming and Peters is the thread of people.[14] Organizations must hire, train, and develop the best people they can. While the government of the United States has passed a variety of laws dealing with various forms of discrimination, including racial, age, and disability,[15] the economy has changed significantly.[16] The world has become a far more competitive place than it was when the Civil Rights Act was passed in 1964, and organizations can no longer afford to discriminate based on criteria that have nothing to do with the jobs that people are doing.

Equal Employment Opportunity and Affirmative Action ■ ■ ■

Today, discrimination in employment based on anything other than the qualifications and abilities to do the job simply does not make very good business sense. This is not to say that discrimination which is in violation of the various civil rights laws does not occur. It does, as does reverse discrimination aimed at white males.[17] But in today's competitive international environment, racial, age, and gender discrimination simply do not make sense. Good employees are hard enough to find, and if a firm limits itself to one or two particular groups to the exclusion of others, it is going to find itself at a competitive disadvantage, because the people who make up their competition will be more talented and productive.

There have been significant swings in national employment policy over the past several decades. The civil rights laws made discrimination based on race illegal and encouraged affirmative action programs.[18] The affirmative action programs essentially said that there are groups of people, which can be identified, that have suffered discrimination in the society based on their ethnic background or the color of their skin. This is wrong and it is going to be made up to them through affirmative action. Although this may be a noble sentiment, like every other policy or action, it has unintended consequences. Those consequences have included the establishment of quotas (although, nobody uses the word, as quotas, by definition, are illegal—affirmative action goals is the preferred terminology) and reverse discrimination. The practice of racial norming to achieve affirmative action is a case in point. If, on a competitive exam for the police department, the highest grade achieved by a white is 90, by an Hispanic, 80, and by a black, 85. The 90, 80, and 85 are all considered equal under racial norming. The resulting consequence is that a white male who scored 81 may never be hired, whereas a black or Hispanic who scored in the low to mid-70s may be hired simply because of his or her racial and/or ethnic background. The white may have a more deprived background than any of the blacks or Hispanics who took the test [over half of the people living below the poverty level in the country are white[19]] but will not get the job. This is an example of an affirmative action tool resulting in reverse discrimination.

The problem is that the bill for the acknowledged injustices of past discrimination in the workplace as well as the rest of society is being presented to selected members of the current workforce and, by extension, their families—specifically, white males. Unfortunately, this is not advisable, for several reasons:

1. White males are not a monolithic group. At the turn of the century, employment notices frequently ended with the word "NINA," which was short for "No Irish need apply." It was later used to include Italians.

2. The white males currently in the workforce are not the ones who are guilty of discrimination. Many of these injustices occurred generations ago. What affirmative action seems to be saying to them is: "Your great-grandfather was a horse thief. We weren't able to catch him, but now we've got you, and we're going to hang you for his crimes."

3. How long can affirmative action last? There seems to be little or no agreement on how long affirmative action should continue. At one end there are those who say

that it never should have been instituted and should be stopped immediately, and at the other, that it should continue forever. Neither position is realistic. The flaw in affirmative action is that it is in direct conflict with the equal protection clause (the Fourteenth Amendment) of the U.S. Constitution. When one group is granted legal advantage over another, it violates the Constitution. This paradox in civil rights law has been tolerated because of acknowledged past injustice. But when will justice be served? This is both a political and a moral question. Moral, from the perspective of trying to right prior wrongs through actions that injure others indirectly, and political from the perspective of being able to

---

BOX 13.1   Ban on Racial Preferences Upheld: California Opponents of Proposition 209 to Appeal to High Court

A federal appeals court on Thursday reaffirmed its ruling upholding California's voter-approved ban on race and gender preferences, meaning that the law could go into effect within a week. The Ninth U.S. Circuit Court of Appeals said a request by civil rights groups for a rehearing on Proposition 209 had failed to gain a majority among the 18 judges eligible to vote. No vote total was announced.

American Civil Liberties Union lawyer Mark Rosenbaum said he would appeal to the U.S. Supreme Court and would ask that court to continue a ban on enforcement of the measure during the appeal. If neither court intervenes immediately, Proposition 209 can be implemented in seven days under the courts' rules, Rosenbaum said. He predicted the Supreme Court would agree to review the case and said that 23 states were considering similar measures. "This is the first time in the nation's history that state and local government have had their hands tied when it comes to remedying past discrimination against minorities and women," he said.

A lawyer for sponsors of the initiative said the appeals court's action makes it less likely that the Supreme Court will review the case. But if the court grants review, "I am confident it will find that the citizens of California acted in the letter and spirit of the Constitution when they voted to end racial preference last November," Michael Carvin of the Center for Individual Rights said in a press release. "So much for the ACLU's Alice-in-Wonderland reading of the Constitution, whereby it is somehow discriminatory to end discrimination," he said. The Clinton administration supported the ACLU's challenge, filed on behalf of minority and female students, employees, and contractors.

Proposition 209, approved by 54 percent of the voters, would prohibit preferences based on race or gender in state and local government employment, education, and contracting. The measure would eliminate a variety of programs, including hiring goals for minorities and women in state employment and consideration of race in public college admissions. University of California regents voted separately to eliminate the schools' affirmative action programs, starting with graduate school admissions this year.

Enforcement of the initiative was barred three weeks after the election by Chief U.S. District Judge Thelton Henderson of San Francisco, who said opponents were likely to prove it unconstitutional. Henderson said the measure, although neutrally worded, would only abolish programs benefiting minorities and women, leaving other groups, such as veterans and children of college alumni, free to ask government agencies for preferential treatment. But a three-judge panel of the appeals court overruled Henderson on April 8, saying that not only were opponents not entitled to injunction against the measure but that it was clearly constitutional.

Source: Associated Press, August 22, 1997.

develop the political will to bring the program to an end. American history is full of examples of minorities being protected from tyrannies of the majority, but excesses of and for a minority will not be tolerated for long in any society.[20]

4. There is a legitimate question as to whether affirmative action is working. Granted, affirmative action worked well in helping to establish a black middle class. It has helped create a cadre of professionals among the various minority groups. Supreme Court Justice Clarence Thomas is a case in point. But poverty, ignorance, and squalor are still evident and certainly not limited to minority groups. Vast numbers of citizens are not part of the mainstream of American life. Frustration, anger, and resentment continue to build in the society as the rich seem to become richer and the poor, poorer. The question is not one based on race but on the opportunities available to all citizens in the society.

Sexual Harassment

One of the more controversial issues facing organizations is sexual harassment. First, it should be understood that sexual harassment has little to do with sex. Sex is only the instrument that is used by one person to wield power over another.[21] There are other ways to do it that are far more subtle, but many people who engage in sexual harassment simply do not have the intelligence to find other ways.

BOX 13.2   Anita Hill and Clarence Thomas

Few congressional hearings have grabbed the country the way the Senate Judiciary Committee's did over the appointment of Clarence Thomas to the Supreme Court. Clarence Thomas, who now serves on the Court, was a prominent conservative African-American attorney who had served in a number of positions in both the Reagan and Bush administrations. Clarence Thomas was appointed to the Court to fill the vacancy left by the retirement of Justice Marshall, the first African American to serve on the Court and a man who had left a distinguished record as his legacy. Thomas was opposed by the Democrats on the committee, mostly along party lines, and although there seemed to be nothing to indicate that there was any reason to oppose the nomination, there was rather little material to support it either. Justice Marshall had held what many viewed as the African-American seat on the Court, and Thomas was viewed by many as a usurper of Marshall's mantle of liberalism, especially in the area of civil rights, where Thomas was known to have very conservative views.

That all changed when Anita Hill, then a law professor but formerly a close associate of Thomas, testified before the committee that Thomas had sexually harassed her and made offensive statements to her. Whether or not the allegations were true became lost in the "He said/she said" arguments that are often typical of sexual harassment charges. People seemed to believe either Thomas or Hill, with the opinion having a high degree of correlation with one's political leanings. Although his reputation was certainly damaged by the allegations, Thomas did eventually assume his current position as an Associate Justice of the Supreme Court.

What Clarence Thomas and Anita Hill did, however, was to raise the consciousness of the country with regard to sexual harassment and make it a major issue. They changed the workplace and the society in which they lived. No longer would such attentions and behavior be ignored. For good or for bad, sexual harassment was on the nation's agenda.

Sexual harassment is based on power in relationships. The harassment can occur in a variety of ways, including man harasses woman, woman harasses man, man harasses man, and woman harasses woman.

Sexual harassment became a national issue during the Senate confirmation hearings of Clarence Thomas, and the nation and the workplace have not been the same since. There are several problems in dealing with sexual harassment.

1. *Attitude.* Many people still have the same attitude toward sexual harassment as they did 30 years ago, and that is not appropriate anymore.
2. *Difficult to prove.* Allegations of sexual harassment often degenerate into a "he said/she said" battle.
3. *Training.* Organizations need to engage in training to protect themselves from lawsuits filed by employees.
4. *Damaging.* Nobody wins in sexual harassment.

It is the obligation of employers to make certain that their employees know what sexual harassment is and not to be put into a situation that would encourage or engender sexual harassment.

Age Discrimination

Perhaps the most common form of illegal discrimination today is age discrimination. This is supported by the fact that there are now more complaints filed with the EEOC based on age discrimination than any other type of discrimination.[22] Essentially, it is against the law to discriminate against people between the ages of 40 and 70 because of their age. Unfortunately, this law is often more honored in its violation than in its practice. The downsizing of U.S. industry, especially of middle management, has been a development that has led to the termination of many people by firms looking to cut costs by going after middle management, and unfortunately, many of these people are in their 40s, 50s, or 60s.

The Americans with Disabilities Act

The Americans with Disabilities Act (ADA) was passed to ensure equal access to employment and services for Americans with disabilities.[23] The ADA and its enforcement go to the heart of the everyday life of Americans. Under the ADA, specific requirements are now in place concerning handicapped access. Such things as the width of a doorway, a hallway, and even the installation of an elevator in a building are covered by the ADA. There have been and will continue to be numerous court decisions concerning the ADA over the key phrase *reasonable accommodation* because often, nobody knows what reasonable accommodation is and this will, of course, be fought out in the courts.

The real problem is that today, because of the advances of medical science, there are far more people with disabilities than there were years ago. This is because we are better able to recognize and define disabilities than was the case years ago, and medical science can now save people who years ago would simply have died of their injuries. The medical experience gained from World War II, Korea, and Vietnam has vastly increased a physician's ability to deal with injuries than was the case 50 years ago, and the same thing can be said for many victims of disease.

For example, 50 years ago, Christopher Reeves, the actor who played Superman and suffered a paralyzing neck injury from a fall from a horse, would have died. Today, Christopher Reeves, although confined to a wheelchair,[24] just finished directing his first movie. He may not be able to play Superman anymore, but that does not mean that he cannot do other things in his field. As with so many other things, the society has not really caught up with the advances of medical science. The ADA represents a forced march to correct and shorten the distance between what the society practices and the reality of the situation. People with disabilities are no longer an oddity in the society, and they are just as capable of making a contribution to the society, in their own way, as anyone else.

The Mommy/Daddy Track

In 1989, Felice N. Schwartz opened a Pandora's box of controversy when she wrote for the *Harvard Business Review*, "Management Women and the New Facts of Life".[25] Among her many points was that women are different from men and should be treated in a different way. This caused her to be attacked from many sides. On one hand, she was accused of trying to destroy all that her fellow feminists had tried to accomplish in attempting to establish that women could be just as good, if not better than, men and deserved the same kinds of opportunities that men have in an organization. On the other hand, she was denounced by some in industry for saying that there was an inherent conflict for many women between work and family. The fact is that Ms. Schwartz was right about many of the things in her article, but more important, touched off a debate in the society on family and work.

Schwartz postulated the mommy track: essentially, where a woman may step out, for a period of time, from the corporate grind to raise her family. This may take many forms, such as a reduced workweek, job sharing, leave of absence, or whatever accommodation can be made. It recognized the difficulty of raising a family and having a full-time career all at the same time. Somebody has to be responsible for the children, and more often than not, that is going to be the mother.

This debate has been carried on in a number of ways and on a number of levels. Perhaps the most public one was between former Vice President Dan Quayle and the TV character Murphy Brown,[26] played by Candice Bergen, on the television show *Murphy Brown*. The Murphy Brown character was one of a highly successful woman in a very competitive field. As a part of the story line, this single woman became pregnant out of wedlock. Vice President Quayle criticized the show and the character in a speech, saying that this was not an appropriate role model for young women. The Vice President was then showered with criticism saying that he was wrong and that women could do whatever they wanted with both their bodies and their lives.

Unfortunately, none of that criticism addressed the central issue of what happens to those women who have children out of wedlock, the vast majority of whom are poor, uneducated, and do not live lives like Murphy Brown. Murphy Brown could have it all: a great career, children, fame, and fortune, but unfortunately, Murphy Brown is a TV character and is fiction. She is not real, and for most people, neither are those kinds of expectations.

The flip side of the mommy track is the daddy track, where men are given the same kind of options that women are given in terms of raising children and responsibility for family life. This type of behavior is so rare that men who do opt for a daddy track are considered suspect and are often written off by their employers. Employers may not like women spending more time with their families, but they find it simply intolerable for a man to exercise the same kind of option, and if he does, he will be forever suspect.

The Glass Ceiling

■ ■ ■

Over the past decade a great deal has been written about the glass ceiling, defined by the U.S. Department of Labor as "those artificial barriers based on attitudinal or organizational bias that prevent qualified individuals from advancing upward in their organizations."[27] Most of the literature in this area has centered around the fact that women and minorities, as a group, are not generally found in the upper reaches of U.S. industry. This can be confirmed by a review of the senior management of almost any company.[28] There are, it should be mentioned, women and minorities who have been successful in entering senior management, but they are comparatively rare.

When considering this situation, two obvious questions arise. First, why is it that more women and minorities have not been promoted to senior management? Second, are there common elements, other than race and gender, that are shared by successful senior executives?

To answer these questions, the relevant labor force environment must first be examined. This is not an examination of conditions today, but rather, of labor market conditions of 30 or 40 years ago, when many of today's senior corporate executives started their careers.

Rarely does a person in his or her early 20s become president of an organization. Even in closely held firms, this would be highly unusual. Rather, high-ranking executives are almost exclusively experienced professional managers who fought their way to the top of their organizations over a period of decades. Despite the recent spate of downsizing, reengineering, mergers, flattening, spin-offs, and takeovers, corporations are still essentially pyramidal in nature. Senior managers climb the organizational ladder by being perceived as more successful than their contemporaries at each level. As they move up, they gain more responsibility, compensation, prestige, and knowledge of how to be successful at the next level.[29]

Many practices that excluded women and minorities from employment and promotion consideration predate the 1964 Civil Rights Act, and most continued for some period afterward. The debate on the 1964 Civil Rights Act was rife with comments by its *supporters* that its passage would not result in minimum employment percentages. Thus the debate indicated that employers would not have to hire minimum percentages of any group or risk losing government contracts and facing possible legal action. It was a matter of time after 1964 before such formal and informal sanctions for businesses with low minority employment became evident. Also, there were often decades of compliance with the letter of this legislation, where such compliance was either mildly supportive or even contrary to the spirit of the civil rights legislation. In education, for example, top schools fought to recruit minority students without apparent regard for their low graduation rates. To satisfy affirmative action goals, they admitted minority students who had SAT scores in the top 10 percent. Such students, who would have been highly successful at state or regional colleges, were frustrated by having to compete with non–affirmative action students who had SAT scores in the top 1 percent.[30]

Employment discrimination by firms is not new. Firms are held accountable for employment discrimination regardless of whether it is based on the employer himself being prejudiced or if the other employees are prejudiced or if the firm's customers are prejudiced against being served by members of certain groups.[31] In the latter two cases, discrimination is driven largely by societal characteristics. However, if discrimination is not to be perpetuated, these "excuses" must be held unacceptable even if the result is to put some firms out of business.

Historically, employment discrimination was not limited to racial minorities and women. Subsets of white males were routinely discriminated against by industrial employers during the nineteenth century and well into the twentieth century. Employment notices at the turn of the century regularly ended with "NINA" for "No Irish need apply," and anti-Semitism was common in many segments of society.

One very obvious characteristic of CEOs and other members of upper management is that they are predominately white males.[32] *Male* is clearly gender and *white* is a common proxy for race. Apart from the race and gender endowments of the accident of birth, are there other common characteristics shared by successful senior executives?

At the time the 1964 Civil Rights Act was passed, the labor force consisted of 62.6 percent males and 37.4 percent females[33] and was 88.9 percent white and 11.1 percent minority.[34] By 1993 the labor force had doubled and its gender composition changed to 55 percent male and 45 percent female, with 82 percent white and 18 percent minority.[35]

Occupations are less stratified by gender today than was the case in 1964. There is ample evidence that in the 1950s and 1960s educated women tended to go into professions such as K–12 teaching, secretarial, and nursing positions. In contrast, educated men went into such occupations as business and engineering. Although men still do not enter nursing in large numbers, women have moved into traditionally male-dominated professions such as business, engineering, law, and medicine.[36]

To date not very many women have risen to the vice-presidential level, so few have been in a position to be considered for a corporate-president vacancy. There are several reasons for this "pipeline problem."

1. The people in line for senior management positions are to some extent a reflection of the labor market that existed 30 to 40 years ago. In the 1950s and 1960s not many women or, for that matter, many minority-group members, went into jobs leading to corporate management positions. It was not until the 1970s that women really started to climb the corporate ladder in large numbers.[37]

2. Many women who did opt for corporate positions left after a few years to get married and raise families. Years later when many of them returned to the labor force, they found themselves behind their former male peers in corporate experience and "time in grade." This was ground that would be difficult to make up.[38]

3. The women who had left the labor force for their family were stigmatized. They might do it again. Beyond this, all women were stigmatized as potential labor

force leavers. Business felt that it could not rationally justify training and promoting someone who might leave after a few years. Although men might leave for various reasons, marriage and childbirth by their spouse was more likely to cement them into their job than cause them to leave it.[39]

4. Women are not as severely penalized as men by the society if they should choose to step out of the corporate world. "Men have responsibilities, and women have choices,"[40] seems to be the attitude of a significant segment of industry. A woman who opts out of the corporate life can go back. On the other hand, opting out is simply not perceived as a feasible alternative for men, so they are forced to continue to pursue their careers whether they want to or not.

5. The passage of civil rights legislation targeting women's rights did not provide an instantaneous remedy to the pipeline problem. Governmental agencies and their suppliers were quickest to respond. However, even for them, it took several years for an awareness of the need to recruit and promote women and minorities to become widespread.

Although much has been written about the glass ceiling, it is mostly opinion and conjecture; there has been little in the way of hard-nosed research into the topic.[41] The reason is obvious: If a private organization were to allow research in this area, the researchers might find evidence of an incidence of discriminatory behavior. No matter how tenuous the connection to the employer, this incidence could cause the corporation to be sued for discrimination. However, the public sector does not have the option to withhold information, as promotions are a matter of public record. Powell and Butterfield[42] conducted a study of a cabinet-level U.S. federal government department focusing on promotions within the department to the Senior Executive Service (SES). The researchers were surprised to find that gender worked to the advantage of the female employees both directly and indirectly. In fact, eligible women were promoted to the SES at twice the rate of their male counterparts. There were many more men promoted, but this reflected that there were many more eligible men than eligible women. This could, at least, be explained partially by the pipeline problem. The point is that once women reached levels where they could be considered for senior management, they were promoted at twice the rate of males. According to the Department of Labor definition cited above, the glass ceiling in this department did not exist. However, the glass ceiling was not shattered to the point where proportionately equal numbers of women and men were being promoted to the SES in this department. So according to the loose definition in apparent widespread use, the glass ceiling in this department continues to be a problem.

Managers do not have to be effective to be successful as these terms are defined by some researchers.[43] In Luthans' study, a manager's success was determined by how fast he or she had been promoted up the managerial ladder. Managerial effectiveness is measured through subordinates' evaluations of their satisfaction, commitment, and subunit performance. This study provided evidence that successful managers spend the most time networking, socializing, interacting with outsiders, and politicking. Effective managers, on the other hand, spend the least time on those same activities. The study indicated that fewer than 10 percent of the managers were considered to be both effective and successful. Luthans provides evidence that effective and successful managers behave in almost exactly opposite ways.

■ ■ ■   **BOX 13.3   Kansas City Corporate Leadership**   ■ ■ ■

In Kansas City there is only one female executive in charge of one of the 100 largest companies in town. All of the others are white males. But these white males have other things in common, not the least of which is where they went to school. These executives have gone to a number of different institutions, but over half of them have gone to the top 25 schools in the country as reported by *U.S. News and World Report.* When the executives from the University of Missouri and the University of Kansas, local large institutions, are added, these schools represent the alma mater of almost 75 percent of the chief executives of the 100 largest companies in Kansas City.

These executives would seem to have more in common than just their gender and race. They reflect a labor market that existed some 30 years ago. For example, the average age of a CEO in Kansas City is about 53, which means that they started their business careers about 30 years ago, in the 1960s. In the 1960s, women did not initially go into business. Many of them were still in the home, and those that went to college and to work were overwhelmingly in teaching and nursing.

Women have been caught in a pipeline problem caused by the fact that many of them did not start in industry until fairly late and those that did often had to step out to raise families. Added to that is the fact that many of them simply did not attend the right schools. Of course, most men did not attend the right schools either. With all the talk about the glass ceiling, one would think that all white males had somehow achieved the rank of CEO, but that is obviously not the case. Getting into the right network with the right credentials is also important.

The number one alma mater among Kansas City CEOs of publicly held companies is an institution that simply did not accept women until the 1960s, and then, initially, only a limited number. It is about as far away from Kansas City as it is possible to get and still be in the United States: a medium-sized institution known as Harvard University.

Source: Peter Soule, Park College.

Job Security   ■ ■ ■

One of the factors that has changed for workers in North America has been job security. Simply stated, there is much less job security today than was the case 10, 20, or 50 years ago. There are many reasons for this, some being:

1. The world economy. Today, companies and their products compete on a global scale.
2. Pressure for increased profits. Organizations are cut to the bone to produce greater profits.
3. Greater demand for more productive workers.

The fact is that the gold watch and the retirement party are over.[44] Loyalty between the employer and the employee are a thing of the past and are only as good as the next paycheck.

This, of course, does not lead to a stable work environment or a long-term view for employees or their employers. It can also lead to decisions that are made with short-term results and objectives in mind that can really hurt the company in the long run.

Both employers and employees need to understand that there is no longer a long-term commitment between them.[45] The workplace has become Darwinian, and the law of the survival of the fittest is the only retirement party now being held for anyone.

Child/Elder Care

An area of continued demand in the human resource arena is child care. In a world where the dual-career family is the norm, taking care of the children is a major concern of every parent. Mother does not stay home anymore. She works, and somebody has to take care of the kids.[46] Child care is a major concern. Companies that have addressed this issue have found that employees who take advantage of some form of child care have a very low turnover rate. The reason is simple: Knowing that one's children are well cared for and are relatively easily accessible can make all the difference in the world to parents. This is a situation that most parents will not want to disturb. It is a situation that is important to them and one they are very unwilling to leave. Unfortunately, many companies have not realized the advantages of assisting with child care and have simply ignored the situation. These organizations are missing the opportunity to increase their employee's productivity and to cut down on their turnover and absenteeism. Enlightened managers of companies realize that providing for the needs of their employees only enhances productivity.[47]

An aspect of family life that is going to be more important in the future is elder care, the care of workers' parents and other senior citizens. As the population ages and more people live longer lives, their health and well-being will become a greater concern to the population as a whole as well as to their children, who will make up the workforce. Elder care is going to be a growing aspect of society,[48] a market and industry that is almost guaranteed to grow in the future. Unfortunately, it is also going to be very expensive. The children of senior citizens may be faced with the decision of staying home to take care of elderly relatives or placing them in elder care facilities costing thousands of dollars a month, often more than the employee takes home in his or her check.

In the future, organizations are going to have to address all of these issues: It won't be child care or elder care, but dependent care. Workers who are members of the sandwich generation are going to need help if they are to be effective employees. These are issues that affect the society, and the society is where the workers come from. For an employer to ignore the problems that face his or her employees is to invite them to seek employment with someone who will not ignore those problems. As the labor market tightens for qualified and capable employees, employers are going to have to meet their demands, and in the future, dependent care is going to be one of them.

AIDS and Other Chronic Diseases

Organizations and their employees are going to be faced with a growing problem of what to do about people with AIDS and other chronic diseases, some of whom may have been cured while others will simply be in remission.[49] This includes not only people with AIDS but also those with diabetes, cancer, heart disease, and other conditions. The fact is that years ago, people simply died from many of these ailments; today many survive and lead full lives. Unfortunately, society, in particular, health insurance, has not caught up with the current state of medical practice.

Many of these conditions are covered by the ADA, but that does not solve many of the problems when it comes to hiring people with these conditions or when discovering that some employees may have developed one of these conditions. Especially in the case of a small business, this type of situation can totally destroy the health insurance of the entire company workforce. Insurance companies are in the business of making money, and if a particular client becomes unprofitable, they are likely to try to find a way to discontinue doing business with that client (i.e., cancel the policy).

Employees with AIDS and other chronic diseases present managers with some highly unique problems. Many employees want to continue to work and, to a perhaps limited extent, are capable of doing so. On the other hand, the organization can be placed in a very uncomfortable and highly unprofitable situation of having to provide for much of the medical care of these employees. True, AIDS patients and diabetics are covered by the ADA, but not everyone is and the health insurance company does not necessarily have to renew or grant a policy. Managers must search their conscience and determine what is the right course of action to follow.

Drugs and Alcohol

Probably the most important problem facing industry in terms of decreased productivity is drugs and alcohol.[50] More time is lost on the job because of these preventable factors than for any other reason. Employees with these problems need counseling and help. Employers need to take an interest in these problems because it affects the quality of their products.

BOX 13.4 Nonfatal Occupational Injury and Illness Incidence Rates per 100 Employees, United States, 1994

Industry	Incidence Rate
Private sector total	8.4
Agriculture, forestry, fishing	10.0
Mining	6.3
Construction	11.8
Manufacturing	12.2
Transportation and utilities	9.3
Wholesale and retail trade	7.9
Finance, insurance, real estate	2.7
Services	6.5

Source: Derived from the *Statistical Abstract of the United States, 1996*, p. 434, table 677.

Drugs can be divided into two basic categories: legal and illegal. Legal prescription drugs often help employees in the performance of their jobs. It is important, however, that the employer know what medications an employee is taking, in case of an emergency or with regard to possible side effects of the drug and how they might affect the employee's performance.

Illegal drugs and alcohol present a real problem for employers.[51] The society is cursed with billions of dollars of illegal drugs entering the country from a variety of locations. Trying to stem the tide of this invasion is one of the major activities of law enforcement in the United States, a situation that would not exist if people did not take the drugs. Any organization that does not think it has a drug problem is fooling itself. Drugs are so common and pervasive in the society that they are a major cause of crime and many other social ills. Organizations must deal with these problems because they have no choice. They can choose to help employees, they can ignore the problem, or they can terminate an employee for using drugs. Ignoring the problem is not the answer, because the problem will not go away. Trying to help an employee with a drug problem is probably the most humane thing an organization can do, but there may come a time when the organization can no longer afford to extend assistance and the employee must be discharged.

Alcohol represents a huge problem for organizations and often is more difficult to deal with than illegal drugs.[52] The reason is that alcohol is a legal drug and is used at all levels of society, including senior management. But alcohol is still a drug and, as such, can have a great impact on an organization. The admonition by consumer groups not to purchase a car made on a Monday is a case in point. The logic is that workers are returning from their weekend binge and are hung over, so will not do as good a job on the car as they would on another day of the week. Although this may or may not be true, the mere fact that people think it might be is an indication of how large the problem is. Alcohol robs people of their ability to perform. It steals productivity and costs the society billions of dollars in direct losses of productivity as well as indirect losses from the effects of alcohol, which include a wide variety of social ills.

Psychological Issues

Employee health is not just a physical concern but a mental one also. Stress is a leading cause of health problems for employees.[53] There are many forms of stress, and some stress is a good thing. But too much stress or too much of the wrong kind of stress can be very harmful to the health of an employee.

Stories of executives slumping over their desks after working late at night are legion. Even on the assembly line, employees have been known to break down. There are documented cases of people having to be led away from their position on the assembly line because they would not have left voluntarily when their shift ended. These people were literally bored into a nervous breakdown.

Perhaps the greatest problem with stress is that it can lead to burnout and depression. People can maintain a certain level of stress only for so long. Everyone is different. One of the first signs that people are beginning to react negatively to stress is when they start to experience burnout. Although there are many medical definitions for burnout, a lay definition might be that a person

BOX 13.5 Fatal Work Injuries, by Cause, United States, 1994

Cause	Number of Fatalities	Percent Distribution
Transportation accidents	2740	42
Highway	1336	20
Nonhighway	407	6
Aircraft accidents	424	6
Workers struck by vehicles	383	6
Water vehicle accidents	92	1
Railway accidents	81	1
Assaults and violent acts	1308	20
Homicides	1071	16
Self-inflicted injury	210	3
Contacts with objects and equipment	1015	15
Struck by object	589	9
Caught in or compressed by:		
Equipment or objects	280	4
Collapsing materials	132	2
Falls	661	10
Exposure to harmful substances or environments	638	10
Contact with electric current	346	5
Exposure to caustic, noxious, or allergenic substances	131	2
Oxygen deficiency	110	1
Fires and explosions	202	3
Other events and exposures	24	Less than 0.5
Total	6588	100

Source: Derived from the *Statistical Abstract of the United States, 1996*, p. 434, table 678.

has become tired, bored, and disillusioned with whatever it is that he or she is doing. Like a piece of firewood, they have burned out and all that is left are some ashes and perhaps a charred hulk of what used to be. Burnout is a serious problem; many people have it and do not know it.[54]

If a person becomes burned out and does nothing to try to combat it, he or she in serious danger of becoming depressed. Depression is a serious health problem in the United States and many people are not aware they are depressed. In its simplest form, depression can simply be an inability to enjoy life, to have fun, and to be able to relate to others in a positive and meaningful way. In its most dangerous form it can lead to suicide, mental breakdown, or perhaps even murder. Organizations, employees, and loved ones need to recognize the symptoms of depression before it is too late for the person who is depressed or those around him or her.

DEVELOPING EFFECTIVE HUMAN RESOURCES   ■ ■ ■

Education   ■ ■ ■

The development of human resources is the responsibility of both the public and private sectors. As has been well documented in numerous studies, such as *A Nation at Risk*,[55] the public education system in the United States is in crisis. In an era when jobs are demanding greater skills and a higher level of education, the school system is failing. Nationwide, the high school dropout rate is about 15 percent[56] with some states having much higher rates. Added to this is the fact that graduating from high school does not mean that students have the basic skills necessary to succeed in the job market. Many leave high school with less than satisfactory reading levels and nominal skills in math. These people become part of the workforce, but they do not have the skills needed for the jobs that are available in the economy, and more important, they do not have the prerequisites necessary to obtain the skills for the jobs.

The problems of public education have been studied, rehashed, and studied again. Some say that it is a failure of the schools, some say the parents, some say the society. Blame is really not important; finding solutions is. If public education is going to be successful, the education of children must be the most important part of the school. It starts at the top of the education system and works its way down. Perhaps the most public problem in dealing with the erosion of education in the United States has been the role of athletics.

Intercollegiate athletics is supposed to foster sportsmanship and fair play, but with the possible exception of the NCAA, there are few who would argue that it does. The most important thing in intercollegiate athletics in the United States is money.[57] The student athletes are certainly not important—a quick glance at the graduation rates of many top collegiate teams is evidence enough of that.[58] Even those graduation rates are suspect. How many "student athletes" have been given grades or put in the courses of "cooperative" teachers or professors without tenure, for whom it is made abundantly clear just how important it is for the point guard to pass the course? This attitude is also found on the high school level, where students are given grades to keep them eligible for sports.

It is also found in the elementary schools of some districts where eighth-grade boys are held back a year so that when they start in the freshman football program in high school, they will be a year older, a year bigger, and a year stronger. The schools, with the cooperation of parents, are willingly sacrificing an entire year of a child's life for ten afternoons of athletic competition. The desire to win, and the money and prestige that goes with winning on any level of athletics in the United States, has had a corrosive influence on the educational system. The use of steroids in high school and undoubtedly in elementary school is just another example.[59] These pills can kill people, but student athletes are still taking them, often with the acquiescence of their coaches.

■ ■ ■ **BOX 13.6 High School Dropouts, by Race and** ■ ■ ■
Hispanic Origin, United States, 1973–1994

Item	1989	1990	1991	1992	1993	1994
Event Dropouts[a]						
Total	4.5	4.0	4.0	4.3	4.2	5.0
White	3.9	3.8	3.7	4.1	4.1	4.7
Male	4.1	4.1	3.6	3.8	4.1	4.6
Female	3.8	3.5	3.8	4.4	4.1	4.9
Black	7.7	5.1	6.2	4.9	5.4	6.2
Male	6.9	4.1	5.5	3.3	5.7	6.5
Female	8.6	6.0	7.0	6.7	5.0	5.7
Hispanic	7.7	8.0	7.3	7.9	5.4	9.2
Male	7.6	8.7	10.4	5.8	5.7	8.4
Female	7.7	7.2	4.8	8.6	5.0	10.1
Status Dropouts[b]						
Total	14.4	14.6	14.2	12.7	12.7	13.3
White	14.1	13.5	14.2	12.2	12.2	12.7
Male	15.4	14.2	15.4	13.3	13.0	13.6
Female	12.5	12.8	13.1	11.1	11.5	11.7
Black	16.4	15.1	15.6	16.3	16.4	15.5
Male	18.6	13.6	15.4	15.5	15.6	17.5
Female	14.5	16.2	15.8	17.1	17.2	13.7
Hispanic	37.7	37.3	39.6	33.9	32.7	34.7
Male	40.3	39.8	44.4	38.4	34.7	36.1
Female	35.0	34.5	34.5	29.6	31.0	33.1

[a]Event dropouts is the percentage of students who dropped out that year.
[b]Status dropouts is the percentage of the population who have not completed high school between the ages of 18 and 24.
Source: Derived from the *Statistical Abstract of the United States, 1996,* p. 175, table 274.

The problem is that the abuses of student athletics have contributed to the decline of education in the United States. The importance of the money and other plums that winning teams generate has not been lost on other students. Corners are cut for those rewards and the rest of the community knows it. Solid A and B students cannot get financial aid to attend college, but a functionally illiterate running back gets a full "scholarship." Grades are altered, student athletes are withdrawn from courses after they have failed final exams, and teachers are pressured to bend the rules. The message is clear to everyone: Education is not important, glory on the gridiron is. It destroys the morale of teachers and makes cynics of students, hypocrites of administrators, and victims of athletes. It is an easy step from giving grades to athletes to lowering the standards for everyone else; from a functionally illiterate running back getting a full "scholarship" to play ball to graduating other ill-prepared students; and for a system of education to sacrifice the entire student body.

Training

Corporations have for many years acknowledged the need to train employees. In the 1870s, the NCR Corporation sponsored the first formal sales training program for its sales force. Corporations are engaged in academic education as well: McDonald's offers an Associate Degree in fast food management; General Motors founded General Motors Institute, which offers a B.S. degree; Arthur D. Little offers a Master's degree in accountancy; and the Rand Corporation has a Ph.D. in policy analysis.[60] American industry spends approximately the same amount of money on formal training of its employees as is spent on all of traditional higher education in the United States and serves approximately the same number of people.[61]

American industry is committed to training because executives are keenly aware of how rapidly the world is changing, and they and their fellow employees must keep up. It is, however, a very expensive proposition and although a great deal of money is spent on educating employees, the benefits are often difficult to determine. Firms also find themselves dealing with the remedial education of new employees. Schools are not producing employable graduates and corporations have gone into the business of bringing them up to a level of skills they can employ.[62]

The point to remember about corporate education and training is that it is far more specific than traditional education. Companies are interested in what their employees can do for the firm. They are not interested in Chaucer. Companies need people who can communicate effectively, not novelists. They have been forced to address the basic skills of new hires and to address the changing needs of their current employees simultaneously. It is not unusual for a corporate training department to be offering courses in basic skills while offering advanced computer courses. This is because people have to be able to read the manual before they can use the machine.[63]

Career and Staff Development

Developing employees is a major function of any organization. Training is a part of that process, but it takes more than training. The experiences that employees have is just as important, perhaps more important, than what is learned in the classroom. Organizations, indeed the society as a whole, need to view workers as an asset that can be improved over time, not just written off on the income statement. Employees are expensive, and that expense must be turned to the maximum benefit of the organization.

Employees also have obligations in career and staff development. They have an obligation to the firm, but they also have an obligation to themselves. The ultimate responsibility for a person's career lies not with the organization but with the person.[64] This lesson has been brought home to a number of employees who have worked for an organization for a long time and have suddenly found themselves out on the street. During the 1980s, many employees suddenly found themselves out of a job because of a merger, takeover, or other event over which they had little or no control. Many of these workers had performed admirably over the years but were now unemployed.[65] It came as a shock to many of them that decades of loyal service to the firm would end with a 10-minute notice to clean out their desk. Many traditions of job security ended in the corporate restructuring of the 1980s. For example, the banks in the financial district in New York used to brag that even during the bottom of the Great Depression of the 1930s, they never laid off employees. These banks have cut back extensively during the past decade. The term *reduction in force* (RIF) was coined by the First National City Bank of New York (Citibank), where the president is one of the ten highest-paid executives in the United States.

The days of the 40-year career with the same organization and a gold watch and retirement party at the end are over. The old implied contract between the white-collar worker and the employer has been breached. Blue-collar workers always knew there was a chance they would be laid off, but white-collar workers seemed immune. Workers today know that they can be gone at any time, and it could have nothing to do with performance. Even workers who have survived cut backs and mergers are nervous because they do not know when their number will come up. As a result, loyalty to the firm is probably at its lowest point in decades. A situation that is not helped when senior managers are quoted in the press expressing uncaring attitudes about employees and their jobs.[66] Not only does this have an impact on the workforce because of the uncaring executive, but it affects other organizations, whose employees begin to wonder how they are viewed by their CEOs.

Performance and merit pay appraisal is an integral part of any career development program. But if it is to be effective, it must be done honestly and objectively. Both the supervisor and the employee must know the rules and the criteria by which the employee is going to be evaluated. There is nothing more damaging to employee morale than an unfair, arbitrary, and capricious evaluation system.[67]

Merit pay is a case in point. Although in theory merit pay sounds like a reasonable and fair approach, it is far from that in practice. For merit pay to work, there must be general agreement on what constitutes merit.[68] Management likes to keep the criteria as fuzzy as possible, while workers generally want them to be as specific as possible. Management prefers hazy criteria, because then they can give out raises as they like, which may or may not reflect true merit. Managers are also often limited as to how many superior, acceptable, and unacceptable performance ratings they can give. Although this is done in an effort to prevent all superior appraisals, it forces the manager to make difficult and often arbitrary and inaccurate decisions. The problem is that for a merit pay system to work, the organization must be willing to invest the time, money, and effort necessary to make it work, and unfortunately, few organizations seem willing to do that.

Compensation

During the past several years there has been a great discussion over the issue of compensation. The fact is that the real wages of U.S. workers have been declining for over 20 years. The other problem is that the middle class has eroded. There is a larger percentage of working poor in the United States in the 1990s than in the 1970s; at the same time, there are more people making over $50,000 per year than at any time in the history of the nation. What has happened is that the nation went from a kind of bell-shaped curve in terms of income in 1970 to a kind of skewed distribution by 1986. (After 1988, the federal government provided figures that were no longer comparable to prior years.) This divided the nation into haves and have nots. Large numbers of people who were middle class have fallen out of the category. Many of these are blue-collar workers who have been displaced from factory jobs in the rust-belt industries. They have gone from making $17 per hour to minimum wage. American workers are no longer the highest paid in the world. In fact, German and Japanese firms are opening plants in the United States, in part, to take advantage of the relatively lower wages of U.S. workers.

BOX 13.7 Theory of the Senior Management Class (with Apologies to Thorstein Veblen)

Over 90 years ago, Thorstein Veblen published *The Theory of the Leisure Class*. At the risk of greatly oversimplifying his thesis, Veblen stated, among other things, that the function of the leisure classes for the rest of the economy was to provide a role model to which the lower social classes in the rest of the economy could aspire. Although the leisure class no longer builds "summer cottages" in Newport, and the excesses of the robber barons have been at least curtailed by the SEC and the antitrust laws, there has arisen a new class of people to which lower-class members of the society may aspire, the senior management class.

The recent controversy over executive pay has only served to focus the attention of the public on these issues. As Ralph V. Whitworth, President of the United Shareholders Association, has said: "Executive pay is irrational. There's no connection between pay and performance." Executives, on the other hand, have become defensive. William P. Stiritz, the CEO of Ralston Purina, who, a few years ago made $13.8 million in salary, bonuses, and stock awards, has called the recent controversy "the lowest form of yellow journalism. . . . It's an easy hit . . . a red herring. It raises highly divisive issues among employees, shareholders, and management." Both are only half right.

Executive compensation is certainly an easy hit and a red herring and it also raises highly divisive issues among employees, shareholders, and management, but it is not "yellow journalism." Rather, it is a reflection of the frustrations that many people feel with regard to the future of U.S. society and the economy in general. The current interest in executive compensation was touched off by President Bush's trip to Japan. A comparison of the pay of the American executives who accompanied President Bush with the compensation of their Japanese counterparts was an embarrassment for the President and the country.

As was obvious by comparing the pay of the U.S. executives to the compensation of the senior management of highly successful Japanese firms, there is no connection between pay and performance. However, it is not irrational. Senior management in the United States is paid huge amounts because it gives the rank and file of the corporate management cadre something for which to aspire. Every year millions of young people enter the workforce. Many of them hope to one day be the CEO of a large corporation. Unfortunately, the chances of any of them reaching that level of success are ridiculously low. The fact is that there are only 500 Fortune 500 firms, and perhaps another several thousand or so organizations in that league, not to mention foreign organizations and their ambitious executives and employees. Since the odds of hitting the jackpot at Atlantic City, Las Vegas, or the state lottery are at least as good and may be better than becoming the CEO of a major organization, senior management has to find a way to keep the lower ranks interested and committed.

BOX 13.7   (*continued*)

Senior management's compensation is the pot of gold at the end of the rainbow. It is the modern version of the Horatio Alger legend of "by pluck and luck the individual will succeed" that is still a strong theme in the American ethos. Luck is something over which a person has little or no control and will probably be used to explain why he or she did not get the "breaks," but *pluck* means hard work. It means at least 60 hours per week, interrupted vacations, moving the spouse and kids away from friends and family, being away on business during the piano recital, and missing Little League games. It means stress and pressure for the person and often, isolation from the society outside the organization. Finally, it often means a bitter taste at the end of decades of devoted hard work for the organization, and the virtual certainty that two weeks after they leave the company, the standard reply to the mention of their names will be, "Who?"

But there will be those few, those lucky few, who will have the use of the corporate jet and other company perks; the vast stock options, bonuses, and princely salaries; the prestige and social status that goes with being the head of a major organization; the ego-inflating interviews with the press; and the obvious wisdom that seems to come to senior executives in areas about which they are woefully ignorant. This is the pot of gold at the end of the rainbow for which middle management strives and aspires and which senior management must continue to use to lure them on.

Benefits

Years ago, the benefits that employees received from their employers as a part of their compensation program were usually referred to as fringe benefits. Today, these benefits can represent over 38 percent of the compensation for a typical employee and nobody calls them "fringe" anymore.[69]

Benefits are often various forms of insurance, including life, health, and disability. They can include subsidized meals, parking places, vacations, recre-

BOX 13.8   Money Income of U.S. Families: Percent Distribution by Income Level in Constant (1994) Dollars, 1970 to 1994

| | Percent Distribution for Income of ($000): | | | | | | | Median |
Year	Under 10	10– 14.9	15– 24.9	25– 34.9	35– 49.9	50– 74.9	75 and over	Income ($000)
1970	7.9	7.0	15.8	18.8	24.1	18.3	8.0	35.4
1975	7.3	7.6	16.3	17.2	22.8	19.6	9.1	36.1
1980	7.7	6.8	15.4	15.7	21.9	20.7	11.8	37.8
1985	8.6	6.6	15.2	15.2	19.8	20.3	14.3	38.2
1990	7.9	6.4	14.4	14.4	19.4	20.6	16.9	40.0
1992	9.1	6.8	14.7	14.7	18.7	20.2	15.7	38.6
1993	9.4	7.0	15.1	14.8	17.7	19.6	16.4	37.9
1994	8.7	6.9	15.0	14.3	18.0	19.9	17.2	38.7

Source: Statistical Abstract of the United States, 1996, p. 466, table 717.

ational facilities—anything provided by the company that is not a direct cash payment. Companies are generally required by law to provide social security and unemployment insurance. The remainder, however, are at the discretion of the employer.

Benefits are at the center of two controversies. The first is the desire of the Internal Revenue Service to tax benefits. Rather than pay higher taxes through higher pay, employees have often opted for increases in benefits, which have generally not been taxed. Sensing that this is a form of tax avoidance, the IRS has sought to tax these benefits, with limited success, the most notable being the taxing of educational benefits.

The second controversy involves health insurance. American society is unique in that health insurance is generally tied to employment. This is not the case, however, for approximately one-third of the workforce, which does not receive this benefit from their employers and must obtain health insurance on their own. There are numerous aspects to this controversy:

1. Americans pay over 11 percent of the GNP on health care, more than any other country in the world.

2. The United States ranks near the bottom in many statistical measures of health care among industrialized nations.

3. Many people in the workforce and the society are considered uninsurable because of prior medical conditions and cannot get insurance.

4. The cost of medical care has been increasing at several times the rate of increase in the GDP.

5. Some of the best health care in the world is available in the United States and some of the worst.

6. Certain sections of inner cities in the United States have higher infant mortality rates than parts of the less developed world.

7. U.S. firms are less competitive in the world economy because they must pay for insurance directly, a cost that is reflected in the price of their goods, whereas their foreign competitors do not.

Perhaps the biggest paradox associated with medical insurance is the fact that people who have had a major illness in the past find it difficult, if not impossible, to obtain health insurance. These people represent the success stories of modern medicine. Yet their very success has made them uninsurable. This is not a small minority. There are millions of people who have survived cancer, heart attacks, and other deadly diseases, but health insurance companies will generally not insure them.

The fact is that the American health system is not working very well. It is broken and needs to be fixed. A crisis exists in the system and is deepening. There will be no easy cures, but people are beginning to make it known that they are concerned. A single medical emergency can easily wipe out *all* the financial assets of a family, which may have taken a lifetime to build. House, car, savings, everything can be used up in just a few short weeks without medical insurance.

Worker Safety

Safety in the workplace has been one of the great success stories of American industry.[70] Working conditions are demonstrably safer than they have been at any time in history for the workforce as a whole. This is not to say that there have not been some gaping exceptions or that the society is not paying a very high price to clean up those exceptions.

The Johns-Manville Corporation is a case in point. For years the company knowingly exposed workers, customers, and the general public to a highly hazardous substance—asbestos. Many of the company's former workers now suffer from brown lung and other respiratory-related diseases. The firm denied any connection, all the while knowing that it was true. Eventually the truth did come out that asbestos is very hazardous. Billions have now been spent in an effort to clean up this economic and environmental disaster, to say nothing of the impact on human beings who have suffered, especially exposed employees. Johns-Manville, of course, was sued in a class action for millions of dollars, which would have put it out of business. The defense the company employed was to file for bankruptcy protection.[71]

The Occupational Safety and Health Act, which founded the Occupational Safety and Health Administration, is the major federal law concerning conditions in the workplace. This law was passed in typical fashion. The federal government of the United States has historically been very reluctant to venture into new realms of regulation. Once it has established that regulation, however, it often pursues it enthusiastically, and OSHA is a case in point. Only with great reluctance and after numerous obvious violations of any standard of safety was OSHA established. Once established, however, the agency pursued its mission with zeal until the Reagan Administration, which cut it back significantly.

Worker safety has also ventured into the realm of personal behavior. Firms have restricted smoking as part of a campaign to improve their workers' health.[72] But do they have the right to tell someone what they can and cannot do? This is an issue that will eventually be settled in the courts, and the issue of secondhand smoke is a health concern. It is again a typical dilemma of having to balance the rights of one person with the rights of another.

Unions

Much of the story of the American worker is the story of the American labor movement. Unions have been important in the workplace because they have led the way in wages, workplace reforms, safety, and other key issues. It would be safe to say that the U.S. worker owes a great deal to the labor movement, whether or not he or she is a union member.

Unfortunately, the union movement has fallen on tough times. Although there have been some bright spots in the movement, notably in the health and civil service areas, unions have been in decline for over 20 years. This is partly because the industries in which unions have been strongest are those that have been in decline and have suffered the most from foreign competition. But there are other reasons:[73]

1. The union leadership is out of touch with the rank and file. In 1984 the AFL–CIO endorsed Walter Mondale for President, but union members voted overwhelmingly for Ronald Reagan.

2. Unions have earned a reputation for corruption and contacts with organized crime. Jimmy Hoffa and the Teamsters are only the most flagrant example.

3. Unions have often stood in the way of progress and technological advancement. One of the nails in the coffin of the railroads was the retaining of firemen on diesel locomotives.

The current perception of unions and their members is that they are overpaid, underworked, and lazy. The perception is incorrect, but the unions have been remarkably inept at dealing with it. As Peter Drucker has pointed out,[74] the unions have provided the society with a counterweight to the influence of industry, and that balance is in danger of being lost. The jury is still out, but if the unions continue on the present course, they will become irrelevant to the society and leave a vacuum that will eventually be filled by something else.

THE INTERNATIONAL HUMAN RESOURCE ENVIRONMENT ■ ■ ■

The world is drawing closer together than at any time in history. As Robert Reich, a former Secretary of Labor, has written, the only factor of production that is essentially stationary is labor.[75] The other classical factors of land, capital, and entrepreneurship are all able to move around the globe, virtually at will. The global transportation system makes the location of raw materials and markets, at worst, an inconvenience; capital markets serve projects around the world with little regard for national boundaries; and entrepreneurship and management skills are being exported around the globe by multinational corporations and colleges and universities. The only factor of production that is not easily portable is labor.

American, British, French, and Japanese workers all compete with each other. The problem is that now, countries can offer only two real advantages to a corporation to locate a plant or other facility in that country. The first is the country's infrastructure: the network of roads, sewers, power and energy production, political stability, and education. The second is the skill level of workers. Highly educated and skilled workers are in demand, low-skilled and poorly educated workers are not, and their pay reflects the level of skill. Low-skill jobs are leaving the United States. Many are going to Mexico, where a worker doing exactly the same job as his or her U.S. counterpart makes in a day only a fraction of what the American worker makes in an hour, with little or nothing in the way of benefits. These are jobs that are easily learned, perhaps in 30 minutes or less, and the people in these countries are glad to have them.

A variation on this problem is foreign-born workers who work for domestic firms outside the United States and outside their home country.[76] An example of this is an Indian national working for a U.S. oil company in Saudi Arabia. Dealing with this person's benefits, retirement, salary, and other allowances can be a problem.

The final challenge is dealing with a diversified workforce, not just in the United States but all over the world.[77] As firms establish a presence outside the United States, they will need to hire a more diverse workforce, the same as the domestic situation where more minorities are entering the labor pool. The fact is that "they" are rapidly becoming "us."[78] The manner in which organizations are able to handle this change in the workforce will go a very long way toward determining which organizations will not be successful in the next century and which will.

THE WORKPLACE OF THE FUTURE ■ ■ ■

The workplace of the future will be characterized by one word—*changes:* changes in the workforce, changes in technology, and changes in the competitive environment. One of the changes that is certain to occur in the workplace will be changes in the workforce.

In the United States, the workforce is going to get older and more minorities will be taking positions than in the past. This change is simply a reflection of the change in the demographics of the population as a whole: proportionately fewer white males and more of everything else. This is going to mean changes in the way the workforce responds to the society and the organization. Employees are going to have a somewhat different agenda today than they do now, or even had years ago.

A second change in the work environment of the future will be in the use of technology. Personal computers are only the beginning of what is bound to be a technological change in the way people do business. Communication devices such as beepers and cellular phones give only a hint of what is to come in the future. Applications of hardware and software are only at the beginning stages of their development, and the technical possibilities are endless. Great technological change is taking place in the workplace and there is no telling where that is going to end.[79]

The third great arena of change in the workplace is going to be in the area of competition. If there is anyone who thinks that today's world is competitive, all they have to do is wait a few years and they will discover that today's world will be looked upon as "the good old days when things were not as cutthroat as they are now." Competition is going to increase, and it is going to increase on all levels and for everyone. Competition for markets will increase; competition for materials will increase; competition for jobs will increase; and competition for outstanding and productive employees will increase. This may seem like a paradox, but it really is not. Organizations will have to search long and hard to find the best employees for their business, while workers will find that they must be willing to work harder, learn more, and be more adaptable than they needed to be in the past. The world of employment and commerce is going to be even more competitive in the future than it has been in the past, and organizations and employers are going to have to adapt or face a future of uncertainty and failure.

SUMMARY ■ ■ ■

Specialization of labor has been going on for thousands of years, even before the advent of recorded history. Up until about 250 years ago most production was craft oriented, but with the advent of the industrial revolution, this changed to the factory system. Mass production became the rule, and the jobs were to be found in the factory. Today, the industrial age has evolved into the information age: an age of international trade, shrinking distances, and virtually instantaneous communication. Workers, companies, and societies are no longer competing on a domestic level. Rather, they compete internationally. Japanese, Americans, and Europeans all compete for the same resources and customers.

Human resources has become recognized as an important part of any organization and the key to competitiveness in a global marketplace. Organizations can no longer afford to discriminate based on such irrelevant criteria as gender, race, or ethnic background. In addition to the fact that it is against the law to do so in the United States, it is not good business. Businesses need the very best people they can get, and those people come in all shapes, sizes, and colors. Successful firms recognize that success in any endeavor is more and more dependent on people.

Other forms of discrimination and harassment are also going to be a thing of the past: Sexual harassment, age discrimination, and discrimination against the disabled are now disappearing. Unfortunately, so is job security. Organizations are now faced with the problem of how to best utilize their resources, and their most important asset is people. The glass ceiling will be slowly shattered as women and minorities slowly move up the corporate ladder to take positions of responsibility.

Other issues facing organizations in the human resources field include dependent care, a combination of child and elder care; AIDS; drug and alcohol abuse; burnout; and other psychological issues.

Organizations need to address the development of effective human resources. Education and training are two essentials for an effective workforce, but as most people know, the education system is failing badly in the United States, with about 15 percent of the students dropping out of high school nationwide. Progressive organizations are furiously training their employees in job-specific tasks just to stay even in an increasingly competitive environment, and career development of employees is a major factor in helping to advance both the organization and the individual. Performance is the key to success in this environment, and reward for performance is a way to keep important employees on the job. Unfortunately, most organizations could do a much better job of this.

Compensation and benefits represent major expenses for most firms, but they should not be thought of as expenses; rather, they should be considered investments. People obviously need to be paid for their work, and a fair and equitable compensation program is necessary to attract and keep employees. These programs need to change with the times. A compensation program designed in the 1950s for a workforce made up primarily of white males simply does not reflect reality. Organizations must tailor their pay to the needs of their employees, and if that means having the option of elder care or child care, the company is foolish if it does not provide it because competitors will. Good employees are hard enough to find, and keeping them is harder still. The best way to do that is to discover and provide for their needs through the compensation program.

Safety and health issues also come into consideration. One of the great success stories of American industry has been the decline in accidents that have resulted in death or injury on the job. Other issues are now under review, including activities that years ago were considered normal. Smoking, in particular, has come under attack. There is evidence that smokers endanger not only their own health but the health of those around them. Dealing with these types of issues will be a task for management in the years to come.

Unions, which for so many years represented the American laborer, are in trouble. For a variety of reasons, some of their own doing and some not, they have been in decline. It is still an open question whether or not they will ever be as effective or influential as they once were.

People must recognize that the economy is no longer domestic in character, but international. This is reflected in what workers do and what they get paid. High pay goes to highly skilled workers and low pay goes to low-skilled workers. Corporations will go where they can get the best value for the money they are spending on labor, and if workers want to have a high standard of living, they are going to have to develop those skills that are well paid. If workers do not, they can expect to experience the wages of poverty and depravation.

The workplace of the future will, in some ways, be very similar to today's workplace, but in many other ways it will be different. The demographics will change and the technology is bound to change, with the advent of the personal computer and various communication devices only the beginning. Competition will also change and become even more intense than it is today, with competition for materials, markets, personnel, and jobs becoming more intense.

Questions

1. How did specialization of labor develop prior to the industrial revolution?
2. What was the major change in production techniques with the advent of the industrial revaluation?
3. According to Alvin Toffler, what change is taking place in modern society?
4. Why does discrimination in employment based on race, gender, and national origin no longer make good business sense?
5. Why do workers need to be highly skilled and educated if they are to maintain a high standard of living in the evolving international economy?
6. What are corporations doing to train and develop their employees?
7. How can performance appraisal be used to help develop and enhance a person's career?
8. How have income patterns changed in the United States over the past 20 years?
9. What are some of the problems facing American society in the area of health care?
10. What are some of the problems facing unions in the changing U.S. economy?
11. What are some of the problems that multinational corporations will face when they have to deal with employees in the future?

CASE I   Mike Franklin was very upset. He had just come from a meeting with the associate dean over Richard Gordon, one of Franklin's students. Franklin, an assistant professor at the college, had been there about a year. He and his wife had purchased their first home and were expecting a baby in about five months. Gordon was a star basketball player who had achieved national prominence, and although the school was not really expected to go to the Final Four of the NCAA tournament, there was reasonable hope for the Sweet Sixteen. Gordon himself was expected to be an early draft pick, probably going in the lottery set aside for the teams with the worst record.

What had started the problem was Gordon's attitude in class. Gordon was not an A student; in fact, Franklin wondered what kind of student he was. Gordon had taken out a newspaper in the middle of class, turned his seat around at the back of the room, and proceeded to read the paper in the middle of class, making certain that Franklin and the rest of the students in the class would notice. Franklin became aware that this particular class was starting to break down, so he dismissed the students with the exception of Gordon, who left the room, ignoring Franklin as he requested Gordon to stay behind. Franklin then went to the associate dean's office because the department chair was out of town. He knew that he was going to have to do something about this situation before the next class session of that course.

The dean listened to what Franklin had to say, and although she was understanding, she made it clear that there was little she could or would do. Gordon was too well known and had too high a profile. The school had too much riding on him remaining eligible to play ball, and she suggested that for the good of Franklin's future at the school, he find a way to deal with the problem.

It was clear to Franklin that the college was not going to support him if he tried to do something about Gordon's attitude, and if he did, his position at the college would be on less than solid ground. He had heard that the school would sometimes place athletes like Gordon in the classes of nontenured or cooperative professors who would make certain that the students would get good grades, and now he knew it was true.

Gordon wondered how he could morally grade the other students on their work in the class while essentially giving Gordon a "bye." It would be an easy step simply to give the grades away to the other, less athletically gifted students once Gordon had received his grade. He was also concerned about his family. The school's teams were known to have an absolutely rabid following. Cross burnings were not exactly unknown in the state, and he did not want to find one in his yard.

For now, he would have to calm down and put his anger aside, as his next class would soon begin. But after class, he would go home and discuss the situation with his wife.

1. What do you think Franklin should do?
2. Do you think that Gordon is entitled to special treatment?
3. How would you feel if you were one of the students in the class?
4. What do you think about the school's position?
5. What does this tell you about what is important to the college?

CASE 2

A local school district board of education decided to put in the teacher contract an incentive for teachers in the district to get advanced degrees and to take courses that, the district hoped, would make them better teachers.

The incentive was that the district would pay for any schooling that would enhance the credentials of the teachers to teach in the school system, and the teachers would receive a $100 addition to their base salary for every credit completed with a grade of B or better. For example, if a teacher took 10 credits, he or she would receive a $1000 raise in base salary. The following year, such a teacher scheduled to receive a 5 percent raise would receive worth $1050; the next year, $1102.50; and so on.

After about five years of the program, the school district was surprised to discover that their teachers had the highest average pay of any district for over 100 miles in any direction. Local taxpayers were up in arms because although this was certainly not the poorest district in the area, it was far from the wealthiest. They felt they were paying a high price for an educational system that was not producing the kind of results they felt they were paying for.

In the new contract negotiations, the school district wanted to cut substantially, if not eliminate, the educational incentive program for teachers, and to give virtually no raises to teachers, explaining that they were already the highest paid in the region, among the five highest-paid groups in the state, and that taxpayers were not happy about the situation.

The teachers' position was that they had the best qualified faculty of any school district in the state and that they deserved their high salaries because they were so highly qualified. The district was, indeed, fortunate to have such a fine faculty, and they should be paid accordingly.

Negotiations had broken down between the teacher's union and the school board. The school year started without a new contract, while both parties attempted to elicit public support for their positions.

1. What do you think about the educational enhancement policy?
2. Why do you think so many teachers took advantage of it?
3. How do you think the school district should present its case to the general public?
4. How do you think the teacher's union should present its case to the general public?
5. If you lived in this community, which side would you support?
6. How do you think agreement can finally be reached on the contract?

CASE 3

A manager is aware that some of his employees must be laid off during a regular seasonal downturn. He is aware that one of his employees is newly pregnant. He has been told by his superiors not to inform the employees of an impending layoff.

1. What are the manager's ethical obligations?
2. What are the ethical obligations of an employer to a pregnant employee?
3. What are the ethical obligations to an unborn child of an employee working in a seasonal business?
4. What are the ethical obligations of a society in such situations?
5. How could such situations be prevented in the future?

CASE 4

You are the member of a state union. You believe that the basic premise underlying the concept of tenure (lifetime employment) for faculty members is that the faculty will stay out of politics and politics will not affect the faculty. In other words, the employment of faculty members will not be affected by their support or lack of support of political candidates. The state faculty union's leadership has endorsed one of the major party candidates for governor. This endorsement has been repeated in both state and local union literature. You believe that such actions jeopardize the tenure system and are unethical.

1. What are your ethical obligations?
2. What is the state union's ethical obligations?
3. What are the ethical obligations of the local faculty union?
4. Why do such situations occur?

References

1. Wells, H. G., *The Outline of history,* Garden City Publishing, Garden City, NY, 1961.
2. Ibid.
3. Toffler, Alvin, *The third wave,* William Morrow, New York, 1980.
4. Wells, *The outline of history.*
5. *Brother against brother: Time-Life Books history of the Civil War,* Prentice Hall, Upper Saddle River, NJ, 1990.
6. Davis, D. B., *The problem of slavery in western culture,* Cornell University Press, Ithaca, NY, 1966.
7. Blair, William, *An inquiry into the state of slavery amongst the Romans,* Negro Press, Detroit, MI, 1970.
8. Greene, L., *Child labor: then and now,* Franklin Watts, New York, 1992.
9. Davis, *The problem of slavery.*
10. Marx, Karl, *The communist manifesto,* H. Regnery Co., Chicago, 1955.
11. Schwartz, Alvin, *The unions; what they are; how they came to be; how they effect each of us,* Viking Press, New York, 1927.
12. "N.Y. court OK's negligence suit," *Business Insurance,* February 24, 1997, v. 31, n. 8.
13. Reich, R., "Metamorphosis of the American worker," *Business Month,* November 1990.
14. Dolyns L., "Ed Deming wants big changes and he wants them fast," *Smithsonian,* August 1990.
15. Haight, G., "Managing diversity," *Across the Board,* March 1990.
16. Maidment, F., "American economy suffers from lack of educated and trained workforce," *Atlanta Journal and Constitution,* December 28, 1987.
17. Eihiejile, Innocent, "We need good managers, not gender stereotypes," *People Management,* November 30, 1995.
18. Haight, "Managing diversity."
19. *Statistical abstract of the United States, 1996,* U.S. Department of Commerce, Washington, DC, 1996, p. 472, Chart 730.
20. Haight, "Managing diversity."
21. Nelton, S., "Sexual harassment: reducing the risks," *Nation's Business,* March 1995.
22. Nye, David, "When the fired fight back," *Across the Board,* June 1995.
23. Hall, F. S., and E. L. Hall, "The ADA: going beyond the law," *The Executive,* 1994, v. 8, n. 1.
24. "Actor Christopher Reeves is paralyzed and unable to breathe on his own after shattering spinal bones in horse-riding accident in Culpeper, VA," *New York Times,* June 1, 1995.
25. Schwartz, F., "Management women and the new facts of life," *Harvard Business Review,* January–February 1989.
26. Rosenthal, A., "Quayle says riots sprang from lack of family values," *New York Times,* May 20, 1992.
27. *Employment and earnings,* U.S. Department of Labor, Washington, DC, v. 39, n. 5 table A-22.
28. *Good for business: making good use of the nation's human capital,* U.S. Government Printing Office, Washington, DC, 1995.

29. Hammermesh, D. S., and A. Rees, *Economics of work and pay*, 5th ed., Harper & Row, New York, 1993.

30. Sowell, T., *Inside American education*, Free Press, New York, 1993.

31. Hammermesh, *Economics of work and pay*.

32. *Good for business*.

33. Goldenpaul, D. C. (ed.), *Information please almanac*, Simon & Schuster, New York, 1966.

34. *Statistical abstract of the United States, 1966*, U.S. Department of Commerce, Washington, DC, 1966, p. 216, table 296.

35. *Statistical abstract of the United States, 1994*, U.S. Department of Commerce, Washington, DC, 1994, p. 398, table 619.

36. *Good for business*.

37. Morris, B., "Executive women confront mid-life crisis," *Fortune*, September 18, 1995.

38. Hammermesh, *Economics of work and pay*.

39. Ibid.

40. O'Reilly, B., "Men at mid-life crisis? What crisis?" *Fortune*, September 18, 1995.

41. *Good for business*.

42. Powell, G., and A. Butterfield, "Investigating the 'glass ceiling' phenomenon: an empirical study of actual promotions to management," *Academy of Management Journal*, 1994, v. 37, n. 1.

43. Luthans, F., "Successful vs. effective real managers," *Academy of Management Executive*, v. 2 (May, 1988).

44. McKendall, Marie A., and Stephen T. Margulis, "People and their organizations: rethinking the assumptions," *Business Horizons*, November–December 1995.

45. Ibid.

46. Maynard, Roberts, "Child-care options for small firms," *Nation's Business*, February 1994.

47. Ezra, Manni, and Melissa Deckman, "Balancing work and family responsibilities: flextime and childcare in the federal government," *Public Administration Review*, July–August 1995.

48. Mineham, M., "The aging of America will increase elder care responsibilities," *HR Magazine*, July 1997, v. 42, n. 7.

49. Slack, J. D., "The Americans with Disabilities Act and the workplace: management's responsibilities in AIDS-related situations," *Public Administration Review*, July–August 1995.

50. Caldwell, Bruce, "Surveys document wellness incentives, link health risks to higher plan costs," *Employee Benefits Plan Review*, June 1995.

51. Ibid.

52. Ibid.

53. Bachler, C. J., "Workers take leave of job stress," *Personnel Journal*, January 1995.

54. Ibid.

55. United States National Commission on Excellence in Education, *A nation at risk: the imperative for educational reform: a report to the nation and the Secretary*, The Commission, Washington, DC, 1983.

56. Gage, N. L., "Dealing with the drop-out problem," *Phi Delta Kappan*, December 1990.

57. Loughran, J., "Unsportsmanlike conduct: exploiting college athletics," *America*, May 11, 1996, v. 174, n. 16.

58. Ibid.

59. "Dying to be bigger," *Seventeen*, December 1991.

60. Maidment, F., "University-based executive education programs," Doctoral dissertation, University of South Carolina, Columbia, SC, 1983.

61. Carnevale, A., "The learning enterprise," *Training and Development Journal*, February 1989.

62. Andresky, J., "The making of a workforce," *Business Month,* September 1989.

63. Walter, J. W., "Human resource planning, 1990s style," *Human Resource Planning,* 1990, v. 13, n. 4.

64. Lucht, J., "Helping your career by expanding yourself," *Industry week,* April 4, 1988.

65. Nulty, P., "Pushed out at 45—now what?" *Fortune,* March 2, 1987.

66. Burroughs, B., and J. Helzer, *Barbarians at the gates: the fall of RJR Nabisco,* Harper & Row, New York, 1992.

67. Halachmi, A., and M. Holzer, "Merit pay, performance targeting, and productivity," *Review of Public Personnel Administration,* Spring 1987.

68. Ibid.

69. "Employers costs for employee compensation," *U.S. Bureau of Labor Statistics News,* June 1988.

70. *Occupational injuries and illnesses in the U.S. by industry, 1988,* U.S. Department of Labor, Bureau of Labor Statistics, Washington, DC, August 1990.

71. Sherrill, R., "Murder Inc.—what happens to corporate criminals?" *UNTE Reader,* March–April, 1987.

72. "All fired-up over smoking," *Time,* April 18, 1988.

73. "Big labour's political gamble may pay off," *Business Week,* April 23, 1984.

74. Drucker, P., "Peter Drucker asks, 'Will unions ever be useful organs of society?'" *Industry Week,* March 20, 1989.

75. Reich, "Metamorphosis."

76. Green, W. E., and D. Walls, "Human resources: hiring internationally," *Personnel Administrator,* July 1984.

77. Copeland, L., "Learning to manage a multicultural workforce," *Training,* May 1998.

78. Reich, R., "Who is them?" *Harvard Business Review,* March–April, 1991.

79. Toffler, *The third wave.*

ETHICS WITH CONSUMERS AND PRODUCTS

Concepts **:** You Will Learn ■ ■ ■

how the Uniform Commercial Code warranty of merchantability has incorporated ethical concepts into the relationship between businesses and their customers

how the concept of a seller's warranty to its customers represents an ethical contract between the buyer and seller

how the concepts of ethics applies to techniques relating to selling

how the concepts of ethics relate to advertising

how the concepts of ethics relate to making decisions about the selection of customers and the relationship with the seller

INTRODUCTION ■ ■ ■

In 1997, Prudential Insurance was negotiating a multimillion-dollar settlement with customers it had defrauded.[1] Prudential salespeople had sold customers insurance policies the customers did not need and had "churned" their premium payments to generate more commissions. These practices may have benefited Prudential and its salespeople in the short run. However, in 1997 it was forced to reimburse its customers and pay substantial fines. In addition, its actions had generated a significant amount of adverse publicity. Combined with a scandal relating to its securities unit several years earlier, Prudential's activities had cost it much of its reputation as an honest institution with which to do business. One former customer told the author, "I'd always done business with Prudential because I trusted them, but now I don't. I'll never do business with them again." Once a business loses its reputation, it is difficult to regain it.

In 1997, a well-known tax preparer settled claims that it had encouraged customers to take tax refunds in a manner that generated high-interest loans. The company made money on the loans but suffered a great deal of poor publicity. In addition, the city of New York was looking to fine the company and recover the profits generated from the loans.

There have been a series of scandals that have shaken the business community. Few hurt a business more than one in which the business takes advantage of its customers for its own benefit. Not only is such conduct unethical, it can have a severely negative impact on profits. The level of public distrust of almost all levels of authority means that one must be especially careful in promoting good customer relationships as well as selling only safe and useful products.

IMPLIED WARRANTY OF MERCHANTABILITY   ■ ■ ■

One of the most important legal concepts in many years was the enactment of the implied warranty of merchantability. This warranty is given by every merchant to every buyer of goods. Under the Uniform Commercial Code, Article 2, which has been adopted by a substantial majority of states, *goods* are defined as tangible, movable items. They would include such items as television sets, automobiles, desks, and refrigerators but would not include land or personal services.

A merchant is someone who deals regularly in goods of that kind. An ethical merchant would sell goods that meet the purposes for which they are sold. The implied warranty of merchantability codifies this ethical principle. The warranty of merchantability provides that every merchant gives to every buyer a warranty (guarantee that the goods will be fit for the purposes for which they are purchased. This means that the goods should work for the purposes intended.

If the goods fail to work as intended, the purchaser has a remedy for breach of contract. That is, the purchaser may recover the amount of money necessary to make the goods work as intended. In some cases, this may be the purchase price. In other cases, it is the amount of money to repair the defect. In rare cases when the goods are unique, the appropriate remedy is to require the merchant to deliver goods that conform to the contract. The remedies in Box 14.1 conform to the ethical principles that one should satisfy one's obligations. Either one should pay money damages to make the injured party whole, or one should be compelled to perform the contract.

More important, a person injured by a defect in a product can bring an action to recover for the injuries under the implied warranty of merchantability. The injured party can recover without showing any specific act of negligence by the defendant merchant. The fact that the injured party does not need to show negligence is a substantial departure from previous law. It has allowed many more plaintiffs to recover than previously. This has also led to the filing

---

■ ■ ■   **BOX 14.1**   ■ ■ ■

EXAMPLE: Mel, a merchant, sells a rare vase to Harold. When the vase arrives, it contains some small cracks, which means that it is incapable of being shown. This is a breach of the implied warranty of merchantability. Harold could bring an action to recover the amount necessary to repair the cracks. Given the unique nature of the vase, he could also obtain a decree of specific performance that would compel Harold to deliver a vase that conforms with the contract.

of a substantially greater number of lawsuits than previously. The result of this has been that many plaintiffs have been able to recover for their injuries; conversely, it has also led to a substantial increase in the cost of litigation and the cost of selling products.[2]

This is one of those areas where ethical principles come into conflict. It is ethical to require a person or business to pay for the injuries caused by a product. However, the cost of allowing people to recover for their injuries must be borne by someone. In our society it is borne primarily by the company and ultimately by the consumer. This is also one of those times that public ethics is decided by a clash of competing interests. Some have suggested that limits be placed on the amount of money that could be awarded in a suit under the implied warranty of merchantability. These suggestions have come largely from the business community.

On the other side of the ethical fence stand the trial attorneys. They believe that awards should not be limited. Both sides are heavy contributors to political campaigns.[3] This may prove to be a case where the competing interests manage to balance each other out and things will remain the same regardless of the merits. Court rulings relating to the warranty of merchantability have tended to construe its provisions rather broadly and give plaintiffs the ability to recover. The defendant merchant can defeat the plaintiff's claim if the merchant can show that plaintiff misused the product.

The legal test for determining the appropriate use of the product was if the merchant could have "reasonably expected" that the plaintiff would use the product in such a manner.[4] This is the standard legal test for resolving many matters. It means that one should look at what a reasonably prudent person would have done under the circumstances. This is not only the appropriate legal standard; it is also the appropriate ethical standard. A merchant should place goods into the marketplace that are safe for the purposes for which they are to be used. Conversely, it should not have to bear the legal responsibility if someone misuses the product.

Some product uses are clearly intended, and it is a relatively simple matter to find that the maker or seller or a product is liable. Similarly, other uses are clearly improper, and the maker or seller should not be held liable. Situations such as the ones in Box 14.2 occur regularly and can result in lawsuits related to the implied warranty of merchantability. In these cases the law supports ethical conduct and protects the customer. It is also good business to produce a product that is safe and works as intended.

Express warranties are guarantees given by the seller to the buyer that a product will work in a particular manner. A seller may give a warranty in a number of ways. The seller may give the warranty in words by stating certain facts about the product. It then becomes the seller's ethical and legal responsibility to perform its promises. The warranty or guarantee must be about a material fact rather than an opinion about the product. Say that a salesman from Ace used cars, Jones, informs Smith that her new car has been driven only 50,000 miles. This is a warranty because it is a promise about a fact. It is Jones' ethical responsibility to ensure that the statement was accurate and that he will take corrective measures if it was not. These ethical concepts are now codified in the law under the Uniform Commercial Code. Jones has the obligation to ensure the accuracy of his statements. If he was incorrect, he will be liable for breach of warranty. But suppose that Jones tells Smith that the new car is a "real

---

BOX 14.2

EXAMPLE: Sally is an 81-year-old woman who buys a hot cup of coffee on her way to work. She takes the coffee and places it between her legs while she is driving. After a couple of miles, the lid on the cup falls off. The coffee spills on her leg. She sues the coffee shop for the burns on her leg. Do you believe that the coffee shop should have reasonably expected that she would place the coffee between her legs? Would you rule for the plaintiff or the defendant?

EXAMPLE: Harry buys a hammer at Hammer City. He uses it to drive in some nails while doing some work in his basement. He also needs to put a large screw through a plank into the foundation. He does not have a screwdriver that will accomplish this. He takes the hammer and attempts to drive in the screw. The head of the hammer flies off and hits Harry in the head. Harry brings suit against Hammer City. Was his use reasonable? Would you rule for the plaintiff or the defendant?

EXAMPLE: Harriet purchases a portable hairdryer from Hair City. One day she finishes giving her cat a bath. She takes the hair dryer and uses it to dry off the cat. Unfortunately, the cat's hair catches on fire and the cat is burned. She brings a suit against Hair City. Should the merchant have reasonably expected that Harriet would use the dryer in this manner? In the lawsuit, would you vote for the plaintiff or the defendant?

EXAMPLE: Bill purchases a new hedge trimmer at Hedge City. He uses the trimmer to cut some hedges on his property. He then takes the trimmer and starts to cut down some small trees. The trimmer catches in the trunk and a piece flies off and catches Bill in the face. Bill files a suit against Hedge City. Was this a reasonable use on his part? Should the plaintiff or the defendant prevail?

---

beauty" and that she will "never have any problems." These are only opinions from a salesperson, and a reasonable buyer should know that it constitutes mere "puffery" and does not constitute a warranty (guarantee).

Warranties may result from a specific statement made from the merchant to a buyer who relies on them. The statement must be about a material fact that helps form the "basis of the bargain" between the seller and buyer (Box 14.3). A warranty may also be given by showing the buyer a sample or model. If the merchant indicates that the goods relating to the contract will conform to the model or sample, the merchant has created a warranty with the buyer (Box 14.4).

Sellers have an ethical duty to deliver what they promised to the buyer. Warranties are a legal guarantee that this ethical duty will be fulfilled.[5] The

---

BOX 14.3

EXAMPLE: Hanson tells Johnson that the car he is selling to Johnson has a new transmission. This is a statement about a material fact that becomes a "basis of the bargain" between Hanson and Johnson. If it is later determined that the transmission was not new, it is a breach of warranty between the merchant seller and the buyer. A breach of legal warranty is also a breach of one's ethical obligation.

BOX 14.4

EXAMPLE: Crawford goes into Furnies Furniture Store to purchase a new dining room table. He is shown a particular model by the salesperson. He agrees to purchase the table based on the model he was shown. When the table arrives, it does not conform to the contract. This is a breach of warranty created by the salesperson's demonstration of the sample. As a result, Crawford can recover damages for breach of contract.

EXAMPLE: Alfred goes to the local commodities exchange to purchase 3 tons of wheat. He is shown a certain type of wheat, which is pulled from a bin. The broker informs him that any wheat ordered from her will conform to this sample. Alfred orders 3 tons of the wheat, but only 1 ton conforms with the sample. Alfred's broker has breached the warranty created by the sample. He is entitled to recover monetary damages representing the difference between the value of the wheat as shown in the bin and the actual value of the wheat that was sent.

Uniform Commercial Code helps place these ethical principles into law. There are a number of other possible warranties that a seller could give to a buyer in any of the ways discussed above. The Magnuson–Moss Act[6] does not require a seller to give warranties. However, it does give the buyer additional powers to enforce them. Similarly, many states have passed "lemon laws," which give added protection to the purchasers of automobiles. These statutes give sellers of cars a certain number of times to repair the automobile. If the seller is incapable of doing so, the seller must either return the purchase price or give the purchaser a new automobile. The states have set up arbitration boards that can adjudicate disputes between the seller and the buyer.

An ethical seller can use the law as a floor for guiding actions. If the seller wants to grant warranties as an inducement to the sale, he or she should recognize that he or she is likely to be bound by them. State and federal laws prevent one from giving a warranty and then not conforming with it. Beyond providing products that will act as guaranteed, a business has other ethical responsibilities with respect to its customers, products, and services. Among these responsibilities is that of meeting the customer's needs in the manner they prefer.

Too many sellers refuse to listen to their customers or to educate them.[7] Although the customer is not always right, the customer is still the customer. A business has the obligation to listen to customers. It also has the obligation to inform if there are better ways of meeting customer needs. Meeting customer needs while achieving a level of respect and a reasonable profit can be a difficult balancing act. A business has an ethical responsibility to both its customers and its owners. It needs to carefully define what it is selling to its customers. This will help clarify both its ethical responsibility to the customer and provide guidance for people selling its products or services.

Many ethical problems relating to customers and products result from a failure to determine what the business is selling, how the business will sell it, to whom it is selling, and how the product or service will be priced. Many businesses get into ethical problems with their customers and products because they failed to accomplish this step. As a result, they find themselves trying to sell the wrong things to the wrong people at the wrong price. This can lead to overzealous salespeople, deceptive pricing techniques, and other improper practices.

BOX 14.5

EXAMPLE: Bacque Enterprises of Linden, New Jersey is a toymaker that employs people with learning disabilities. The owner proactively reaches out to parent groups to obtain their suggestions about product safety and to obtain their approval of the product. As the company has grown, the owner has continued to improve product safety, which has resulted in an ever more successful company. Bacque has received national recognition for his toys through appearances on the *Managing with Lew Dobbs* and *Oprah Winfrey* shows.

Promoting Positive Relations

The legal responsibility of merchants with respect to product safety is well defined by the Uniform Commercial Code warranty of merchantability.[8] As noted above, the legal responsibility also requires a high level of ethical responsibility. However, it may be inadequate from an ethical standpoint simply to follow the law. A merchant should want to proactively promote product safety rather than simply to avoid legal liability. A company can obtain a positive reputation by searching out opportunities to encourage public input into issues of public safety (Box 14.5).

Sales Techniques

One area that can lead to a large number of ethical issues involves sales to the customer. A salesperson is an agent of the business.[9] If the agent commits an unethical act, it will be imputed to the organization. If unethical practices among salespeople become commonplace, it reflects poorly on the entire organization. Despite past scandals relating to unethical sales practices, they seem to continue. Another unethical practice is to deceive a customer into making repairs that are not necessary.[10] This is a common complaint among people who go to service stations to have work done on their automobiles.

The examples in Box 14.6 illustrate how instances of unethical conduct can severely jeopardize the entire existence of a business. Although good service is expected by customers, they are quick to complain if they receive poor service. Reports of unethical conduct appear regularly in the media and can severely harm a business. Complaints about products and services are so common that state and local governments have established a variety of boards and commissions to regulate the activities of businesses that deal regularly with the public.[11] It can take some time to obtain a license, but only a few unethical acts to lose it.

Advertising

An organization's advertising is a method of communicating its values to the public.[12] It should reflect the highest ethical standards of a firm. Unfortunately, too many companies slide into the trap of looking at advertising only as a way of promoting sales. At its best, advertising is a way of informing potential buy-

BOX 14.6

EXAMPLE: Ralph's Department Store regularly advertises television sets for sale at $100. Ralph's store has only a few sets to sell. When customers come into Ralph's, they find that there are no sets to purchase. However, Ralph's salespeople then show customers a variety of other furniture at higher prices. This is called "bait and switch." It occurs when a seller indicates that one product is for sale, but then offers customers another product. Such conduct is not only unethical, it is unlawful. Still, many sellers continue to engage in such practices despite the risks to their businesses.

EXAMPLE: Mary goes into Joe's Repair Station after hearing some knocks in her car's engine. The problem could be solved with a simple repair. However, Joe knows that Mary is an elderly woman who knows very little about automobiles. Mary is also busy taking care of an ailing sister. Joe tells Mary that she will need to have a complete transmission overhaul. She tells Joe to go ahead and make the repairs. Later, the city's department of consumer affairs releases a report indicating which service stations were cited for making repairs that were not necessary. Joe's service station is listed among them. Mary has her car checked at another station and decides to bring suit against Joe's. She also informs all her friends about her negative experience at Joe's.

EXAMPLE: Fly-by-Night Investments purchases stock of new companies when the stock is offered to the public. These stock investments are suitable for very aggressive investors. They are not suitable for conservative investors such as elderly people who need a steady source of income rather than speculative long-term gains. Fly-by-Night hires a number of young salespeople who begin to market the stocks to almost anyone who answers the phone and is willing to talk with them. They sell a significant number of shares to elderly people who needed conservative investments rather than stocks of new companies. The prices of the new stocks drop sharply and the elderly people lose most of their money. Several of these investors go to an attorney, who brings suit against Fly-by-Night. The suit is covered by the local media, which portrays Fly-by-Night as a company willing to "cheat" older citizens. The unfavorable publicity severely hurts its business. Its failure to define its services and customers has led to ethical problems.

ers that an organization has the resources and skills that are capable of meeting a buyer's needs. At its worst, advertising becomes a way of manipulating people into purchasing products or services they do not need. Deceptive advertising is not only unethical, it is unlawful.[13] The Federal Trade Commission and state agencies have the authority to stop advertising or other promotional activities that are deceptive (Box 14.7).

Another area of unethical conduct has been the use of "sound-a-likes" by some advertisers. A well-known automobile maker was held liable for committing a tort by using the voice of a singer who sounds similar to the well-known entertainer Bette Midler. Sellers of various products seem to be able to find singers who sound like the legendary rock star Elvis Presley. Although "sound-a-like" commercials may be entertaining, they send an immediate message to the listener that the seller does not have high ethical standards. A seller who would deceive its customers about its advertisement would probably deceive the customer about the product or service. Sellers tell the customer more than just information about the product with their advertisement. The advertisement represents the seller's way of telling the world what it represents.

BOX 14.7

EXAMPLE: Pounds-Away makes a pill that it claims will help people lose weight. In its advertisements it claims that a person will lose a pound per day by taking a pill every eight hours. The company has only a few examples to support its claims. It has no medical evidence to bolster its statements. The few people who did lose weight may have done so for other reasons. The state Department of Consumer Affairs asks Pounds-Away to stop its advertising because it is deceptive. When it refuses, the department brings an action that enjoins Pounds-Away from engaging in any more advertising which claims that its product will cause people to lose a pound every day. The agency has the legal authority to impose substantial fines for violating its orders.

A poor or dishonest advertisement tells the buyer that the seller is likely to be the same. Ethical advertisements tell the other person what the seller can do to meet the buyer's needs. An unethical advertisement is too much concerned with "making the sale." It is too little concerned with the buyer. Advertisements that appeal to people's insecurities rather than their values are unethical.[14] Too many sellers are willing to appeal to man's baser instincts to persuade them to purchase their product (Box 14.8). Tobacco advertisements which suggest that the smoker will be healthy and popular fall into this category; beer commercials which suggest that a purchase will increase one's sex appeal also raise ethical issues.[15]

Personal Promotions and Sales

Many organizations use personal selling as a technique to increase revenues. There are a number of ethical issues that relate to the sale of products on a person-to-person basis. For a valid contract to exist, the sale must meet basic legal requirements relating to reaching a bargain between the two parties.[16] In addition, organizations engaging in person-to-person selling must conform with other legal and ethical requirements. Person-to-person "sales" should be a dialogue between the parties. However, they often have been episodes which involved high-pressure techniques of salespeople who had little interest in the needs of the buyer. As a result, legislators have enacted laws that require salespeople to give buyers some period of time to cancel the sale.[17] Depending on the state in nature of the transaction, the period of time is likely to be one to three days.

An ethical salesperson seeks to meet the needs of the client rather than merely selling them a particular product or service. In this case, good ethics

---

BOX 14.8

EXAMPLE: Virile Vitamins markets a series of vitamin products. However, they also advertise that their product will increase male libido. Advertisements show swimsuit-clad men and women embracing each other. Their ads also feature testimonials from men identified by their initials. They claim that their sex drive and attractiveness to women has increased because they took vitamins made by Virile Vitamins. There is no evidence that the pills actually do increase male libido or attractiveness to women. There are a number of ethical issues relating to these advertisements. They contain dubious claims that may deceive the purchaser. They also appeal to lower rather than higher values.

BOX 14.9

EXAMPLE: NXY Bank sells home equity loans over the phone to people who live in affluent areas. The bank hires young people who call people at night and try to persuade them to borrow money based on the value that the owner has in the home. The salespeople have little or no training in finance or banking. As a result, they make little effort to determine the needs of the people. Potential borrowers tend to be annoyed by the calls and refuse to deal with the caller. It is unethical to waste people's time talking about products they do not need or want. In addition, it creates a negative impression for the organization.

EXAMPLE: Third National Bank hires two recent college graduates. One uses the telephone to solicit new credit card customers while the other solicits home equity loans. Each calls people who live in a specific zip code during evening hours. Often, they reach people during dinner or after they have gone to sleep. In addition, they try to continue their presentations even after the prospective customer informs them that they are not interested. As a result, many people hang up in anger.

also equal good salesmanship. The best salespeople know that it is more important to keep a good customer and make repeat sales than it is to make the first sale. A relatively new problem relates to issues involving telemarketing. Young people are being trained to try to make sales over the phone. However, their approach seems to be more "hard sell" than the newer sales approach, which requires a great deal more listening than previously.

An organization gives an impression of itself through its salespeople.[18] If they appear to be uninterested in the customer as a person with individual needs and problems, the prospective purchaser is unlikely to have a favorable impression of the organization. Direct marketing has many useful purposes. It provides a way for sellers to communicate with potential buyers and provide them with information about products and services. Although some people find phone calls and direct mail solicitations annoying, they are free to ignore them. One can hang up the phone or throw out the mail. The seller has the obligation not to use its freedoms in an improper manner (Box 14.9). Used correctly, direct marketing can be an effective tool for conveying information and selling goods and services (Box 14.10). It is an inexpensive method of contacting potential consumers.[19]

BOX 14.10

EXAMPLE: ABC Corporation uses its direct marketing approach to talk with potential customers. The corporation hires people to ask such customers about their financial conditions. After they have determined the needs of the survey's respondents, they design a product that meets the respondents' long-term financial objectives and goals. After the products are designed, ABC Corporation again calls potential customers to test their reaction to the proposed products. After receiving customer input, ABC makes some minor changes to the products. ABC then mails literature regarding the products and services to potential customers and asks them to respond if they are interested in using them. Telemarketers then call people who have responded and work with them to determine how the products can meet their financial needs.

Closing the Sale

There are a significant number of ethical issues that relate to the decision of whether the "consumer" should actually become a customer of the seller. In some cases it would be more ethical not to accept someone as a customer if the organization cannot actually meet the customer's needs. This means that the organization's salespeople must take the time to determine carefully what customers need. This means that the salesperson must listen carefully to what the customer is telling him. It also means that the salesperson must know precisely what his organization offers and whether it will meet the customer's objectives.

In some cases it may be more ethical to suggest that the customer does not need the product or refer him or her to another organization. This is a case when good ethics would also be good business. Customers are impressed by people who place their interest above the company's short-term economic interests. The unethical company or salesperson drives too hard to close a sale regardless of whether it would meet the customer's needs.[20] This can result from excessive top management pressure to achieve results. This may be especially true in today's extremely competitive business climate.

The example in Box 14.11 is a case where low ethical standards can lead to poor business results. People want to do business with those they can trust and with whom they can develop long-term relationships. Organizations that are incapable of developing such relationships are not likely to do well in the future. Firms that engage in behavior raising ethical questions will pay a long-term price.

BOX 14.11

EXAMPLE: Sam works as a salesperson for MZX Corporation. He regularly calls on customers who might purchase his products. He obtains 80 percent of this business from existing long-term customers. He cultivates his existing customers very carefully by giving them excellent service. Sam has learned that customers will reorder only if they are pleased with the products and services they receive currently. Sam regards it as his ethical duty to meet his customers' objectives. As a result, Sam will not accept a customer unless he is certain that his company is capable of meeting the new customer's objectives. Sam finds that he obtains additional business even if he tells potential customers that their needs might be better met by another seller. In some cases, this has resulted in an excellent long-term, profitable relationship.

EXAMPLE: Frank is the sales manager for HBX Corporation. He demands that his salespeople exceed their sales quotas, which are established by upper management. As a result, Frank's salespeople place excessive pressure on customers to buy their products in order to achieve quarterly and annual sales quotas. There are negative consequences to this pressure. Many customers later complain that they are not satisfied with the products. This results in some customers returning the products. Others have written letters to the company president complaining about the organization's products. Some have written to the state Division of Consumer Affairs to complain about the products and excessive pressure by salespeople. These events have made it difficult for HBX Corporation to develop many long-term relationships with customers. Therefore, the salespeople do not obtain very much repeat business.

Maintaining high ethical standards is particularly important if one manages financial assets on behalf of others.[21] As this is being written, it has become public that a well-known New York bank made a series of large loans to an illiterate, alcoholic butler of a famous and wealthy woman in order to obtain related business. As a result of questions about the handling of the transactions raised by other parties, a judge ruled that the bank had acted improperly.[22] The episode generated considerable adverse publicity for the bank. As a result, the bank's reputation has been severely tarnished. Affluent people do not like to have their money handled by institutions whose ethics and judgment have been questioned. They also do not like to have publicity generated about financial matters. As a result of the bank's questionable conduct, it is likely to forfeit future business.

Selling to Children

Children are major consumers in our economy.[23] However, selling to children raises significant ethical questions. The law recognizes that children need protection against exploitation. As a result, the law allows minors to cancel any contract other than for goods and services necessary for them to live. However, even if it is lawful to sell one's products and services to minors, the organization may still have to answer numerous ethical questions relating to the sales. Some sales to minors may be legal but still questionable ethically. Minors are particularly unable to make thoughtful decisions about what is in their long-term interest. Sellers know that children are willing to purchase products or services that offer fun. Some are tempted by the opportunity to earn easy dollars by selling to young people. Sellers have an ethical obligation not to do any harm to their young customers.

The example in Box 14.12 illustrates ethical problems into which sellers can slide. They are caught between earning profits and doing what is best for the minors who purchase the product. As a result of the Warranty of Merchantability, the seller could be held legally liable for selling unsafe products.

BOX 14.12

EXAMPLE: Ronald's sells a variety of convenience foods. Its customers consist primarily of adults looking to save time, and minors who want to eat "fun food." Ronald's does considerable advertising on television. The primary thrust of the advertising is to persuade minors that eating can be fun for children. The advertisements show young people at Ronald's playing and having a meal of hamburgers and hot dogs. What Ronald's does not tell the minors is that they would be healthier if they ate salads and other vegetables.

EXAMPLE: Tommy's Toys sells toys to children under the age of 8. Recently, competitors have begun to take away some of Tommy's business. As a result, Tommy's has had to cut expenses. One of the areas Tommy's decided to cut was its safety program, by reducing the number of inspections that each toy receives. As a consequence of the reduction in inspections, Tommy's toys are not as safe as they were previously. Tommy's continues to sell the toys. Their advertisements stress that the products are "safe for all ages."

If the products are alleged to be unsafe, the seller could receive considerable negative publicity, which can make it the target of lawsuits.

Products Taken into/onto the Body

Few sellers are faced with as many ethical issues as those selling products that are placed on the body or are ingested into it.[24] Many firms walk a thin line between producing products that can benefit people and those that could cause harm. This is a difficult dilemma (Box 14.13). These industries are heavily regulated by the federal and state governments. As a result, the laws are explicit with respect to many decisions. However, there are still many ethical questions that need to be decided.

In a market-driven economy, an ethical businessperson would ask whether one should supply what the customer seems to "want" or what the customer actually needs.[25] This requires one to think about placing others' interests above one's own. The violations of "product ethics" does not have to be as blatant as the examples in Box 14.14. Marketing and salespeople regularly encounter situations when they must decide the level of quantity or quality of a product or service that a customer actually needs. The salesperson may be pulled

BOX 14.13

EXAMPLE: Joe works for the Richard Hamilton Tobacco Company, which sells cigarettes to the general public. Joe knows that the company complies with all legal requirements relating to the sale of cigarettes. Despite this, Joe is aware that his company's products could cause cancer in the user and others who inhale the smoke. Joe is responsible for marketing the company's products. Despite the reports of the health risks of this company's products, Joe regularly approves the company's marketing campaign.

EXAMPLE: Sam works for HPX Company, which makes breast implants that women use for cosmetic purposes. Sam's job is to sell the implants to doctors. Sam has some internal memorandums which indicate that the breast implants tend to leak and could cause physical injury to the women who use them. Sam decides to discuss the memorandums with his boss. Sam's boss tells him to "forget them; keep selling to the doctors!" Sam does what he is told. Later, it is determined that the implants have injured a significant number of women. What is Sam's liability and responsibility for these injuries?

BOX 14.14

EXAMPLE: Children tend to be attracted to various types of junk food rather than to food that is good for them. If you are a manufacturer of food, do you promote "healthy" food or "junk" food? There is some evidence that cereal manufacturers have placed sugar in cereals to make them more appealing to children. Tobacco manufacturers have been accused of placing additional nicotine into cigarettes to make them more addictive.

between various interests with respect to the sale of a particular product. The company may want to sell certain products, but the customer may actually need another product.

OTHER CONSUMER ISSUES

It is the seller's responsibility to meet the customer's needs and in a way that meets the customer's ability to pay. It is also the seller's responsibility to earn a profit for the owners of the business. Finding the proper balance between the interests of the business and the interests of the customers is not an easy matter (Box 14.15). There have been many cases of businesses that have exploited their customers rather than helping them. This is a breach of a seller's ethical responsibilities. Meeting customer needs while satisfying the company's need to earn a profit can be a difficult problem. Well-run organizations help their salespeople by placing the long-term interests of the customer ahead of the organization's short-term interests.[26] Customers appreciate an organization that is willing to place their interests first. They are also likely to look out for the long-term interests of the organization. They are also likely to send other people to the organization as future customers.

BOX 14.15

EXAMPLE: KIP Corporation sells educational products to students who are about to take tests relating to attending college or obtaining professional licenses. It offers students a number of separate packages with various services. The packages have different prices depending on how many services students want.

The company encourages its telephone salespeople to sell the most expensive packages, for which the salespeople also receive the highest commission. The students are not told that the salespeople work on commission. The salespeople regularly try to sell students the most expensive package. Failing that, they try to sell students the next-most-expensive. The salespeople are encouraged not to let the prospective customer get off the phone without buying at least one of the packages.

There are a number of organizations with similar but slightly different student courses. In some cases the student's needs would be better satisfied if they purchased another company's product or services. Despite this, the salespeople never urge such a course of action. Are they meeting their ethical responsibilities?

EXAMPLE: Alan owns a car lot that sells both new and used automobiles to a number of customers with different needs and income levels. Alan inherited the business from his father and often thinks of the advice he received from him about running a business. His father would tell him, "Meet most of your customer's needs, even if you send him to your competitor."

Alan has instructed his salespeople to meet the customer's needs regardless of who sells the automobile to the customer. Alan has instructed his salespeople to listen closely to the customer to determine what their needs are with respect to transportation. If Alan is able to meet the client's needs, the salesperson may sell an automobile to the customer. If not, the client is to be referred to another lot.

This policy has paid rich dividends for Alan. Although he has lost some customers, he has gained many more from satisfied clients. These clients have remained long-term customers who have

■ ■ ■ **BOX 14.15** *(continued)* ■ ■ ■

bought car after car from Alan. In addition, many of them have brought family and friends into Alan's lot to buy automobiles.

EXAMPLE: William needs a special type of oven to use in his restaurant. He goes to Olga, who specializes in making stoves and ovens. Olga designs an oven that she believes will meet William's needs. William gives Olga approval to move ahead with construction of the oven. Unfortunately, the oven does not turn out to be sufficient for William's restaurant's needs. He can recover the amount of money to either upgrade the oven or to obtain one that will meet his needs.

EXAMPLE: Millie is an attorney who practices in a large urban area. She has a significant number of people who walk into her office with various legal problems. Although Millie believes that she is capable of handling a wide variety of legal matters, she does not accept every case. She is careful to refer matters that require a certain level of expertise in particular areas to other attorneys. By doing so, Millie may lose some fees, but she serves her clients better. As a result of these actions, she receives a considerable number of referrals from other attorneys related to her own area of specialization. She discovers that she also earns more money by doing so.

Customers often have very specific needs which may or may not be satisfied by the seller. If the seller's standardized product does not meet the customer's needs, the seller must make an ethical decision as to whether it can make modifications that will meet those needs. If the buyer relies on the seller's skill in developing the product specifications for the contract, the seller has given a contractual warranty that the product will be fit for the particular purpose desired by the buyer. The seller will be held liable for breach of contract if the contract does not meet the specifications in the contract. The seller will be held liable for the amount of money necessary to place the buyer in the same position that the buyer would have been in had there been no breach of this warranty of fitness.[27]

This issue of meeting the specialized needs of customers raises a number of ethical questions as well as legal ones. The first issue is whether one has the ability to meet the specialized needs of the purchaser. One should ask oneself if one should undertake the job or refer it to someone who may have more ability in particular areas. An ethical decision maker recognizes that it is more important to meet customer needs than to try to make quick profits. Usually, this emphasis on customer needs will result in longer-term profits as well as a more ethical approach to dealing with customers.

EMERGING CONSUMER ISSUES ■ ■ ■

There are a number of other ethical issues that can and will relate to customers. As these new issues develop, the ethical decision maker will need to be sensitive to these issues and develop effective solutions to them. An emerging issue relates to the differences in prices that men and women pay for similar products and services[28] (Box 14.16). In U.S. society it was traditional for men to go to work and for women to take care of the home and the children. In recent

BOX 14.16

EXAMPLE: Dry cleaning establishments often charge higher prices to clean women's blouses than to clean men's shirts. Some women and consumer groups have argued that this is unethical and unfair. Since, at first glance, this does appear improper, the cleaning establishments will have the responsibility of explaining the reasons for the differences in price. Below are some questions the establishments could ask themselves:

■ Are there good reasons for the differences in prices? Can they be justified in terms of differences in costs?

■ Are there any collateral reasons that would justify a change in prices (e.g., women bring in more clothes to the cleaner, thus justifying a lowering of prices for women's blouses).

■ Even if there are justifications for the differences in prices, would it be better, from a public relations perspective, not to charge different prices? Are you able to publicly justify the differences in prices? Do you want to do so?

■ What are the consequences of your organization's actions? Would you want to read about your deliberations in the newspaper?

■ Do you believe that the entire process can pass the "smell test"? That is, does it look as if you have done the right thing?

EXAMPLE: Women students have also argued that they are treated differently by their instructors. They contend that instructors are more likely to call on their male counterparts and also treat the comments of male students more seriously. Female students also state that certain instructors do not treat their career aspirations with the same seriousness as those of male students. Female students suggest that colleges hire more female instructors and give sensitivity training to male instructors. Male instructors may want to look at this as an ethical question and examine their own conduct by asking the following questions:

■ Do you call equally on male and female students?

■ Do you treat the responses of male and female students equally?

■ Do you encourage both male and female students to pursue careers?

■ Do you demand equal quality and quantity of work from both genders?

EXAMPLE: Women and others often complain that they are treated differently at car service stations. They often find that the service station attendants will inform women that their automobiles need a higher level of repairs than they would if a man were to bring in the same vehicle. Again, one should ask oneself certain questions:

■ Are you concerned primarily with the needs of your customer or with the need to earn short-term profits?

■ Do you treat all customers similarly?

■ Do you regard customers as people to be served, or merely as sources of revenue?

■ Would you be willing to give up short-term revenues to achieve long-term benefits?

years it has become common for women to enter the workplace.[29] There are different issues that arise in the workplace because of the different styles of men and women.

The standard communication styles of men and women are different and these differences can lead to difficulties as well as opportunities.[30] Men often tend to communicate in a top-down style, while women are more likely to try to build relationships based on "supportive, personal" statements. Generally, men are more willing to give orders, while women are more likely to make requests. These differences may mean that customers may phrase their needs differently or have different requirements based on their gender. This can be a difficult balance to maintain. One has an ethical obligation to treat people equally. However, one also has the obligation to take gender differences into account and recognize how these differences may affect the delivery of products and services.

Issues Relating to Children ■ ■ ■

The law has always recognized the special position of children in our society. It is presumed that a child does not have adequate knowledge and experience to purchase items other than those necessary to live. Under the law, a minor may cancel contracts prior to reaching the age of majority. The law clearly favors the rights of the minor as opposed to those of the seller. As a result of these legal provisions, a seller who sells items to children carries an extra burden. If the item is expensive, the seller should only sell it to the adult parent or guardian. Adults are bound by contracts, while minors are not.

In addition to the legal issues involved with selling to children, there are a considerable number of ethical issues. Children are by nature very impressionable. One has a special ethical responsibility when selling to children. One should be promoting positive products. At the very least, one should not be selling harmful products to children (Box 14.17). An ethical decision maker would also not sell toys, such as guns or knives, which promote violence. An ethical decision maker would also not sell toys that encourage children to have unrealistic fantasies about being superheroes or villains. Such fantasies are not healthy for children because they may try to act them out in inappropriate ways.

In general, sellers have an obligation to sell minors products that are constructive, healthy, and promote positive values.[31] It is ethical to sell products to children that promote a desire to learn, life-affirming conduct, and a willingness to treat other people with dignity and respect. The growth of the use of computers and the Internet by children in the United States raises additional ethical issues for sellers of products and services to children. The computer can be used in the home. Sending marketing and sales messages into the child's home means that one has an even greater ethical responsibility. There are regulations that govern advertising to children on television. However, the Internet is a new vista for marketing and selling products to children, and the old rules do not apply. Some parent groups have urged the Federal Trade Commission to adopt regulations that would govern the sale of products and services to children over the Internet. They argue that the Internet offers an opportunity to send children a seamless web that combines programs and marketing messages. They contend that such a medium offers a new opportunity to exploit

BOX 14.17

EXAMPLE: One of the hottest political issues in recent years has related to the sale of cigarettes to minors by tobacco companies. Although the companies deny targeting children, the evidence seems to be to the contrary. Certain of the representations and advertisements seem clearly intended to sell cigarettes to minors. Although tobacco companies have the legal right to sell products to adults, it is unethical to sell products to children that could be harmful to their health. The tobacco companies knew that their products are addictive; it is unethical for them to sell their products to children.

The tobacco companies have a difficult ethical position to defend with respect to the sale of their products. There are numerous reports linking cigarettes to health problems. It would clearly be unethical for cigarette companies to aim marketing and advertising at minors who are not able to make intelligent decisions about their health. It would be particularly unethical to portray cigarettes as a product that promotes good health.

EXAMPLE: Although some companies, such as Bacque Enterprises, take special care to produce toys that are safe and positive, many corporations do not meet their ethical responsibility to produce safe toys. Often, this failure is not deliberate but a type of carelessness. Companies often become too concerned with earning short-term profits and too little concerned with developing toys that are safe and promote positive values. Toys that can be put into a child's mouth or body are inherently dangerous.

children.[32] Marketing and salespeople argue that they will be responsible and that there is no need for additional regulations.

The proponents of new regulations point out that many businesses have not had a record that inspires confidence among the public. They argue that the parents have no ability to control what comes into one's house. They contend that they are unable to monitor what their children see and need the help of government. This has been the traditional argument between those who favor governmental intervention and those who oppose it. Those who oppose governmental intervention argue that the free market system should be allowed to work its "magic" and that parents can be trusted to protect their children.[33] Those who favor more governmental intervention would argue that it is necessary to curb the excesses of the marketplace.

Marketing by Professionals   ■ ■ ■

Many people attend school because they hope to become professionals, such as physicians, attorneys, accountants, architects, and psychologists. It takes a considerable amount of education and training to become a qualified professional. However, little of this education or training prepares one to attract patients or clients. The questions of how to attract people who will pay for the services of a professional is one that has always been of concern to the professions. Although other businesses are free to advertise and engage in other marketing activities, the professions have generally frowned on their colleagues who are too aggressive in seeking business. However, the Supreme Court has ruled that the professions may not prohibit individual members from soliciting new business.

Nevertheless, seeking out new business can be difficult for professionals because they must obtain new business while not acting in a manner that is perceived as unprofessional (Box 14.18).

Many professionals believe that advertising tends to demean their profession and lowers its standards.[34] They argue that a professional should be chosen based on her abilities rather than being based on who has the better advertising agency. Opponents also argue that advertising hurts the entire profession. They contend that poor advertising makes the members of the profession look like self-seeking "money grabbers." They also contend that advertisements overemphasize price and that a person who makes a selection based on price may be making a mistake. Opponents contend that selection of a professional should be based on his or her ability to meet the client's needs.

Proponents of professional advertising have a number of arguments in their favor. They contend that advertising provides information to people who would otherwise not have access to it. These people often are the poor, the elderly, and others not familiar with professionals. This promotes a greater sense of justice within the community. A second argument is that the First Amendment was designed to promote economic as well as political free speech. The Supreme Court has noted that such businesses as banking advertise and that they remain dignified. The Court ruled that professional advertising could not be forbidden.[35]

The Federal Trade Commission has found that advertising lowered the fees of the professionals in the area. This benefits the consumers of professional services and contributes to the effective functioning of our market-driven society. Professionals who are just entering the market have a better opportunity to gain access to the market if advertising is allowed. Jacoby and Myers is a law firm begun by young lawyers who filled a market niche by opening store-front law offices designed to serve the legal needs of the middle and lower segments of the legal services market.

The professional associations now have a different ethical obligation than previously. They may no longer simply forbid advertising. Rather, the professional associations now have the responsibility of helping their members decide whether to advertise and to help them produce ethical advertisements if

BOX 14.18

EXAMPLE: Like other businesses, professionals walk a thin line between wanting to suggest good results while trying to avoid promising more than they can deliver or more than the law permits them to promise. This can be a difficult accomplishment.

Lawyers should be able to promise good representation, but not that they will win every case or obtain vast sums of money for their clients.

Investment advisers should be able to promise that they will diversify an investor's portfolio effectively and make intelligent investment decisions. They should also be able to promise that they will collect the dividends and interest derived from the investments. They should not be able to promise that they will achieve extraordinary returns or regularly outperform the market averages.

Plastic surgeons should be able to promise that they can correct defects and make one look better. They should not be able to promise that they will enable their patients to look like Tom Cruise or Kim Basinger.

they decide to advertise. Professionals have still another different obligation than other businesses. A professional may be disciplined by his or her professional association or state regulatory agency. As a result, ethical advertising is not just desirable, it is a necessity. One does not want to lose one's license to practice a profession in order to obtain additional revenue.

Ethics and Sales

Many schools do not emphasize salesmanship in the curriculum. Nevertheless, more workers will need to think of themselves as salespeople in the future. The fierce international competition[36] will require people who are able to explain the benefits of the product and convince people that the product will meet their needs. As noted above, professionals are engaging in advertising and other marketing activities. Colleges and universities are now competing for student's time and money. This is a type of salesmanship.

Some people have argued that one of the reasons that the United States has had difficulties with respect to international trade is that Americans have lost their ability to sell to customers in foreign countries. How this happened is a puzzle because Americans traditionally have been known as good salespeople. After World War II, the only major economy remaining was that of the United States.[37] Many businesspeople began to believe that the world would learn to speak English and would always buy American products. Unfortunately, this did not occur. Although many citizens of other countries did learn English, they did not roll over and accept American products.

Some analysts believe that U.S. business schools are to blame for the decline in the ability of Americans to sell effectively. They argue that business schools became too involved with numbers and too little involved with meeting the needs of people. Somehow, the sales process became regarded as beneath a graduate of a business school. This trend has been reversed in recent years as Americans have been compelled to "sell" their products to real customers rather than simply "crunching the numbers." The new emphasis on "sales" also raises ethical issues relating to the process. American business needs to recognize that the "right" to sell their products includes certain responsibilities with respect to the methods of making the sale.

Unfortunately, salespeople have developed a poor reputation in recent years. Like some politicians, they have been seen as people who will promise the customer almost anything to obtain business (Box 14.19). Even colleges and universities have become marketing and sales oriented.[38] They are not only

---

BOX 14.19

EXAMPLE: One of the troubling images of salespeople involves the used car salesman, who is perceived as a fast-talking, smooth-selling, promise-them-anything type of person who has few ethical standards. The differences between promised and actual performance was one of the reasons for the decline of the U.S. automobile industry. People expect salespeople to live up to their promises. If the product or service does not work out in accordance with a customer's expectations, he or she will go to another supplier. This is one reason why salespeople need to think about promises before they make them.

■ ■ ■   **BOX 14.20   Ethics and Grade Inflation**   ■ ■ ■

You are an instructor at a local college, where you teach a number of undergraduate courses. You have been there for about 10 years. Generally, you are perceived as a difficult but fair grader of students. Lately, you have come under increasing pressure to award higher grades so that your students can attend graduate school. You believe that this will diminish the value of the degree granted by the college. What are an instructor's ethical obligations to the college? to the students? What is the ethical obligation of the college to the students? How should schools resolve issues about grades? Should grades be granted? Why or why not?

competing for students but also for people's time. People could do a variety of things other than going to school and college. Colleges now spend their time and resources to convince people that going to classes would be an effective use of their time and money.

An ethical issue relating to this new emphasis on college salesmanship is whether it has a positive or a negative impact on a student's education, that is, whether instructors are being encouraged to treat students as "consumers." If this means that instructors spend more time considering students as people, this may be positive. However, if instructors begin to "pander" to student desires, the impact is likely to be negative. Students are at colleges to learn. If instructors begin to lower standards to try to please their consumer students, they are doing them an injustice. They are also acting in an unethical manner. They are not giving students the best possible education under the circumstances (Box 14.20).

Clarifying Expectations (an Ethical Necessity)   ■ ■ ■

An ethical decision maker is careful to clarify expectation from the very beginning. This is part of being an ethical person and being an ethical decision maker. This requires that all parties seek first to understand the positions and circumstances of the other. The parties should then try to be understood by the other party. The parties should then be able to reach agreement as to what each expects from the relationship (Box 14.21).

■ ■ ■   **BOX 14.21**   ■ ■ ■

EXAMPLE: Employment is a type of customer service. A worker offers his or her labor to the customer (the employer) for a price. It is essential for both parties to carefully define each other's responsibilities. The parties should reach agreement on the following matters:

■ What is to be the exact nature of the employee's duties?
■ How will the performance of the employee be appraised?
■ Is the method of appraisal a fair one?
■ Could it be improved?
■ Is it defensible in court?
■ Is employee performance capable of being measured?

- Does the employer have a clear direction as to where it wants its business to go in the future?
- Have the two parties reached agreement on the skills that the employee will need in the future?
- Will the employer provide training and coaching opportunities for the employee?
- What are the employee's responsibilities with respect to taking advantage of the training and coaching opportunities?
- Are there any understandings with respect to the long-term employment of the employee?
- Should there be a commitment to long-term employment on the part of both the employee and employer?
- Should this commitment be placed into writing?
- How will the employee be compensated by the employer?
- What are the provisions for additional compensation or for increases in future compensation?
- Would any other provisions be material to the relationship between the employer and employee?

EXAMPLE: NCD Corporation is contracting to obtain management consulting services from Hanson and Associates. NCD Corporation has been a reasonably successful company but believes that it needs to do a better job planning for the future and positioning itself in the marketplace. Hanson and Associates is a firm that specializes in strategic management and marketing. Hanson has helped a number of other corporations put together strategic plans and new marketing approaches.

    After some initial discussion, it becomes apparent that NCD Corporation is uncertain as to the direction it would like this consulting agreement to take. The company does not want to upset its managers by making them feel that there is a lack of confidence in their abilities. However, it is clear that its managers do not have the appropriate managerial skills to achieve the success the company will require in the future.

    More particularly, the managers do not have long-term planning, goal-setting, and marketing abilities. A review of the company's history indicates that NCD Corporation was built upon the success of some early products built by the engineers who started the company ten years earlier. The company still has strong technological skills and still earns a reasonable profit. However, the company's president is concerned that the company's revenues have not been increasing at an acceptable rate. In addition, the president believes that the company has not been successful in adapting to changing economic and market conditions.

    The consultants believe that the company needs to think through its future strategy and rely less on past successes. The company has been earning a reasonable profit based on its product successes. However, it has not had a major product success in several years. The consultants have done some marketing studies to determine the attitudes of customers toward NCD and its products. The survey, although rather general, indicated that although the company was generally well regarded, it did not have a reputation as an innovator. Neither was it perceived to be an effective marketing company. Because it has been dominated by engineers, it is not seen as being exceptionally "customer friendly."

    Hanson and Associates wants to resolve a number of questions before moving forward.

- How long will this assignment last?
- Hanson believes that additional marketing surveys will be required. Who will pay for these surveys?
- Hanson believes that some one-on-one consulting with individual managers is necessary. Is this something that the company wants to have Hanson do? Is the company willing to pay for this?
- Hanson believes that consulting tends to be effective only when it changes the culture of the organizations. This can take a considerable period of time. Is this something the company wants? There are some ethical issues involved in making cultural changes. How will they be resolved?

SUMMARY ■ ■ ■

Many organizations, both large and small, have sought to defraud the public. Laws and government regulations have been the result of these actions and more are certain to follow as people find new and different ways to defraud the public. In the United States, most commercial activity is governed by the Uniform Commercial Code. This code includes a number of provisions, including the implied warranty of merchantability, which means that every merchant gives every buyer a warranty that the goods will be fit for the purpose for which they were intended.

Many of the lawsuits that are the mark of our litigious society stem from this warranty that goods are sold as safe for normal use. Court rulings relating to the warranty of merchantability have tended to construe its provisions rather broadly and give plaintiffs the ability to recover. Sellers have an ethical duty to deliver what they promised to the buyer. The ethical seller can use the law as a floor for guiding his or her actions.

Beyond providing products and services that will act as guaranteed, a business has other ethical responsibilities with respect to its products, customers, and services. Too many sellers refuse to service their customers or to educate them. Meeting customer needs while still achieving a level of respect and a reasonable profit can be a difficult balancing act. Many ethical problems relating to customers and products result from a failure to determine what a business is selling, how will the business sell it, to whom it is selling, and how the product or service will be priced.

One area that can lead to a large number of ethical issues involves sales to a customer. Complaints about products and services are so common that state and local governments have established a variety of boards and commissions to regulate the activities of business that deal regularly with the public. An organization's advertising is a method of communicating its values to the public. At its best, advertising is a way of informing potential buyers that an organization has the resources and skills capable of meeting the buyer's needs.

Many organizations use personal selling as a technique to increase revenue. Person-to-person sales should be a dialogue between parties. An ethical salesperson seeks to meet the needs of the client rather than merely selling a particular product or service. There are a significant number of ethical issues that relate to the decision of whether the consumer should actually become a customer of the seller. This means that the organization's salespeople must take the time to determine carefully what customers need. In some cases it may be more ethical to suggest that the customer does not need the product or refer him or her to another organization.

Maintaining high ethical standards is particularly important if one manages financial assets on behalf of others. Organizations that do not do so are likely to suffer, at the very least, severe damage to their reputations.

Children are major consumers in our economy. However, selling to children raises significant ethical questions. Some sales to minors may be legal but still questionable ethically. Sellers know that children are willing to purchase products or services that offer fun. Sellers have an obligation not to do any harm to their young people.

Few sellers are faced with as many ethical issues as those selling products that are placed on or ingested into the body. These industries are heavily regulated by federal and state governments.

In a market-driven economy, an ethical businessperson would ask whether one should supply what the customer seems to "want" or what the customer actually needs. Marketing and salespeople regularly encounter situations when they must decide the level of quantity or quality of a product or service that the customer actually needs.

It is the seller's responsibility to meet the customer's needs and it is the customer's ability to pay. Finding the proper balance between the interests of the business and the customers is not an easy matter. Meeting customer needs while satisfying the company's need to earn a profit can be a difficult problem. Customers often have very specific needs which may or may not be satisfied by the seller. This issue of meeting the specialized needs of customers raises a number of ethical questions as well as legal ones. The first issue is whether one has the ability to meet the specialized needs of the purchaser. An ethical decision maker recognizes that it is more important to meet customer needs than to try to make quick profits.

There are a number of other ethical issues that can and will relate to customers. One issue is the difference in prices that men and women pay for similar products or services; another is how much women and men are paid for similar or identical services.

The law has always recognized the special position of children in our society. Under the law, a minor may cancel contracts prior to reaching the age of majority. The law clearly favors the rights of a minor as opposed to those of the seller and expects the seller to maintain a special ethical responsibility. In general, people have an obligation to sell minors products that are constructive, healthy, and promote positive values. There are regulations that govern advertising to children on television. However, the Internet is a new vista for marketing and selling to children. Some have urged the Federal Trade Commission to adopt regulations that govern the sale of products to children over the Internet.

Many people attend school because they hope to become professionals. It takes a considerable amount of education and training to become a qualified professional. Some professionals have used advertising to attract new business, and although their peers and professional associations have discouraged such practices, the Supreme Court of the United States has ruled that such practices are perfectly legal.

Sales is, perhaps, the area where ethics and ethical behavior are most at risk. It is also the one area where people need to pay more attention than they have in the past. Everyone is in the process of selling: selling ideas, selling services, selling products, but most of all, selling themselves. Because of ethical abuses and lapses, selling, as a profession, has fallen on hard times. People view salespersons as some of the least ethical people in the society, but sales is necessary to the success of any organization. Schools and colleges have tended to downplay sales as a role for their students, but sales remains an attractive career for many students and an important element in the success of organizations and individuals.

Questions

1. What is the warranty of merchantability?
2. To what products does the warranty of merchantability apply?
3. What are the consequences of the warranty of merchantability with respect to breach of contract actions by the buyer?

4. What are the consequences of the warranty of merchantability with respect to tort suits brought by the buyer injured by the product?

5. What are the consequences of the warranty of merchantability with respect to tort actions by other persons injured by a product?

6. With respect to product safety, what are the ethical responsibilities to the seller created by the implied warranty of merchantability?

7. What is the major legal defense to a tort claim based on a breach of the warranty of merchantability?

8. How does the tort liability of a seller under the warranty of merchantability and defenses to it reflect the ethical responsibilities of the seller and the buyer?

9. Discuss the ethics of product safety issues for the seller.

10. Discuss the ethical responsibilities of selling products to children.

11. Discuss the ethics of selling based on commission.

12. Discuss the warranty of fitness for a particular purpose.

13. Discuss some of the ethical issues with respect to selling to men and women.

14. Discuss the ethical issues involved with charging different prices to different customers.

15. Discuss some of the ethical issues involved with selling over the Internet.

16. Discuss some of the ethical issues involved with marketing.

17. Discuss some of the ethical issues involved with selling college classes to students.

18. Discuss some of the ethical issues involved with treating students as consumers.

19. What ethical issues would you consider in accepting new employment?

20. Why is clarifying expectations so important to ethical decision making?

21. What is a "bait and switch"?

22. What are "sound-a-likes"?

23. What do you think of the ethics of using sound-a-likes?

24. Name some ethical principles involved with marketing products over the phone.

25. Would you want to be a salesperson?

26. What ethical conflicts exist with respect to being a salesperson?

27. What ethical considerations relate to selling to children?

28. What products would you not sell to children?

CASE I

Hapland Corp. offers paid courses to students who are taking standardized tests for college admissions, professional licensing, and other purposes. It charges a substantial amount for lectures, personal tutoring, tapes, and computer software. It markets these courses to young people who are afraid that they will fail the examinations. In its advertisements, Hapland Corp. offers little scientific evidence that its products actually help students do well on the tests. One of its products is designed to look as if it is a computer game. Hapland charges a higher price for the computer game than for similar written materials, although there is no evidence that it is more effective than the written materials.

1. Is it ethical for Haplan to charge a higher price for the game than for the written materials?
2. Given the lack of scientific evidence that their products actually help the young people to whom they are sold, is it ethical to continue to make these sales?

CASE 2

Lou develops a new fast-food restaurant called Hoagie and Stoagie. He sells long sandwiches and cigars at the restaurant. Many minors come to his stores and ask for cigars after their sandwiches. Lou sells the cigars to them. Lou also takes his idea to a large consumer company. One of its senior vice presidents tells Lou that it is not interested in buying either his restaurant or his idea. Later, the consumer company begins to sell cigars at its own fast-food restaurants.

1. What are the ethical issues involved for each of the parties who are part of this case?

CASE 3

Jones works for NDZ Corp., which makes hand and power tools for home use. Jones notices that there has been an increase in customer complaints regarding the malfunction of the tools. Jones also knows that NDZ Corp. is working on a very close profit margin.

1. What are his ethical responsibilities to customers?
2. What are his ethical responsibilities to the company?

CASE 4

You are an editor for a large publishing firm. Your job is to acquire written material that can be published for the college textbook market. You regularly work with college professors who are paid for the writing they do either on a per job or on a royalty basis.

You recently asked one of your authors to revise one of his works for possible inclusion in another of your company's textbooks. The two of you had an oral agreement but no written contract. The author prepared the work you requested, and you sent it out for the review of other professors in the field. Some of the reviewers indicated that they would be unlikely to use the materials because they do not need any new materials. Some of the reviews indicated that the materials were excellent and they would probably use them.

You are now uncertain that your company will go ahead with the scheduled project. In addition, your boss has told you to cut costs and to move forward only with those projects that will make money. You do not think that this project will move ahead. You can pay the author of the materials the amount of money you promised him. However, you can also find a way to avoid paying him.

1. What do you do?

CASE 5

Plump A' Part markets a variety of products to people (mostly women) who want to lose weight. The company is aware that 97 percent of the people who purchase weight-loss programs are not able to keep weight off. Despite this knowledge, the company regularly sells a variety of products and services to consumers who believe these items will help them to lose weight. The company charged a price of 100 percent above what it cost the company to obtain the product. Several of its customers have lost a substantial amount of weight. Plump A' Part uses these customers in its advertisements. The company pays them several thousand dollars to appear in the advertisements. There is little evidence to support the contention that the products actually help people lose weight.

1. What are the ethical issues involved with this case?

References

1. King, Carole, "Raters keeping an eye on Pru," *National Underwriter*, August 18, 1997, v. 10, n. 33.
2. Paskell-Mede, Mindy, "The high cost of losing," *CA Magazine*, October 1997, v. 130, n. 8.
3. Ullmann, Owen, "What Republicans learned from donorgate: new rules," *Business Week*, November 10, 1997.
4. Eldridge, William, *Core concepts of business law*, South-Western, Cincinnati, OH, 1995.
5. Ibid.
6. Ibid.
7. Anderson, Kristin, *Knock your socks off answers: solving customer nightmares and soothing nightmare customers*, AMACOM, New York, 1995.
8. Eldridge, *Core concepts*.
9. Corcoran, Kevin, *High performance sales organizations: achieving competitive advantage in the global marketplace*, Irwin Professional Publishing, Burr Ridge, IL, 1995.
10. Seebacher, Noreen, "Homes: savvy women avoid scams," *Detroit News*, October 21, 1997.
11. Ibid.
12. Arena, William F., *Contemporary advertising*, 5th ed., Irwin Publishing, Burr Ridge, IL, 1994.
13. Ibid.
14. Ibid.
15. Davis, Mike, "Time to write rules for ads that are out of bounds," *Campaign*, London, September 9.
16. Eldridge, *Core concepts*.
17. Ibid.
18. Van Der Lewn, Gerad, "Zen and the art of cold calling," *Success*, November 1997.
19. Reilway, Jerry, *Beyond 2000: the future of direct marketing*, NTC Business Books, Lincolnwood, IL, 1995.
20. Van Der Lewn, "Zen and the art of cold selling."
21. Sutton, Reiner, "What's wrong with this picture?" *Credit Union Magazine*, September 1997.
22. *Estate of Doris Duke*, Surrogates Court, City of New York, 1995.
23. Gunther, Marc, "This gang controls your kids brains," *Fortune*, October 27, 1997.
24. Ibid.
25. Assael, Henry, *Consumer Behavior and Marketing Action*, 4th ed., PWS-Kent, Boston, 1992.
26. Peters, Thomas, and Robert Watermann, *In search of excellence: lessons from America's best-run companies*, Harper & Row, New York, 1982.
27. Eldridge, William, *Contracts*, Prentice Hall, Upper Saddle River, NJ, 1997.

28. Ayers, Ian, "Race and gender discrimination in bargaining for a new car," *American Economic Review,* June 1995.

29. "The in box," *Supervisory Management,* September 1994.

30. Gray, John, *Men are from Mars, women are from Venus: a practical guide to getting what you want,* HarperCollins, New York, 1992.

31. Gunther, "This gang controls."

32. Ibid.

33. "Finally, some light for parents in the TV issue: better ratings system opens the way for use of the 'V' chip," *Los Angles Times,* July 11, 1997.

34. Stevens, Robert E., C. William McConkey, and David L. London, "Professional attitudes toward advertising: a comparison of attorneys, dentists and physicians," *Akron Business and Economic Review,* Fall 1991.

35. *Bates v. Boor of Arizona,* 433 U.S. 350 (1976).

36. Maidment, Fred (ed.), *Annual editions: international business, 1997–1998,* Dushkin/McGraw-Hill, Guilford, CT, 1997.

37. Ibid.

38. Falls, Joe, "College football: clever marketing gives WMU a boost," *Detroit News,* August 29, 1997.

STRATEGIC RESPONSE TO A CHANGING GLOBAL ENVIRONMENT

Concepts : You Will Learn ■ ■ ■

the basic steps of strategic management

how to apply the steps of strategic management to one's personal life and to a businesses

the importance of applying the concepts and steps of strategic management in a changing global environment

how the increasing global competition is placing greater pressure on U.S. business

how to use the steps of strategic management to help solve ethical problems

REASONS FOR STRATEGIC MANAGEMENT

The world's economy is becoming increasingly complex and competitive. It is necessary to have a clear understanding of what one wants to accomplish in one's career and in one's business. One also needs to have a clear understanding of where one is going if one is going to achieve one's goals. In addition, many ethical problems arise because of a failure to define the business clearly: how the business will satisfy customer needs and how the business will market its products to its customers. As a result, the business is tempted to cut ethical corners to earn profits. A good strategic plan will reduce the likelihood of later problems developing. It should also reduce the pressure on people to commit unethical acts in the future. A good organization regularly updates its strategic plan as conditions change.[1]

STEPS IN THE STRATEGIC MANAGEMENT (PLANNING) PROCESS ■ ■ ■

1. *One should define the purpose (mission) of one's career or business.*[2] That is, one should determine what is one's reason for existing. One needs to decide what one does that will allow one to achieve satisfaction and to earn a living. This can be a difficult process and should be done carefully and with precision. If one does not understand one's objectives from the beginning, one is unlikely to achieve a satisfactory result.

The mission statement should also provide a way to uplift the organization's employees and to provide a sense of guidance for its employees when they are compelled to make decisions.[3] That is, the organization's mission statement would indicate its values and provide employees with a clear idea of which activities it wants to do and which it does not. The written mission statement provides a handy reference point for employees to guide them in their actions.

2. *The next step is to determine if there are quantitative goals that the organization could establish that would help the organization achieve its mission.*[4] The establishment of goals is a way of pointing people toward the achievement of meaningful objectives that will help the organization achieve its mission. If the goals are achieved, the organization's mission will also be achieved. If the organization has no goals, it is likely to engage in many pointless activities and make little progress.

3. *The organization should then look to determine if it has current goals that will help it to achieve its mission.*[5] If not, the organization needs to establish goals that will help the organization accomplish its mission. The primary function of a manager is to develop a mission and goals for the employees. If the company has no goals, it is unlikely to succeed.[6] It is essential that the managers work with their employees to determine and achieve their objectives. This step is designed to find out if the organization has current goals that will allow it to achieve its mission. Some organizations discover that they have no meaningful quantitative objectives or that their current goals are not consistent with the organization's new mission statement.

4. *The organization should then perform an environmental scan, which means that it should look into its environment to determine what factors could affect its ability to achieve its mission.*[7] Every organization will encounter environmental factors that will affect its ability to achieve its mission. Some factors will be favorable and may help the organization achieve its goals and mission. Others may have a negative effect. The organization should develop plans for coping with these environmental factors.

In a rapidly changing environment, organizations that are able to anticipate environmental changes will perform well. Those organizations that do not are likely to disappear. It is essential for organizations to find ways to benefit from environmental changes. It is no longer useful for a manager to expect that what has worked in the past will work in the future. Regardless of the successes of organizations, it will not be sufficient to support future achievement. In some cases, success may become the enemy of the future. An organization that bases its future on what has worked in the past is likely to find that it has headed down the wrong path.

5. *The organization should also perform an internal resources analysis that examines the organization's strengths and weaknesses.*[8] This step helps the organization determine if its internal resources and culture will help it achieve its mission. If the

BOX 15.1 Market Targeting

It is no longer sufficient simply to define oneself or one's business in general terms. The world's economy has become too competitive and too specifically niche oriented for one to think of oneself as being in a general business. The organizations that succeed are those that have carefully defined their customer and market niche.

Professionals have recognized that they need to develop a specialty practice if they are going to succeed. One should also think of oneself as being a specialist in some area. An attorney might specialize in criminal defense or plaintiff work. A physician might focus on internal surgery or injuries related to athletics.

Similarly, a business needs to find a distinct focus that sets it apart from its competition. A bank may decide to find its market focus in the lower end of the consumer market or by filling the borrowing needs of large institutions. A supermarket may aim its efforts at the low end or high end of the market, but it needs to make a decision.

BOX 15.2 Business Mission Statement

YTC Corporation defines its mission as "to be the state's premier seller of highest-quality health foods products to high-income customers in the suburban areas of the state." This statement tells its employees what activities the organization wants its employees to engage in. It wants them to obtain only the highest-quality health food and sell only this type of food. It does not want them to obtain or sell any different type of food. Although this seems rather straightforward and simple, it has been the authors' experience that organizations often waste a great deal of time discussing and rehashing irrelevant issues because they do not clearly define their business. In addition, the mission statement above also provides a clear regional market focus of the employees of YTC Corporation. It lets the employees know that the corporation only wants to have facilities in high-income suburban areas. This means that they do not need to waste their time considering placing their facilities in other areas.

BOX 15.3 Business Flexibility

The growth of some companies in the computer field has been rapid because of their ability to utilize new technologies to find opportunities and to solve problems. However, one's strengths can also become weaknesses if one is not careful. A company that has achieved success through computer technology may be tempted to believe that it can simply apply the technology to any situation and achieve good results. The environmental landscape changes too quickly for this type of assumption. One must analyze all the options in light of changing conditions and needs. Although the past can provide useful guideposts for the future, it is no substitute for clear thought and careful analysis. This illustrates what can happen to many organizations. They fail to analyze their past adequately or explore what is occurring in their own environment. As a result, this failure in the future can lead to poor results.

answer appears to be in the affirmative, the organization probably does not need to change. Conversely, the organization may not have the resources to achieve its mission.

The internal resources analysis may be the most difficult step of the strategic management model. It requires the organization to take an honest look at itself. Many organizations will find that they do not have the skills necessary to achieve its mission and goals. In this step, the organization should realistically assess its abilities.[9] In this complex economy, it is extremely important that one build good products or services and have the marketing and sales ability to convince people to buy them. Many organizations will find that they lack one or more of these critical talents. This presents the organization with a problem that must be solved.

One can obtain these skills by hiring people from the outside or by training people who are employees within the organization. Either of these alternatives can create severe problems for the organization, depending on the skills that are necessary for the organization's success. If the necessary skills are easily developed, there may be few problems finding people who have them or obtaining the services of qualified trainers. However, if the organization lacks management abilities, it has significant difficulties. It takes considerable time to develop good managers. Without them, the organization will not succeed.

Too often, organizations do not take seriously their obligations to develop quality managers who have the ability to help the organization to achieve its goals. Many organizations believe it is sufficient to find "smart" people and make them managers. However, being smart does not mean that one will be a good manager. It takes considerable time and training to develop the managerial skills that are necessary for people to help their organizations succeed. Organizations expect a level of "loyalty" from their employees, but too often are unwilling to spend the time or resources necessary to help them. It is not ethical for the organization to allow managers to fail because it does not devote the resources necessary for them to succeed.

If one must hire managers from the outside, it is an indication that the company has not adequately developed its own people to assume managerial positions. It is also an indication for the outsider that he is not likely to discover a solid managerial infrastructure when he moves into the organization. This will make the new manager's job extremely difficult. It is also useful to analyze the organization's culture during this step. An organization's culture consists of the values, norms, beliefs, and ways of doing things; If the organization has a strong, positive culture, it is far more likely to succeed than if it has an unclear or unfocused culture.[10]

Organizational cultures can help or hinder the organization's ability to achieve its mission. If the culture of the organization is not consistent with its mission, there will need to be some changes. An organization's culture can swallow up its plans for the future and make them impossible to implement.

When an organization is required to implement policies that run contrary to its culture, there is likely to be considerable resistance, which will create problems and friction.[11] As a result, one is faced with considerable ethical and practical difficulties.

In an increasingly competitive world, organizations that are unwilling to change will not survive. However, change is difficult and carries costs. The organization's senior management must take these costs into account and plan for change. Senior management must decide whether the mission of the organization should be changed or the culture needs to be changed.

BOX 15.4 Organizational Culture

The leaders of the executive and legislative branches of the federal government have insisted that the composition of the U.S. armed forces should more adequately reflect the diversity of the citizenry. Although the senior management of the military has agreed to the program of the civilian leaders, such a policy runs somewhat contrary to the established culture of the military. The military has traditionally been a white male organization. It has also been characterized by a strong sense of masculine pride and values. Introducing large numbers of women and minorities into the military represents a very significant change for its members. In addition, President Clinton's first order was to give homosexuals greater rights in the military. After a series of negotiations, the military adopted a "don't ask, don't tell" policy, which states the military will not ask about a person's sexual orientation, and a member of the military would not inform anyone regarding one's sexual orientation. Many members of the military may feel overwhelmed by these changes and their implementation. They are being asked to carry out policies that are contrary to their culture, beliefs, values, and ways of doing things.

In Box 15.4, regarding the military, the nation's leaders need to decide if the implementation of the policies is worth the costs of changing the organization's culture.[12] The military has had a difficult time implementing these changes and some people have argued that the costs of the change may be too high. The proponents of change in the military argue that it is essential that various members of the community be able to obtain positions of responsibility in the armed forces. Opponents of the change argue that the mission of the military is unique and that it should not be subject to the same social standards as the remainder of society. The same clash between cultures often exists in various organizations or between the organization and the remainder of society. Senior managers need to recognize the possibility that the culture will prevent the accomplishment of the organization's mission.

6. *At this stage, the senior managers might wish to reconsider the mission and goals.*[13] Their analysis of environmental factors and of the strengths and weaknesses may cause them to decide that the mission and goals should be changed. At least, the senior managers may want to look at whether its mission and goals continue to make sense. However, one should not be afraid to continue to make necessary internal changes if the mission of the organization continues to make sense. It may be necessary to implement significant and wrenching changes within the organization.

7. *After the organization has reassessed its mission for the future, it needs to determine if its current "strategy" will succeed in the future.*[14] The organization must also determine if it actually has a strategy for dealing with the future. Sometimes the organization will decide that its current strategy will not enable the organization to achieve its goals. An organization's mission statement indicates what the organization wants to accomplish, while its strategy is a decision as to what the organization will do to achieve its goals. Often, organizations will discover that they have no concrete plan to attain their goals.

A strategy is a detailed plan for accomplishing the mission and goals of the organization. It establishes the outline for the individual's actions that will permit the organization to achieve success. A strategy answers the questions regarding who is responsible for accomplishing the specific tasks necessary for the organization to achieve its mission and specific goals. If the organization has no strategy, it is not likely to succeed. Implementing changes is a difficult process that requires considerable planning and ability. Almost any new strategy will require some change. As a result, one of the most important functions of a manager is to develop an effective strategy to enable the organization to achieve its mission and goals.

Common Strategies Adopted by Organizations

a. *Do the same as before.*[15] This may be an appropriate strategy for organizations that are succeeding in accomplishing their mission and goals. Some organizations may be so well positioned that they can continue what they are doing. However, this is also a very dangerous strategy because it presumes that the future will be the same as the past. This is a dangerous assumption because often an organization's success makes it too sure of itself. This becomes the basis for future failure.[16]

b. *Do everything.*[17] This is a strategy that can result from a desire to please too many groups and individuals. It may also result from trying to combine too many opinions into a plan. As a result, the organization does not have a program to achieve its mission. Effective planning does involve receiving input from a variety of people. However, the organization's plan needs a focus that will differentiate the institution from other organizations. If the institution wants to make an ethical difference, it should choose a particular area and focus its energies on that area.

In a democratic society, this "do everything" strategy is common because of the tendency in the United States to allow people to express their "opinions." Consensus is a useful concept when developing a strategy. However, a consensus with no theme is not a strategy likely to work in this environment. This may be a reason that government does not seem to work very well. Because it has so many purposes, it has no specific focus. As a result, the government does not have a specific purpose on which to focus. In addition, governments tend not to do long-term planning, which often leads to crisis management.

c. *Hit another home run.*[18] An organization may have had a success in the past which it continues to try to duplicate rather than formulating an effective plan for the future. Baseball clubs tell hitters to try for singles rather than to swing for the fences. This strategy is likely to be adopted by organizations that have had a major technological achievement. In government, a politician may have been able to enact a new program or cut taxes. The political leader continues with the same policies despite changing conditions.

Herbert Hoover was a tremendous success in business and later as Secretary of Commerce. Hoover believed that the free enterprise system would generate economic growth and jobs if government would not interfere with the workings of the free market. When the Great Depression hit in 1929, Hoover believed that it was a temporary condition and that the free market system would solve the problems associated with the Depression. Unfortunately for Hoover and the country, the Depression continued for much longer than Hoover expected. Hoover refused to change his policies. Ultimately, this resulted in the election of Franklin Roosevelt as President.

d. *Go in different directions.*[19] A creative person often can see a number of different courses of action that would be desirable. It can be useful to explore different alternatives, but it is important to select one and to pursue it. The most successful

BOX 15.5   Public Office

Some people decide to run for public office on a full- or part-time basis. They may do so for a variety of reasons, which may range from the desire to serve the public, feed one's ego, gain power, or earn some money. In our system of democracy, it is possible for anyone to run for office even if they have no qualifications whatsoever. Serving in public office can be extremely time consuming and frustrating. The public expects one to be available at all times. Governmental employees want you to consider their interests, and various other groups want you to pursue their agendas. Such activities can take one's energies away from one's full-time job. One should consider carefully if one is spreading oneself too thin in either one's personal life or one's business.

people in our country tend to be those who are excellent in one particular area. In an increasingly competitive world it is extremely difficult to be good in more than one area at a time. The Age of the Renaissance Man is over. Much of the same is true of organizations. If they pursue too many alternatives, they dilute the resources that are available to pursue any one alternative. This may be a mistake. It is particularly a mistake if the alternatives head the organization in different directions. This will make it unclear to both insiders and outsiders as to how the organization perceives itself.

e. *Pursue a high-end niche strategy.*[20] Another strategy is to pursue an upscale market niche approach. This strategy aims the organization's products and services at the more affluent end of the marketplace. This provides focus to the organization's activities. Many retailers select the more affluent customer as their primary focus. Clothing stores may offer only items for working men and women with high incomes. A high-end niche strategy permits the organization to develop a consistent marketing strategy that aims its products, pricing, and promotional activities in one direction.

f. *Employ a low-price strategy.*[21] Another potential winning strategy is to be able to produce a product or service at the lowest possible cost and to be the low-price supplier of a particular item. There is evidence that people will purchase some products based on the organization that is able to supply them at the lowest price. Although some products are not price sensitive, many people buy products based on the price of the service or product. One can make a considerable amount of money selling based on volume. Just as there are clothing stores that make money focusing on the upscale portion of the market, others, such as Kmart, can earn money by selling to people who are price sensitive.

The *New York Times* earns considerable amounts of money by appealing to a more educated and affluent market segment. Conversely, the *National Enquirer* makes a considerable amount of money by appealing to the least educated and lower-income segment of the market. It is possible to make money by appealing to the upper- or lower-income segments. To achieve such profits, organizations need to develop a consistent plan and process that will achieve the results one wants.

g. *Allow oneself to fall into the middle.*[22] In this economy it is dangerous to allow one's organization to fall within the muddled middle of the marketplace. These organizations lose their focus, and potential customers find it difficult to figure out what constitutes the "distinctive competence" of the organization. As a result, potential customers are not certain as to the reasons for buying the organization's services or for working with it. The customer is often looking for a specific type of product or service that meets a particular need.

In the earlier part of this century, it was common to try to appeal to the entire market or to develop products and services that appealed to everyone. Some organizations still think in this manner. In the early age of television, the most popular shows were those that featured a variety of acts that appealed to different segments of the audience. A classic example was the Ed Sullivan Show, which featured acts appealing to children, teenagers, adults, and senior citizens. The popularity of the variety shows of the 1950s has been replaced by cable television shows, which appeal to specific segments of the population. People can now watch all of what they want. No longer must they watch large segments of a program in order to see a few minutes of what they really want to see. In other areas, there has also been a shift from strategies that try to appeal to the unclear middle of the market. If customers want to buy a particular product or service, they are able to do so.

If the organization is caught in the middle, it is not likely to do well. Generally, people are more likely to gravitate toward a particular area that satisfies their specific needs rather than to an organization that tries to appeal to some vague middle ground. Similarly, organizations may offer too many alternatives of similar products or services. This may tend to confuse potential customers. They may also begin to wonder if the organization has adopted an unethical "bait and switch" approach to their products and services.[23] Bait and switch tactics can involve a variety of techniques. One of them is to show people one product and then try to convince them to buy a more expensive product. Another tactic is to pretend that the product is available when it is not. A third unethical tactic is to try to encourage people to buy immediately by pretending that a product or service is in short supply.

An organization that cannot provide a sense of focus risks looking as if they will sell anything to anybody. This is not the image that one wants to project in this environment. Consumers want to have a sense of consistency about their purchases and about the supplier.

8. *The next step is to select a strategy among the alternatives generated.*[24] This is a critical step that many organizations pass over too quickly. As a result, they may select one of the general strategies outlined above even though it is not appropriate for the organization. It is often a good idea to assign people to argue for and against each of the alternative strategies developed during the previous stage. If that step was performed correctly, the organization should have many different alternatives from which to choose.

One should be careful not to fall into one of several traps that are common at this stage. One trap is to quickly choose a strategy without adequate consideration of other possible approaches. This is one reason that it is useful to assign people to present each option. The organization should also try to avoid the trap of group think,[25] which occurs when a group rushes into a decision while rejecting the opinions of people who question the group's decision.

The classic example of group think was the ill-fated Bay of Pigs invasion, which was authorized by President Kennedy in an attempt to overthrow Fidel Castro's government in Cuba. Kennedy's advisors urged him to authorize an invasion of Cuba by a small band of anti-Castro rebels. When the invasion failed,

Kennedy searched for the reasons. It became clear that the people advising the president had been prevented from exercising independent judgment, which could have stopped the invasion. The research revealed that certain people acted to discourage different points of view that could have prevented the fiasco.

It is a relatively easy matter to make decisions without sufficient thought. It is useful to designate specific people to act as devil's advocates who will argue against a decision that a group is about to make. However, a devil's advocate may pay a price for his opposition to the proposed actions of the organization. Research indicates that devil's advocates help organizations reach better decisions but may tend to be disliked by other members of the group.

The foregoing considerations should encourage the organization to adopt a specific approach to decision making that will permit adequate consideration of all the options that are available to the organization. If the organization selects a strategy that runs contrary to its culture, it will need to work at changing its culture. Many organizations become so rigid that they have difficulty in adjusting to a rapidly changing world.

Organizations built on highly technical products may find that they need to shift from a technical culture to one that is more marketing and sales oriented. People with strong technical or professional skills often fail to appreciate the importance of marketing and selling the product or service to the customer. People do not just obtain products because they are of high quality. There are many excellent products that people do not purchase for a number of reasons. Ultimately, they must be persuaded to purchase the product or service by someone who is familiar with the needs of the customer.

9. *Strategies are of little use until they are actually implemented.*[26] Well-run organizations are able to develop ways to help their employees "buy into" a strategy so that they will be cooperative in implementing it.[27] It is useful if the employees have a sense of ownership of the strategy and believe that they will benefit from its successful implementation. The best organizations are those that are able to blend together the employee's self-interests with the organization's interest. During the development of strategic alternatives, to develop a feeling of commitment, the organization should have involved employees. Selection of the strategy also should have allowed people to discuss the pros and cons of each alternative.

There are a wide range of plans for paying employees based on performance, and it may be useful to have these implemented before reaching this stage.[28] If they have not been implemented previously, it is appropriate to do so. Employees who have a stake in their organization are likely to maintain a high ethical level. They are also likely to be more productive employees. Possible programs to foster implementation of the strategy while maintaining high ethical standards are discussed in the paragraphs below.

Employee stock option plans allow employees to purchase the stock of their company below market price.[29] This allows employees to build up a substantial ownership interest in their employer. If the business performs well, the employees will benefit directly as the price of the stock rises. This will help ensure successful implementation of the organization. An organization could also pay directly for specific work performed by an employee. This could be done on an old-fashioned piecemeal basis or based on some other specific "pay for performance" mechanism.

In Japan, managers often spend a great deal of time and energy building agreement among their employees to implement future plans and strategies. This can take a great deal of time, but employees will actually implement the strategy because they have had a chance to be involved and give input.[30] In the United States, managers are more likely to develop the plans by themselves and order their implementation by employees. The managers then discover that employees are not willing to implement the plans because they have no opportunity to provide input or to be involved in putting the plans together.

Much of the business system in the United States has been built on the traditional military model, which emphasizes a tops-down mentality. In this structure, people are told what to do by their superiors. They are then supposed to carry out their superiors' orders. The military model has a number of advantages. It provides a structure that offers "certainty" for the people within the system. Each person understands how he or she fits into the system. Generally, people accept their positions and strive to make the process work. However, the system also builds in a type of rigidity that prevents new ideas and promotes a rather "slavish" obedience to the rules, to bosses, and to the organization. It may also create resistance to any change and a commitment to policies and procedures that are no longer useful.

10. *The organization needs to monitor progress toward achieving implementation of the strategy.*[31] It is useful to try to measure progress as much as possible. Many people who are knowledgeable about the management process believe that it is essential that an organization measure its progress. An organization tends to obtain what it measures. If it measures specific quantitative progress, it is likely to receive it. If it does not measure its progress, it is not likely to achieve much progress. Management by objectives is a method by which an organization can measure progress toward its goals and implementation of its strategy.[32]

The first step of management by objectives is for the organization to establish its own quantitative objectives. It needs to determine what quantitative benchmarks would measure its progress toward achieving its mission. Generally, it is considered useful to have about five or six quantitative objectives (goals) for the organization. Some possible examples of objectives are:

- We will increase our sales revenue by 8 percent this year.
- We will hold our cost increase this year to no more than 3 percent.
- We will develop three profitable new products this year.
- We will expand the sale of our products into a new market this year.
- We will increase our profits by 15 percent this year.

After the organization has developed its goals, it should then develop objectives for its subunits which are consistent with those of the larger organization. In the example above, the subunits should develop goals that feed into the objectives of the organization.

The next step is to develop quantitative objectives for each employee who will contribute to the achievement of the organization's objectives. It is useful to make this process one in which the subordinate and the superior discuss the objectives of the employee. The superior is in a better position to understand the objectives of the organization. The subordinate is in a better position to explain the nature of his or her duties and how he or she can contribute to the organization's objectives. It would be useful for both the subordinate and superior to suggest approximately five goals for the subordinate to achieve in the upcoming year. The two parties could then reach agreement on the subordinate's objectives and how the employee's performance will be evaluated.

Some possible individual objectives that fall into the broader goals of the organization include:

- I will help my unit increase its sales revenues by 7 percent this year.
- I will help our unit hold its cost increase to 2 percent this year.
- I will help our unit develop two new profitable products this year.
- I will help our unit expand its products into two new areas this year.
- I will help our unit increase its profits by 15 percent this year.

11. *The next step in the strategic management model is to give rewards to the employees and subunits that achieve their goals and objectives.*[33] People have a low level of trust in their organizations. If people do not receive adequate rewards for their contributions to the organization's success, they will become resentful and are less likely to make similar contributions in the future.[34] These rewards could be either monetary or nonmonetary. Organizations should make some effort to determine what rewards employees would like to receive. Too often, managers presume incorrectly that they know what types of rewards employees want. Employers tend to overemphasize the importance of monetary rewards to employees.[35] As a result, they forget to give employees different types of rewards. Surveys of employees show that they are less concerned with monetary rewards and more interested in being recognized for good work and on being involved with major decisions that affect their work and their lives.

12. *If the organization has done a good job at the previous steps, it should achieve good results.*[36] It should then have distributed rewards that will reinforce the desire for additional achievement. The organization can then start the process of objective setting for the following year. Research indicates that the process of goal setting will lead to increasingly better results for the individuals and the organization. Research also indicates that organizations which perform management by objectives will achieve better results than those that do not.[37]

THE IMPORTANCE OF PLANNING FOR THE FUTURE ■ ■ ■

The global economy has become fiercely competitive, and the United States is at a disadvantage because of certain factors. Workers in the United States are seen by many as no longer being competitive with workers in other countries. Some employers argue that American workers have lost their work ethic and are sometimes outworked by workers outside the United States. Conversely, American workers have little confidence in American management. They have seen their fellow workers "downsized" while watching managers continue to receive high salaries and other benefits. As a result, there is a very high level of distrust between managers and workers.

Planning is a method of improving the chances of success for the organization. It may also be a way of reducing the level of distrust among the parties. When planning is done well it enhances communication among the various parties. It permits a discussion of how the organization can move forward together. Excellent managers ask questions of their workers about what is going well in the organization and how the organization can do more of what is working. People and organizations tend to get those things on which they focus. If they tend to focus predominantly on problems, they are likely to have more problems. If they focus on success, they are likely to achieve more success.[38]

Excellent managers recognize that it is important for employees to be able to make decisions without consulting senior management continually. However, many employees have had little practice in making decisions. Instead, they have been told what to do. As a result, they have learned not to make decisions or even to make suggestions. Senior management should not be surprised that this is the reaction of its employees. They have been conditioned not to think, and receive little credit if they do. If performed correctly, the process of strategic management should foster a high level of communication among all managers and employees.[39] Well-run strategic planning sessions have elements of top-down and bottom-up communication.

The goal-setting process clarifies expectations among the individuals involved. This is of critical importance in managing well. It is a fundamental premise of good management that both the manager and subordinate need to have a clear idea as to what each expects from the other. When expectations are clear, the superior and the subordinate are likely to find a way to achieve their mutual goals. If expectations are not clear, they are likely to have poor results. The most common failure of management is to neglect setting clear standards. However, this is a mutual responsibility. It is not sufficient for an employee to "whine" about lack of clear goals. Although the employer has a responsibility to set clear goals, an equal responsibility rests with the employee to seek out opportunities to clarify goals and to contribute to the organization's objectives.

TOTAL QUALITY MANAGEMENT AND TEAM MANAGEMENT ■ ■ ■

Closely related to strategic management are the concepts of total quality management and team management.[40] A well-developed strategic plan can consider the organization's need for high quality and build in goals to help it achieve them. Quality can be important to an organization and to its subunits.[41] If it is, the strategic planners should develop objectives that focus on achieving these quality goals. It is important to define these objectives with precision. If "quality" becomes merely a slogan, the organization is not likely to achieve the level of quality it desires.

Team management is another concept that can be used or abused by the organization's senior management.[42] The values that one wants should be connected to specific goals and statements as to how these values will be achieved. If managers want people to work as a team, they need to establish team and individual goals and back them up with adequate rewards when they are achieved. Team management should not be utilized as an excuse to extract more work from employees. Genuine team management allows both the organization and the individual to achieve their goals. Great strengths can often become great weaknesses. Concepts such as teamwork can be an excuse for an overly dominant leader to coerce fellow workers into performing unwise or unethical actions. Organizations that stress teamwork need to guard against an unethical type of group think that leads people into bad decision making.

BOX 15.6 Employee Characteristics

Individuals tend to become what their organization demands. That is, employees are likely to conform their actions to activities that their superiors demand. "Hunker down and go along" is a motto that employees adopt in poorly run organizations. These are institutions that have created a culture that is resistant to new ideas and ways of doing things. As a result, new managers will tend to imitate managers who had an influence on them. They are likely to adopt both the strengths and weaknesses of previous managers. In addition, they may resent efforts to change their current style.

A well-considered decision-making process encourages people to develop new options and to have them explored by the organization. Managers should recognize that most employees want to contribute to their organization. They do not need new slogans. In most cases, what they need is better managers and better decision makers. It would be too easy to ascribe evil motives to most managers. Some may be uncaring or evil, but many just do not have the skills to do an adequate job of managing. Too often, people are selected for management but are not given adequate training for the position. As a result, they can make mistakes that cause harm to their employees and others.

Some people are promoted to management because they are perceived as "smart." Although being smart is an asset to a manager, it is not sufficient to being an excellent manager. Organizations have an obligation to give their managers adequate training to include sufficient developmental activities, such as prior lower-level supervisory activities.[43] The authors of this book have had experience in the world of business, government, and education. In these instances, the authors observed that managers often adopt cultural "values" that may no longer be applicable in a changing marketplace. Furthermore, they often lack skills in dealing with people and with new ideas suggested by subordinates.

The above should not be construed as critical of managers. Rather, it suggests that organizations need to provide more training for its managerial cadre. The schools and colleges can only teach certain skills. Learning is a lifelong process, and a good manager needs to engage in continual education.[44]

BOX 15.7 Loyalty and Ethical Decision Making

One issue that may confront an employee in the future relates to the concepts of loyalty to his or her organization as opposed to loyalty to society's interests. This has been a problem that has been faced by employees for many years and is a problem that will be faced by employees in the future. Many organizations place a high value on their employees' loyalty. They ask employees to sign covenants not to compete and other agreements which bind the employee to the organization. In exchange, the organization offers a job, wages, medical benefits, and other inducements to remain with the organization. In past years, this represented a fair trade of services for benefits.

However, this equation has changed in recent years as the employment relationship has been altered between employer and employee. But there is a larger ethical decision-making issue involved with loyalty to the organization. Although loyalty can be a noble virtue, it is not without its dark side.

BOX 15.7 (continued)

Loyalty to the organization can be a virtue. However, loyalty is abused if it is raised to a level higher than loyalty to society or loyalty to specific principles. One may be unable to find ways of reconciling the various types of ethical loyalties. If one's loyalty to one's employer comes in conflict with loyalties to society or to other principles, one has a difficult problem to solve. First, one should look for help from other people.

In our U.S. society, individualism is highly regarded. As a result, it can be difficult for many people to admit that they need or want assistance. However, few ethical issues can be solved in a vacuum. That is, it is not a simple matter to resolve ethical conflicts between loyalty to one's employer and other values.

Organizations may have resources that are available to people who face loyalty and ethical issues. That is, they have people who can help resolve these questions. Because of various scandals, organizations have devoted new resources to ethical issues. One should be able to discuss these types of issues with specialists in the area of ethics.

One should recognize that large organizations now may have people who can help an employee who has conflicts between loyalties to the organization and loyalties to other entities. They can help sort out these conflicting loyalties for workers and managers. Below are some steps that one might take to resolve these conflicts.

1. Discuss the issue with your immediate supervisor. This person is usually in the best position to help one resolve such conflicts. A new employee may see difficulties that can easily be solved by someone with more experience. One of the duties of a boss is to help employees resolve difficulties, and although a superior's first responsibility is to the organization, the supervisor is also responsible for helping employees.

2. Discuss the issue with the organization's designated ethical advocate. This person is trained to deal with issues involving ethics. They should be able to resolve ethical issues that are encountered by employees. These would include issues of potentially conflicting loyalties. A good ethical advocate is trained in resolving ethical issues on behalf of both the organization and the employee. They may be able to find solutions to these issues which others cannot. If the organization does not have a designated ethical advocate, one may want to discuss the issue with a member of the department of human resources. These people often have considerable experience dealing with complex issues involving the organization's employees.

3. Consult an attorney. Although the image of lawyers has taken a beating in recent years, lawyers are able to inform people of their legal rights, are capable of advising people about the state of the law, and can often find ways of resolving disputes among parties. A skilled attorney is able to recognize the strengths and weaknesses of the positions of various people involved in the situation. Lawyers are able to look at the situation from an objective point of view and advise clients regarding their future direction. It is especially important to consult an attorney in an environment of corrupt police officers and drug-influenced law enforcement officials.

The U.S. law enforcement community has always been seen as among the most corrupt and lawless elements of our society. In American society there are a variety of gangs that defy the law. In a society of drugs, alcohol, and other unlawful activities, law enforcement officials have sometimes been just another gang involved in criminal activity. The purpose of *Miranda* and other warnings is to protect citizens from their own law enforcement authorities. As this is being written, new scandals regarding police brutality have erupted in New York, Philadelphia, and other cities in the United States. Similar situations exist within other organizations in the workplace. That is, units designed to

BOX 15.7 (continued)

protect people become oppressors. A good attorney may represent a person when no one else will. An attorney is able to be objective regarding the situation while providing support for the client. In complicated situations, the services of a skilled attorney can provide a different dimension which is necessary to resolving the situation. An attorney can ensure that the organization's rules and regulations have been followed. Although an organization has the right to expect loyalty from its employees, it does not have the right to dictate every aspect of an employee's life.

4. The parties involved should also look at cases that have dealt with conflicting loyalties. A good attorney can determine how courts have resolved similar situations. These cases can act as a guide for the parties in resolving matters of conflicting loyalties. The courts have held that organizations may not interfere with employees' political or religious liberties. Courts have also held that employees may not be told to commit acts that violate laws or public policy. Various government bodies have also enacted statues that prohibit organizations from engaging in reprisals because people exposed wrongdoing within their organization. These are sometimes called "whistle-blower" laws because they protect people who report misconduct by their organizations. A person who is confronted with conflicting loyalties should immediately check any rules and regulations of the organization to see if the situation is covered by organizational policies or procedures.

5. If one believes that one has been treated unfairly, one can file a grievance against an organization. This is a serious matter that should not be taken lightly. Organizations do not like people who file complaints against them. As this is being written, President Clinton has issued new guidelines regarding the display of religious symbols in the workplace. Although the guidelines seem about as clear as possible, they are likely to provide problems of understanding and clarification. Questions about religion and the workplace are bound to arise in the future. However, the guidelines also give protection to employees so that their religion cannot be used against them. In some cases it is improper for employees to engage in political activity. For example, people who hold certain governmental positions give up their right to engage in politics. One should check into the limitations on one's activities before one takes actions that may violate the explicit or implicit contract with one's employer.

6. New employees should be aware of the importance that many employers place on loyalty to the organization. The economy has become even more fiercely competitive. Many U.S. companies have come under strong pressure from foreign competitors. In this environment, few organizations or jobs are safe. Concepts such as "team management" can be transmogrified into a desire that employees exercise loyalty to them. A good manager cares about his or her employees as much as about his or her own career. Unfortunately, some managers look at their positions as an opportunity for self-aggrandizement. The high level of distrust in U.S. business leaders may result from the tendency of some to misuse their positions.

7. Look for "servant leaders" to be in charge of your organization. A servant leader sees himself as a leader whose job is to succeed by helping others achieve. Although the servant leader has a position of power, he or she recognizes that it is to be used for the benefit of the people in the organization. This is a difficult line to walk. One of the functions of a leader is to set an agenda and to lead. Unfortunately, the level of distrust in the country's private and public leaders is so high that it is extremely difficult for anyone to lead. To succeed in this environment, one must have other skills. Since the Vietnam War and the scandals that involved leaders in various sectors of the economy, the concept of leadership in U.S. society has become unclear and uncertain. The faces on Mount Rushmore represent U.S. leaders who have been largely forgotten. As a result, it is difficult for leaders to define their role in such a climate. More commentators are suggesting that leaders think of

■ ■ ■   **BOX 15.7   (continued)**   ■ ■ ■

themselves as servants as well as leaders. That is, they need to establish a climate for their employees to grow in terms of work-related and other accomplishments. A good leader now establishes the ground rules and environment that reward ethical and productive work.

One is less likely to encounter issues relating to conflicting loyalties in a work environment with a servant leader. Servant leaders would be sensitive to these issues and would have policies and procedures in place that would help resolve them. The culture of an organization is determined by the actions of senior managers. One should look for a productive culture in which to work.

SUMMARY   ■ ■ ■

In a changing world economy, it is important that managers plan for the future. Organizations that depend on their past successes to survive are likely to fail. Although the future may be similar to the past, it will not be the same as the past. Good managers must be continually looking for new ideas and ways of doing things. The good manager is proactive and is searching constantly for additional sources of revenues. Many businesses that were successful in the earlier part of this century have disappeared by the end of the century. Companies that do not engage in strategic management are not likely to succeed in an increasingly competitive international economy. A good manager recognizes that an organization needs to develop "distinctive competencies," which are special abilities to accomplish certain objectives possessed by the organization or the individual. Research indicates that organizations and individuals that possess distinctive competencies are likely to achieve success.

Those organizations that do not have a specific distinctive competence are not likely to succeed in the future. Organizations that do not have a specific focus are unlikely to achieve their objectives. They tend to fall into a muddle that confuses the consumer, who cannot find a focus for the organization. It will no longer be sufficient to offer customers a panoply of products and hope that they choose one of the seller's. Successful organizations are those that find a consistent focus and theme that specifically meets consumers' individual needs. Organizations that do not find a specific niche in the marketplace are not likely to succeed.

Questions _____

1. What is a mission statement?
2. What are the elements of a good mission statement?
3. What are distinctive competencies?
4. How do they relate to an organization's mission?
5. How does the concept of distinctive competencies relate to the possibilities of the success of the organization?
6. What is the value of a mission statement for an organization?

7. What are the basic steps of strategic management?

8. What is the purpose of having the organization establish quantitative goals during the strategic management process?

9. What is the purpose of establishing quantitative objectives for individual employees?

10. What is an environmental scan?

11. What is the purpose of an environmental scan?

12. What is an internal resources analysis?

13. How would you develop alternative strategic options?

14. How would you evaluate the alternatives generated during the strategy development stage?

15. Name some generic strategies that you would want to consider or avoid during the decision-making phase.

16. What is a devil's advocate?

17. What are the advantages and disadvantages of being a devil's advocate?

18. What are the advantages and disadvantages of having a devil's advocate in your work group?

19. How do you prevent an organization from engaging in groupthink?

20. What is groupthink?

21. Give some examples of groupthink.

22. How would you monitor the progress of an organization?

23. How would you help an organization achieve its mission and goals?

CASE 1

You are the chief executive officer of a medium-sized bank in a major urban area. Your organization has done reasonably well but has never adopted a formal strategic planning process. The bank is in a variety of businesses but has no particular specialty area.

Your institution was founded to serve the banking needs of affluent persons living within the city. The bank has a trust and estate department, an investment area, and a banking section. Each of them has some earnings, but none of them has had significant earnings growth or has shown indications of being able to propel the bank forward into the future. There are many other financial institutions in the city that provide similar services. Most of these banks are much larger than your institution. They have significantly greater resources to market and advertise their financial service.

As you look at the skill of the managers and employees at your bank, you believe that its major strength lies in the area of estate planning and administration. One of its weaknesses is that the bank does not have strong marketing or sales skills. You are concerned that it may not be possible to train the people at your institution to be good salespeople in a short period of time.

1. What steps would you take at this moment in time?
2. How would you develop a strategy for this organization?

CASE 2

You are the manager of a new unit in the Department of Transportation of a large urban state. You have been given the assignment of developing a plan for getting roads built in shorter periods of time. This is a project that is of significant importance to the commissioner of the department. The commissioner was recently appointed and wants to demonstrate to the governor that he is a good manager and is capable of making improvements in the department. When roads are built quickly, it creates jobs and improves the state's transportation system. The governor is very concerned about improving the state's economy.

Your staff is composed of professional engineers who have been employees of the department for a significant number of years. The staff is used to doing things a certain way and has not suggested any new methods of getting roads built. You are disappointed with this lack of response from your staff. You have a few ideas about how to move ahead. You discussed this matter with your boss, but he stated that this is your project to handle.

1. What do you do?
2. How might you approach this problem?

CASE 3

You work for a large corporate utility doing management information systems work. You have a direct boss who supervises your work and a human resources manager who provides support in the area of worker development. Ranking above these managers are directors who are responsible for supervising a number of managers. These directors have a considerable amount of influence and power within the organization.

One day the director of human resources told you how much he values a positive attitude within the organization. He also told you that he dislikes complainers within the organization. He adds that he would like you to inform him about any people who complain or have a "bad attitude." You are aware that "bitching" about the company is a fairly common practice among your fellow employees. You also realize that most of these comments are harmless among people who work very hard for the company. However, there are some people who do complain on a regular basis and tend to bring down the morale of the entire unit. However, you dislike "snitches" and would not like to be placed in a position of informing on your fellow employees. The director's comments also made you realize that he has probably asked other people to snitch on their fellow employees. This has made you very cautious in your dealings with your fellow employees.

You recognize the value of a positive attitude at work. However, you also recognize that people are not going to be positive all the time. In addition, you are concerned that a quest for a perpetual positive attitude could discourage legitimate suggestions for improvement. There has been considerable discussion in the organization about people being part of a team. In addition, you have read a great deal of literature about being a team player. The materials do stress having a positive attitude, but they do not state that you are expected to be an informant for your boss.

1. What do you think about the ethics of the director who told you that he would like you to snitch on your fellow employees who complained or had a bad attitude?
2. What does it tell you about the organization of which you are a part?

3. Do you want to be part of his team?
4. How do you think his team is likely to do in the future?
5. What does it mean to be a team player within a large organization?
6. What would you do in this situation?
7. To whom should your loyalties lie within an organization?

CASE 4

H. L. Mencken, a great American journalist, once stated that "no politician in America could be trusted because they all appealed to the mob." Mencken, who believed that the United States had failed to develop an "enlightened aristocracy" to lead it, was an antidemocratic man in a society dominated by democratic ideas.

Other American thinkers have argued that the United States has been able to find a middle road between the concepts of "egalitarianism" and "merit," which have torn apart other societies. In the United States, great political leaders have found a balance between these conflicting concepts.

President Franklin Roosevelt was able to save the free enterprise economic system while expanding the role of government in society. Confronted with enemies such as Stalin and Huey Long to his left and Hitler to his right, Roosevelt was able to find a middle ground to guide the nation during the Great Depression.

President Eisenhower, who grew up in Kansas and Texas, the center of the nation, also built a strong center which resisted the appeals of the far left or right spectrums of the political process. Just as Roosevelt could reject Huey Long and Father Coughlin, Eisenhower could resist the appeals of Joe McCarthy.

American voters have continued this tradition in the 1990s by choosing a Democratic President and a Republican Congress. This tradition allows U.S. business to function within certain rules and guidelines that can be understood by the business community.

1. What are the benefits of a centrist political system?
2. What are the disadvantages of such a system?
3. Where do you stand in the political system?
4. Do you believe that such a system is ethical?

References

1. Drucker, Peter, *Concept of the corporation,* John Day & Co., New York, 1946.
2. Ibid.
3. Ibid.
4. Eldridge, William, "Where angels fear to tread," in Jack Rubin, Gerald Miller, and W. Bartley Hildreth (eds.), *Handbook of strategic management,* Marcel Decker, New York, 1989.
5. Ibid.
6. Drucker, *Concept of the corporation.*
7. Eldridge, "Where angels fear to tread."
8. Ibid.
9. Glueck, William, and Lawrence Jauch, *Business policy and strategic management,* McGraw-Hill, New York, 1984.
10. *Corporate culture,* American Management Association, New York, 1988.
11. Ibid.

12. Ibid.

13. Eldridge, "Where angels fear to tread."

14. Ibid.

15. Glueck and Jauch, *Business policy.*

16. Ibid.

17. Ibid.

18. Eldridge, "Where angels fear to tread."

19. Harvey, Donald, *Strategic management,* Merrill/Prentice Hall, Columbus, OH, 1982.

20. Woodruff, Robert, and Gerald Hill, *Marketing management perspectives and applications,* Richard D. Irwin, Homewood, IL, 1976.

21. Ibid.

22. Ibid.

23. Hosmer, Larue T., *The ethics of management,* Richard D. Irwin, Homewood, IL, 1987.

24. Eldridge, "Where angels fear to tread."

25. Janis, Irving Lester, *Groupthink: psychological studies of policy decisions and fiascoes,* Houghton Mifflin, Boston, 1982.

26. Drucker, *Concept of the corporation.*

27. Vroom, Victor, and Arthur Jago, *The new leadership: managing participation in organization,* Prentice Hall, Englewood Cliffs, NJ, 1988.

28. Belcher, David, *Compensation administration,* Prentice Hall, Upper Saddle River, NJ, 1974.

29. Ibid.

30. Pascale, Richard, *The art of Japanese management,* Simon & Schuster, New York, 1981.

31. Trundle, George (ed.), *Managerial control of business,* Wiley, New York, 1948.

32. Glenn H. Varney, Ph.D., *Management by objectives,* Management Advisory Association Inc., Cleveland, OH, 1971.

33. Ibid.

34. Henderson, Richard, *Compensation management: rewarding performance,* Prentice Hall, Upper Saddle River, NJ, 1989.

35. Ibid.

36. Ibid.

37. *Management by objectives.*

38. Peters, Thomas, *A passion for excellence: the leadership difference,* Random House, New York, 1985.

39. *Management by objectives.*

40. Brelin, Harvey, *Focused quality: managing for results,* St. Lucie Press, Delray Beach, FL, 1994.

41. Peters, *A passion for excellence.*

42. Brelin, *Focused quality.*

43. Lawler, Edward, *High involvement organizations,* Jossey-Bass, San Francisco, 1986.

44. Ibid.

16

MEETING THE CHALLENGES OF THE FUTURE

Concepts ⋮ You Will Learn ■ ■ ■

the future will not be the same as the past. The world's economy is changing too rapidly for people to assume that anything is constant.

successful people and organizations will be those that can satisfactorily adapt to a rapidly changing environment. The marketplace changes continually and it is important for people and organizations to adapt to it.

there will be new challenges in the future that will be different from those of the past.

changes in technology, communication, and the international economy will present completely different opportunities for the future.

the workers of tomorrow will also be different. In the past, the workplace was composed of a majority of white males; in the future, the workforce will consist of a majority of women and minorities. It will take different types of management skills to lead this new workforce.

INTRODUCTION ■ ■ ■

The challenges of the future will be met by managers who have the ability to create a vision for their employees and organizations. The future is likely to be confusing for many people, and employees will benefit from having a mission with which they can identify.[1] The new manager will need to have different abilities from those they have had in the past.[2] While people tend to do what is familiar to them, tomorrow's managers will face different problems and opportunities, and older methods are not likely to be successful.

Decisions regarding how to deal with the public will need to be pushed down to the lowest possible level. This means that managers will need to treat their employees differently. Rather than issuing orders, they will need to ask questions in order to solicit suggestions and ideas.[3] It will not be sufficient for management simply to do things better than they have done in the past. Rather, managers will need to focus on doing completely different things.[4]

Managers will need to be leaders much more than previously. It will not be sufficient simply to act as supervisors. Senior-level management will help establish the vision and mission of the organization. The junior-level manager will be responsible for building support for the mission and for implementing it.

THE CHALLENGE FOR BUSINESS ■ ■ ■

The challenge for American business is to outperform their international competitors by finding market niches and other competitive advantages. This will not be easy to accomplish. The United States has fallen far behind other countries in many areas.

The schools in the United States continue to rank in the middle among schools in developed nations. Graduates of this country's schools are regarded by the nation's businesses as being unprepared for their work assignments.[5] This means that U.S. businesses will need to work more closely with educational institutions to develop the types of programs that will allow students to become good employees. In addition, businesses should develop in-house training programs that help ease the transition between being a student and being an employee. Many businesses previously had lengthy training periods for supervisors and employees when they assumed their new positions. Businesses cut back on these programs to save money. This is not in the interests of either the employer or the employee.

Most new employees find new employment rather frightening. They need the help of a mentor who can teach the more junior employee how to succeed in his or her new environment. Surveys indicate that the employee's initial experiences will determine how the employee will regard the organization for the remainder of his or her career. Well-run companies recognize these consequences and provide methods of helping the employee. It costs the organization too much in terms of time and money to have employees leave in frustration.

Business leaders suggest that educational institutions need to do a much better job of developing their students' communication skills and ethical decision-making abilities. One of the reasons that students may not develop these talents is the instruction in the high schools, colleges, and universities. The U.S. educational system has never developed consistent standards throughout the country. As a result, the country seems to have become more bipolar with respect to educational achievement. That is, some students seem to reach high educational achievement while many others attain much less achievement. These results have unfortunate consequences for businesses that need managers and employees who can quickly adapt to changing conditions.

Building the Vision ■ ■ ■

The top challenge for senior-level managers is to establish a vision for the organization and a culture that will permit employees to succeed.[6] The new international economy will demand that employees be able to react to rapidly changing conditions. They will not be able to accomplish these tasks unless senior management has given the employees the tools to achieve them.

Employees want to work for organizations that are accomplishing valuable objectives. Employees want to have a reason to go to work each day. Although some people believe giving them a regular paycheck is sufficient, many employees have higher values. They want to believe they are doing something valuable for society.

A vision gives employees guidance when dealing with fellow workers and customers. The organization's vision statement should be built on a number of factors based on the external environment and the internal strengths and weaknesses of the organization. The first of these factors is to determine the distinctive competencies of the organization, that is, what the institution does better than anyone else.[7] People and institutions that succeed are those that build on their strengths rather than worry about their weaknesses.

There are different ways of helping the organization determine their distinctive competencies. One method is to write a history about themselves or about the organization. People can learn a great deal about their strengths from analyzing their job and personal history. For example, an organization can look at how it started to build its revenues. This can be an indication of what it does extremely well. Some businesses get away from their core competencies as they expand into different areas, and they forget to build on their strengths.

Similarly, people spend too little time analyzing what they do extremely well when choosing a career. Often, they become what their parents want or make other uniformed decisions. A person who takes the time to write out a history is more likely to determine one's strengths that could lead to a more satisfying career and life.

Another method of determining one's distinctive competence is to ask a number of other people what they believe one's strengths are. An organization can ask its customers, suppliers, and others about the organization's strengths. Outsiders are often in a better position to evaluate the organization objectively and to determine it strengths. This is sometimes called a marketplace analysis. In other words, what does the market believe the organization's distinctive competencies are?

One could conduct market surveys, which are questionnaires that ask people about the organization. The survey might be done in writing or over the phone. People will often use the surveys as an opportunity to tell them things that they would not tell the organization's representatives.

A third method is to ask the organization's members what they believe its distinctive competencies are. Although this is likely to be less objective than other opinions, they have some validity. People know what they like to do and may have a good idea what they do well.

After the organization has determined its distinctive competencies, it should determine if they could fill specific economic needs in the marketplace. The determination of distinctive competencies resolves what the organization can do very well. This next step is designed to resolve the question of what needs doing.

There are many objectives that need to be accomplished in an international economy. The revolutions in technology and communications allow individuals and organizations to market their products and services throughout the world in a very short period. This opens up the international marketplace to individuals and organizations that want to share their distinctive competencies with others.

There are a number of trends in the marketplace that could mean success in the future for organizations able to take advantage of them.

1. The general population of the United States is aging rapidly.[8] Far more people are living into their seventies, eighties, and nineties. In addition, the large numbers of people born within the ten years following the end of World War II are now reaching their fifties. This Baby Boom generation will be reaching retirement age in about another 15 years. As a result, there will be a dramatic change in purchasing habits of consumers. Organizations that can find ways of appealing to this newly elderly group should do well in the future. Older people buy completely different products and services than those bought by younger people.

2. The Earth will need to be cleaned in the future because of the pollution that has been dumped into the environment.[9] There are toxic waste dumps throughout this country that need to be cleaned. In addition, the United States needs to clean its air and water as well as its land. People with new technologies and new ideas should be able to do well by contributing to this process.

3. The economy will become increasingly international.[10] U.S. businesses will need to be able to compete with companies that will market their products and services in the United States. This means that U.S. companies must be able to compete in other countries. Although most people in other countries speak languages other than their own native tongue, the same is not true among Americans. Non-U.S. citizens are able to sell in English to U.S. customers, but few U.S. citizens are capable of selling in a language other than English. This puts U.S. companies at a severe disadvantage in international trade. U.S. companies are often advised to enter foreign markets. However, they should do so only if they have the distinctive competencies to succeed. People in the organization should be able to work in the language of the country in which they want to do business. In addition, they should be familiar with the customs of the countries in which they will be working.

4. There is renewed interest in topics such as ethics, decision making, and leadership.[11] Among the reasons for this interest include the perception that these are areas that have been in decline within the United States. However, these are areas that are critical to an organization's success. If a business has low ethical standards, makes bad decisions, or has ineffective leadership, it is unlikely to succeed in this competitive economy.

Ethical decision making has become of special importance in our society. As noted throughout this book, there is a belief in much of the country that the ethical standards of the individuals and organizations have declined. In many cases, poor ethics are the result of poor decision-making skills.

Leadership has become a topic of increasing importance because of a perception among many that leadership skills have declined as managerial skills increased. The nation's business schools have tended to emphasize "number crunching" as opposed to leading people in a manner that will achieve the vision of the organization.

Leaders are more than mere managers. They do much more than simply supervise the activities of their employees. They work with their employees to build a vision and goals that allow the organization to achieve great accomplishments. Leadership will be discussed more later in this chapter.

5. The technological and communication revolutions will continue to have an enormous impact on organizations.[12] Use of these improvements allows senior managers to conduct business differently than in the past.

BOX 16.1   Lt. Kelly Flinn and the Air Force

In 1997, the Air Force career of Lt. Kelly Flinn came to an end as a result of an agreement that resulted in her general discharge from the service. Lt. Flinn had been accused of adultery with the spouse of an enlisted woman and refusing to obey a superior's order to stop her conduct. The case became public as a result of Lt. Flinn's attorneys' contact with the media and Lt. Flinn's status as a pilot whose plane carried nuclear weapons. Lt. Flinn's superiors decided to bring criminal charges against her because her actions violated the "good order and discipline" of the Air Force. These actions caused an explosion of controversy among the public and in Congress. Lt. Flinn was later given a general discharge, which allowed her to leave the Air Force.

This is an example of how a culture can affect the decision-making process. It is also an example of a decision-making process that needs to inject a higher degree of flexibility with respect to the consideration of options. Like the other armed forces, the Air Force has procedures that allow senior officers to impose punishment without going through the judicial process. This could have been an additional option. The Air Force would have been able to punish Lt. Flinn without generating a great deal of adverse publicity.

The probable result of the case is that Congress will enact legislation governing ethical conduct in the military. This is likely to result in many more changes that the military will find objectionable. This represents a case of when the application of better decision-making skills would have resulted in better results.

There is less need for middle-level managers because senior executives can communicate directly with their workers. This has been reflected in the high level of downsizings in the private-sector and the reorganizations in the public sector.

Many tasks previously performed by workers can now be performed by computers. Businesses can now reach many potential customers on the Internet or through other means of worldwide communication.

New marketing and sales techniques will be developed to take advantage of the new technologies available. Businesses in foreign countries will be able to reach into U.S. markets very rapidly. Similarly, American firms will be able quickly to capture significant segments of the market outside the United States.

Following the determination of what it does well, what it likes to do, and what needs doing, the organization should develop a short mission statement which outlines what the organization intends to become and where it is going in the future. The statement should not contain vague generalities that could be applied to almost any organization. This is a common mistake that many organizations make.

The Vision Statement in Box 16.2 is so broad that it could be applied to almost any organization. It provides no guidance to the employees of ZBN as to how they are to act when there are choices to be made. The final statement is actually a contradiction. One cannot produce products of highest quality and

BOX 16.2   ZBN Corporation's Mission Statement

At ZBN Corporation we are committed to developing an organization that treats people with dignity and care. We offer our customers the highest-quality products at the lowest-possible price.

■ ■ ■   **BOX 16.3 Examples of Vision Statements**   ■ ■ ■

1. We are the state's leading seller of fertilizing equipment, which helps our customers grow food.
2. We are one of the state's leading suppliers of inexpensive clothing for the work and relaxation needs of our female customers.
3. We are the city's leading supplier of financial services to entrepreneurs and business people. Our financial services allow them to build the economy and create jobs.

sell them at the lowest prices. This will only serve to confuse both customers and employees. In addition, a statement that is too broad will cost the senior executives credibility with people who read the statement.

The vision statement should be inspiring, but it should also be specific enough to give the organization its own unique purpose. The vision statement should be neither too broad nor too narrow. It should provide guidance to the organization's managers and employees by telling them in which businesses the organization wants to engage and in which it does not. It provides a sense of purpose for members of the organization.

It has been the authors' experience that companies spend a great deal of time "spinning their wheels" trying to decide what to do about their business. A carefully crafted mission statement should allow people to focus on what they should be doing and prevent them from heading into areas that will be unproductive.

The vision statement should also provide inspiration for employees. A large number of people dislike going to work. People want to believe that their work has some larger meaning. They want to work for an organization that is accomplishing something meaningful.

Implementing the Vision   ■ ■ ■

The major function of senior managers is to create and implement a vision for the organization.[13] Many people have excellent ideas but do not do a good job of implementing them. Great executives are also leaders who are able to achieve the mission and objectives of the organization. They are capable of persuading their subordinate managers and workers to implement the plan and objectives.

Good managers are not necessarily good leaders,[14] and of course, the opposite is also true. As a result, there has been renewed interest in the topic of leadership. Some of the differences between a manager and a leader are outlined in Box 16.4. The effective leader motivates his or her employees to achieve the organization's mission and objectives. Being an effective leader is not easy. Most people have had little training in leadership. Furthermore, we are in an age that is not friendly to leadership.

The double-barreled impact of the Vietnam War and the Watergate scandal eroded confidence in governmental leadership. Subsequent scandals in law enforcement, in the clergy, and on Wall Street further undermined confidence in leadership. The downsizings of the 1980s and 1990s demonstrated a failure of corporate leadership.

Box 16.4 Leader versus Manager

Manager	Leader
Tells people what to do	Asks questions
Is neutral	Is proactive
Is self-oriented	Is others-oriented
Sees self as boss	Sees self as colleague
Does things right	Does right things
Focuses on short term	Focuses on long term

As this is being written, the tobacco industry has admitted to deceiving the American public for decades. Cartoons will no longer be used to induce young people to smoke. Similarly, the Marlboro Man will no longer be used in advertising and the tobacco companies will be required to attempt actively to reduce the level of underage smoking in future years. The company's advertising has been shown to be deceptive. Similar actions have been taken against other private-sector firms. Drexel Lambert went out of business because of the corruption of its partners.[15] Entire police departments have been sent to jail and prosecutors' offices have been convicted of abusing their power.

New leaders will need to demonstrate the highest ethical standards. In addition, organizations and their leaders will need to see themselves as servants who are capable of meeting the needs of their customers and society. As public trust in leaders has reached a new low, it will become important for new leaders to demonstrate conduct that will inspire confidence among employees and customers.

The authors' discussions with various people indicate that a pervasive distrust of nearly everyone's motives permeates the United States. The nation's optimism that followed World War II has given way to different feelings about our nation's institutions.

The future leaders of business will need to be both persons of thought and persons of action. They will need to be excellent planners as well as excellent implementers. The great business leaders will be those who have a passion about their products and their people.[16] A great leader will place a high priority on empowering his or her employees by focusing on what they are doing well and how they can do more of it. Decisions will need to be made at the level closest to the customer. However, many employees have little experience at making decisions.

"I want assertive, fiercely independent workers who will do exactly as they are told" seems to be the attitude of many senior managers. They know that they should surround themselves with managers who can help them in areas in which they are weak. But they hang onto the idea that the job of managers is to tell people what to do. However, this has a corrosive effect on the ability of junior-level managers and employees to contribute to the organization. They lose their ability to think and to make decisions because they are told what to do instead.

Businesses that are run from the top down are not likely to do well. Those that find ways of involving their employees are likely to do better in a competitive

BOX 16.5 Ethically Managing Your Career

One must now draw out plans for ethically managing one's career. Ethical and educational standards in the United States have fallen so low that one no longer can presume that the ethical standards and abilities that existed previously at various institutions are actually present.

EXAMPLE: Many inner-city high schools have become armed camps. Some bear more resemblance to prisons than institutions of learning. As a result, students have to spend more time defending themselves from violence than engaging in actual learning.

Often, the consequences are that high school students graduate without the skills necessary to enter the workplace or to study at the college level. However, some students get pushed through college with good grades but are then unable to study at the graduate level or perform the functions associated with that of an employee.

The need of employees to "punch their tickets" with a variety of degrees has resulted in a significant number of diploma mills which turn out graduates with degrees but little knowledge or ability. Sometimes, such people pursue additional education for which they are also unprepared.

The private-sector, governmental agencies, and academia are filled with people who have the appropriate credentials but are not adequately prepared for their positions. This means that a person developing a career must be prepared to cope with people who are not prepared for their positions.

How does one navigate around the people one is likely to encounter during one's career? One needs to have a specific plan to reach one's goals. Some possible action steps might include some or all of the following:

1. One should try to obtain as much education as possible. This will help broaden one's ethical perspectives and give one additional points of view. In addition, the world's economy is being driven by people with technical and knowledge-based skills. A person with a good education will be able to move to different jobs if confronted with insurmountable ethical problems in a particular job position.

2. Examine carefully the claims of the organization for which you are going to work. As this is being written, the Catholic Church is raising ethical questions about ethics in advertising which some people consider to be oxymoronic. Just as it is difficult to determine how much truth is behind advertising claims, an organization may present a false front to a potential employee.

3. Intelligent consumers learn to investigate different products to determine which will best meet their needs. They investigate a number of different products, evaluate their strengths and weaknesses, and then select one. A person searching for a new job or career should take similar actions. It is important that one ask other employees about the values, beliefs, and practices of the organization. If ethical standards are important to a job candidate, he or she should ask other employees about the organization's ethical standards and codes of conduct. One should also look at the organization's reports and approaches to attracting customers.

4. If one listens to employees, managers, and customers, one can obtain a good idea of the ethical standards of an organization. An ethical organization would do several things very well. Among them would be the ability to plan exceptionally well for both the financial and ethical success of the organization.

5. An organization that fails to plan is planning to fail. In this turbulent economic environment, the organization must plan or it will not do well. Organizations that run into financial difficulties are also likely to run into ethical difficulties. Therefore, it is important to plan for both financial and ethical success.

BOX 16.5 **(continued)**

6. An ethical organization knows what it is trying to accomplish and how it is going to do so. Its ethical plan should include codes of conduct for its employees which will cover situations that employees are likely to encounter. These might include the following:

a. Policies that deal with items such as expense accounts and gifts from customers

b. How employees deal with ethical problems they might encounter

c. Information about resources available to an employee who encounters ethical issues

d. The basic ethical standards and values of the organization

Although these seem rather general, they do provide guidance for employees to assess their conduct. It is important for employees to know what is expected of them.

7. It is important that senior management establish ethical values and then follow them. Recent scandals involving major companies revealed that senior management was aware of the unethical practices of their subordinates. Does the organization have an ethical advocate who can advise senior management about the ethical consequences of their proposed actions? Employees will be guided by the example set by senior managers. Too many organizations have senior managers who fail to establish high ethical standards for their organizations.

8. If the organization fails to pay constant attention to their ethical standards, there will be a steady decline in the organization's values. Ethical values have a tendency to slide downward with the passage of time unless senior management pays constant attention to reinforcing good practices. The organization also ought to have a designated devil's advocate who will challenge the actions of the organization when he or she believes they are incorrect. This is likely to reduce the likelihood that the organization will make serious ethical errors. Many of the most recent scandals could have been prevented if some senior-level people had spoken out against the practices that caused them.

9. One should also determine if the organization has regular training in ethical standards, policies, and procedures. Ethical standards often slip under the pressure to earn profits and with the passage of time. The report on the ethical standards of advertising by the Catholic Church reflects a legitimate concern that the pressure to achieve profits could result in practices that are harmful to society. Too often, organizations and others are unwilling to look at themselves and allow others to do it for them. The iron-clad rule of responsibility states that people who use their positions irresponsibly will lose them. Well-run and ethical organizations will regularly review their own standards. Members of learned professions constantly review the conduct of their members and impose disciplinary actions if the person has violated their canons of ethics. It would be useful if all organizations conducted similar reviews.

10. Save your money. Some people get into ethical difficulties because they need the money. It becomes easy for a new employee to start spending money beyond his or her means. Big-ticket items are available for relatively small down payments, and it is a simple matter to buy items on credit.

11. Some people in certain occupations find themselves surrounded by people with a great deal of money. They find it difficult to resist the lure of having a similar lifestyle. This is one of the reasons that law enforcement officers can be tempted by people who engage in unlawful activities. It is difficult to live on small salaries when others are living lavishly on illegal activities.

12. One is less likely to be tempted if one has saved up a sufficient amount of money to meet living expenses. One can walk away from an unethical situation if one is in a strong financial position. One may not be in a position to refuse to obey unethical orders if one cannot feed one's family.

■ ■ ■ **BOX 16.5** *(continued)* ■ ■ ■

13. Some people find themselves in a difficult financial position because they do not budget their money sufficiently. As a result, they find themselves in difficulty because their outgo exceeds their input. One needs to monitor both the revenue and the expenses. One should want the highest-possible salary, but one should also monitor the expenses that one has which are associated with that revenue. The best financial planners suggest that one immediately put a certain percentage of one's after-tax income into savings and then budget the remainder based on project categories of necessary expenditures.

14. Be committed to your organization, but be more committed to principles and society as a whole. This may be difficult in the "pressure cooker" economic environment of the 1990s, but it will lead to a more ethical career.

15. As noted above, it is useful to save some money and obtain a broad-based education to help one accomplish this objective. It is also useful to have additional irons in the fire in case one wants to move to another position. It is important to be committed to one's career, but one should also have available some other options.

economy.[17] Although we all tend to feel comfortable with what we know, businesses will need to be able to change rapidly in order to succeed. Their ability to change will depend on their willingness to develop the skills to make proper decisions.

THE CHALLENGE FOR GOVERNMENT ■ ■ ■

The challenge for government will also be different in the future than in the past. One of the challenges for government is to be able to fend off attempts by private-sector firms that want to take over governmental activities. This trend is called *privatization*. It reflects a desire by government officials to have governmental services performed more efficiently and at less cost. Private-sector companies believe that they can earn a profit by performing governmental services.

Private companies are looking for ways to earn new profits as old sources become less reliable with the advent of international competition. There are a significant number of private firms that run prisons.[18] Certain groups are urging the dismantling of many public services.

Advocates of vouchers that allow public school students to attend private schools say that more choice and competition would improve all education. This, they contend, would improve the educational process and would benefit the students. Although opponents argue that such a voucher system would hurt the public school system, proponents remain convinced that private competition is necessary to help the nation's students compete with young people from the rest of the world.[19]

Governments would also do well to consider which of its purposes it wants to achieve and which purposes are less important. Government has so many different purposes to fulfill that it may not do an excellent job of fulfilling any of its purposes. The public school system may fall into this category.

The school system has had many different purposes thrust upon it by school boards and state legislatures. America's public schools were founded to teach reading, writing, arithmetic, and a sufficient amount of civics to allow citizens to participate in the nation's democracy. However, the schools have also been charged with teaching driver's education, health, physical education, sex education, drug education, and other subjects. It is difficult to do something very well when an organization has so many tasks to accomplish. Challenges for the educational system will be discussed later.

FUTURE CHALLENGES

In 1999, the national government was divided between the Republicans, who retained control of Congress, and the Democrats, who retained control of the presidency. Neither the President nor Congress has proposed any major new initiatives. The nation's government may have reached an agreement that the federal government should do little more but little less.

Although some people may regret the lack of major issues at the national level, this may be an opportunity to consolidate the government's activities and improve the services that are currently delivered. People tend to distrust the ability of government to take over new areas of the economy, but they are reluctant to terminate the services that government currently provides. For example, the national health care proposals put forth by various governmental officials have been rejected. However, the citizens are reluctant to support reductions in popular programs such as Medicare or Medicaid. Citizens also complain about taxes, but they are unwilling to cut governmental programs to achieve this result.

Government leaders may want to think about what government ought to be doing and what should be left to the private sector. The law of unintended consequences states that certain actions lead to results that are totally unexpected. Many people believe that some governmental programs have been affected by that law. They argue that programs designed to help people have created a sense of dependency that diminishes their willingness to work. This is one of the reasons that both President Clinton and the Republican leaders in Congress agreed to the welfare reform law.

It may be that many governmental programs fall into this category. Fewer people are interested in expanding the welfare state. The leaders of the liberal parties in the United States and England, Bill Clinton and Tony Blair, are trying to govern from the center of the political spectrum. In a televised interview in June 1997, Tony Blair stated that his goal was to create a society that rewarded ambition and enterprise but that also had room for compassion for others. He argued that the new role for government was to provide people with the education and skills that would allow them to compete within the international economy.

Although Blair's formulation is rather general, it does have some elements of a good mission statement. It helps provide some sense of direction and closure because it eliminates the traditional struggle between those who favor private industry and those who want the major industries to be owned by the government. The reelection of Bill Clinton and the election of Tony Blair signal the end of the old form of socialism and a new type of debate. This new debate can be productive if it provides a specific focus on which programs are valuable and which are not.

Certain activities can be performed only by government. For example, the nation's armed forces must be controlled by a national government. It would be unthinkable for a private-sector company to own the Army, Navy, or Air Force. Some people point out cases of overexpenditure of moneys by the armed forces, but in past years the military was often underfunded. In the 1970s many people argued that the military did not have the resources to defend the country adequately. The overfunding and underfunding have tended to balance each other out and the military has generally managed its resources well. Turning the military over to the private-sector would make no sense.

Similarly, law enforcement activities must be controlled by the government. Although there is room for private police forces, only the affluent could afford to hire police departments to protect themselves. Only by pooling resources of individuals can the community provide protection against the criminals of our society.

In other chapters, problems in the environment have been discussed. Protecting the environment could not be left entirely to the private sector because it is not in the interests of the private sector to spend a great deal of money to clean up the environment. Some argue that only massive governmental intervention can solve problems in the environment.[20] In our society, effective governmental action balances growth of the economy with the need to protect the environment.

The process of educating the nation's young people is one that has been controversial since the advent of the republic. The country's most prestigious educational institutions were founded as private organizations that would educate the nation's youth. Conversely, the country's sense of "equality" resulted in the founding of "public" institutions which offered an education to those who had ability but could not afford college or university degrees.

The establishment of public schools and universities changed the nature of the society in which they operated. An entire industry has been built around public education. There are many thousands of public grammar, high school, and college teachers and support staff. These people form a powerful voting and lobbying group. They continually ask for more funding for public education. They argue against using public funds for any form of private education. There are many who argue that the near monopoly that the public schools have on education is not beneficial for students.

What Should Government Be Doing?

Lincoln once stated that government should only do what the people cannot do for themselves.[21] Although this has a Lincolnesque ring to it, it is still so general as to provide little help in resolving these issues. It does not give criteria for deciding which programs the people can do for themselves. It also does not give criteria for deciding issues relating to efficiency and costs. Neither does it help decide issues relating to who will exercise control over these programs and institutions.

Below are some suggested criteria that may help decide issues with respect to whether programs should be public or private.

1. Can we measure the success of the program in a quantitative manner? If so, can we compare private and public performance in a quantitative way?

2. Can we measure the costs of implementing the programs in some quantitative way? If so, can we compare the costs of implementing the program in the private sector versus the governmental sector?

3. Can we make decisions based on the comparisons between the performance and costs in the private and public sectors? If so, can we make a decision as to which sector would control the program?

4. Are there other considerations that would affect a decision as to whether a program should be placed in the private or public sector? For example, would the decision concentrate too much power in one sector or another?

As an example, many people believe that the wave of mergers and acquisitions has concentrated too much power in the hands of a few corporate leaders. Conversely, one of the problems with communism and Nazi Germany was that too much power was placed in the hands of governmental leaders. One of the virtues of U.S. society is that power is widely diffused among various groups. As a result, no one person or group controls an excessive amount of power. This prevents the horrible abuses of power that have been seen in totalitarian societies.

Are there any other values that society would like to encourage that should affect the decision? For example, certain activities might demand a higher level of "compassion." It might be more appropriate to place these activities into the governmental sector rather than the private-sector. The primary concern of the private sector must be to earn profits, while the government sector may be able to demonstrate a greater level of compassion.

BOX 16.6   Job Training and Welfare

The issue of job training for people who are no longer eligible for welfare has become more significant since President Clinton signed the welfare reform bill. Although this issue has been delegated to county governments, it is not clear how and by whom the job training should be carried out.

The first issue is how general or specific the job training should be. An argument could be made that these people will first need to be taught basic work attitudes before they can be taught job skills. In other words, they will need to be taught such matters as getting out of bed, getting to work on time, learning to take instructions, dealing with others, and other ordinary skills that are essential to succeeding at work. These skills could be taught by either the public or private sector. However, these are rather general skills and it may be more appropriate to have them taught by the government because it is accepting responsibility for the lack of preparation many of these people have. In addition, governmental instructors are likely to demonstrate a greater degree of tolerance and caring.

After these skills have been learned, the people can be taught more specific skills. Many will need to be taught basic skills such as reading, writing, and simple arithmetic, subjects that might better be taught by the governmental sector, which has had much greater experience at teaching these skills. These people could also use additional training with respect to specific job skills. For example, some people could be trained to be toolmakers. These activities might better be handled by the private sector because they can train people in the specific methods employed at the private-sector employer.

Often, private employers complain that educational institutions do not train their graduates in any specific hands-on skills.[22] After students are given basic work skills by governmental entities, it may be appropriate to turn the training over to private-sector institutions that can train workers exactly as they want. This would be useful for employers. The people responsible for the programs should be able to measure the results of the training programs by both the governmental and private entities. They could also measure the costs of the program. The program's sponsors could then make decisions as to whether the private or public sector could do better.

Although control of job training is important, it does not give any group so much power that it should pose no threat to society regardless of who controls the job training program. However, in the past, some job training programs have been used as sources of political patronage. As a result, in some cases it may be better to place at least some job training programs in the hands of private-sector firms. This analysis could be employed with respect to various programs. This should help people decide in which sector these programs belong. Although this analysis may not be perfect, it is more useful than ideological statements with little underlying thought.

Challenges for Educators   ■ ■ ■

Education is likely to be conducted differently than in the past because of the changing economic realities and the greater competition for jobs.[23] Citizens are also likely to demand greater accountability for the dollars spent on education in this nation. The higher test scores of students in other countries has caused many to ask if our education system is giving consumers value for the money spent.

One difficulty for the U.S. system of education is that it has remained relatively constant for many years. Curriculum and learning methods have changed hardly at all in many years. In addition, the emphasis on personal styles, academic freedom, and home rule has helped prevent the establishment of nationwide standards. As a result, it is difficult to figure out what it means to graduate from a high school, college, or other program.

One can no longer expect that the people one encounters will have the consistent level of knowledge and skill that one associates with a particular level of education or profession. This is a dangerous trend because it lowers the level of competencies throughout all of society. Some research indicates that the general level of knowledge and competence in our society is declining. Despite these facts, our nation's educational institutions remain largely committed to continuing past practices. The national teachers' unions tend to resist almost any changes in the nation's educational system.

Many people go into "teaching" because they love their subject, they like school, they like young people, or some other reason. Most cultures tend to become rather rigid, and the nation's educational institutions are not an exception. Teacher's unions often become committed to protecting the least competent of its members.

Furthermore, teachers are as reluctant as anyone to admit that they could perform their jobs even better than previously. The most recent research indicates that students would benefit from more self-learning. This is especially true at the college level. The research indicates that the traditional lecture method does not promote critical thinking or long-term learning. There are a variety of alternative approaches to the lecture method that would promote a more effective education experience for students.

However, teachers are not the only ones who resist positive change. Students tend to want clarity in their courses. They have also been given the power to evaluate college professors. Some students tend to resent instructors who depart from the lecture method. It represents change and may also represent a lack of clarity for students who are used to the lecture approach.

English universities place less emphasis on conducting classes and more emphasis on tutoring students who request it. However, U.S. higher education is based on the number of contact hours that students have with instructors. In addition, instructors are paid based on the number of hours in which they are in class with students. This also tends to foster a lecture method, regardless of its effectiveness.

In any organization it is important to do the right things as opposed to simply doing things right. In the American educational system, a great deal of emphasis is placed on process as opposed to measuring results. The new emphasis on accountability that the public is demanding will create a different culture of the various educational establishments. They will need to find methods of measuring results without losing their ability to impart long-term learning techniques.

Educational institutions will also need to meet the challenges of more carefully defining their mission and developing purposes distinct from those of other educational establishments. They will need to do more consulting with private-sector corporations and governmental organizations to determine their needs and the skills they want graduates to possess.

In a survey of corporate leaders it was indicated that the graduates needed greater communication skills and more training in ethics and decision-making skills. Despite these findings, few educational institutions offer courses that deal directly with these issues. Although some instructors are willing to initiate such courses, they are faced with problems such as turf battles and faculty who oppose new programs.

Institutions often become very rigid and opposed to change. Educational institutions often fall into this category. Some people do not like change, for a variety of reasons. This will make it difficult for educational institutions to change to meet the various needs of the business and governmental communities.

American businesses need to catch up with many of their foreign competitors. U.S. governmental institutions are changing to better compete with private firms that want to earn profits performing governmental activities. U.S. educational institutions will also need to change their methods of instruction, methods of evaluation, and basic purposes.

SUMMARY

American business is going to have to meet the challenge of outperforming international competitors in the future. To do this the entire society is going to have to overcome a number of challenges. The first is as old as the practice of management itself: the development of a vision for the organization. This is even more important today than it was years ago because the environment is far more competitive. Organizations need to know who they are and what they are trying to do if they want to be successful.

Other situations involve the general aging of the population, not only in the United States but in the rest of the industrialized world and the problems of pollution, to say nothing of cleaning up the mess that has already been made. Technological and communication advances have also changed the world, and the implications are huge. Things happen, and the world knows instantly, unlike 100 years ago, when it was easy to hide events that were simply not acceptable to the outside world.

Leadership is going to be a commodity that will be in great demand, but there will probably be insufficient quantities of it. Leadership will require a new paradigm. People will want to be inspired, not just ordered, and successful managers will be the ones who master that ability.

Governments will also face a more difficult time on the road ahead. The idea and scope of government is changing; privatizing is now the watchword, but not all things should be privatized.

Of all the aspects of society, education is probably the most important in the long run. Given the ability of the other factors of production to move from society to society and country to country, the labor force will be the key to the prosperity of the society in the future. The skills of the labor force and the ability of that labor force to acquire new skills will determine the long-term success of a particular society as the world becomes a smaller place. Without an educated and trained workforce a society is doomed to remain second class at best, and the country will be relegated to, at best, second-tier status among nations.

Questions

1. What is a mission statement?
2. What is the purpose of a mission statement?
3. What are the elements of a well-crafted mission statement?
4. What factors are involved in developing a mission statement?
5. What are distinctive competencies?
6. What is the importance of distinctive competencies in developing a mission statement?
7. Name some important trends that may affect the success of American businesses.
8. What is a mentor?
9. What is the importance of a mentor to a new employee?
10. Explain why the topic of leadership has become more important in recent years.
11. How would you define leadership?
12. What are some characteristics of a good leader?
13. What are some differences between managers and leaders?
14. What is the importance of high ethical standards for an effective leader?
15. What does the concept of *empowering* mean?
16. What does *privatization* mean?
17. How would you define the responsibilities of government?

18. How would you decide what programs government should be engaged in?
19. How would you develop a process for deciding these questions?
20. What are the procedures relating to decision making?
21. Name some future challenges for America's business community.
22. Name some future challenges for America's governmental community.
23. Name some future challenges for America's educational community.

CASE 1

You are the chief executive officer of a large American corporation. Your company has been earning reasonable profits but has also been subject to fierce international competition. You are in the process of reviewing your plans for the future. You have discovered that the internal safety standards that your company applies to its products are higher than those required by law. In addition, they are much higher than required by the laws of foreign countries in which your company does business. If you lowered your company's safety standards, you could increase your profits significantly. The added profits would also be sufficient to satisfy any additional judgment against you.

1. What should you do?

CASE 2

You are the administrator for a large governmental agency. You observe that senior administrators earn high salaries, and will receive a generous pension when they retire. You believe that younger people could do the same work as the senior administrators for substantially lower salaries. This would save your agency a considerable amount of money. You have the power to dismiss the senior administrators.

1. What should you do?

CASE 3

You are a teacher at a small college. You have traditionally used a lecture approach to convey your knowledge of the subject matter. You have just read some research indicating that the lecture method is not very effective at developing critical thinking skills or long-term learning. Your student evaluations have always been high and you have been told that your students enjoy your classes. You are also aware that your students like a high degree of clarity and have become used to the lecture method. In addition, you have tenure and there is no need for you to change your teaching methods. You believe that you have an ethical duty to promote the maximum amount of learning for students.

1. Should you change or explore different methods of teaching your course material?

References

1. Huey, John, "Managing in the midst of chaos," *Fortune,* April 5, 1993.
2. McClenahan, John S., "Can you manage in the new economy?" *Industry Week,* April 5, 1993.

3. Kuritko, Donald F., Jeffrey S. Hornsby, Douglas W. Naffziger, and Ray V. Montagno, "Implement entrepreneurial thinking in established organizations," *SAM: Advanced Management Journal*, Winter 1993.

4. Weiner, Edith, "Business in the 21st century," *The Futurist*, March–April, 1992.

5. United States National Commission on Excellence in Education, *A nation at risk: the imperative for education reform: a report to the nation and the Secretary*, The Commission, Washington, DC, 1980.

6. Morgan, Malcolm J., "How corporate culture drives strategy," *Long Range Planning*, April 1993.

7. Eldridge, W., "Where angels fear to tread: a practitioner's guide to strategic management in government," in Jack Rabin, Gerald J. Miller, and W. Bartley Hildreth (eds.), *Handbook of strategic management*, Marcel Dekker, New York, 1989.

8. Nelton, Sharon, "Golden employees in the golden years," *Nation's Business*, August 1993.

9. Seas, Andrew, "Environmental inequalities: literature review and proposals for new directions in research and theory," *Current Sociology*, July 1997, v. 45, n. 3.

10. Graham, Edward M., "Beyond borders: on the globalization of business," *Harvard International Review*, Summer 1993.

11. Bok, Derek, "Social responsibility in future worlds," *Readings in management*, South-Western, Cincinnati, OH, 1986; in F. Maidment (ed.), *Annual editions: management, 1997–1998*, Dushkin/McGraw-Hill, Guilford, CT, 1998.

12. Weiner, "Business in the 21st century."

13. Joplin, Janice R., "Developing effective leadership: an interview with Henry Cisneros, Secretary, U.S. Department of Housing and Urban Development," *Academy of Management Executive*, May 1993.

14. Ibid.

15. Stewart, James, *Den of thieves*, Simon & Schuster, New York, 1991.

16. Peters, Thomas, *A passion for excellence*, Random House, New York, 1986.

17. Ibid.

18. Vinocur, Barry, "The ground floor: investors rush into a prison REIT, though some view it as pricey," *Barrons*, July 14, 1997, v. 77, n. 2.

19. Lee, Susan, "Trustbusters," *Forbes*, June 2, 1997.

20. *The global 2000 report to the President: entering the 21st century*, U.S. Government Printing Office, Washington, DC, 1980.

21. Thomas, John (ed.), *Abraham Lincoln and the American political tradition*, University of Massachusetts Press, Amherst, MA, 1986.

22. United States National Commission, *A nation at risk*.

23. Ibid.

INDEX